CULTURAL PSYCHOLOGY

CROSS CULTURAL AND MULTICULTURAL PERSPECTIVES

Christine Ma-Kellams

University of La Verne

ROWMAN & LITTLEFIELD

Lanham • Boulder • New York • London

Executive Editor: Nancy Roberts
Assistant Editor: Megan Manzano
Senior Marketing Manager: Amy Whitaker
Interior Designer: Ilze Lemesis
Cover Designer: Sarah Marizah
Cover Art: iStock.com/PeopleImages

Credits and acknowledgments for material borrowed from other sources, and reproduced with permission, appear on the appropriate page within the text.

Published by Rowman & Littlefield
An imprint of The Rowman & Littlefield Publishing Group, Inc.
4501 Forbes Boulevard, Suite 200, Lanham, Maryland 20706
www.rowman.com

Unit A, Whitacre Mews, 26-34 Stannary Street, London SE11 4AB, United Kingdom

British Library Cataloguing in Publication Information Available

Library of Congress Cataloging-in-Publication Data

Names: Ma-Kellams, Christine, author.
Title: Cultural psychology: cross-cultural and multicultural perspectives / Christine Ma-Kellams.
Description: Lanham, Md.: Rowman & Littlefield, [2018] | Includes bibliographical references and index.
Identifiers: LCCN 2018011820 (print) | LCCN 2018012715 (ebook) | ISBN 9781442265295 (Electronic) | ISBN 9781442265271 (cloth: alk. paper) | ISBN 9781442265288 (pbk.: alk. paper)
Subjects: LCSH: Ethnopsychology.
Classification: LCC GN502 (ebook) | LCC GN502.M32 2018 (print) | DDC 155.8/2—dc23
LC record available at https://lccn.loc.gov/2018011820

♾️™ The paper used in this publication meets the minimum requirements of American National Standard for Information Sciences—Permanence of Paper for Printed Library Materials, ANSI/NISO Z39.48-1992.

Printed in the United States of America

Contents

Preface   vii

Acknowledgments   ix

Introduction — Half of the World's Population Is . . .   xi

PART I Cross-Cultural Psychology, or the Question of How We Differ

CHAPTER 1 Race, Ethnicity, and Nationality   1

Defining Race, Culture, and Ethnicity   1

East Asians versus European Americans   4

African Americans   18

Latino/a Americans   24

American Indians   28

White Identity   33

Key Concepts   37

CHAPTER 2 Class   49

A Brief History of Class   49

Defining Social Class   50

Key Concepts   63

CHAPTER 3 Religion   69

How Religious Are We, Really?   72

Brief History of Religion as Culture: The Protestant Work Ethic   74

Defining Religion: Culture, Religion, and Spirituality   74

Explaining Religion's Effects   82

Summary   86

Key Concepts   87

CHAPTER 4 Gender   95

Development of a Gendered Identity   95

Defining Gender versus Sex   97

How Different Are Men and Women, Really?   100

Key Concepts   110

CHAPTER 5 Region   117

Regional Variation in the United States: A Tale of Three Cities   117

Regional Variation in Homicides   119

The History of the South   121

Global Regional Variation: The Urban versus Rural Difference   126

Global Regional Variation: The Role of Environmental Threats   128

Key Concepts   131

CHAPTER 6 Human Universals   135

A Reasonable (but Wrong) Conclusion   135

Levels of Universality   138

Psychological Universals in the Four Fs: Fighting/Fleeing, Flirting, and Feeding   142

Morality Universals   152

Religious Universals   155

Key Concepts   157

PART II Multicultural Psychology, or When Cultures Collide

CHAPTER 7 Intergroup Conflict: Stereotypes, Prejudice, and Discrimination   161

Stereotypes versus Prejudice versus Discrimination   163

The Automatic Nature of Stereotypes and Prejudice   164

The Self-Confirming Nature of Stereotypes   165

Prejudice and Discrimination   167

Positive Stereotypes: Fact or Illusion?   172

Knowing Is Half the Battle: What Alleviates Stereotype Threat?   173

Summary   174

Key Concepts   175

CHAPTER 8 Ingroup Derogation and Self-Stereotyping 179

The Story of Race, Revisited 180

Ingroup Derogation among Racial Minorities 181

Ingroup Derogation among Low-Status Groups 181

Self-Stereotyping among Advantaged Groups 183

Explaining Ingroup Derogation and Self-Stereotyping 184

Ingroup Derogation versus Self-Stereotyping 185

Key Concepts 192

CHAPTER 9 — Identity and Acculturation 195

What Are You? (I Mean, Where Are You From?) 195

Defining Identity, Because It's Complicated 196

Having an Identity, Because Identification Matters 198

Changing Identity, Because Identity Is Fluid 199

Not All Immigrant Experiences Are Created Equal 201

Unpacking Minority Group Identities, Because Identity Is Socially Constructed 203

Key Concepts 206

CHAPTER 10 Navigating Diversity: Multiculturalism versus Culture-Blindness 211

Racism without Racists? Multiple Approaches to Diversity 211

Multiculturalism 212

Moderators and Mediators: Explaining the Ideology-Prejudice Link 216

The Role of Intergroup Contact in Shaping Attitudes toward Diversity 217

Key Concepts 221

PART III: The Future of Culture

CHAPTER 11 Where Does Culture Come From? 225

A Lesson from *Breaking Bad* 225

A Brief History of Cultural Psychology 226

Culture as Ecology 228

Culture as Social Epidemiology 229

Culture as Gene-Environment Interactions 230

Explaining Between-Culture Variation 232

The Bottom Line   238

Key Concepts   238

CHAPTER 12 Culture and the Brain: Frontiers in Cultural Neuroscience   243

A Brief History of Neuroscience   243

Your Brain, on Culture: Universals across Ethnic Contexts   244

Your Brain, on Culture: Cultural Differences by Ethnicity   246

The Same, but Different (Again)   247

Additional Forms of Culture, Revisited   248

Key Concepts   250

CHAPTER 13 Predicting the Future: Tracking Cultural Change   253

Mechanisms for Cultural Change   253

Cultural Changes within the United States   254

Cultural Changes Outside the United States   255

Global Trends in Cultural Change   257

Conclusion   261

Key Concepts   261

Epilogue   263

Index   267

Preface

How do beliefs associated with one's social milieu change psychological tendencies? *Cultural Psychology: A Cross- and Multicultural Approach* will explore the specific ways one's cultural background shapes one's sense of self, emotions, motivation, judgments, relationships, and more. It discusses race, politics, God, sex, money, and how you like your coffee. In the process, this book will unpack "culture" in all its various forms, including (but not limited to) ethnic, socio-economic, gender, and religious culture (for a popular psychology book on these forms of culture, see Markus & Connor, 2013); it will also cover what happens when cultures collide (e.g., diversity issues and multiculturalism) and present insights into the future of culture.

The goals of this book are to help you gain a better appreciation for the ways in which human culture and psychological processes interact and to enhance your ability to deal with and understand variations in human behavior across populations and groups. In order to achieve these goals, this book will rely heavily on empirical psychological research on culture, examining theoretical and methodological foundations of both cross-cultural and multicultural research in psychology and applying them to real-world issues, like whether money makes one happy (Vohs, Mead, & Goode, 2006) or how Obama influenced White identity (e.g., see Knowles & Peng, 2005). It will present the mounting evidence suggesting that much having to do with psychological processes is culture-specific, theory-driven, and context-dependent. It will discuss several basic questions of cultural psychology, such as

1. What is culture? What is ethnicity?
2. How does culture relate to psychological processes? How does the human psyche affect human cultures?
3. How does one apply cultural psychology to understand and deal with real-life cultural conflicts or ethnic tensions?

Cultural Psychology: A Cross- and Multicultural Approach will include chapters on the newest, most groundbreaking issues facing the study of culture, including how to unpack the origins of culture—where it comes from—and how to test the history of culture in modern-day laboratory studies, how culture shapes the brain (and how the brain changes culture), and the question of cultural change in the era of globalization.

References

Knowles, E., & Peng, K. (2005). White selves: Conceptualizing and measuring a dominant-group identity. *Journal of Personality and Social Psychology, 89*, 223–241.

Markus, H. R., & Conner, A. (2013). *Clash! 8 cultural conflicts that make us who we are.* New York, NY: Penguin Group.

Vohs, K. D., Mead, N. L., & Goode, M. R. (2006). The psychological consequences of money. *Science, 314*(5802), 1154–1156.

Acknowledgments

I would like to thank the reviewers who read parts or all of this manuscript:

Steven L. Berman, University of Central Florida

Lilia Briones, California State University, San Bernardino

Brenya Buchalski, University of Texas, San Antonio

Vannee Cao-Nguyen, University of West Florida

Matt J. Goren, Social Science for Industry

Gustavo Gottret, University of Ottawa

Graciela Espinosa Hernandez, University of North Carolina, Wilmington

Special thanks to Glenn Gamst, for providing material on multicultural practices in clinical settings; Thai Chu, for sharing his teaching materials when I taught my first Multicultural Psychology class; all the cultural researchers and psychologists whose work made this possible; and my RAs—ShaiAsia Wanamaker, Brianna Bishop, Brian Villagrana, Matthew Farah, Reina Aldape, and Tatiana Hoapili—for all their assistance.

Half of the World's Population Is . . .

Asian (United Nations, 2015). There are 22 countries in the Middle East and the 15 largest cities in the world have two things in common: (1) none of the cities is in Europe, and (2) none of them is in the United States ("Largest Cities in the World," 2018). These stark realities alone may explain the fact that most people in the world are Yellow, Black, Brown, poor, female, non-Christian, and do not speak English (Central Intelligence Agency, 2016). So, the answer to the tacit question of who cares about culture (and why should we?) is: You do, I do, we all do. As the rest of this book will reveal, race, God, money, sex, and who you voted for changes all that we know about "human nature," from how you like your coffee and who you vote for to how you raise your kids and who you sleep with. This is the story of how culture changes (almost) everything.

We Are a (Uniquely) Cultural Species

Veronica Rutledge and her husband loved everything about guns. They practiced at shooting ranges. They hunted. And both of them, relatives and friends say, had permits to carry concealed firearms. Veronica typically left her Blackfoot, Idaho, home with her gun nestled at her side. So on Christmas morning last week, her husband gave her a present he hoped would make her life more comfortable: a purse with a special pocket for a concealed weapon. The day after Christmas, she took her new gift with her on a trip with her husband and her 2-year-old son. (McCoy, 2014, para 1.)

On Tuesday morning, Veronica went to Walmart with her son, her gun "zippered closed" inside her new purse. She left her purse unattended for a moment (McCoy, 2014). "An inquisitive 2-year-old boy [her son] reached into the purse, unzipped the compartment, found the gun and shot his mother in the head" (T. Rutledge, as quoted in McCoy, 2014).

PHOTO 1.1. The tragedy of Veronica Rutledge

Source: Facebook

Afterward, reporters interviewed her father-in-law, Terry Rutledge, who perhaps not surprisingly was extremely devastated. But Rutledge wasn't merely heartbroken, he was angry—not with his grandson or his deceased daughter-in-law. Rather, he was "angry at the observers [he perceived to be] already using the accident as an excuse to grandstand on gun rights" (McCoy, 2014, para. 8).

Why a grandfather would respond to his grandson fatally and accidentally shooting his daughter by being concerned about gun laws and his lawful, Second Amendment right to bear arms may be a puzzle to economists, liberals, and everyone who doesn't live in Idaho, apparently, but it's not a puzzle to cultural psychologists, because cultural psychologists study culture. And if there is one thing you will walk away from this class knowing, it's that your culture—whether it's gun culture or midwestern culture or California culture or American culture or whatever other culture you subscribe to—can fundamentally change the way you think, feel, and respond to the world around you. As the rest of the book will cover, this is the story of how culture has changed (almost) everything.

Said differently, we are a uniquely cultural species. What makes us so different from all the other life-forms around us is not simply a matter of our opposable thumbs or binocular vision—which are useful but not all that unique since all primates have those. It is also not just our capacity for language—even prairie dogs can speak, as scientists discovered a few years ago, after listening to them chirp for 30 years. Apparently they can talk about your height, build, and what you're wearing—yes, prairie dogs will gossip about your weight, apparently, to their prairie dog friends ("Prairie dogs' language decoded by scientists," 2013), so watch out!

So humans are uniquely cultural, more so than any other species, and we are so cultural that it may just be the most unique thing about us. How do we know this? We know, because we are the only animal that

- Is afraid to die (e.g., see discussion of terror management theory in chapter 3), and dies for our ideas.
- Managed to hurl ourselves onto the moon. Think about it! There're no great restaurants up there, no hot members of the opposite sex with whom we can procreate; there is not even oxygen. Nevertheless, a group of humans got together and said among themselves, "Hey, this seems like a good idea to throw millions of dollars at," and the rest of the humans sat mesmerized, watching it live the day it happened.
- Tires of interacting with other members of our species and opts for cloning ourselves in the nontraditional way—that is, via robots or love dolls (e.g., "Strange Love," n.d.).
- Thinks birth control is a good idea, that will go out of our way not to have kids and then sometimes change our mind when we're too old to have kids (and then develop crazy loopholes that will allow us to have kids anyway like freeze our eggs or donate our sperm or get other members of our species to be injected with our egg and sperm so that they can have our children for us and then give them back to us after the birth).

You get the point. Humans are incredibly cultural, and our culture may be one of the most defining and interesting features of our species. But what is culture?

Before we explain how culture changes (almost) everything, we must first define our terms. Culture can be broadly defined in at least three ways.

Definition 1: Culture as information (e.g., Kashima & Gelfand, 2012). Here, culture is acquired from other members of one's species through mechanisms such as social learning, and it includes values, beliefs, and practices as norms. For example, your culture will largely determine what you know about emotion display rules (Matsumoto, 1990) and how familiar you are with different hand gestures (photo I.2), as in how you interpret the meaning of strangers pointing their index and pinky fingers at you.

Definition 2: Culture as the people, or a group of individuals, living in a shared social context (for review, see Lehman, Chiu, & Schaller, 2004). To say that culture is defined by having a group of people is not as obvious as it sounds and shouldn't be taken lightly.

Here's why having a group of people is important: To borrow a concept from economics and game theory, consider the "Prisoner's Dilemma" (Rapoport & Chammah, 1965). Say you go into the test-stealing business with a fellow student (Gilbert, 2012). The two of you go to introductory psychology courses at large universities and steal copies of exams and then turn around and sell them for $100 a pop to anyone who wants an easy A, but alas, you and your business partner get found out (Gilbert, 2012). Law enforcement agents detain you, separate you in different rooms, and interrogate you (Gilbert, 2012). You know that if you both stay silent, they have no case, but if you both confess, you're both going to jail—so obviously, you and your partner should both keep your mouths shut (Gilbert, 2012). But they want to induce you to talk, so they also let you know that if you stay silent and your partner snitches, you go to jail and your partner walks, but if your partner stays silent and you betray him or her, your partner goes to jail and you go free (Gilbert, 2012). If you study these possible outcomes, you'll find that you're in a prisoner's dilemma (Gilbert, 2012).

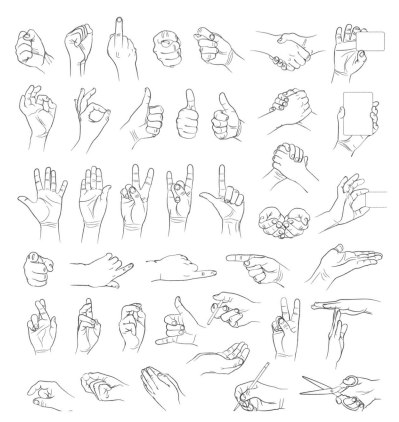

PHOTO 1.2. Culture as information: The meaning of hand gestures

Source: iStock

Say that you are going to a Prisoner's Dilemma (PD) tournament, one in which you'll be playing PD with all kinds of people (Gilbert, 2012). What would be your winning strategy? Ideally, you would need to find a large group of people you know to play the tournament and decide that whenever you're playing with each other, you'll cooperate; that way, you'll maximize the chance that one of you will win and split the money with everyone else, but for this to work, you have to have a way of knowing who is willing to participate in this strategy (Gilbert, 2012). How would you do that?

You could wear matching outfits, come up with a secret handshake, or memorize each other's names and faces, but there is also an easier way to ensure cooperation: you do it all the time, and it's called being part of a group (Gilbert, 2012). You're members of teams, clubs, cliques, families, races, nations—groups that you belong to with visible signs such as matching costumes and secret handshakes; being part of groups is a way of knowing whom you can trust (Gilbert, 2012). Human beings are wired to favor those in their own group because doing so offers tangible benefits, and culture is often part of that process.

Definition 3: Culture as a shared way of life among a group of people, that is human-made, collective, enduring, and organized (Hofstede, 1980a). *Human-made* refers to the idea that culture is created by people; as such, culture will invariably change as people change (see chapters 11 and 13). *Collective* means that culture is, by definition, a shared phenomenon rather than a solitary or isolated occurrence. Culture is transmitted across time (it endures), over generations, in groups. Culture is also organized in that cultures typically vary systematically rather than randomly. As we will discuss in chapter 1, there are underlying cultural dimensions that can be used to understand and distinguish between just about all cultures, and they often relate to one another in predictable ways.

Cross-Cultural Psychology Approaches and Methods

As with all psychological science, the approach to understanding culture and the human psyche is twofold. On the one hand, we can take a top-down approach, where we take a specific theory and test how that theory plays out in different cultures. As we will discuss in chapter 11, many of the initial studies in cultural psychology in the first two decades since its inception have been about taking Western concepts and testing their applicability and generalizability in non-Western contexts. On the other hand, we can also take a bottom-up approach, where we start with observations about a given cultural group or context and then create a theory from our observations.

In both approaches, the overarching goal of cross-cultural psychology is the same as the rest of psychology—namely, to describe, explain, and predict human behavior. As such, we rely on the scientific method of making observations, formulating a specific hypothesis or prediction, testing said hypothesis in an experiment, analyzing our data using statistical techniques, drawing conclusions, and using the findings from our studies to formulate theories.

Threats to Validity in Cross-Cultural Research

Although we rely on many of the same empirical methods and theoretical approaches as the rest of psychology, cross-cultural research is nevertheless subject to a unique set of threats to validity (outlined below), given the nature of our studies.

- Translations. Unlike mainstream psychological studies, the very words we use in cross-cultural studies can be problematic because not all languages share equivalent words. To illustrate, the English word *procrastinate* does not always have a direct translation in many other languages, and the German word *schadenfreude*, which refers to a feeling of joy at your enemy's suffering (e.g., Leach, Spears, Branscombe, & Doosje, 2003), does not have a direct translation in English. Beyond issues of equivalency, similar issues arise when translating expressions, given that most languages have idioms that may or may not always translate literally (e.g., the English expression *kick the bucket* cannot be literally translated). To address these potential translation issues, **back-translations** are often used in cross-cultural research in cases where experimental materials need to be used in more than one language (Brislin, 1970). That is, original materials are typically first translated to the second language by one person, and then a different person will back-translate—that is, translate the translated material back into the original language, and the two versions (the original version and the back-translated version) will be compared to establish equivalency.

- Response bias. Beyond translation issues, cultural psychology is also subject to some of the other threats to validity found in psychology more generally. One of the major biases is response bias, which can be particularly problematic when comparing answers to surveys by different cultural groups. Some cultures are likely to show a **moderacy bias** when they answer questions—that is, choosing middle-of-scale answers (Heine & Lehman, 1995)—whereas other groups might show an **extremity bias**—opting for the ends of the scales when answering questions (Schulman, 1973). These biases have less to do with how the cultures actually perceive or think and more to do with the way they like to answer questions. If you discover a difference between groups, you do not know if it's because they are actually different or just different in terms of their preferred response styles. To address these response biases, researchers can opt to use dichotomous questions that rely on yes/no answers (rather than Likert-type scales that have clear extremes and a middle; e.g., Flaskerud, 1988). Alternatively, if Likert-type scales are used, researchers can rely on individual standardized z-scores instead of raw scores to capture how much each participant deviates from his or her own average response (e.g., Fischer, 2004). A related response bias is **acquiescence bias,** or the tendency for participants to agree with the statement regardless of its content or the participant's actual thoughts and feelings (van de Vijver & Tanzer, 1997). In the context of cross-cultural research, acquiescence bias is more prevalent in cultures that hold holistic views (van Dijk, Datema, Piggen, Welten, & van de Vijver, 2009; see chapter 1), in which many possible truths are viable. To deal with acquiescence bias issues, researchers can reverse score responses to statements worded one way and the same statement worded in the opposite way (e.g., "I feel like I am a person of worth" and "I feel like I have no worth at all") to determine whether a participant is endorsing contradictory views by agreeing with two opposite statements (e.g., Watson, 1992).
- Reference group effects: To illustrate the reference group effect (Heine, Lehman, Peng, & Greenholtz, 2002), consider these two questions: How smart are you? How physically attractive are you? How did you come up with your answer?

At the core of the reference group effect is the issue of who people are comparing themselves to when answering questions—that is, what their reference point is (Heine et al., 2002). If I ask you, "How smart are you?" are you comparing yourself to (1) other students at your university, (2) other college students in general, (3) the general population in the city you live in, (4) the general population of the world, or (5) something else?

There are various strategies to cope with reference group effects. One way is to simply be more concrete and specific about the precise behavior at hand, and to avoid overly general questions (Heine et al., 2002). So instead of asking you how smart you are, I can ask you what your IQ score is (or give you an IQ test). A related strategy is to ask for quantitative descriptions (e.g., what percentage of people are smarter than you?) or offer predetermined reference points (Heine et al., 2002). Another option is to avoid self-report all together and rely on behavioral or physiological measures that are not prone to reporting biases (for review, see Heine et al., 2002).

Goals and Nongoals of This Book

The study of culture is, at worst, misinterpreted as the study of a long and illustrious history of **stereotypes**. In stereotyping, as in culture, people make generalizations about groups of people based on a limited sample of data that may or may not represent everyone from that group. What, then, is the difference?

On the one hand, cultural psychology acknowledges that **generalizations** are a key part of the endeavor to understand human behavior, and one that is not unique to the study of culture. Indeed, in every subfield of psychology—and many other sciences—generalizations are made about types of people (e.g., about introverts versus extroverts, in personality psychology, or 4-year-olds versus 7-year-olds, in developmental psychology) or people in types of situations (e.g., people under cognitive load versus no cognitive load, in cognitive psychology). As in these other contexts, between-group differences are the focus, but within-group variation is also an assumed norm. In cultural psychology, this within-group heterogeneity means that not all members of a given group will behave in a predicted, culturally normative way.

The other truth about the study of culture that distinguishes it from the study of stereotypes is that cultural differences themselves are changeable—they can evolve. As we will discuss in chapter 13, culture changes as people change, and there is growing empirical evidence that even minor tweaks in one's environment can produce substantive changes in one's cultural behavior. Thus, rather than being something stable and essential that is assigned to you (as in the case of stereotypes), culture represents a socially learned feature that you can change.

A second nongoal of this book is overknowledge. The aim of this book is to highlight the fact that differences are not to be confused with deficits and that to appreciate diversity we must first recognize and understand where such differences exist. However, even though there are real and substantive cultural differences between people that should not be ignored, it is also important to not jump to immediate conclusions when interacting with a person from a different cultural background. After all, within-group heterogeneity means that not everyone within a cultural group will act in a similar way or necessarily identify with being a member of that culture to the same extent.

Instead, the goal of this book is to use theoretical and empirical findings to demonstrate that there is no such thing as a "general" or "neutral" person but that people always behave in shared, culture-specific ways. To this end, the aim is for you to understand the world from various different points of view, including your own. In doing so, you may end up broadening your understanding of how people define what is good, beautiful, true, useful, efficient, beneficial, and real; as a result, you might become slower to jump to premature (or unfounded) conclusions and more informed before taking a stance.

References

Brislin, R. W. (1970). Back-translation for cross-cultural research. *Journal of cross-cultural psychology*, *1*(3), 185–216.

Central Intelligence Agency (2016). *Country comparison: Population*. Retrieved from https://www.cia.gov/library/publications/the-world-factbook/rankorder/2119rank.html

Fischer, R. (2004). Standardization to account for cross-cultural response bias: A classification of score adjustment procedures and review of research in JCCP. *Journal of Cross-Cultural Psychology*, *35*(3), 263–282.

Flaskerud, J. H. (1988). Is the Likert scale format culturally biased? *Nursing Research*, *37*, 185–186.

Gilbert, D. (2012). Survival. Retrieved from Harvard University course, Science of Living Systems.

Heine, S. J., & Lehman, D. R. (1995). Social desirability among Canadian and Japanese students. *The Journal of Social Psychology*, *135*(6), 777–779.

Heine, S. J., Lehman, D. R., Peng, K., & Greenholtz, J. (2002). What's wrong with cross-cultural comparisons of subjective Likert scales? The reference-group effect. *Journal of Personality and Social Psychology*, *82*(6), 903–918. doi:10.1037/0022-3514.82.6.903

Hofstede, G. (1980a). Culture and organizations. *International Studies of Management & Organization*, *10*(4), 15–41.

Kashima, Y., & Gelfand, M. J. (2012). A history of culture in psychology. In A. W. Kruglanski & W. Stroebe (Eds.), *Handbook of the history of social psychology* (pp. 499–520). New York, NY: Psychology Press.

Largest cities in the world. (2018). City Mayors Statistics. Retrieved from http://www.citymayors.com/statistics/largest-cities-population-125.html

Leach, C. W., Spears, R., Branscombe, N. R., & Doosje, B. (2003). Malicious pleasure: Schadenfreude at the suffering of another group. *Journal of Personality and Social Psychology*, *84*(5), 932–943.

Lehman, D. R., Chiu, C., & Schaller, M. (2004). Psychology and culture. *Annual Review of Psychology*, *55*(1), 689–714. doi:10.1146/annurev.psych.55.090902.141927

Matsumoto, D. (1990). Cultural similarities and differences in display rules. *Motivation and Emotion*, *14*(3), 195–214.

McCoy, T. (2014, December 31). The inside story of how an Idaho toddler shot his mom at Wal-Mart. *The Washington Post*. Retrieved from https://www.washingtonpost.com/news/morning-mix/wp/2014/12/31/the-inside-story-of-how-an-idaho-toddler-shot-his-mom-at-wal-mart/

Prairie dogs' language decoded by scientists (2013, June 21). *CBC News*. Retrieved from http://www.cbc.ca/news/technology/prairie-dogs-language-decoded-by-scientists-1.1322230

Rapoport, A., & Chammah, A. M. (1965). *Prisoner's dilemma: A study in conflict and cooperation*. Ann Arbor: University of Michigan Press.

Shulman, A. (1973). A comparison of two scales on extremity response bias. *The Public Opinion Quarterly*, *37*(3), 407–412.

Strange love. *National Geographic*. Retrieved from http://channel.nationalgeographic.com/taboo/episodes/strange-love

United Nations (2015). Population. Retrieved from the World Population Dashboard website: http://www.un.org/en/sections/issues-depth/population/

Van de Vijver, F., & Tanzer, N. K. (1997). Bias and equivalence in cross-cultural assessment: An overview. *European Review of Applied Psychology*, *47*(4), 263–279.

Van Dijk, T. K., Datema, F., Piggen, A. L. J. H. F., Welten, S. C. M., & van de Vijver, F. J. R. (2009). Acquiescence and extremity in cross-national surveys: Domain dependence and country-level correlates. In A. Gari & K. Mylonas (Eds.), *Quod erat demonstrandum: From Herodotus' ethnographic journeys to cross-cultural research* (pp. 149–158). Athens, Greece: International Association for Cross-Cultural Psychology.

Watson, D. (1992). Correcting for acquiescent response bias in the absence of a balanced scale: An application to class consciousness. *Sociological Methods & Research*, *21*(1), 52–88.

CHAPTER 1

Race, Ethnicity, and Nationality

Since the inception of cultural psychology as a breakthrough new field in the early 1990s that suddenly challenged everything mainstream psychology thought it knew about "human nature," the study of culture—at least in Western psychology—has largely been the study of racial, ethnic, and national differences. Thus the first—and longest—chapter of this book pays homage to the extensive and rich literature on comparative differences between European Americans and other groups. The chapter will begin with a brief discussion of the meanings assigned to terms like *race*, *ethnicity*, and *nationality*, including how they are operationalized in the context of cross-cultural research methods. The chapter will then be organized by race/ethnicity and include separate sections for cross-cultural studies on East Asians/Asian Americans, Latinos/Latino Americans, Africans/African Americans, and Native Americans. Given that the overwhelming majority of cross-cultural research has been conducted on East Asians, this section will be the largest and include cultural differences in the self, emotion, cognition, morality, and psychopathology. Sections on Latinos/Latino Americans, Africans/African Americans, and Native Americans will focus on variations in the self, cognition, and psychopathology.

Defining Race, Culture, and Ethnicity

The terms *race*, *ethnicity*, and *culture* are often used interchangeably, but theoretical distinctions exist in their actual definitions. **Ethnicity** refers to the affiliation a person has with a specific ethnic group, whereas **racial identity** refers to how racial minorities develop a concept of the self through the experience of racial oppression (Gamst, Liang, & Der-Karabetian, 2011). Racial identity is also distinct from **race**, which often refers to the notion of presumably biologically based group differences (Smedley & Smedley, 2005). While ethnicity, culture, and racial identity all refer to subjective senses of belonging to social groups (e.g., "tiger moms" may be seen as one of them; see Insight Box 1.1), race typically implies an objective, biological distinction—a distinction that modern science has not been able to locate (Smedley & Smedley, 2005).

INSIGHT BOX 1.1

Were You Raised by a Tiger Mom?

In 2011, Amy Chua made national headlines and raised many pointed eyebrows when she came out with her polemic book on parenting, *Battle Hymn of the Tiger Mom*. In doing so, she raised all kinds of thorny questions about culture and parenting, some of which will be discussed in more detail in this chapter. For a quick diagnostic of whether you were raised by a so-called "tiger mom," consider the following checklist:

- attend a sleepover
- have a playdate
- be in a school play
- complain about not being in a school play
- watch TV or play computer games
- choose their own extracurricular activities
- get any grade less than an A
- not be the #1 student in every subject except gym and drama
- play any instrument other than the piano or violin
- not play the piano or violin (excerpt from Chua, 2011, pp. 3–4)

If you checked all (or most) of the above rules, you may have likely been raised by a "tiger mom" yourself. Keep in mind that although tiger-parenting is largely construed as a Chinese phenomenon in Chua's book, she also acknowledges that the term is loosely used to mean any mother who practices the kind of strict parenting style outlined above—a style psychologists refer to as authoritarian parenting—a style of parenting not specific to Asian countries (and not practiced by all Asian parents; e.g., see Rudy & Grusec, 2001, 2006).

Although there is not direct research on "tiger parenting," there is a rich body of literature on how culture shapes parenting styles. **Authoritarian parenting** imposes absolute standards and values obedience and respect for authority, whereas **authoritative parenting** believes in firm control and exerts high demands for maturity but also endorses a willingness to reason and negotiate (for a review, see Dornbusch, Ritter, Leiderman, Roberts, & Fraleigh, 1987). However, whether authoritarian or authoritative parenting is more effective at producing high levels of internalization of parental values depends on cultural context (e.g., authoritarian parenting is linked to low internalization among middle-class Anglos but not necessarily among other groups; see Rudy & Grusec, 2001, for review). Authoritative parenting styles are more common in the United States and parts of Europe, whereas authoritarian parenting is more common in Asia, Mexico, Egypt, and among African Americans in the United States, to name several (e.g., Brody & Flor, 1998; Leung, Lau, & Lam, 1998; Rudy & Grusec, 2001, 2006; Varela, Vernberg, Sanchez-Sosa, Riveros, Mitchell, & Mashunkashey, 2004).*

The question everyone wants to know is: Which type of parenting is better? As with much of psychology, the answer is "it depends." In other (i.e., non-American) cultural contexts, authoritarian parents encourage children to align themselves with group values without much discussion, but this is under the assumption that the group will work to fulfill the child's needs. As a result, in these non-American contexts, authoritarian parenting is associated with positive outcomes, such as warmth (Brody & Flor, 1998) and concern for the child's success (Rudy & Grusec, 2001). In North America, however, authoritarian parenting is associated with negative outcomes: negative parental emotion, a less positive view of the child, and a lack of warmth (Rudy & Grusec, 2006). Moreover, authoritarian parents tend to blame children's misbehavior on the children's dispositions or traits and as a result, feel a loss of control (Coplan, Hastings, Lagacé-Séguin, & Moulton, 2002; Rudy & Grusec, 2001, 2006).

How do we make sense of these opposing effects of parenting in different cultural contexts? In my first semester in college, I had this political science professor whose name has long escaped me but whose catchy New York accent and no-nonsense, Dr. Phil-esque attitude I could not help but take notice of. I've forgotten everything he taught us about South Africa apartheid, the Gorbachev phenomenon, the prerequisites for a civil society, and the problem with bringing democracy to the rest of the world (it was, after all, Berkeley). The only thing I do remember—and the one thing I'd like to leave you with now—is the difference between "normative" and "descriptive." **Normative** is the way things should be. **Descriptive** is the way things are. With much of cultural psychology, the findings are descriptive rather than normative; the science will tell us how things are but remain silent on the much harder question of how things should be. Thus, if there is one bottom line to culture and parenting, it would be this: If culture changes everything, so does context. In other words, culture happens in specific contexts, and taking cultural phenomena out of context doesn't always produce the same effects.

*A third type of parenting, **permissive parenting**, also exists, and there is little research to suggest positive outcomes associated with this kind of laissez-faire style (e.g., Dwairy, 2004; Querido, Warner, & Eyberg, 2002).

APPLYING WHAT WE KNOW: CONTENT ANALYSIS OF CULTURAL PRODUCTS

Culture isn't magic; it always comes from somewhere. But where? Often, culture is perpetuated via cultural products. Consider:

• The most popular children's TV shows
• The most iconic artists and their most popular songs
• Beloved movies and books
• Popular cultural products and their ads

For each product above, try to find what cultural idea it expresses. For example, consider Grover's "I am Special" song on *Sesame Street* (the most watched children's TV sitcom in American history; Hymowitz, 1995), or Madonna's hit single, "Express Yourself" (the third most popular single in Madonna's prolific career; Jacobs, 2014). For best results, compare products across cultures and see if you can spot the differences.

To illustrate, consider *My Sassy Girl*, the highest grossing Korean comedy of all time (until recently; Chu, 2016). If you have seen the movie, you may know that it is essentially Korea's equivalent of *Grease*, or *When Harry Met Sally*, or *Titanic*. The basic storyline—based on a true story—goes something like this:

• Boy meets inebriated girl on the subway
• Boy is pressured into helping her because the other passengers mistake him as her boyfriend

- After he helps her, he feels responsible for her, leading to a relationship that allows him to tolerate her many abuses.

It's interesting to note that an American version of the movie got made and few saw it— which bring us to the question of how Asian cultural norms and values and European American ones diverge.

As an additional illustrative example, consider these classic fairy-tale endings across East versus West:

- Cinderella: Indentured by her stepsisters, Cinderella escapes to a prince's ball and captures his heart. (In the Brothers Grimm version, pigeons pluck the eyes of the stepsisters).
- Japanese Cinderella: The stepsisters fall down and apologize (also in an early French version); Cinderella forgives them and invites them to live in the castle with her, suggesting that they all live happily ever after—together (Kristoff, 1999).
- Goldilocks: Goldilocks goes in the bears' empty home, eats their porridge, and breaks their furniture. Caught in their bed, she runs out and goes unpunished, never to return to the forest again.
- Japanese Goldilocks: Goldilocks apologizes; the bears accept and invite her to visit again (Kristoff, 1999).

East Asians versus European Americans

The Self

When I was in graduate school, I worked in a lab headed by a Korean professor named Heejung Kim, a cultural psychologist whose work will reappear in this book. The first time I met with her at her office, I noticed an interesting sign on her door that I'd never seen before (photo 1.1).

PHOTO 1.1. Uniqueness is not always valued everywhere.

Source: iStock

It single-handedly captures one of the primary differences between different cultural selves, which are further elaborated below.

Self-Construal Unique attributes are at the core of the European American model of the self. For many European Americans, the self is a stable, bounded, internal collection of innate abilities and traits that is separate from others, guides behavior, and is relatively less influenced by situational context or social norms (Markus & Kitayama, 1991). This is in contrast to the East Asian model of the self, which is a more permeable, situationally dependent entity that is fundamentally connected to the thoughts, feelings, and behaviors of others (Markus & Kitayama, 1991; see figure 1.1).

These differences in cultural selves can be observed in everyday life. Consider the ads we encounter (photo 1.2). After analyzing the content of magazines, Kim and Markus (1999) found that rebellion, individual choice, freedom, and uniqueness were the common recurrent themes in American magazines, whereas respect for collective values, group harmony, and following trends were the most prevalent themes in Korean magazines.

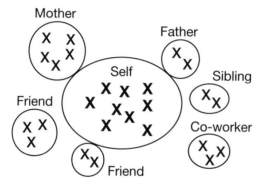

A. Independent View of Self

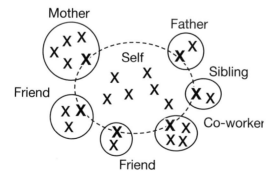

B. Interdependent View of Self

FIG. 1.1. Markus and Kitayama's (1991) notion of independent versus interdependent selves

Source: Based on Markus, H. R., & Kitayama, S. (1991). Culture and the self: Implications for cognition, emotion, and motivation. *Psychological Review, 98*(2), 224–253.

PHOTO 1.2. Cultural products include the ads we see.

Source: Getty

These differences in self-construal can also be seen in actual behaviors. Interviews with Olympic athletes often reflect the same cultural script of independent Western selves and interdependent Eastern selves. Consider the following quotes by Japanese versus American athletes:

"Here is the best coach in the world, the best manager in the world, and all the people who support me—all these things were getting together and became a gold medal. So I think I didn't get it alone, not only by myself."—Naoko Takahasi, marathon (Yamamoto, 2000, as cited in Markus, Uchida, Omoregie, Townsend, & Kitayama, 2006)

"I don't want to sound selfish in saying that I'm swimming for myself, you know? There's a lot of influences and motivating factors. But when I stand up on the blocks, it has to be coming from within me."—Gary Hall, swimming (Neal, 2000, as cited in Murphy-Berman & Berman, 2003)

Empirical analyses of the media's coverage of Olympic events yielded a similar pattern of results: While American media focused on the individual characteristics of the athlete, Japanese media were far more likely to focus on the emotional features of the event and the athlete's training and background, including their relationship with their coaches and the support of their families (Markus et al., 2006; and see table 1.1).

TABLE 1.1. Summary of European American versus East Asian Cultural Selves

European American selves	East Asian selves
Separate from other people, stable, consistent	Fundamentally <u>inter</u>dependent individuals
Individual traits, preferences, goals as basis of the self	Must actively adjust self to fit into one's <u>ingroup</u>
Well-developed personal sense of self	Important to know and occupy one's proper place within the group
Try to control the situation	Adjust the self to fit the social situation
Maintain sense of self as positive and unique.	Committed to maintaining group harmony

Sources: Lebra, 1976; Markus & Kitayama, 1991

APPLYING WHAT WE KNOW: THE "I AM . . ." TASK

What kind of self-construal do you have? To answer this question, complete the prompt, "I am ____," 20 times (Cousins, 1989):

I am_____.
I am_____.
I am_____.
I am_____.
I am_____.
I am_____.
I am_____.
I am_____.
I am_____.
I am_____.
I am_____.
I am_____.
I am_____.
I am_____.
I am_____.
I am_____.
I am_____.
I am_____.
I am_____.
I am_____.

Afterward, group your responses together in meaningful categories, like individual attributes (e.g., "I am blonde"; "I am tall"; "I am smart"), social group membership or relationships (e.g., "I am a daughter"; "I am in love"; "I am a member of ___"); universals (e.g., "I am a human"; "I am a living thing"), and so forth. Pay special attention to the first five responses you gave. The type of statement you made in your top five responses should be a relatively good reflection of your self-construal.

When Japanese and European American participants completed the same "I am" task as part of a study, Cousins (1989) found that while U.S. participants focused primarily on "pure attributes"—individuating features of the person that made them unique, Japanese participants focused primarily on social roles. Thus how people see and talk about themselves are also a good indication of the kind of selves their culture promotes.

Self-Esteem Culture doesn't only change how you see yourself; culture also conditions how you feel about yourself. In mainstream psychology, the assumption has long been that people everywhere need self-esteem, or positive self-feelings, and as such, it was also assumed that people everywhere use the same kinds of self-enhancing strategies to boost and maintain their self-esteem (Heine, Lehman, and Markus, 1999). However, when Heine, Lehman, and Markus (1999) administered the Rosenberg Self-Esteem Scale (Rosenberg, 1965) to Japanese and Canadian participants with varying degrees of exposure to American culture (from Japanese who have never been abroad on one end to long-term Asian immigrants in the middle, to European Canadians on the other end), they found that self-esteem increased as exposure increased. Japanese who had never been abroad exhibited the lowest self-esteem, whereas third-generation Asian Canadians and European Canadians exhibited the highest self-esteem; Asian immigrants exhibited self-esteem levels that were in-between (Heine et al., 1999; see figure 1.2).

What accounts for these cultural differences in self-esteem? To answer this question, Kitayama and his colleagues (Kitayama, Markus, Matsumoto, & Norasakkunkit, 1997) asked three groups of participants—(1) Japanese living in Kyoto, Japan, (2) Japanese Americans living in Eugene, Oregon, and (3) European Americans living in Eugene, Oregon—to describe different situations in their everyday life that raised versus hurt their self-esteem, or success versus failure situations. They subsequently took these situations and presented them to a new group of Japanese, Japanese Americans, and European Americans; they asked the new group of participants to imagine themselves being in these Japan-made versus U.S.-made situations and rate how each situation would make them feel (Kitayama et al., 1997). They found two interesting and parallel sets of effects. First, Kitayama et al. (1997) found that overall, American participants reported self-esteem increases whereas Japanese participants reported self-esteem decreases in response to these scenarios; this was consistent with the previous data showing that self-esteem is generally higher in the United States than in Japan. Second, they found that whether the situation was made in Japan or made in the United States also made a difference; among all participants, situations made in the United States lead to more increases in self-esteem than situations made in Japan do (Kitayama et al., 1997).

Emotion

The American poet Mark van Doren once observed that there are "two statements about human beings that are true: that all human beings are alike, and that all are different." The trick is figuring out when the first statement is true and when the second statement is truer. In the case of cultural difference in emotion, both statements apply.

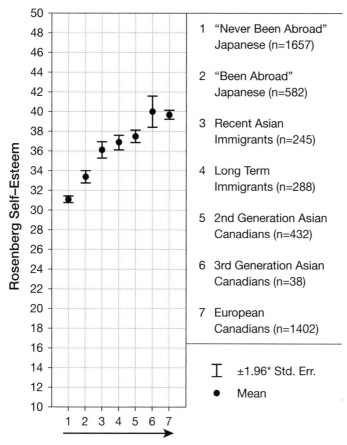

FIG. 1.2. Heine, Lehman, Markus, and Kitayama (1999) found self-esteem to change as a function of exposure to American culture.

Source: Based on Heine, S. J., Lehman, D. R., Markus, H. R., & Kitayama, S. (1999). Is there a universal need for positive self-regard? *Psychological Review*, *106*(4), 766–794.

Ideal versus Actual Affect When Jeannie Tsai and her colleagues in 2006 set out to study culture and emotion at her laboratory in Stanford, they found a seemingly irreconcilable paradox: On the one hand, ethnographies compiled by ethnic studies researchers and anthropologists seemed to suggest that a great deal of variation existed in how people experienced emotions across different countries. Not surprising, numerous theorists by the 1980s and '90s assumed that this meant that culture fundamentally shaped how people experienced emotion (e.g., Kleinman & Good, 1985; Shweder, 1995; Tsai, Knutson, Fung, 2006; Wierzbicka, 1994). On the other hand, a number of empirical studies that were just beginning to emerge at the time found no real evidence for cultural variation in reported emotional responses among people from different countries (e.g., Scherer, 1997), and related studies on people's physiological and facial responses to emotional situations similarly found little evidence for cultural differences (e.g., Tsai & Levenson, 1997; Tsai, Levenson, & Carstensen, 2000).

To reconcile this paradox, Tsai and her colleagues proposed a new framework named Affect Valuation Theory, which posited that (1) ideal and actual affect are distinguishable forms of feeling, with ideal affect referring to feelings people want to feel and actual affect referring to feelings people actually feel; and (2) culture changes ideal affect more than actual affect (Tsai, Knutson, & Fung, 2006). In other words, the enormous cultural differences captured by ethnographers might reflect variation in ideal affect, whereas the small to nonexistent cultural differences found in empirical cross-cultural studies might be capturing actual affect (Tsai et al., 2006). Consistent with this idea, they found that while European Americans liked feeling excited and other kinds of high-arousal positive emotions (HAP emotions), East Asians prefer to feel calm and other kinds of low-arousal positive emotions (LAP emotions), presumably because excitement facilitates being unique whereas calmness allows one to be like others and fit in (Tsai et al., 2006).

A subsequent study by Tsai, Louie, Chen, and Uchida (2007) found that these cultural differences in ideal affect are learned through cultural products and socialization. In their analyses of children's storybooks (photo 1.3), Tsai and her colleagues (2007) found that best-selling children's books in the United States contained bigger smiles, more excited emotions, and more arousing situations than best sellers in Taiwan did. Moreover, exposure to these different kinds of storybooks changed children's preferences for exciting versus calm activities (Tsai et al., 2007). Consistent with what is discussed in "Applying What We Know: Content Analysis of Cultural Products," these findings confirm that observed cultural differences may be largely perpetuated via the cultural artifacts we produce and consume.

Emotional Expression versus Suppression Here's the thing: Things are not always what they seem. You don't need to be a psychologist to figure out that people are often motivated to hold back or "suppress" what they are automatically motivated to do and, instead, behave differently (Gazzaniga, 2008). For example, you might sometimes smile when you are not happy. People hold back surprise and disgust when the situation calls for them to do and they may even laugh when they feel like crying or are nervous. Given East-West cultural differences in values, norms, self-perceptions, and other-construals (for review, see Markus & Kitayama, 1991), it is not surprising that cultural differences exist in both the self-reported use of emotional expression and suppression (Butler, Lee, & Gross, 2007). Here the term **emotion expression** refers to behaviors that veridically reflect a felt emotion, while the term **emotion suppression** refers to the intentional act of reducing or inhibiting such expressive behaviors during emotional experiences (Gross & Levenson, 1993).

Mainstream psychology has extensively highlighted the functions of emotional display or expression. On the most basic level, emotional expression allows communication of internal states to others (e.g., Ekman & Davidson, 1993), which, in turn, facilitates the development and maintenance of social relationships (Ekman,

PHOTO 1.3. Storybook covers reflect cultural values

1993). Keltner (1995), for example, demonstrated that embarrassment displays can redress a transgression and appease the transgressed (other). Failure to express emotions has been associated with detriments to well-being, including increased negative affect (Gross & John, 2003) and more negative relational as well as physical outcomes (Richards, Butler, & Gross, 2003). With few exceptions, the general assumption is that emotional expression is an adaptive psychological practice with clear benefits for well-being and social functioning.

However, cultural psychologists have increasingly observed that this emphasis on emotional expression might be specific to American culture and that there is a link between Western European values of independence and the norm of open emotion expression (Markus & Kitayama, 1991; Oyserman, Coon, & Kemmelmeier, 2002; Tsai & Levenson, 1997; Wierzbicka, 1994). Recall the independent self-construal, where the individual is a unique entity who needs to assert his own independence and autonomy; thus emotions—as part of the independent self—need to be expressed in an open and frank manner. Emotion suppression has generally been associated with negative life outcomes in European American samples (e.g., Gross & John, 2003), and necessary only under conditions of self-protection (Wierzbicka,

1994). In contrast, recall the East Asian model of the interdependent self, where the self is not seen as its own autonomous entity but as one fundamentally connected to the needs and concerns of others (Markus & Kitayama, 1991). Hence, Asians tend to be highly concerned about the effect of their emotional expression (particularly of negative emotions) on others. Consequently, in order to maintain group harmony, emotional suppression is more valued than veridical emotional expression (Tsai et al., 2002). Indeed, Asians have been shown to report greater habitual suppression of emotional cues, both positive (Camras, Kolmodin, & Chen, 2008) and negative (Gross & John, 2003). Moreover, among Asians, suppression tends to be unrelated to negative social outcomes (Butler, Lee, & Gross, 2007) and actually related to positive life outcomes for cultural members (Huang, Leong, & Wagner, 1994), although these findings have not always been replicated with physiological measures (Roberts, Levenson, & Gross, 2008). Emotional expressivity, on the other hand, has been associated with poor psychological functioning (Chentsova-Dutton, Chu, Tsai, Rottenberg, Gross, & Gotlib, 2007).

Emotion Recognition and Accuracy Beyond the question of how individuals choose to express (or suppress) their true feelings, cultural differences also exist in how well people recognize and perceive feelings in other people. Several studies indicate that, in general, people are relatively poor at differentiating between emotional displays that are nonnormative in their culture. For example, Jack, Blais, Scheepers, Schyns, and Caldara (2009) found that in their eye-tracking study, East Asians tended to ignore facial cues when looking at negative, socially threatening emotions, making them unable to distinguish between "disgust" versus "fear." No such cultural differences emerged on socially acceptable emotions like "happy," "surprise," or "sad" (Jack et al., 2009). Jack et al. (2009) go on to argue that East Asians hold an emotion-processing bias against emotions (i.e., disgust, fear) that they do not want to see (or is considered inappropriate—in both themselves and others); disgust and fear may be particularly avoided for East Asians because they go against the collectivist goals of social harmony.

It is important to note that the tendency to detect culturally normative emotional displays more accurately than culturally nonnormative displays is not specific to one culture. East Asians are actually better than European Americans at differentiating between emotional displays that are valued in Eastern culture (and not valued in Western culture). For example, East Asians tend to be better discriminators between "guilt" and "shame" than European Americans are, apparently due to the major role these two emotions play in promoting Eastern values of "saving face" (Ho, Fu, & Ng, 2004). Thus it appears that in general, cultural norms surrounding the kinds of emotional displays that are acceptable (and their presumed accompanying practices) have strong influences on the accuracy with which individuals are able to detect such emotion-related facial displays.

Relationship context also plays a role. The interdependent self means that for East Asians, their emotional states are largely determined by interpersonal concerns (e.g., Mesquita & Karasawa, 2002), and emotions are typically perceived in the context of relationships (Masuda, Ellsworth, Mesquita, Leu, Tanida, & Van de Veerdonk, 2008). Not surprisingly, these cultural members dedicate much time and energy into knowing others' wants and moods. Consistent with this idea, Yamagishi (1988) found evidence that the Japanese monitor others' wants and needs more than their Western counterparts do. However, this phenomenon appears to apply predominantly in the context of close relationships. As Ma-Kellams and Blascovich (2012) found, East Asians were better at inferring the emotions experienced by close others (i.e., friends), but also worse at inferring the emotions experienced by strangers. Thus there are limits to interdependence, and East Asians' concerns are limited to close others and do not apply to strangers (Cousins, 1989; Ma-Kellams & Blascovich, 2012).

Emotion and the Body Evidence from both empirical and ethnographic studies suggests that emotions are fundamentally more linked to bodily events for members of East Asian cultures than for members of European American cultures. Chinese Americans use more somatic words than European Americans when talking about emotional events, including their relationships and childhood; furthermore, less acculturated Chinese exhibited greater reliance on somatic words (Tsai, Simeonova, & Watanabe, 2004). This finding is consistent with ethnographic research showing that in Chinese culture the body and psyche are connected: In the Chinese language, for example, multiple idiomatic emotional expressions use the body parts as metaphors (e.g., fear: Yu, 2009).

Interestingly, this bodily emphasis in the context of understanding emotions also means that East Asians are less accurate than European Americans when discerning the causes of physically arousing emotional events. In lab studies, they were more likely to misattribute the cause of their bodily changes—namely, when East Asians met an attractive person after crossing a dangerous, physically arousing (virtual) bridge, they were more likely to misattribute their bodily arousal from the bridge-crossing (sweaty hands, racing heart, butterflies in the stomach) to the attractive other person and mistakenly assume they were romantically interested; European Americans were less likely to make this error (Ma-Kellams et al., 2012).

Cognition

As with emotion, the study of culture and cognition is also marked by tension between presumably universal versus culturally specific processes. For much of the 20th century, mainstream psychology, following the ways of 18th- and 19th-century philosophers like Locke, Hume, and Mill, assumed that all adults relied on the same cognitive processes of categorization, learning, induction and deduction, and causal reasoning more generally (Nisbett, Peng, Choi, & Norenzayan, 2001). However, over the past three decades, cultural psychologists have uncovered major differences among cultures both in terms of specific beliefs and processes as well as in terms of lay epistemological theories more generally.

Broadly speaking, East Asian systems of thought are characterized by a greater emphasis on context, or field; the interrelationships or connectedness between objects; and dialectical ways of reasoning (Nisbett et al., 2001). As a result, East Asian cognitive styles are more holistic, contextual, field-dependent, intuitive, and relationship-based than Western cognitive styles are. This is in contrast to the Western or European American system of thought, which is characterized by a greater focus on central or focal objects, discreteness, and linear, Aristotelian thinking (Nisbett et al., 2001).

Attention In a classic study by Masuda and Nisbett (2001), Japanese and Americans viewed underwater scenes containing fish and other objects; afterward, they simply reported what they had seen. While (European) Americans focused primarily on the large, focal fish in the scene, Japanese focused on the various background elements (e.g., the surrounding water, smaller animals and plants, etc.; Masuda & Nisbett, 2001). In addition, Japanese also mentioned relationships between the different elements in the scene, whereas European Americans talked about the elements as discrete objects (Masuda & Nisbett, 2001). Afterward, Masuda and Nisbett (2001) gave both groups a recognition task in which the experimenter modified the background of the scene and tested participants' memory for the focal objects; European American participants' memory for the objects were unaffected by the change in background, whereas Japanese participants' memory was impaired.

Causality and Attribution A longstanding, paradigmatic feature of human cognition (according to mainstream psychology) has been the so-called **fundamental attribution error,** or **correspondence bias**—namely, the tendency for individuals to assume another person's behavior is the result of their dispositions rather than features of the situation (Ross, 1977; Gilbert & Malone, 1995). However, given the aforementioned tendency for Asians to attend to contextual elements of the environment, they should also be less likely to commit this "fundamental" error in making attributions about others' behavior. Consistent with this idea, various studies have shown that while European Americans tended to explain behavior via traits, Asians (including Hindu Indians, mainland Chinese, Hong Kong Chinese, and Koreans) tended to explain behavior via social roles, obligations, societal factors, and other features of the social or physical environment (Morris, Nisbett, & Peng, 1995; Morris & Peng, 1994; Norenzayan, Choi, & Nisbett, 2001). This tendency to emphasize contextual cues rather than dispositions emerged across a variety of situations, including when explaining mass murders (Morris et al., 1995; Morris & Peng, 1994) and sports events (Lee et al., 1996), as well as when predicting or explaining both people's behavior more generally (Norenzayan et al., 2001) and the actions of animals and objects (Morris & Peng, 1994).

Judgments of Association and Categorization East Asians' tendency to emphasize contextual cues in the environment also has implications for more basic cognitive processes like categorization. Emphasis on the field suggests that the field plays an important role in understanding the object, and knowing the relationship between object and field is fundamental to knowing the nature of the object itself; not surprisingly, East Asians tend to use relationships based on similarity as a basis of judgment of associations, which is in contrast to the tendency to rely on rules and categories as the basis of association that is more prevalent among European Americans (for a review, see Nisbett et al., 2001).

As a classic illustration of this, an early study by Chiu (1972) presented to Taiwanese and European American schoolchildren a series of pictures of related items (e.g., a man, a woman, and a child) and asked them to associate two objects. The Taiwanese children tended to make associations based on relationships and context (e.g., pairing the woman with the child because the former takes care of the latter), whereas the European American children tended to make associations based on category membership or shared features (e.g., pairing the man and the woman because they are both adults; Chiu, 1972). Similar patterns of spontaneous association on the basis of relationships versus rules have been demonstrated in East Asian and European American adult populations (e.g., Osherson, Smith, Wilkie, Lopez, & Shafir, 1990), and other studies have shown that East Asians also experience more difficulty with category- or rule-based learning than their European American counterparts but are just as apt at exemplar (e.g., example-based) learning (Norenzayan et al., 2000).

Holistic and Dialectical Cognitive Styles Beyond cultural differences in these specific cognitive processes outlined above, there is also evidence that Easterners and Westerners differ more fundamentally in their basic epistemological outlook. **Epistemology** refers to the origins of knowledge—how we come to know what we know. Here the argument is that Easterners follow a different set of principles when reasoning about the world. According to Peng and Nisbett (1999) Westerners rely on three laws of reasoning:

1. The law of identity, which states that an object is identical with itself;
2. The law of noncontradiction, which states that a statement cannot be both true and false;
3. The law of the excluded middle, which states that a statement must be either true or false (as opposed to neither).

These three laws may appear obvious to the lay American, until you contrast them with the three alternative approaches to rationality and knowledge that are more prevalent in Eastern cultures, outlined by Peng and Nisbett (1999):

1. The principle of change, which states that reality is dynamic and constantly changing;
2. The principle of contradiction, which states that contradiction is a natural feature of existence;
3. The principle of relationship/holism, which states that everything is interrelated.

Let's unpack these three principles of **dialectical thinking** outlined above. The **principle of change** is based on the Eastern concept of yin/yang, which states that change and transformation between two opposite states is a natural part of life—that is, a perpetual alternation between one state, yin, and its opposite state, yang. In an empirical demonstration of this principle, Ji, Nisbett, and Su (2001) presented European American and Chinese university students with a series of hypothetical scenarios and asked them to predict the future of the targets involved. For example:

> "Lucia and Jeff are both seniors at the same university. They have been dating for two years. How likely is it that they break up after graduation?"

> "Vincent has been the chess champion for three years in high school. How likely is it that he will lose in the next game against his strongest opponent?" (Ji et al., 2001, p. 451)

Consistent with the notion of the principle of change, Chinese students were more likely to predict a change in behavior across situations, expecting Lucia and Jeff to break up and anticipating that Vincent would lose the next chess competition

(Ji et al., 2001). Moreover, Ji et al. (2001) found that not only did Chinese students predict more change but they also perceived change as wiser than did European American students.

Related to the principle of change is the **principle of contradiction**, which posits that opposing and contradictory features are a natural and normative part of reality. To illustrate, Peng and Nisbett (1999) gave European American and Chinese students hypothetical scenarios involving conflict or contradictory views between two parties (e.g., a conflict between mothers and daughters) and asked the students to resolve them. While European American students tended to choose one side and favor it, Chinese students were more likely to find merit and fault with both sides (Peng & Nisbett, 1999).

Finally, the **principle of holism or relationship** states that things can only be understood in relation to one another rather than in isolation. We have already seen this at work in the fish studies outlined above, where East Asians alluded to contextual features of the underwater scene more often than their European American counterparts did. Additional studies have shown parallel effects: When drawing landscape pictures, East Asians drew the horizon at a higher location than European Americans did, which allowed them to capture more of the context or background (Masuda, Gonzalez, Kwan & Nisbett, 2008); similarly when drawing and taking photographs of individuals in portraits, East Asians used a smaller face-to-frame ratio than European Americans (Masuda, Ellsworth et al., 2008). This effect not only appeared with modern East Asian and European American participants, but also in archival analyses of classic East Asian versus European landscape art and portraiture (Masuda et al., 2008; and see table 1.2).

Psychopathology

Mental Health Disparities In the context of Asian Americans, the most striking mental health disparity is the rate at which Asians (versus other Americans) seek help. Past studies have shown that among those Asians who needed mental health services, only 17% actually sought help, and of that minority, only 6% sought help from an actual mental health professional (other common sources of help came from medical doctors or religious leaders; Office of the Surgeon General, 2001).

TABLE 1.2. **Summary of Major Differences between Western Analytic Cognition and Eastern Holistic Cognition**

Analytic cognition	Holistic cognition
Dispositional attribution	Situational attribution
Avoidance of contradiction	Dialectical thinking
Formulaic, rule-based logic	Experience-based knowledge
Focus on object	Focus on context/relationships

As a result, similar to the finding among Blacks/African Americans, those who finally receive help are more likely to be at an acute stage of their illness than are White Americans receiving the same services (Office of the Surgeon General, 2001). According to the Surgeon General and U.S. Department of Health and Human Services (2001), this underutilization of mental health services likely reflects a variety of factors including:

1. Stigma and shame associated with mental illness;
2. Unavailability of services provided in Asian languages;
3. Differential rates of diagnoses for specific psychopathologies.

Culture-Specific Disorders

Amok refers to a dissociative disorder observed in parts of Southeast Asia (including Malaysia, Laos, the Philippines, Polynesia, and Papua New Guinea) that involves violent, aggressive outbreaks and occasionally homicidal behavior (see Carr & Tan, 1976, for a review).

Dhat is an anxiety disorder found in Indian, Chinese, and Sri Lankan communities that involves feelings of weakness, exhaustion, and the belief that semen is being involuntarily discharged (Ranjith & Mohan, 2006).

Koro is another anxiety disorder similar to *Dhat* in that it also involves fears surrounding the involuntary actions of a man's penis—in this case, the fear that it will retract into the body and lead to death (e.g., Cohen, Tennenbaum, Teitelbaum, & Durst, 1995).

Taijin kyuofusho is an anxiety-based disorder that involves feelings of guilt over embarrassing others and timidity resulting from the belief that one's own body is offensive to others (Phillips et al., 2010).

Somatization of psychological distress is a more controversial disorder. It was originally assumed that, compared to individuals of European descent, those from Asian countries are allegedly more likely to manifest bodily symptoms when experiencing psychological distress. To illustrate, Kleinman and Good (1985) found that while depression was rare, neurasthenia (a similar disorder characterized by somatic symptoms) was not; they concluded that neurasthenia might be a cultural version of depression. Other studies have found similar patterns of Chinese people focusing on somatic instead of psychological symptoms when distressed (e.g., Chan, 1990; Parker, Cheah, & Roy, 2001), and the longstanding assumption was that this was because of **stigma** or cultural differences (for a review, see Ryder et al., 2008).

More recent research has challenged this idea: When Ryder et al. (2008) used three different modes of assessment (self-report, clinical interview, questionnaire) to evaluate symptoms among European Canadians and Chinese, they found that cultural differences appears to reflect more of a Western tendency to "psychologize" rather than Eastern tendency to somatize. Similarly, Zaroff, Davis, Chio, and Madhavan (2012) found that rates of somatic symptoms are comparable among different cultural groups when methods are controlled for or held constant—in other words, cultural differences may be more due to biases in reporting than actual experiences.

INSIGHT BOX 1.2

Hofstede's Cultural Dimensions

The origins of cultural psychology didn't happen in the United States or Asia or in a university or a lab. They happened at IBM, when a social psychologist by the name of Geert Hofstede started working as a management trainer and manager of personnel research (Minkov, 2012). There he introduced employee opinion surveys in national subsidiaries of IBM around the world, traveling to interview people and conduct surveys regarding people's behavior in large organizations and how they collaborated (Minkov, 2012). Forty countries and 116,000 surveys later, he came up with key cultural dimensions to capture cultural variation across countries (Hofstede, 1980b; Hofstede, 2011), including:

- Individualism-collectivism: the most oft-studied and paradigmatic of Hofstede's cultural dimensions. While individualism emphasizes concern for the self and one's primary ingroup, collectivism emphasizes concern for others, as well as traditions and values (Hofstede, 1980b). As a result, members of individualistic cultures prefer competitive strategies while collectivists tend to rely on harmony in conflict resolution. Individualism is more prevalent in Western countries (e.g., the United States/Canada, Western Europe, Australia, etc.), whereas collectivism is more prevalent in Asia, Latin America, Africa, and former communist countries (although see Oyserman, Coon, & Kemmelmeier, 2002, for more in-depth coverage of cultural differences).

- Power distance: the degree to which members of a culture accept that power in organizations is unevenly distributed (Hofstede, 1980). Power distance and individualism-collectivism are related in that collectivistic societies also tend to have larger power distance, whereas individualistic societies tend to have smaller power distance (Robert, Probst, Martocchio, Drasgow, & Lawler, 2000).

- Uncertainty avoidance: a preference for certainty and conformity. Cultures high in uncertainty avoidance value rules, procedures, and institutions; in contrast, cultures low in uncertainty avoidance prefer nonconformist attitudes, unpredictability, creativity, and divergent forms of thinking and behavior (Hofstede, 1980). High uncertainty avoidance countries include Japan, South Korea, France, and Germany, whereas low uncertainty avoidance countries include United States, Great Britain, and China (van Oudenhoven, Mechelse, & de Dreu, 1998).

- Femininity/masculinity: one of the more controversial and less empirically supported of Hofstede's dimensions (Constantinople, 1973). In theory, feminine cultures prefer consensus and are more caring and gentle, whereas masculine cultures are more responsible, decisive, and ambitious. Hofstede (1983) labeled the Netherlands, France, Portugal, Costa Rica, and Thailand as feminine cultures and Japan, Germany, Great Britain, Mexico, and Italy as masculine cultures.

- Time orientation: centering on long-term versus immediate outcomes. Countries with long-term time orientations are focused more on long-term outcomes and include countries like those in East Asia; in contrast, countries with short-term time orientations are more concerned with immediate outcomes and include the United States, Latin America, Africa, and the Middle East (Hofstede, 2011).

African Americans

The Self

On the one hand, the longstanding assumption has been that the previous model of the independent, Western self versus the interdependent, Eastern self applied (see Insight Box 1.2) to other non-Western groups, including African Americans and

Latino/a Americans (Gaines et al., 1997; Triandis, 1980). Consistent with this idea—that Western selves are independent and non-Western selves are interdependent—past studies have shown that models of African American selves center on both the person and the immediate nuclear family but also take into account the important roles of extended (biological) family members and "fictive" (i.e., nonbiological) kin, along with the ideas of Afrocentricity and spirituality (Der-Karabetian, Dana, & Gamst, 2008). The fact that terms like **fictive kin** exist in the context of African American relationships to mean non-kin, platonic relationships that are so strong that they are comparable to biological family ties suggests that a high degree of emphasis is placed on interdependent ties (Chatters, Taylor, & Jayakody, 1994; Johnson & Barer, 1990; Scott & Black, 1989). Empirical studies have shown that on the whole, "Americans of color" in general (Gaines et al., 1997; Oyserman, Coon, & Kemmelmeier, 2002) are more collectivistic than European Americans, and African Americans in particular are more collectivist, less individualistic, and more familistic than European Americans (e.g., Oyserman, Gant, & Ager, 1995).

On the other hand, more recent research suggests that the picture may be far more complex. Although the previous findings suggest that independence versus interdependence (and in parallel fashion, individualism-collectivism) appear to be dichotomous, oppositional constructs, other data suggest that they are orthogonal—that is, individualism can be high and low on either dimension, and being high on one dimension does not necessarily equate to being low on the other dimension (Bontempo, 1993).

A meta-analysis of 83 cross-cultural studies showed that European Americans were no more individualistic or independent than African Americans; if anything, African Americans showed a small but significant tendency to be more individualistic than European Americans across studies (Oyserman et al., 2002). On measures of collectivism or interdependence, European Americans and African Americans were comparable (Oyserman et al., 2002). To further complicate things, additional studies have also demonstrated that the degree of collectivism among African Americans is related to their level of racial/ethnic identity and awareness; those who self-identify more as African American are more collectivistic, and this relationship emerges among African Americans but not European Americans (e.g., Phinney & Chavira, 1992).

Emotion

Self-Construal and Emotion In mainstream psychology, researchers have observed a relationship between self-construal and distress. According to the cognitive diathesis-stress model (Beck, 1983), highly interdependent individuals are more likely to express distress and depression in response to a relationship-threatening event, whereas independent individuals are more likely to experience these negative emotions in response to an event that threatens the independent achievements of the self. Although this model was originally tested and supported among European American college students (e.g., Bieling, Beck, & Brown, 2004), subsequent studies have found that the same link also emerges among African American students (Christopher & Skillman, 2009).

Emotional Expression The limited number of studies done on comparisons between African Americans' and European Americans' emotional expressions suggest that African Americans' emotional expressions may be less accurately judged relative to their European American counterparts. In a study comparing African American and European American perceivers reading emotions on African American and European American targets, Gitter, Black, and Mostofsky (1972) found that European American targets were judged with greater accuracy overall, with the only exception being judgments of pain, for which African American targets were judged more accurately. The pattern of misjudgment was specific to certain kinds of negative emotions—namely, African Americans were misjudged to be expressing anger, disgust, and sadness (Gitter et al., 1972). In interpreting those findings, the researchers contended that contentious racial issues in the public sphere have contributed to the caricature of African Americans as angry and disgusted; outside of responding to racial turmoil, African American emotional expression is perceived as less than desirable, at least historically speaking (Gitter et al., 1972).

More recent data have challenged this idea by suggesting that overall, there should exist a general **ingroup advantage** in emotion recognition, with members of all cultures being better at recognizing emotions among their own group relative to an outgroup (Elfenbein & Ambady, 2002). However, given the small number of studies involving African or African American participants that were included in Elfenbein and Ambady's (2002) meta-analysis that led to this conclusion, the jury may still be out; more research is still needed.

Emotional Perception and Accuracy Although the findings on emotional expression may be less than clear-cut, the data on emotion perception and accuracy suggest that, overall, members of minority groups are more accurate at detecting emotion than members of majority groups. Direct comparisons of African Americans reading European Americans versus European Americans reading African Americans have shown that the former is far more accurate than the latter (Gitter et al., 1972), sometimes by an immense magnitude of difference (i.e., 72% accuracy versus 42–47% accuracy; Nowicki, Glanville, & Demertzis, 1998). Subsequent meta-analyses have further confirmed that this effect is so large that minority group members are often better at perceiving majority group members' emotions than their own group members' emotions—displaying an **outgroup advantage** rather than an ingroup one in the majority of studies (Elfenbein & Ambady, 2002). This suggests that in matters of emotion recognition, power and exposure may play a critical role in explaining why minority groups are necessarily better at reading majority groups than vice versa.

Emotion and the Body Beyond expression and perception, emotions may be construed in more visceral terms in African cultural context. For example, there are cultural expressions that refer exclusively to bodily experiences that cannot be easily translated to (e.g. *seselelame*), and many West African languages use the body to reference emotional words (Chentsova-Dutton & Dzokoto, 2014), much like the way it is used in Chinese and Japanese. In line with these cultural practices, it is not surprising that West Africans report being more sensitive to changes in their bodies relative to European Americans (Chentsova-Dutton & Dzoko, 2014;

Dzokoto, 2010). Cultural schemas about the body, the existence of culturally specific words (e.g., *seselelame*), and the use of emotional expressions that involve body parts (e.g., fear as "heart-fly") can potentially explain West Africans' emphasis on the body in emotional situations (Chentsova-Dutton & Dzoko, 2014). Despite this focus on the body, studies have shown that West Africans—like East Asians— also appear to be less accurate in assessing what their bodies are actually doing in response to emotional events. Chentsova-Dutton and Dzokoto (2014) argued that West African's awareness of their bodies may also promote inaccuracy in interpreting what their body is doing in emotional situations. According to their argument, West African culture holds a cultural **schema** that associates fear with the heart racing; although this might be generally true, it may not serve to accurately describe in-the-moment bodily changes (Chentsova-Dutton & Dzokoto, 2014). In their study, they had West Africans guess their own heart rates while seeing a scary film; the strong emotional content likely made the West Africans anticipate increases in heart rate (because of the schema) but neglect the actual changes going on in their body (Chentsova-Dutton & Dzokoto, 2014).

Cognition

Cognitive Styles As with the self, a similar distinction has been made between Western, European American styles of analytic, dispositional, and decontextualized thinking versus the more holistic, contextual, and intuitive thinking that is presumed to be more prevalent in the non-West, including not only Asia but also Africa and Latin America. This has been confirmed by both ethnographic and anthropological reports (e.g., Hirschfeld, 1995), as well as empirical studies (e.g., Lechuga, Santos, Garza-Caballero, & Villarreal, 2011; Lechuga & Wiebe, 2011; Malloy & Jones, 1998; Zarate, Uleman, & Voils, 2001). Like East Asians, African Americans have a distinct cognitive style from European Americans (e.g., Hale, 1982). Although fewer studies have been conducted on African American cognitive styles, a number of empirical studies have suggested that relative to European Americans, African Americans are more **field-dependent** (Shade, 1986; Stiff, 1990) and reason more holistically and contextually about problems (Malloy & Jones, 1998). This is consistent with a larger body of work that suggests that learning in African American contexts includes an emphasis on social and emotional factors and typically in a communal context that values expressivity, creativity, flexibility, and nonverbal communication (Willis, 1992).

Social Cognition When examining specific cognitions that African Americans, on the whole, tend to hold about their social world, an interesting dichotomy—if not outright contradiction—emerges. On the one hand, African Americans have consistently reported valuing, identifying with, and feeling good about their **ingroup,** or their own group, as well as themselves (for review, see Gray-Little & Hafdahl, 2000). In other words, on both measures of **collective self-esteem** and **personal self-esteem,** African Americans typically score higher than European Americans (Rowley et al., 1998; Twenge & Crocker, 2002). Consistent with this evidence, other studies have shown that being stigmatized—that is, being part of a negatively valued group in society—appears to have little bearing on self-esteem or its correlates, including depression and life satisfaction (Crocker et al., 1994). In the attempt to explain these findings, researchers argued that stigma also offers protective defenses by allowing stigmatized group members to attribute negative feedback to prejudice rather than something about themselves, compare themselves with fellow (disadvantaged) ingroup members rather than advantaged outgroup members, and devalue dimensions on which the ingroup does poorly but value dimensions on which the ingroup does well (Crocker & Major, 1989). On the other hand, more recent evidence shows that on **implicit measures,** African Americans do not exhibit these positive views of their own group. Despite their **explicit** ingroup favoritism, on implicit measures they either tend to favor European Americans (Ashburn-Nardo, Knowles, & Monteith, 2003) or show no group preference at all (Ashburn-Nardo, Monteith, Arthur, & Bain, 2007).

It is important to note that this dichotomy between implicit and explicit social cognition is not specific to African Americans. Indeed, a growing number of studies within mainstream psychology have highlighted this possibility of dissociating implicit versus explicit attitudes (Greenwald & Banaji, 1995; Hetts & Pelham, 2001). In addition, the finding that African Americans tend to have more negative views of their own groups on an implicit level is psychologically consequential: Other research has shown that implicitly favoring European Americans leads to worse outcomes, including lower self-esteem, lower life satisfaction, greater likelihood of depression, and more discrimination toward ingroup members (i.e., preferring to work with an outgroup member instead of an ingroup member) among African Americans (Ashburn-Nardo et al., 2007).

How do we explain this paradox of positive explicit attitudes paired with negative implicit attitudes toward the ingroup? The current data suggest that implicit and explicit measures may be tapping distinct psychological constructs and systems (e.g., Gawronski & Bodenhausen, 2006)—for example, explicit attitudes may reflect up-to-date, conscious endorsements whereas implicit attitudes may reflect a lifetime of acquired subconscious associations. A related interpretation is the idea that explicit attitudes reflect personal beliefs, whereas implicit attitudes reflect cultural influences (Arkes & Tetlock, 2004).

Psychopathology

Discrimination and Well-Being Discrimination remains an issue in contemporary American society (Smedley & Smedley, 2005) and has negative psychological consequences for African Americans, including depression and suicide ideation (e.g., Klonoff, Landrine, & Ullman, 1999). For African Americans, discrimination from adults (as opposed to peers) is especially common, particularly in the context of interactions with law enforcement, teachers, and shopkeepers (Fisher, Wallace, & Fenton, 2000; Rosenbloom & Way, 2004). Relative to other minority groups in the United States, African Americans report experiencing the most discrimination (Asian Americans report the second most discrimination, and Latinos report the third; Landrine, Klonoff, Corral, Fernandez, & Roesch, 2006). Despite the fact that experiencing prejudice and discrimination has a direct and negative effect on African Americans' well-being, research has shown that strong group identification can buffer these negative effects (Branscombe, Schmitt, & Harvey, 1999). In other words, African Americans who strongly identify with their group are less likely to suffer the negative psychological consequences of discrimination.

Mental Health Disparities Health disparities between Blacks/African Americans and European Americans stemming from psychopathology stand as a function of both differential rates of susceptibility to certain kinds of disorders as well as socioeconomic factors. Overall, it is well established that socioeconomic differences are a powerful contributor to health disparities in the United States (Gallo & Matthews, 2003): Not only are Black Americans less likely to receive outpatient treatment but twice as likely to receive inpatient treatment (Snowden, 2001) but they are more likely to rely on emergency room services for mental illness and are more likely to be misdiagnosed (Snowden, 2001; Office of the Surgeon General, 2001). The fact that Black Americans are overrepresented in inpatient and ER treatment settings suggests that delays in receiving timely treatment are common; as a result, illnesses are likely to be in a more acute stage and relapse more likely (Dana, Gamst, & Der-Karabetian, 2001).

Differential Rates of Diagnoses for Specific Psychopathologies Black Americans, relative to White Americans, exhibit higher rates of phobias and schizophrenia and lower rates of depression (Office of the Surgeon General, 2001). However, given that misdiagnosis is also more common among ethnic minorities in general, this difference in rates may reflect true differences in susceptibility or biases in assessment. Several studies have found that using more structured clinical assessments (as opposed to unstructured assessments) diminish or eliminate these differences in depression and schizophrenia, suggesting that bias on the part of the mental health provider may indeed play a major role (Office of the Surgeon General, 2001).

In addition to differential rates of diagnoses, differences also exist in prescribed courses of treatment. Relative to White Americans, medication is less likely to be prescribed. Certain medications—namely, antidepressants—also appear to be less effective among Black American patients than White American patients (Office of the Surgeon General, 2001).

Culture-Specific Disorders

Falling-out refers to seizure-like symptoms (e.g., collapsing) that have been reported by African Americans, Haitians, and Bahamians (Weidman, 1979).

Hex, *root-work*, and *voodoo* all refer to unnatural illnesses or death resulting from the work of evil spirits (Tinling, 1967).

Odde Ori refers to a disorder characterized by a perceived crawling sensation in the body. Found in Nigeria, it has been linked to somatization (Makanjuola, 1987).

Somatization, if you recall, refers to the tendency to report bodily symptoms instead of psychological ones when experiencing psychological distress. Generally speaking, even in the context of physical illness, African Americans are more likely to report bodily symptoms after exercise or surgery and in response to a variety of diseases (Edwards, Fillingim, & Keefe, 2001; Faucett, Gordon, & Levine, 1994). In the context of psychological distress, members of both African and African American cultures are more likely to report bodily symptoms rather than purely affective ones (Dzokoto & Adams, 2005; Friedman & Paradis, 2002).

Latino/a Americans

The Self

Similar to the case of African Americans and East Asians, Latino/a Americans have long been presumed to exhibit more collectivistic cultures and more interdependent selves. According to Dana (1998), *la familia* ("family") is at the center of Latino/a selves. In this case, family consists of not only the nuclear and immediate family but also members of the extended family (i.e., including but not limited to grandparents, aunts/uncles, cousins, friends, and godparents). Moreover, similar to the African American–related term *fictive kin*, the term *compadrazgo* is sometimes used in Latin American contexts to refer to the special relationship between a child's parents and godparents (Delgado, 1980; Kutsche, 1983; Segura & Pierce, 1993), once more suggesting that interdependent connections form an important part of the self. Additional studies have further affirmed that relative to European Americans, Latino/a Americans are more familistic (e.g., Valenzuela & Dornbusch, 1994).

However, recent research has also challenged this simplistic model. Meta-analysis of numerous cross-cultural studies shows that Latino/a Americans and European Americans did not differ in the degree to which they saw themselves in an individualistic manner and that, even outside of the United States, international comparisons showed that Americans were no more individualistic than Latin Americans living in South or Central America (Oyserman et al., 2002). (This is in contrast to the comparison with Asians, who did show a consistent tendency to be lower in individualism both in the United States and in international comparisons; however, Latino/a Americans did show slightly higher collectivism scores than European Americans; Oyserman et al., 2002).

In Latino/a American contexts, there are also specific cultural scripts that prescribe what a good "self" is like—most notably, **simpatía** is attributed to a person who is simpatico—that is, likable, easygoing, expressive, affectionate, polite, and fun (Triandis, Marin, Lisansky, & Betancourt, 1984). It is related to the interdependent self insofar as people who are simpatico tend to promote harmony in relationships by demonstrating respect, minimizing conflict, emphasizing the positive, and de-emphasizing the negative (Diaz-Loving & Draguns, 1999; Triandis et al. 1984). In this way, simpatico is related to the Big 5 personality construct of Agreeableness, which has a similar association with positive relationship outcomes and interpersonal harmony (e.g., Graziano & Eisenberg, 1997).

Interestingly, a number of studies had shown that despite this cultural script, Latino/as tend to score lower on *simpatía* and agreeableness than European Americans, despite the fact that Latin American culture highly values this personality dimension as a desirable way of being (e.g., Schmitt, Allik, McCrae, & Benet-Martinez, 2007). To reconcile this paradox, Ramirez-Esparza, Gosling, and Pennebaker (2008) assessed Mexican bilinguals' reports of their *simpatía* in English and Spanish, as well as behavioral manifestation of their actual simpatico behavior (i.e., via interactive interviews). They found that speaking in English activated self-enhancement values and led the bilinguals to self-report greater *simpatía* (compared to when they were speaking in Spanish); in contrast, speaking in Spanish increased their actual *simpatía*-related behaviors, in line with the cultural script (Ramirez-Esparza et al., 2008). Taken together, this suggests that language can be an important vehicle for transmitting culture.

Emotion

Ideal and Actual Affect Similar to the findings on the self, research on cultural variation in emotion among Latinos and European Americans also reveals a complex picture. On the one hand, past research has found that, like European Americans, Latinos prefer to emphasize good feelings, self-enhancement, and enhancement of positive feelings (Heine, Lehman, Markus, & Kitayama, 1999; Triandis et al., 1984). In line with this idea, both Latinos and European Americans find positive emotions to be more appropriate and preferable than negative emotions (Diener, Scollon, Oishi, Dzokoto, & Suh, 2000; Diener & Suh, 1999), which—despite sounding like an obvious pattern—is actually not a universal trend (East Asians, for example, do not show this preference for positive over negative emotions; Diener & Suh, 1999).

Consistent with these preferences, the empirical evidence on actual felt and recalled emotion suggests that Latinos experience high levels of positive emotion. When Scollon, Diener, Oishi, and Biswas-Diener (2004) compared reports of felt emotion across cultures (including European American, Latino, Asian American, Japanese, and Indian), findings revealed that Latinos felt the most pride, and this was the largest cultural difference that emerged for positive emotion. In terms of negative emotion, Latinos and European Americans felt the least guilt (e.g, relative to Japanese, Indians, and Asian Americans; Scollon et al., 2004). Taken together, this suggests that Latino and European Americans are similar in that they both value positive emotions over negative ones and report experiences in line with these preferences.

Emotional Expression and Regulation Interestingly, studies on the actual expressiveness of Latinos do not show that they are as expressive as the cultural value of *simpatía* would suggest. Early studies comparing Costa Ricans and European Americans found that the latter were more comfortable expressing a wide array of emotions (including both **independent emotions** like proud, capable, critical, annoyed, and **interdependent emotions** like sympathetic, respectful, fearful, apologetic) than the former (Stephan, Stephan, & Vargas, 1996). Although this pattern held across types of emotions, it was especially pronounced in the context of negative emotions like annoyance, distrust, and disapproval—feelings that Costa Ricans were especially reluctant to show (Stephan et al., 1996). Stephan et al. (1996) suggested that one possibility might be that, in collectivistic societies like Costa Rica, people might feel pressure to express emotions to promote harmony and relationships even when they may not be feelings those emotions, and as a result, individuals may be less comfortable with unfiltered, open emotional expression.

Additional studies have further confirmed that members of Latino cultures are not highly expressive. For example, in their large-scale, cross-national study, Matsumoto, Yoo, and Fontaine (2008) found that Latin American countries like

Mexico and Brazil were lower in their endorsement of emotional expressivity than European American countries (e.g., Canada, the United States), although nevertheless higher than East Asian countries (e.g., China, Japan, South Korea). Consistent with these findings, studies on **emotion regulation strategies**—that is, techniques to influence which emotions you have and when you have them, including the use of **suppression,** or effortfully inhibiting your felt emotion—versus **cognitive reappraisal**—construing the event differently so as to change one's feeling about it—found that European Americans were less likely to suppress relative to Latino/a Americans (or African Americans or Asian Americans), although the cultures did not differ on their reliance on reappraisal (Gross & John, 2003).

Cognition

Cognitive Styles and Reasoning As with East Asians, Latinos also reason more holistically and contextually than European Americans (Lechuga, Santos, Garza-Caballero, & Villarreal, 2011). When compared to European Americans, Mexican Americans were more accepting of contradiction and more likely to view the whole rather than simply the parts; however, when compared to Koreans, Mexican Americans scored lower on these holistic thinking measures (Lechuga et al., 2011). In other words, Mexican Americans reason more holistically than European Americans but less holistically than East Asians.

Latinos and East Asians also exhibit some of the same cognitive biases (Lechuga & Wiebe, 2011; Zarate, Uleman, & Voils, 2001). One such bias is the overconfidence bias, which refers to the tendency to exhibit less doubt or more certainty about a judgment than one's knowledge warrants (Johnson & Fowler, 2011). As a classic judgment and decision-making bias, overconfidence has been well demonstrated in mainstream psychology (Griffin & Tversky, 2002). In cross-cultural contexts, overconfidence is more common not only in East Asian cultures but also in Latin American cultures relative to the United States/Europe, including Argentina, Peru, Mexico, and Brazil (Lechuga & Wiebe, 2011; Stankov & Lee, 2014).

Taken together, these findings suggest that Latino/as are both similar and different from European Americans and East Asians. Researchers have explained these similarities and differences via the complex historical influences present in Latin American culture: For example, the influence of Western Greek thought during the colonization period along with the Aztec and Mayan civilization practices that are devoid of European practices and more closely resemble Chinese practices (Garcia, Sierra, & Balam, 1999; Lechuga & Wiebe, 2011).

Social Cognition How do Latino Americans view themselves (and others) in the context of their social world? Recent data show that, as a group, Latino Americans are the fastest growing ethnic minority in the United States and one that is approximating majority status in certain states, like California (Therrien & Ramirez, 2000). Despite this strength in numbers, Latino Americans nevertheless still experience underprivileged incomes, susceptibility to poverty, and disadvantaged education (Marotta & Garcia, 2003). Moreover, they are also viewed as less "American" than their European American counterparts, despite the fact that studies have shown higher levels of patriotism among Latino/a Americans than European Americans (in this case, Mexican Americans; de la Garza, Falcon, & Garcia, 1996). On both implicit measures—that is, an Implicit Association Test (IAT) associating Latino Americans versus European Americans with American versus foreign concepts—and explicit survey questions, both Latino/a American and European American participants rated Latinos as less American (Devos, Gavin, & Quintana, 2010). In addition, Latino/a Americans also reported feeling less strongly identified with U.S. nationality (Devos et al., 2010).

Perhaps of even more concern is the finding that Latino/a Americans (along with African Americans) also tend to endorse the same stereotypes about their own group that are held by majority group members (Jost & Banaji, 1994; Ma-Kellams, Spencer-Rodgers, & Peng, 2011). Although these stereotypes include both positive and negative attributes (e.g., Latino/a American participants rated themselves as being more attractive, hardworking, committed to family, and their men as more masculine but also rated themselves as less intelligent and with less leadership skill), implicit attitudes show that overall, Latino/a Americans did not show the same level of ingroup favoritism typically observed among European Americans (Ma-Kellams et al., 2011). Recent work by Cuddy et al. (2009) has shown that this tendency is not specific to minority groups in the United States; rather, collectivistic cultures in general tend to show weaker endorsement of positive ingroup stereotypes relative to individualistic cultures.

Psychopathology

Discrimination and Well-Being Like African Americans and East Asians, Latino Americans are also subject to discrimination (Landrine et al., 2006). Perceiving discrimination, in turn, is related to psychological distress, depressive symptoms, suicide ideation, and state and trait anxiety (e.g., Araujo & Borrell, 2006). Notably, the patterns of discrimination may differ: Although Asian Americans are more often discriminated against by peers, Latino and African American students report more discrimination by adults, including police, teachers, and shopkeepers (Fisher, Wallace, & Fenton, 2000; Rosenbloom & Way, 2004). The content of the discrimination also is distinct for each cultural group—for example, Latinos are seen as likable but disrespected, whereas Asian Americans are seen as unlikable and envied (Fiske, Cuddy, Glick, & Xu, 2002; Lin, Kwan, Cheung, & Fiske, 2005). In line with these ideas, Latino/a Americans were more likely to be discriminated against in the context of the law (i.e., being accused of cheating or violating a rule), and more likely to experience stress in response to discrimination (Hwang & Goto, 2008).

Mental Health Disparities Although differences in rates of psychopathology between different subgroups of Latino/a Americans are complex, the disparity in the likelihood of receiving care is clear: A large subset of Latino/a Americans do not receive adequate mental health services (Office of the Surgeon General, 2001). This lack of access is especially pronounced among Latino/as who do not speak English, given the limited number of Spanish-speaking mental health providers; those with the highest need (i.e., the incarcerated, those with substance-abuse problems, refugees, and veterans); and the under- or uninsured. Relative to White

Americans, Latino/as are more likely to be uninsured or underinsured, which may be a product of employer coverage and immigration status (Office of the Surgeon General, 2001).

Differential Rates of Diagnoses for Specific Psychopathologies The patterns of prevalence rates vary for different subgroups of Latino/a Americans. On the one hand, Mexican-born Mexican Americans exhibit similar rates of mental illness overall compared to the general U.S. population; on the other hand, U.S.-born Mexican Americans exhibit higher rates of depression and phobia, as do Puerto Ricans living in the United States compared to Puerto Ricans living in Puerto Rico (Office of the Surgeon General, 2001). Similar patterns emerge among Latino/a American youth, who exhibit higher rates of depression, anxiety disorders, and substance abuse (Office of the Surgeon General, 2001). Although a host of factors may contribute to these differential rates of diagnoses, one possibility is that the process of acculturation and other features of living in the United States may contribute to the increased susceptibility to mental disorders (Office of the Surgeon General, 2001).

Culture-Specific Disorders

Ataque de nervios, or "attack of nerves," refers to an out-of-consciousness state that allegedly results from the actions of evil spirits; it stands as an unexplained distress syndrome found in parts of Latin America. Somatization has been linked to a variety of anxiety-based disorders, including *ataque de nervios* (Lopez, Ramirez, Guarnaccia, Canino, & Bird, 2011).

Mal puesto is similar to hex, root-work, and voodoo death in that it also refers to unnatural illnesses—or in some cases, death—that result from the use of evil spirits (Martinez & Martin, 1966).

Susto, *espanto*, *pasmo*, *miedo* all refer to feelings of tiredness and weakness that result from frightening or unexpected experiences (for review, see Der-Karabetian, Dana, & Gamst, 2008).

Somatization and the presence of somatic symptoms have also been linked to more generalized reports of anxiety and depression (e.g., in Mexico; Varela et al., 2004).

American Indians

As with all other ethnic groups, there is enormous heterogeneity among American Indian or Native American groups (Swisher & Deyhle, 1989). There are about 567 federally recognized American Indian entities (Bureau of Indian Affairs, 2018), and within them, there are at least 200 traditional tribal languages (Fleming, 1992), with considerable variation in language, values, spiritual beliefs, and degrees of acculturation (Whitbeck, Hoyt, Stubben, & LaFromoise, 2001). Nevertheless, there may also be commonalities across these different subgroups, and the goal of this section is to cover the limited research done on American Indians in terms of the self, emotion, cognition, and psychopathology.

The Self

For American Indians or Native Americans and Alaskan Natives, the self is comprised of a complex conglomeration of not only the self and family/extended family, but also important places, community members, the tribe, animals, plants, and both natural as well as supernatural forces (Dana, 1998). Studies have shown that although there is considerable variability across tribes, subtribes, and clans, the majority of Native Americans believe that the self is composed of spirit, mind, and body, that other living things also are part of the spirit world, and that wellness happens when there is harmony between these different entities (Locust, 1988).

Self-Construal Ethnographic studies have shown that American Indians' self-construals contain both independent and interdependent features (Deyhle & LeCompte, 1994; Tharp, 1994). Studies on Navajo, Pueblo, and Swinomish Indian tribes have shown, for example, that cooperation is emphasized, but autonomy and individuality are also encouraged, and children are seen as both individuals as well as reflections of their family (Suina & Smolkin, 1994; Swinomish Tribal Mental Health Project, 1991). More recent empirical studies on American Indians' versus European Americans' spontaneous self-descriptions, views of their possible selves, and their endorsement of independence/interdependence found that American Indians were more interdependent in their self-descriptions, describing themselves in terms of how their actions relate to other people, but they also displayed independence by emphasizing self-improvement, achievement, and self-knowledge (Fryberg & Markus, 2003).

Self-Esteem In addition, American Indians tended to hold more negative self-views, reporting more feared selves relating to poverty and deviance (Fryberg & Markus, 2003) and showing lower self-esteem relative to other cultural groups (Twenge & Crocker, 2002).

Yet the American Indian self is largely an absent construct for most other Americans: A large proportion of American Indians—who only comprise 1.5% of the population—live in rural areas; given that relative to other ethnic groups, far fewer of them live in large cities, this likely means they have less contact with outside groups (for review, see Office of the Surgeon General, 2001). To exacerbate this problem, American Indians are also rarely portrayed in the media and at a far lower rate than other minority groups (Fryberg & Markus, 2003; Mastro & Behm-Morawitz, 2005). When they are portrayed, they are typically construed as spiritual (e.g., *Pocahontas*), warrior-like (e.g., *Dances with Wolves*), or in the context of negative life outcomes (e.g., suicide, teenage pregnancy, or dropping out of school; Fryberg, 2003).

The only exception to this general invisibility is in the context in which American Indians are used as mascots for popular professional sports themes, or in the occasional film representation, as mentioned above. Although these popular representations of Native Americans are well known by most Americans, research shows that they actually have negative psychological outcomes for the Native American self. Being exposed to images of Chief Wahoo and Pocahontas led to lower self-esteem among high school students who were Native Americans and did so even more than being exposed to negative stereotypes about Native Americans (Fryberg, Markus, Oyserman, & Stone, 2008). Similar effects emerged when the outcome of interest was feelings of community worth and achievement-related possible selves—that is, images of the self that a person hopes to become (Fryberg et al., 2008). Additional research has shown that overall, Native Americans in general have lower self-esteem than both African Americans and Latino/a Americans, at levels similar to that of Asian Americans (Twenge & Crocker, 2002).

Emotion

Emotion Recognition and Accuracy Consistent with the previous studies on ingroup advantage when it comes to emotion recognition (Elfenbein & Ambady, 2002), research with American Indians have also found that accurate perception of expressed emotions is more difficult in cross-cultural interactions involving American Indian and European American partners, compared to intracultural interactions where both partners are from the same group (Albas, McCluskey, & Albas, 1976). In other words, American Indians are more accurate at recognizing emotions in each other than they are at recognizing emotions in European American targets, just as European Americans are more accurate at recognizing emotions in each other than in American Indian targets. In line with this empirical evidence, ethnographic research has shown that American Indian students often misinterpret their (European American) teachers' emotions and mistake them for being mean or angry, usually in contexts where teachers are speaking in loud tones (Key, 1975, as cited in Albas et al., 1976).

Felt Emotional Experiences Another cultural difference in emotion is the finding that American Indians might be subject to higher levels of certain types of emotional experiences due to their unique history. Some theorists argue that they may experience higher levels of unresolved historical grief stemming from the many historical crimes inflicted upon them over the course of U.S. history, including current-day institutional discrimination (Heart & DeBruyn, 1998). Empirical survey studies confirmed that many American Indians who live on reservations report feeling historical grief (Whitbeck, Adams, Hoyt, & Chen, 2004).

On the positive side, social connectedness and support can alleviate these negative experiences of historical grief. Given Native Americans' interdependent selves, it is not surprising that being connected to one's family and school predicts academic persistence (Gloria & Robinson Kurpius, 2001).

Cognition

Cognitive Styles Similar to East Asians, American Indians tend to be highly field-dependent and rely on a global processing style (for review, see Pewewardy, 2002). Rather than perceiving elements in isolation, American Indians tend to learn and process information holistically, focusing on the whole and the background in conjunction with the foreground (Pewewardy, 2002). Other studies have shown that European Americans were better at sequential processing—considering pieces of information one at a time—and prefer information presented concretely and in order, which are features central to analytic and linear thinking, whereas American Indians were better at simultaneous processing—considering multiple pieces of information at once—and preferred information presented abstractly and randomly, features central to holistic or global cognition (Backes, 1993; Davidson, 1992). This pattern is consistent with the broader link between field-dependence and collectivistic, familial cultures more generally (Nuby, Ehle, & Thrower, 2001). In addition, American Indians also tend to emphasize visual, auditory, and kinesthetic properties when perceiving the social and natural world (e.g., Gilliland, 1999; Wilcox, 1996). Native American students from the Ojibwa and Mohawk tribes showed better performance on visual/spatial processing tasks, while non-Indian students performed better at verbal tasks (Morton, Allen, & Williams, 1994).

More unique to Native Americans is the emphasis on maintaining a dynamic balance between the individual, society, and the natural world. In addition, knowledge is not only derived via observation and empiricism but also via the authoritative traditions and customs of the previous generations, including the accumulated wisdom of leaders and elders (Gill, 1999). In this way, Native American cognition is similar to East Asians' emphasis on experiential knowledge, or information and reasoning based on personal experiences rather than just hard and fast rules.

Normative Cognitive Development Although few studies have been done on American Indian cognition, the existing research has largely focused on the poor educational outcomes experienced by American Indian youth, who suffer drop-out rates of approximately 15% (second only to Latino/as, who have a drop-out rate of 21%; National Indian Education Association, 2008). These gaps in cognitive development may have little to do with cultural values—if anything, many American Indian leaders maintain that education and achievement are critical to strengthening the sovereignty and self-determination of their communities (Inglebret, Jones, & Pavel, 2008; Rivera & Tharp, 2006). Instead, as is the case with cultural achievement gaps in other contexts, these differences appear to stand both as a function of how we define and measure "achievement" (Mueller, Mulcahy, Wilgosh, & Walters, 1986), as well as socioeconomic factors and the availability of resources (Bigelow, 2006; Hoff, 2003, 2006; Hoff & Tian, 2005; Tsethlikai, 2011). In the larger context, Fryberg and Markus (2007) found that American Indian college students viewed education as important for success for not only the individual but also the larger community, but they also had more negative associations with educations and considered academic concerns secondary to family and community concerns.

Psychopathology

Identity and Well-Being As with African Americans, a strong sense of group identification can protect against psychological distress. American Indians who strongly identify with being American or Indian were less likely to experience hopelessness, alcoholism, and suicide relative to those who didn't (Berlin, 1987). Subsequent studies have shown similar effects of ethnic/cultural identity being positively linked to psychological well-being and adjustment and lower rates of depression among Native American groups like the Navajo (e.g., Jones & Galliher, 2007; Rieckmann,

Wadsworth, & Deyhle, 2004), although a more recent study by Albright and LaFromboise (2010) found that identifying with being Native American had no relationship with feelings of hopelessness; rather, identifying with White culture actually alleviated hopelessness. These contradictory findings suggest that much more research is needed to figure out the precise conditions under which cultural identification helps versus hurts mental health outcomes.

Mental Health Disparities Unfortunately, there are relatively few epidemiology surveys conducted on mental health outcomes among American Indians. However, related data show that suicide and alcohol abuse rates are substantially higher among American Indians than the general population. Alaskan Natives have one of the highest rates of suicide out of any group in the world, and fetal alcohol syndrome is more common in American Indian children (Office of the Surgeon General, 2001) than in other groups. The potential reasons for this disparity are multifold and include both individual differences (e.g., expectations about the positive effects of alcohol; traits), situational features (problem-drinking for reservation-dwelling American Indians does not reduce access to rewards like housing, family closeness, economic security, and work opportunities to the same degree as it does for European Americans), and group factors (e.g., historical oppression, discrimination, socioeconomic status; for review, see Spillane & Smith, 2006). More generally, depression and low self-esteem appear to be especially prevalent among Native American teens (e.g., Twenge & Crocker, 2002).

Differential Rates of Diagnoses for Specific Psychopathologies Among U.S. veterans, American Indians are more likely to be diagnosed with PTSD than European Americans (Beals et al., 2002). In their studies comparing Vietnam veterans from two different American Indian tribes (one from the Northern Plains and one from the Southwest) Beals et al. (2002) found that this ethnic difference could be explained by exposure to wartime atrocities and violence. Although ethnic differences emerged on a variety of variables—including demographic factors like marital status (American Indians were less likely to be married), age (American Indians were younger at the time of enlistment), and other reported experiences (e.g., American Indians reported more deprivation, like not having enough water), differences in exposure to terrorizing, wounding, and killing emerged as the only factor that mediated the aforementioned cultural differences (Beals et al. 2002).

Culture-Specific Disorders Ghost sickness refers to symptoms of weakness, anxiety, hallucinations, and dizziness that result from actions by witches, ghosts, and other evil forces; moreover, these supernatural forces are often believed to be able to cause illness and death (Jackson, 2006). In response to these fears, the person with ghost sickness may come up with rituals in the attempt to ward off the evil spirits (Jackson, 2006).

Other, more controversial cases of alleged culture-specific disorders include *kayak angst*, a condition whereby hunters and fishermen from Greenland display symptoms that resemble a panic attack (Amering & Katschnig, 1990; Jackson, 2006); *arctic hysteria*, whereby Eskimos react to upsetting situations with intense fits (Foulks, 1985); and *winding psychosis*, whereby Algonkian natives express a cannibalistic desire for consuming human meat (Marano, 1985).

APPLYING WHAT WE KNOW: HANDS-ON ACTIVITIES

Different cultural selves produce different cultural self-schemas—organized systems of knowledge, emotion, cognition, values, and ways of being (see Insight Box 1.3). Construct a "box" (*cajita*) that illustrates the cultural elements that contributed to your ethnic/racial group's sense of self (Kanagala & Rendón, 2013). Your box can be as creative as you choose: You do need to choose a literal "box"; you can also rely on alternative containers (e.g., a crate, suitcase, basket) that may better reflect your cultural group's identity.

INSIGHT BOX 1.3

Multicultural Competency

Given the wealth of cultural differences discussed in this chapter, one practical question is how professional psychologists can effectively work with culturally diverse populations. Although the American Psychological Association has grappled with this question for more than three decades, implementation remains a challenge. The Office of the Surgeon General (2001) emphasizes that while mental illnesses affect all populations, striking health disparities exist especially in the context of mental health outcomes among U.S. racial and ethnic minorities (see table 1.3). To this end, facilitating multicultural competency in a mental health setting requires: (1) multicultural knowledge, including topics like acculturation and multicultural education (covered in chapters 1 and 10 in this text); (2) awareness of existing cultural barriers, including the notions of White privilege—see chapter 7—and culture-specific clinical practices; (3) sensitivity and responsiveness, including issues of microaggression (see chapters 7 & 8); and (4) other sociocultural diversities apart from race, including class and gender (see chapters 2–5). (For full review of these ideas, see Gamst, Der-Karabetian, & Dana, 2008).

White Identity

Growing up, Ben Folds was a white boy from North Carolina with dreams of being Elton John (Fricke, 1998). Said dreams eventually came true when he formed his punk rock band, the Ben Folds Five, surprising the '90s with their fuzzy bass and piano riffs and happy-go-lucky anger. When the band broke up in 2000, Folds decided to come out with his solo album, *Rockin' the Suburbs*. In its title track, he sings about his hard-knocks life as someone stuck in a nuclear family with two intact parents ("mom and dad you made me so uptight") and who struggles with anger management issues but is tormented by social norms ("I'm pissed off but I'm too polite"). Bottom line to Ben Folds's suburban anthem? It's hard "being male, middle-class, and white."

Regardless of what you make of pop-esque punk rockers or whether you were a fan of Ben Folds during his college circuit days, his lyrics highlight an important but often overlooked point: White people have identities, too. Everything we have talked about so far about race and ethnicity has proven the obvious—that being part of and identifying with a particular racial or cultural group predict important

TABLE 1.3. Summary of Cultural Selves

	European American	Black American	Latino/a American	Asian American	American Indian
Cultural model of "the self"	Individualistic: independent, autonomous, separate entity	Social and collectivistic self that includes family and community members, along with spiritual entities	Social and collectivistic self that includes extended family members	Interdependent self that is contextualized and relational	Extended self that includes spiritual and natural world entities
Implications for mental health practices	Mental health services provided on a one-on-one basis to focus on individual goals and processes	Group-, family-, and community-based therapy are more common; authenticity and identification with the client on the part of the practitioner are important	Group-, family-, and community-based therapy are more common; *simpatía*, respect, trust, and a casual personal style of relating can be helpful	Family-based therapy is more common; competence, structure, and practical, immediate benefits should be emphasized	Group- and community-based therapy are more common; a preexisting relationship or mutual contacts in the larger community can be helpful

Sources: Dana, 1993; Gamst, Der-Karabetian, & Dana, 2008; Khoo, Abu-Rasain & Hornby, 1994; Katz, 1985; Sue & Zane, 1987.

behaviors, from how you see yourself, to the feelings you feel, to the disorders you are susceptible to. It shapes whether your mother hugged you enough and the likelihood of you getting PTSD. However, the overwhelming majority of research focuses on ethnic and cultural minority identification—namely, how nonmajority groups think and feel about their groups. But European Americans have thought and feelings about their race, too (Delgado & Stefancic, 1997).

The Tricky Part: Measuring White Identity

Unlike attempts to measure and research minority group identity, measuring White identity is rare and much more difficult to pull off. Part of the reason is the notion of **colorblind ideology** (an idea we will revisit in chapter 10). Colorblind ideology is the idea that we are blind to race, and many people assume that being nonprejudiced means not seeing race at all. Given the negative associations we have made historically in the United States (and abroad) about people who really strongly endorse being White (cue the KKK and Nazi Germany's Aryan propaganda), asking people explicitly how they feel about being White is methodologically questionable.

The alternative we are left with is an indirect measure of White identity. Knowles and Peng (2005) came up with the **White Identity Centrality Implicit Association**

Test (**WICIAT**), which is modeled after the original Implicit Association Test (IAT) but is adapted to specifically measure implicit White Identity: In an initial practice trial, participants simply have to categorize White and non-White sounding names, like "Chip" and "Connor" versus "Jamal" and "Tyrese"; they use one key if it is a White name and a different key if it is a non-White name. In a second practice trial, participants categorize pronouns associated with the self (e.g., I, my, mine) versus the other (e.g., they, theirs, them), once again using different keys; finally, in the critical test trials, participants have to categorize both names and pronouns, except in the compatible trial, they are using the same key to categorize both White and Self (and a different key to categorize non-White and other; Knowles & Peng, 2005). In the incompatible test trial, the association is switched, such that they are using the same key to categorize non-White and Self (and a different key to categorize White and other; Knowles & Peng, 2005). The idea is that the faster a person associates White with self (i.e., quicker reaction times in the compatible trial), the more central the person with White identity is (Knowles & Peng, 2005).

What Does White Identity Predict?

Knowles and Peng (2005) went on to test the psychological potency of this indirect measure of White identity by giving (White) participants who completed the WICIAT a host of other measures, including collective self-esteem, self-reported overlap with the White ingroup, reaction time in completing the self-reported overlap with the White ingroup, modern racism, White versus Black preference on the IAT, hometown diversity, racial categorization, and White guilt. Below, each measure is broken down.

Collective self-esteem refers to how much you value your ingroup; it is a self-reported survey measure with items like "overall, my racial/ethnic group is considered good by others," and "in general, I'm glad to be a member of my racial/ethnic group" (Crocker & Luhtanen, 1990).

Overlap with the White ingroup involves asking participants to rate a series of traits (e.g., smart, generous, hardworking) for themselves (i.e., whether it describes them) and their ingroup (i.e., whether it describes White people in general); the overlap refers to the extent to which traits that are highly characteristic of you are also characteristic of your ingroup (Knowles & Peng, 2005). In other words, how much are you like other White people? The **reaction time** part simply refers to how long it takes you to answer the question, especially on items where you and your ingroup diverge (i.e., traits that describe you but not your ingroup, or vice versa). In a related measure of overlap, participants are given a series of overlapping Venn diagrams with one circle representing them (labeled "me") and another circle representing the ingroup (labeled "White people") and they have to pick the diagram that best represents the degree of overlap (Knowles & Peng, 2005).

Modern racism is what it sounds like: classic racism wrapped up in more politically correct terms, with items like "discrimination against Blacks is no longer a problem in the United States" and "It is easy to understand the anger of Black people in America" (the latter item is reverse-coded; McConahay, 1986).

White versus Black preference on the IAT is an implicit measure of racial bias; it measures how quickly a person associates European American names or faces with good and African American names or faces with bad, or vice versa (for more details, see Knowles & Peng, 2005).

Hometown diversity is also what it sounds like: the degree to which a person was exposed to non-Whites growing up. Union County, Pennsylvania, is 98% White, whereas Honolulu is only 20% White (Knowles & Peng, 2005).

Racial categorization refers to how participants categorize a series of computer-morphed Black-White faces. Knowles and Peng (2005) started the process by taking two original faces of a Black man and a White man; the computer than creates Black-White racial blends (e.g., 60% Black, 40% White, etc.); the participant views the blended faces and simply has to judge whether the face belongs to a White person or not. Their reaction times were also recorded (Knowles & Peng, 2005). How White do you have to be to be considered White?

White guilt involves showing participants a film of atrocities inflicted on Black individuals by White individuals and asking participants how guilty they felt afterward (Knowles & Peng, 2005).

Of these, (1) reaction time overlap with the White ingroup, (2) hometown diversity, (3) racial categorization, and (4) White guilt predicted performance on the WICIAT: People who had a high White identity centrality on the WICIAT tended to have longer reaction times when a trait was discrepant between themselves and their ingroup, came from towns with greater diversity, were more "strict" in their racial categorization (i.e., requiring a higher percentage of Whiteness to be considered White), and reported feeling more White guilt (Knowles & Peng, 2005). This suggests that White identity and identifying with the White ingroup do *not* equate to being racist, since WICIAT scores were uncorrelated with the two measures of racial bias (modern racism and the Black-White preference IAT; Knowles & Peng, 2005).

Obama and White Identity

On Tuesday, November 4, 2008, crowds across the country (and even the world) went crazy. In Kimisu, Kenya, people made out with strangers and sold Obama wall clocks; in Buenos Aires, those inside a bar aptly named "Sacramento" started a new soccer chant that involved only two words (hint: "olé" and "Obama"), and not that far away, those in Petare, Caracas's largest slum, poured makeshift whiskey screwdrivers in plastic cups; for the first time in their lives, they did *not* switch the channel to baseball when the news came on ("Reactions," 2008). But not everyone was so thrilled—after Obama's reelection in 2012, college students at the University of Mississippi burned his effigy to the ground during an on-campus riot, and the McDonald's in Follansbee, West Virginia, decided that the occasion was so dire it warranted hanging the American flag upside down (Manuel-Logan, 2012). Donald Trump took to Twitter and decided that America was no longer a democracy, while like-minded Republicans vowed to leave the country.

More severe responses were coming. Regardless of how people felt about Obama, some took the election as a sign that race relations in America had at long last been reconciled. Ward Connolly, a social activist, proclaimed, "How can you say there is institutional racism when people in Nebraska voted for a guy who is a self-identified Black man?" (Williams & Negrin, 2008). Will Bennett, the former U.S. secretary of education, voiced a similar sentiment when he said, "You don't take excuses anymore from anybody that says, 'the deck is stacked,' 'I can't do anything,' 'there's so much in-built this and that' " (as cited in Bush, 2011, p. 254).

But the story was not so simple (good stories almost never are). If anything, White identity researchers suspected that Obama's election was actually a boon for the very racists that opposed him. Their argument was this: Obama's election posed as a challenge to racial hierarchy in America, and antiegalitarians—people who oppose equality—might initially oppose him for racial reasons; however, most antiegalitarians do not want to be that obvious, so they needed an alternative strategy (Knowles, Lowery, & Schaumberg, 2009). Knowles et al. (2009) argued that their best bet was Obama winning, because doing so could signal that we live in a "postracial era" where no efforts to undercut racism are needed. And that is exactly what he found. After recruiting nearly 300 voting-age and predominantly White participants, he measured their antiegalitarian attitudes (i.e., about how they felt about group dominance and social hierarchy) and asked how likely they were to vote for Obama; he also asked them whether or not racism was over in this country; ironically, those who were most antiegalitarian and who perceived that racism was over were the ones most likely to vote for Obama (Knowles et al., 2009).

Key Concepts

Ethnicity, racial identity, race
Emotion expression vs. suppression
Fundamental attribution error, or correspondence bias
Epistemology
Dialectical thinking (principles of change, contradiction, holism or relationship)
Fictive kin
Ingroup vs. outgroup advantage (in emotion recognition)
Schema
Field dependent
Collective vs. personal self-esteem
Stigma
Implicit vs. explicit measures
Simpatía
Independent vs. interdependent emotions
Emotion regulation strategies (suppression, cognitive reappraisal)
Colorblind ideology
White Identity Centrality Implicit Association Test (WICIAT): Collective self-esteem, overlap with ingroup, modern racism, IAT, hometown diversity, racial categorization, White guilt

References

Albas, D. C., McCluskey, K. W., & Albas, C. A. (1976). Perception of the emotional content of speech: A comparison of two Canadian groups. *Journal of Cross-Cultural Psychology*, 7(4), 481–490.

Albright, K., & LaFromboise, T. D. (2010). Hopelessness among White-and Indian-identified American Indian adolescents. *Cultural Diversity and Ethnic Minority Psychology*, 16(3), 437.

Amering, M., & Katschnig, H. (1990). Panic attacks and panic disorder in cross-cultural perspective. *Psychiatric Annals, 20*(9), 511–516.

Araújo, B. Y., & Borrell, L. N. (2006). Understanding the link between discrimination, mental health outcomes, and life chances among Latinos. *Hispanic Journal of Behavioral Sciences, 28*(2), 245–266.

Arkes, H. R., & Tetlock, P. E. (2004). Attributions of implicit prejudice, or would Jesse Jackson "fail" the Implicit Association Test? *Psychological Inquiry, 15*(4), 257–278.

Ashburn-Nardo, L., Knowles, M. L., & Monteith, M. J. (2003). Black Americans' implicit racial associations and their implications for intergroup judgment. *Social Cognition, 21*(1), 61–87.

Ashburn-Nardo, L., Monteith, M. J., Arthur, S. A., & Bain, A. (2007). Race and the psychological health of African Americans. *Group Processes & Intergroup Relations, 10*(4), 471–491.

Backes, J. S. (1993). The American Indian high school dropout rate: A matter of style? *Journal of American Indian Education, 32*(3), 16–29.

Beals, J., Manson, S. M., Shore, J. H., Friedman, M., Ashcraft, M., Fairbank, J. A., & Schlenger, W. E. (2002). The prevalence of posttraumatic stress disorder among American Indian Vietnam veterans: Disparities and context. *Journal of Traumatic Stress, 15*(2), 89–97. doi:10.1023/A:1014894506325

Beck, A. T. (1983). Cognitive therapy of depression: New perspectives. In P. J. Clayton & J. E. Barrett (Eds.), *Treatment of depression: Old controversies and new approaches* (pp. 265–290). New York: Raven Press.

Berlin, I. N. (1987). Suicide among American Indian adolescents: an overview. *Suicide and Life-Threatening Behavior, 17*(3), 218–232.

Bieling, P. J., Beck, A. T., & Brown, G. K. (2004). Stability and change of sociotropy and autonomy subscales in cognitive therapy of depression. *Journal of Cognitive Psychotherapy, 18*(2), 135–148.

Bigelow, B. J. (2006). There's an elephant in the room: The impact of early poverty and neglect on intelligence and common learning disorders in children, adolescents, and their parents. *Developmental Disabilities Bulletin, 34*(1-2), 177–215.

Bontempo, R. (1993). Translation fidelity of psychological scales: An item response theory analysis of an individualism-collectivism scale. *Journal of Cross-Cultural Psychology, 24*(2), 149–166.

Branscombe, N. R., Schmitt, M. T., & Harvey, R. D. (1999). Perceiving pervasive discrimination among African Americans: Implications for group identification and well-being. *Journal of Personality and Social Psychology, 77*(1), 135–149.

Brody, G. H., & Flor, D. L. (1998). Maternal resources, parenting practices, and child competence in rural, single-parent African American families. *Child Development, 69*(3), 803–816.

Bureau of Indian Affairs (2018). Indian entities recognized and eligible to receive services from the United States Bureau of Indian Affairs. Retrieved from https://www.federalregister.gov/documents/2018/01/30/2018-01907/indian-entities-recognized-and-eligible-to-receive-services-from-the-united-states-bureau-of-indian

Bush, M. E. (2011). *Everyday forms of Whiteness: Understanding race in a "post-racial" world*. Lanham, MD: Rowman & Littlefield.

Butler, E. A., Lee, T. L., & Gross, J. J. (2007). Emotion regulation and culture: Are the social consequences of emotion suppression culture-specific? *Emotion, 7*(1), 30–48.

Camras, L., Kolmodin, K., & Chen, Y. (2008). Mothers' self-reported emotional expression in Mainland Chinese, Chinese American and European American families. *International Journal of Behavioral Development, 32*(5), 459–463.

Carr, J. E., & Tan, E. K. (1976). In search of the true amok: Amok as viewed within the Malay culture. *The American Journal of Psychiatry, 133*(11), 1295–1299.

Chatters, L. M., Taylor, R. J., & Jayakody, R. (1994). Fictive kinship relations in Black extended families. *Journal of Comparative Family Studies, 25*(3), 297–312.

Chentsova-Dutton, Y. E., Chu, J. P., Tsai, J. L., Rottenberg, J., Gross, J. J., & Gotlib, I. H. (2007). Depression and emotional reactivity: Variation among Asian Americans of East Asian descent and European Americans. *Journal of Abnormal Psychology, 116*(4), 776–785.

Chentsova-Dutton, Y. E., & Dzokoto, V. (2014). Listen to your heart: The cultural shaping of interoceptive awareness and accuracy. *Emotion, 14*(4), 666–678.

Chiu, L. H. (1972). A cross-cultural comparison of cognitive styles in Chinese and American children. *International Journal of Psychology, 7*(4), 235–242.

Christopher, M. S., & Skillman, G. D. (2009). Exploring the link between self-construal and distress and African American and Asian American college students. *Journal of College Counseling, 12*(1), 44–56. doi:10.1002/j.2161-1882.2009.tb00039.x

Chu, K. (2016). South Korean zombie hit "Train to Busan" becomes highest-grossing Asian film in Hong Kong. *Hollywood Reporter*. Retrieved from https://www.hollywoodreporter.com/news/south-korean-zombie-hit-train-933674

Chua, A. (2011, January 19). "Battle hymn of the tiger mother." *The New York Times*. Retrieved from http://www.nytimes.com/2011/01/19/books/excerpt-battle-hymn-of-the-tiger-mother.html

Cohen, S., Tennenbaum, S. Y., Teitelbaum, A., & Durst, R. (1995). The koro (genital retraction) syndrome and its association with infertility: a case report. *The Journal of Urology, 153*(2), 427–428.

Constantinople, A. (1973). Masculinity-femininity: An exception to a famous dictum?. *Psychological Bulletin, 80*(5), 389–407. doi:10.1037/h0035334

Coplan, R. J., Hastings, P. D., Lagacé-Séguin, D. G., & Moulton, C. E. (2002). Authoritative and authoritarian mothers' parenting goals, attributions, and emotions across different childrearing contexts. *Parenting, 2*(1), 1–26.

Cousins, S. D. (1989). Culture and self-perception in Japan and the United States. *Journal of Personality and Social Psychology, 56*(1), 124–131. doi:10.1037/0022-3514.56.1.124

Crocker, J., & Luhtanen, R. (1990). Collective self-esteem and ingroup bias. *Journal Of Personality and Social Psychology, 58*(1), 60–67. doi:10.1037/0022-3514.58.1.60

Crocker, J., & Major, B. (1989). Social stigma and self-esteem: The self-protective properties of stigma. *Psychological Review, 96*(4), 608–630.

Cuddy, A. J., Fiske, S. T., Kwan, V. S., Glick, P., Demoulin, S., Leyens, J. P., . . . Htun, T. T. (2009). Stereotype content model across cultures: Towards universal similarities and some differences. *British Journal of Social Psychology, 48*(1), 1–33.

Dana, R. H. (1993). *Multicultural assessment perspectives for professional psychology*. Needham Heights, MA: Allyn & Bacon.

Dana, R. H., Gamst, G., Der-Karabetian, A., & Kramer, T. (2001). Asian American mental health clients: Effects of ethnic match and age on global assessment and visitation. *Journal of Mental Health Counseling, 23*(1), 57–71.

Davidson, K. L. (1992). A comparison of Native American and White students' cognitive strengths as measured by the Kaufman Assessment Battery for Children. *Roper Review, 14*(3), 111–115.

De la Garza, R. O., Falcon, A., & Garcia, F. C. (1996). Will the real Americans please stand up?: Anglo and Mexican-American support of core American political values. *American Journal of Political Science, 40*(2), 335–351.

Delgado, M. (1980). Providing child care for Hispanic families. *Young Children, 35*(6), 26–32.

Delgado, R., & Stefancic, J. (Eds.). (1997). *Critical white studies: Looking behind the mirror*. Philadelphia, PA: Temple University Press.

Der-Karabetian, A., Dana, R. H., & Gamst, G. C. (2008). *CBMCS multicultural training program: Participant workbook*. Thousand Oaks, CA: Sage Publications.

Devos, T., Gavin, K., & Quintana, F. J. (2010). Say "adios" to the American dream? The interplay between ethnic and national identity among Latino and Caucasian Americans. *Cultural Diversity and Ethnic Minority Psychology, 16*(1), 37–49.

Deyhle, D., & LeCompte, M. (1994). Cultural differences in child development: Navajo adolescents in middle schools. *Theory in Practice, 33*(3), 156–166.

Diaz-Loving, R., & Draguns, J. G. (1999). Culture, meaning, and personality in Mexico and in the United States. In Y.-T. Lee, C. R. McCauley, & J. G. Draguns (Eds.), *Personality and person perception across cultures* (pp. 103–126). Mahwah, NJ: Erlbaum.

Diener, E., Napa-Scollon, C. K., Oishi, S., Dzokoto, V., & Suh, E. M. (2000). Positivity and the construction of life satisfaction judgments: Global happiness is not the sum of its parts. *Journal of Happiness Studies, 1*(2), 159–176.

Diener, E., & Suh, E. M. (2000). Measuring subjective well-being to compare the quality of life of cultures. In E. Diener and E. M. Suh (Eds.), *Culture and Subjective Well-being* (pp. 3–12). Cambridge, MA: MIT Press.

Dornbusch, S. M., Ritter, P. L., Leiderman, P. H., Roberts, D. F., & Fraleigh, M. J. (1987). The relation of parenting style to adolescent school performance. *Child development*, 1244–1257.

Dwairy, M. (2004). Parenting styles and mental health of Palestinian–Arab adolescents in Israel. *Transcultural psychiatry, 41*(2), 233–252.

Dzokoto, V. A. (2010). Different ways of feeling: Emotion and somatic awareness in Ghanaians and Euro-Americans. *Journal of Social, Evolutionary, and Cultural Psychology, 4*(2), 68–78.

Dzokoto, V. A., & Adams, G. (2005). Understanding genital-shrinking epidemics in West Africa: Koro, juju, or mass psychogenic illness? *Culture, Medicine and Psychiatry, 29*(1), 53–78.

Edwards, C. L., Fillingim, R. B., & Keefe, F. (2001). Race, ethnicity and pain. *Pain, 94*(2), 133–137.

Ekman, P. (1993). Facial expression and emotion. *American Psychologist, 48*(4), 384–392.

Ekman, P., & Davidson, R. J. (1993). Voluntary smiling changes regional brain activity. *Psychological Science, 4*(5), 342–345.

Elfenbein, H. A., & Ambady, N. (2002). On the universality and cultural specificity of emotion recognition: A meta-analysis. *Psychological Bulletin, 128*(2), 203–235.

Faucett, J., Gordon, N., & Levine, J. (1994). Differences in postoperative pain severity among four ethnic groups. *Journal of Pain and Symptom Management, 9*(6), 383–389.

Fisher, C. B., Wallace, S. A., & Fenton, R. E. (2000). Discrimination distress during adolescence. *Journal of Youth and Adolescence, 29*(6), 679–695.

Fiske, S. T., Cuddy, A. J., Glick, P., & Xu, J. (2002). A model of (often mixed) stereotype content: Competence and warmth respectively follow from perceived status and competition. *Journal of Personality and Social Psychology, 82*(6), 878–902.

Fleming, C. M. (1992). American Indians and Alaska Natives: Changing societies past and present. In M. Orlandi (Ed.), *Cultural competence for evaluators: A guide for alcohol and other drug abuse prevention practitioners working with ethnic/racial communities* (pp. 147–171). Rockville, MD: U.S. Dept of Health and Human Services.

Foulks, E. F. (1985). The transformation of arctic hysteria. In R. C. Simons & C. C. Hughes (Eds.), *The culture-bound syndromes: Folk illnesses of psychiatric and anthropological interest* (pp. 307–324). Dordrecht, Netherlands: Springer Netherlands.

Fricke, D. (1998, March 5). Three men and a baby grand. *Rolling Stone*. Retrieved from https://www.rollingstone.com/music/features/3-men-and-a-baby-grand-19980305

Friedman, S., & Paradis, C. (2002). Panic disorder in African-Americans: Symptomatology and isolated sleep paralysis. *Culture, Medicine and Psychiatry, 26*(2), 179–198.

Fryberg, S. A., & Markus, H. R. (2003). On being American Indian: Current and possible selves. *Self and Identity, 2*(4), 325–344. doi:10.1080/714050251

Fryberg, S. A., & Markus, H. R. (2007). Cultural models of education in American Indian, Asian American and European American contexts. *Social Psychology of Education*, 10(2), 213–246.

Fryberg, S. A., Markus, H. R., Oyserman, D., & Stone, J. M. (2008). Of warrior chiefs and Indian princesses: The psychological consequences of American Indian mascots. *Basic and Applied Social Psychology*, 30(3), 208–218.

Gaines Jr, S. O., Marelich, W. D., Bledsoe, K. L., Steers, W. N., Henderson, M. C., Granrose, C. S., . . . Yum, N. (1997). Links between race/ethnicity and cultural values as mediated by racial/ethnic identity and moderated by gender. *Journal of Personality and Social Psychology*, 72(6), 1460–1476.

Gallo, L. C., & Matthews, K. A. (2003). Understanding the association between socio-economic status and physical health: Do negative emotions play a role? *Psychological Bulletin*, 129(1), 10–51.

Gamst, G. C., Der-Karabetian, A., & Dana, R. H. (2008). *CBMCS Multicultural Reader*. Thousand Oaks, CA: Sage Publications.

Gamst, G. C., Liang, C. T., & Der-Karabetian, A. (2011). *Handbook of multicultural measures*. Washington, D.C.: Sage Publications.

García, H., Sierra, A., & Balám, G. (1999). *Wind in the blood: Mayan healing and Chinese medicine*. Berkeley, CA: North Atlantic Books.

Gawronski, B., & Bodenhausen, G. V. (2006). Associative and propositional processes in evaluation: An integrative review of implicit and explicit attitude change. *Psychological Bulletin*, 132(5), 692–731.

Gazzaniga, M. S. (2008). *Human: The science behind what makes us unique*. New York, NY: Ecco.

Gilbert, D. T., & Malone, P. S. (1995). The correspondence bias. *Psychological Bulletin*, 117(1), 21–38.

Gill, J. H. (1999). Knowledge, power, and freedom: Native American and Western epistemo-logical paradigms. *Philosophy Today*, 43(4), 423–438.

Gilliland, H. (1999). *Teaching the Native American*. Dubuque, IA: Kendall/Hunt.

Gitter, A. G., Black, H., & Mostofsky, D. (1972). Race and sex in the perception of emotion. *Journal of Social Issues*, 28(4), 63–78.

Gloria, A. M., & Robinson Kurpius, S. E. (2001). Influences of self-beliefs, social support, and comfort in the university environment on the academic nonpersistence decisions of American Indian undergraduates. *Cultural Diversity and Ethnic Minority Psychology*, 7(1), 88–102. doi:10.1037/1099-9809.7.1.88

Good, B. J., & Kleinman, A. M. (1985). Culture and anxiety: Cross-cultural evidence for the patterning of anxiety disorders. In A. H. Tuma & J. D. Maser (Eds.), *Anxiety and the anxiety disorders* (pp. 297–323). Hillsdale, NJ: Erlbaum.

Gray-Little, B., & Hafdahl, A. R. (2000). Factors influencing racial comparisons of self-esteem: A quantitative review. *Psychological Bulletin*, 126(1), 26–54.

Graziano, W. G., & Eisenberg, N. (1997). Agreeableness: A dimension of personality. In *Handbook of Personality Psychology* (pp. 795–824). San Diego, CA: Academic Press.

Greenwald, A. G., & Banaji, M. R. (1995). Implicit social cognition: Attitudes, self-esteem, and stereotypes. *Psychological Review*, 102(1), 4–27.

Griffin, D., & Tversky, A. (1992). The weighing of evidence and the determinants of confidence. *Cognitive Psychology*, 24(3), 411–435.

Gross, J. J., & John, O. P. (2003). Individual differences in two emotion regulation processes: Implications for affect, relationships, and well-being. *Journal of Personality and Social Psychology*, 85(2), 348–362. doi:10.1037/0022-3514.85.2.348

Gross, J. J., & Levenson, R. W. (1993). Emotional suppression: physiology, self-report, and expressive behavior. *Journal of Personality and Social Psychology*, 64(6), 970–986.

Hale, J. E. (1982). *Black children: Their roots, culture, and learning styles.* Baltimore, MD: Johns Hopkins University Press.

Heart, M. Y. H. B., & DeBruyn, L. M. (1998). The American Indian holocaust: Healing historical unresolved grief. *American Indian and Alaska Native Mental Health Research*, 8(2), 56–78.

Heine, S. J., Lehman, D. R., Markus, H. R., & Kitayama, S. (1999). Is there a universal need for positive self-regard? *Psychological Review*, 106(4), 766–794. doi:10.1037/0033-295X. 106.4.766

Hetts, J. J., & Pelham, B. W. (2001). A case for the nonconscious self-concept. In *Cognitive social psychology: The Princeton symposium on the legacy and future of social cognition* (pp. 105–123). Mahwah, NJ: Erlbaum.

Hirschfeld, L. A. (1995). Anthropology, psychology, and the meanings of social causality. In D. Sperber, D. Premack, & A. Premack (Eds.), *Causal cognition: A multidisciplinary debate* (pp. 313–350). Oxford, U.K.: Oxford University Press.

Ho, D. Y. F., Fu, W., & Ng, S. M. (2004). Guilt, shame and embarrassment: Revelations of face and self. *Culture & Psychology*, 10(1), 64–84.

Hoff, E. (2003). The specificity of environmental influence: Socioeconomic status affects early vocabulary development via maternal speech. *Child Development*, 7(4), 1368–1378. doi: 10.1111/1467-8624.00612

Hoff, E. (2006). How social contexts support and shape language development. *Developmental Review*, 26(1), 55–88. doi:10.1016/j.dr.2005.11.002

Hoff, E., & Tian, C. (2005). Socioeconomic status and cultural influences on language. *Journal of Communication Disorders*, 38(4), 271–278. doi:10.1016/j.jcomdis.2005.02.003

Hofstede, G. (1980b). Motivation, leadership, and organization: Do American theories apply abroad? *Organizational Dynamics*, 9(1), 42–63.

Hofstede, G. (1983). The cultural relativity of organizational practices and theories. *Journal of International Business Studies*, 14(2), 75–89.

Hofstede, G. (2001). *Culture's consequences: Comparing values, behaviors, institutions, and organizations across nations* (2nd ed.). Thousand Oaks, CA: Sage Publications.

Hofstede, G. (2011). Dimensionalizing cultures: The Hofstede model in context. *Online Readings in Psychology and Culture*, 2(1), 1–26.

Huang, K., Leong, F. T., & Wagner, N. S. (1994). Coping with peer stressors and associated dysphoria: Acculturation differences among Chinese-American children. *Counselling Psychology Quarterly*, 7(1), 53–68.

Hwang, W. C., & Goto, S. (2008). The impact of perceived racial discrimination on the mental health of Asian American and Latino college students. *Cultural Diversity and Ethnic Minority Psychology*, 14(4), 326–335.

Inglebret, E., Jones, C., & Pavel, D. M. (2008). Integrating American Indian/Alaska Native culture into shared storybook intervention. *Language, Speech, and Hearing Services in Schools*, 39(4), 521–527.

Jack, R. E., Blais, C., Scheepers, C., Schyns, P. G., & Caldara, R. (2009). Cultural confusions show that facial expressions are not universal. *Current Biology*, 19(18), 1543–1548.

Ji, L. J., Nisbett, R. E., & Su, Y. (2001). Culture, change, and prediction. *Psychological Science*, 12(6), 450–456.

Johnson, D. D., & Fowler, J. H. (2011). The evolution of overconfidence. *Nature*, 477(7364), 317–320.

Jost, J. T., & Banaji, M. R. (1994). The role of stereotyping in system-justification and the production of false consciousness. *British Journal of Social Psychology*, 33(1), 1–27.

Katz, J. H. (1985). The sociopolitical nature of counseling. *The counseling psychologist*, 13(4), 615–624.

Keltner, D. (1995). Signs of appeasement: Evidence for the distinct displays of embarrassment, amusement, and shame. *Journal of Personality and Social Psychology*, 68(3), 441–454.

Key, M. R. (1975). *Paralanguage and kinesics: Nonverbal comunication.* Metuchen, NJ: Scarecrow.

Khoo, P. L. S., Abu-Rasain, M. H., & Hornby, G. (1994). Counseling foreign students: A review of strategies. *Counseling Psychology Quarterly, 7*(2), 117–131.

Kim, H., & Markus, H. R. (1999). Deviance or uniqueness, harmony or conformity? A cultural analysis. *Journal of Personality and Social Psychology, 77*(4), 785–800.

Kitayama, S., Markus, H. R., Matsumoto, H., & Norasakkunkit, V. (1997). Individual and collective processes in the construction of the self: Self-enhancement in the United States and self-criticism in Japan. *Journal of Personality and Social Psychology, 72*(6), 1245–1267. doi:10.1037/0022-3514.72.6.1245

Klonoff, E. A., Landrine, H., & Ullman, J. B. (1999). Racial discrimination and psychiatric symptoms among Blacks. *Cultural Diversity and Ethnic Minority Psychology, 5*(4), 329–339.

Knowles, E. D., Lowery, B. S., & Schaumberg, R. L. (2009). Anti-egalitarians for Obama? Group-dominance motivation and the Obama vote. *Journal of Experimental Social Psychology, 45*(4), 965–969.

Knowles, E. D., & Peng, K. (2005). White selves: Conceptualizing and measuring a dominant-group identity. *Journal of Personality and Social Psychology, 89,* 223–241.

Kristoff, C. (1999, December 1). Big wolves aren't so bad in Japan. *The New York Times.* Retrieved from http://www.nytimes.com/1996/12/01/weekinreview/big-wolves-aren-t-so-bad-in-japan.html

Kutsche, P. (1983). Household and family in Hispanic northern New Mexico. *Journal of Comparative Family Studies, 14*(2), 151–165.

Landrine, H., Klonoff, E. A., Corral, I., Fernandez, S., & Roesch, S. (2006). Conceptualizing and measuring ethnic discrimination in health research. *Journal of Behavioral Medicine, 29*(1), 79–94.

Lebra, T. S. (1976). *Japanese patterns of behavior.* Honolulu: University Press of Hawaii.

Lechuga, J., Santos, B. M., Garza-Caballero, A. A., & Villarreal, R. (2011). Holistic reasoning on the other side of the world: Validation of the Analysis-Holism scale in Mexicans. *Cultural Diversity and Ethnic Minority Psychology, 17*(3), 325–330. doi: 10.1037/a0023881

Lechuga, J., & Wiebe, J. S. (2011). Culture and probability judgment accuracy: The influence of holistic reasoning. *Journal of Cross-Cultural Psychology, 42*(6), 1054–1065.

Leung, K., Lau, S., & Lam, W. L. (1998). Parenting styles and academic achievement: A cross-cultural study. *Merrill-Palmer Quarterly, 44*(2), 157–172.

Locust, C. (1988). Wounding the spirit: Discrimination and traditional American Indian belief systems. *Harvard Educational Review, 58*(3), 315–330.

Lopez, I., Ramirez, R., Guarnaccia, P., Canino, G., & Bird, H. (2011). Ataques de nervios and somatic complaints among island and mainland Puerto Rican children. *CNS Neuroscience & Therapeutics, 17*(3), 158–166.

Lundeberg, M. A., Fox, P. W., Brown, A. C., & Elbedour, S. (2000). Cultural influences on confidence: Country and gender. *Journal of Educational Psychology, 92*(1), 152–159.

Ma-Kellams, C., & Blascovich, J. (2012). Inferring the emotions of friends versus strangers: The role of culture and self-construal. *Personality and Social Psychology Bulletin, 38*(7), 933–945.

Ma-Kellams, C., Blascovich, J., & McCall, C. (2012). Culture and the body: East–West differences in visceral perception. *Journal of Personality and Social Psychology, 102*(4), 718–728.

Ma-Kellams, C., Spencer-Rodgers, J., & Peng, K. (2011). I am against us? Unpacking cultural differences in ingroup favoritism via dialecticism. *Personality and Social Psychology Bulletin, 37*(1), 15–27.

Makanjuola, R. O. (1987). "Ode Ori": A culture-bound disorder with prominent somatic features in Yoruba Nigerian patients. *Acta psychiatrica scandinavica, 75*(3), 231–236.

Malloy, C. E., & Jones, M. G. (1998). An investigation of African American students' mathematical problem solving. *Journal for Research in Mathematics Education*, 143–163.

Manuel-Logan, R. (2012). 10 crazy GOP meltdowns after Obama's re-election. *NewsOne.* Retrieved from http://newsone.com/2082964/republicans-against-obama/

Marano, L. (1985). Windigo psychosis: The anatomy of an emic-etic confusion. In R. C. Simons & C. C. Hughes (Eds.), *The culture-bound syndromes: Folk illnesses of psychiatric and anthropological interest* (pp. 411–448). Dordrecht, Netherlands: Springer Netherlands.

Markus, H. R., & Kitayama, S. (1991). Culture and the self: Implications for cognition, emotion, and motivation. *Psychological Review, 98*(2), 224–253.

Markus, H. R., Uchida, Y., Omoregie, H., Townsend, S. S., & Kitayama, S. (2006). Going for the gold: Models of agency in Japanese and American contexts. *Psychological Science, 17*(2), 103–112.

Marotta, S. A., & Garcia, J. G. (2003). Latinos in the United States in 2000. *Hispanic Journal of Behavioral Sciences, 25*(1), 13–34.

Martinez, C., & Martin, H. W. (1966). Folk diseases among urban Mexican-Americans: Etiology, symptoms, and treatment. *Journal of the American Medical Association, 196*(2), 161–164.

Mastro, D. E., & Behm-Morawitz, E. (2005). Latino representation on primetime television. *Journalism & Mass Communication Quarterly, 82*(1), 110–130.

Masuda, T., Ellsworth, P. C., Mesquita, B., Leu, J., Tanida, S., & Van de Veerdonk, E. (2008). Placing the face in context: Cultural differences in the perception of facial emotion. *Journal of Personality and Social Psychology, 94*(3), 365–381.

Masuda, T., Gonzalez, R., Kwan, L., & Nisbett, R. E. (2008). Culture and aesthetic preference: Comparing the attention to context of East Asians and Americans. *Personality and Social Psychology Bulletin, 34*(9), 1260–1275.

Masuda, T., & Nisbett, R. E. (2001). Attending holistically versus analytically: Comparing the context sensitivity of Japanese and Americans. *Journal of Personality and Social Psychology, 81*(5), 922–934.

Matsuki, K. (1995). Metaphors of anger in Japanese. In John R. Taylor and Robert E. MacLaury (Eds.), *Language and the Cognitive Construal of the World* (137–151). Berlin, Germany: Walter de Gruyter.

Matsumoto, D., Yoo, S. H., & Fontaine, J. (2008). Mapping expressive differences around the world: The relationship between emotional display rules and individualism versus collectivism. *Journal of Cross-Cultural Psychology, 39*(1), 55–74.

McConahay, J. B. (1986). Modern racism, ambivalence, and the Modern Racism Scale. In J. F. Dovidio & S. L. Gaertner (Eds.), *Prejudice, discrimination, and racism* (pp. 91–125). San Diego, CA: Academic Press.

Mesquita, B., & Karasawa, M. (2002). Different emotional lives. *Cognition & Emotion, 16*(1), 127–141.

Minkov, M. (2012). *Cross-cultural analysis: The science and art of comparing the world's modern societies and their cultures.* Thousand Oaks, CA: Sage Publications.

Morris, M. W., Nisbett, R. E., & Peng, K. (1995). Causal attribution across domains and cultures. In D. Sperber, D. Premack, & A. J. Premack (Eds.), *Symposia of the Fyssen Foundation. Causal cognition: A multidisciplinary debate* (pp. 577–614). New York, NY: Clarendon Press/Oxford University Press.

Morris, M. W., & Peng, K. (1994). Culture and cause: American and Chinese attributions for social and physical events. *Journal of Personality and Social Psychology, 67*(6), 949–971.

Morton, L. L, Allen, J. D., & Williams, N. H. (1994). Hemisphericity and information processing in North American Native (Ojibwa) and non-Native adolescents. *International Journal of Neuroscience, 75*(3-4), 189–202.

Mueller, H. H., Mulcahy, R. F., Wilgosh, L., & Walters, B. (1986). An analysis of WISC—R item responses with Canadian Inuit children. *Alberta Journal of Educational Research.*

Murphy-Berman, V., & Berman, J. J. (Eds.). (2003). *Cross-cultural differences in perspectives on the self.* Lincoln: University of Nebraska Press.

National Indian Education Association. (2008). Native Education 101: The history of Natives in the American education system. Retrieved from http://www.niea.org/our-story/history/native-101/

Nisbett, R. E., Peng, K., Choi, I., & Norenzayan, A. (2001). Culture and systems of thought: Holistic versus analytic cognition. *Psychological Review, 108*(2), 291–310.

Nowicki Jr., S., Glanville, D., & Demertzis, A. (1998). A test of the ability to recognize emotion in the facial expressions of African American adults. *Journal of Black Psychology, 24*(3), 335–350.

Nuby, J. F., Ehle, M. A., & Thrower, E. (2001). Culturally responsive teaching as related to the learning styles of Native American students. In J. Nyowe & A. Sehlaoui (Eds.), *Multicultural education: Diverse perspectives* (pp. 231–271). Victoria, BC: Trafford Publishing Company.

Office of the Surgeon General, Center for Mental Health Services, National Institute of Mental Health (2001). *Mental health: Culture, race, and ethnicity.* A supplement to *Mental health: A report of the Surgeon General.* Rockville, MD: Substance Abuse and Mental Health Services Administration. Retrieved from https://www.ncbi.nlm.nih.gov/books/NBK44243/

Osherson, D. N., Smith, E. E., Wilkie, O., Lopez, A., & Shafir, E. (1990). Category-based induction. *Psychological Review, 97*(2), 185–200.

Oyserman, D., Coon, H. M., & Kemmelmeier, M. (2002). Rethinking individualism and collectivism: Evaluation of theoretical assumptions and meta-analyses. *Psychological Bulletin, 128*(1), 3–72. doi:10.1037/0033-2909.128.1.3

Oyserman, D., Gant, L., & Ager, J. (1995). A socially contextualized model of African American identity: Possible selves and school persistence. *Journal of Personality and Social Psychology, 69*(6), 1216–1232.

Parker, G., Cheah, Y. C., & Roy, K. (2001). Do the Chinese somatize depression? A cross-cultural study. *Social Psychiatry and Psychiatric Epidemiology, 36*(6), 287–293.

Peng, K., & Nisbett, R. E. (1999). Culture, dialectics, and reasoning about contradiction. *American Psychologist, 54*(9), 741–754.

Pewewardy, C. (2002). Learning styles of American Indian/Alaska Native students: A review of the literature and implications for practice. *Journal of American Indian Education, 41*(3), 22–56.

Phillips, K. A., Wilhelm, S., Koran, L. M., Didie, E. R., Fallon, B. A., Feusner, J., & Stein, D. J. (2010). Body dysmorphic disorder: Some key issues for DSM-V. *Depression and Anxiety, 27*(6), 573–591.

Phinney, J. S., & Chavira, V. (1992). Ethnic identity and self-esteem: An exploratory longitudinal study. *Journal of Adolescence, 15*(3), 271–281.

Querido, J. G., Warner, T. D., & Eyberg, S. M. (2002). Parenting styles and child behavior in African American families of preschool children. *Journal of Clinical Child and Adolescent Psychology, 31*(2), 272–277.

Ramírez-Esparza, N., Gosling, S. D., & Pennebaker, J. W. (2008). Paradox lost: Unraveling the puzzle of Simpatía. *Journal of Cross-Cultural Psychology, 39*(6), 703–715.

Ranjith, G., & Mohan, R. (2006). Dhat syndrome as a functional somatic syndrome: Developing a sociosomatic model. *Psychiatry, 69*(2), 142–150.

Reactions from around the world (2008, November 5). *The New York Times*. Retrieved from http://thecaucus.blogs.nytimes.com/2008/11/05/reactions-from-around-the-world/?_r=0

Richards, J. M., Butler, E. A., & Gross, J. J. (2003). Emotion regulation in romantic relationships: The cognitive consequences of concealing feelings. *Journal of Social and Personal Relationships*, 20(5), 599–620.

Rieckmann, T. R., Wadsworth, M. E., & Deyhle, D. (2004). Cultural identity, explanatory style, and depression in Navajo adolescents. *Cultural Diversity and Ethnic Minority Psychology*, 10(4), 365–382.

Rivera, H. H., & Tharp, R. G. (2006). A Native American community's involvement and empowerment to guide their children's development in the school setting. *Journal of Community Psychology*, 34(4), 435–451.

Robert, C., Probst, T. M., Martocchio, J. J., Drasgow, F., & Lawler, J. J. (2000). Empowerment and continuous improvement in the United States, Mexico, Poland, and India: Predicting fit on the basis of the dimensions of power distance and individualism. *Journal of Applied Psychology*, 85(5), 643–658. doi:10.1037/0021-9010.85.5.643

Roberts, N. A., Levenson, R. W., & Gross, J. J. (2008). Cardiovascular costs of emotion suppression cross ethnic lines. *International Journal of Psychophysiology*, 70(1), 82–87.

Rosenberg, M. (1965). Rosenberg self-esteem scale (RSE). *Acceptance and commitment therapy: Measures package*, 61, 52.

Rosenbloom, S. R., & Way, N. (2004). Experiences of discrimination among African American, Asian American, and Latino adolescents in an urban high school. *Youth & Society*, 35(4), 420–451.

Ross, L. (1977). The intuitive psychologist and his shortcomings: Distortions in the attribution process. In Leonard Berkowitz (Ed.), *Advances in experimental social psychology, volume 10* (pp. 173–220). San Diego, CA: Academic Press.

Rudy, D., & Grusec, J. E. (2001). Correlates of authoritarian parenting in individualist and collectivist cultures and implications for understanding the transmission of values. *Journal of Cross-Cultural Psychology*, 32(2), 202–212.

Rudy, D., & Grusec, J. E. (2006). Authoritarian parenting in individualist and collectivist groups: Associations with maternal emotion and cognition and children's self-esteem. *Journal of Family Psychology*, 20(1), 68–78.

Ryder, A. G., Yang, J., Zhu, X., Yao, S., Yi, J., Heine, S. J., & Bagby, R. M. (2008). The cultural shaping of depression: somatic symptoms in China, psychological symptoms in North America? *Journal of Abnormal Psychology*, 117(2), 300–313.

Scherer, K. R. (1997). The role of culture in emotion-antecedent appraisal. *Journal of Personality and Social Psychology*, 73(5), 902–922.

Schmitt, D. P., Allik, J., McCrae, R. R., & Benet-Martínez, V. (2007). The geographic distribution of Big Five personality traits: Patterns and profiles of human self-description across 56 nations. *Journal of Cross-Cultural Psychology*, 38(2), 173–212.

Scollon, C. N., Diener, E., Oishi, S., & Biswas-Diener, R. (2004). Emotions across cultures and methods. *Journal of Cross-Cultural Psychology*, 35(3), 304–326.

Segura, D. A., & Pierce, J. L. (1993). Chicana/o family structure and gender personality: Chodorow, familism, and psychoanalytic sociology revisited. *Signs*, 19(1), 62–91.

Shade, B. J. (1986). Is there an Afro-American cognitive style? An exploratory study. *Journal of Black Psychology*, 13(1), 13–16.

Shweder, R. A. (1995). The confessions of a methodological individualist. *Culture & Psychology*, 1(1), 115–122.

Smedley, A., & Smedley, B. D. (2005). Race as biology is fiction, racism as a social problem is real: Anthropological and historical perspectives on the social construction of race. *American Psychologist*, 60(1), 16–26. doi:10.1037/0003-066X.60.1.16

Smith, G. T., Spillane, N. S., & Annus, A. M. (2006). Implications of an emerging integration of universal and culturally specific psychologies. *Perspectives on Psychological Science*, *1*(3), 211–233.

Snowden, L. R. (2001). Barriers to effective mental health services for African Americans. *Mental Health Services Research*, *3*(4), 181–187.

Stankov, L., & Lee, J. (2014). Overconfidence across world regions. *Journal of Cross-Cultural Psychology*, *45*(5), 821–837.

Stephan, W. G., Stephan, C. W., & De Vargas, M. C. (1996). Emotional expression in Costa Rica and the United States. *Journal of Cross-Cultural Psychology*, *27*(2), 147–160.

Stiff, L. V. (1990). African-American students and the promise of the curriculum and evaluation standards. In T. J. Cooney & C. R. Hirsch (Eds.), *Teaching and learning in the 1990s: Mathematics in the 1990s. 1990 Yearbook of the National Council of Teachers of Mathematics* (pp. 152–158). Reston, VA: National Council of Teachers of Mathematics.

Sue, S., & Zane, N. (1987). The role of culture and cultural techniques in psychotherapy: A critique and reformulation. *American Psychologist*, *42*(1), 37–45.

Suina, J. H., & Smolkin, L. B. (1994). From natal culture to school culture to dominant society culture: Supporting transitions for Pueblo Indian students. In P. M. Greenfield & R. R. Cocking (Eds.), *Cross-cultural roots of minority child development* (pp. 115–130). Hillsdale, NJ: Erlbaum.

Swinomish Tribal Mental Health Project. (1991). *A gathering of wisdoms: Tribal mental health: A cultural perspective*. Mount Vernon, WA: Veda Vangarde.

Swisher, K., & Deyhle, D. (1989). The styles of learning are different, but the teaching is just the same: Suggestions for teachers of American Indian youth. *Journal of American Indian Education* (August 1989), 1–14.

Tharp, R. G. (1994). Intergroup differences among Native Americans in socialization and child cognition: An ethnogenetic analysis. In P. M. Greenfield & R. R. Cocking (Eds.), *Cross-cultural roots of minority child development* (pp. 87–105). Hillsdale, NJ: Erlbaum.

Therrien, M. R. R., & Ramirez, R. R. (2001). The Hispanic population in the United States. *Current Population Reports*, P20–P535.

Tinling, D. C. (1967). Voodoo, root work, and medicine. *Psychosomatic Medicine*, *29*(5), 483–490.

Triandis, H. C. (1980). Reflections on trends in cross-cultural research. *Journal of Cross-Cultural Psychology*, *11*(1), 35–58.

Triandis, H. C., Marin, G., Lisansky, J., & Betancourt, H. (1984). Simpatía as a cultural script of Hispanics. *Journal of Personality and Social Psychology*, *47*(6), 1363–1375.

Tsai, J. L., Knutson, B., & Fung, H. H. (2006). Cultural variation in affect valuation. *Journal of Personality and Social Psychology*, *90*(2), 288–307.

Tsai, J. L., & Levenson, R. W. (1997). Cultural influences on emotional responding: Chinese American and European American dating couples during interpersonal conflict. *Journal of Cross-Cultural Psychology*, *28*(5), 600–625.

Tsai, J. L., Levenson, R. W., & Carstensen, L. L. (2000). Autonomic, subjective, and expressive responses to emotional films in older and younger Chinese Americans and European Americans. *Psychology and Aging*, *15*(4), 684–693.

Tsai, J. L., Louie, J. Y., Chen, E. E., & Uchida, Y. (2007). Learning what feelings to desire: Socialization of ideal affect through children's storybooks. *Personality and Social Psychology Bulletin*, *33*(1), 17–30.

Tsai, J. L., Simeonova, D. I., & Watanabe, J. T. (2004). Somatic and social: Chinese Americans talk about emotion. *Personality and social psychology bulletin*, *30*(9), 1226–1238.

Tsethlikai, M. (2011). An exploratory analysis of American Indian children's cultural engagement, fluid cognitive skills, and standardized verbal IQ scores. *Developmental Psychology, 47*(1), 192–202.

Twenge, J. M., & Crocker, J. (2002). Race and self-esteem: Meta-analyses comparing whites, blacks, Hispanics, Asians, and American Indians and comment on Gray-Little and Hafdahl (2000). *Psychological Bulletin, 128*(3), 371–408.

Valenzuela, A., & Dornbusch, S. M. (1994). Familism and social capital in the academic achievement of Mexican origin and Anglo adolescents. *Social Science Quarterly, 75*(1), 18–36.

Varela, R. E., Vernberg, E. M., Sanchez-Sosa, J. J., Riveros, A., Mitchell, M., & Mashunkashey, J. (2004). Parenting style of Mexican, Mexican American, and Caucasian-non-Hispanic families: Social context and cultural influences. *Journal of Family Psychology, 18*(4), 651–657.

Weidman, H. H. (1979). Falling-out: A diagnostic and treatment problem viewed from a transcultural perspective. *Social Science & Medicine. Part B: Medical Anthropology, 13*(2), 95–112.

Williams, J., & Negrin, M. (2008, March 18). Affirmative action foes point to Obama, say candidate is proof effort no longer needed. *Boston Globe*. Retrieved from http://archive. boston.com/news/nation/articles/2008/03/18/affirmative_action_foes_point_to_obama/

Whitbeck, L. B., Adams, G. W., Hoyt, D. R., & Chen, X. (2004). Conceptualizing and measuring historical trauma among American Indian people. *American Journal of Community Psychology, 33*(3-4), 119–130.

Whitbeck, L. B., Hoyt, D. R., Stubben, J. D., & LaFromboise, T. (2001). Traditional culture and academic success among American Indian children in the upper Midwest. *Journal of American Indian Education*, 48–60.

Wierzbicka, A. (1994). Emotion, language, and cultural scripts. In S. Kitayama & H. R. Markus (Eds.), *Emotion and culture: Empirical studies of mutual influence* (pp. 133–196). Washington, DC: American Psychological Association.

Willis, W. (1992). Families with African American roots. In E. W. Lynch & M. J. Hanson (Eds.), Developing cross-cultural competence: A guide for working with young children and their families (pp. 121–150). Baltimore, MD: Paul H. Brookes Publishing.

Yamagishi, T. (1988). Exit from the group as an individualistic solution to the free rider problem in the United States and Japan. *Journal of Experimental Social Psychology, 24*(6), 530–542.

Yu, N. (2009). *The Chinese HEART in a cognitive perspective: Culture, body, and language.* Berlin, Germany: Mouton de Gruyter.

Zarate, M. A., Uleman, J. S., & Voils, C. I. (2001). Effects of culture and processing goals on the activation and binding of trait concepts. *Social Cognition, 19*(3), 295–323.

Zaroff, C. M., Davis, J. M., Chio, P. H., & Madhavan, D. (2012). Somatic presentations of distress in China. *Australian & New Zealand Journal of Psychiatry, 46*(11), 1053–1057.

CHAPTER 2

Class

In many ways, class is the new race (Sutter, 2013). Historically, research on race has been invariably confounded with socioeconomic status (SES), but a growing body of research in psychology on class as culture is showing that SES, independent of race, can shape a multitude of psychological processes and real-world outcomes. As this chapter will unveil, class determines both abstract conceptions of the self (e.g., as individualists or collectivists) as well as practical downstream consequences, including preferences, prosociality, and ethical behavior. As a result, class wars (e.g., between working class and upper class) may be less about who owns what and more about the cultural beliefs and values that come with chronically possessing much or little.

A Brief History of Class

Consider this: Social class is arguably one of the most enduring features of human civilization. Over the course of history, political systems have alternated between theocracies, oligarchies, tyrannies, monarchies, parliamentary systems, democracies, socialist systems, and communism; economic systems have ebbed and flowed; empires have come and gone (Corfield, 1991). Even our conceptions of race have changed over time; as a species, we've alternated between basing race on melanin and skin color to geography to family lineage to the shape of our skulls (Herzstein, 1969). But throughout all this time, social class has remained; in just about every society documented, there have existed discrepancies between the haves and the have-nots.

Interestingly, despite the ubiquity and constancy of class, much debate remains as to whether class is here to stay. Back on November 9, 1989, the Berlin Wall fell; afterward, many presumed that the death of communism equated to the death of class warfare, because a single wall falling in Germany was supposed to mean that everyone was suddenly middle class (Roth, November 7, 2014). In the

United States, despite our history with slavery and the rise and struggle of the labor movement over the last century, popular conception nevertheless has long heralded us as a "classless" society, or at least a society where talking about class makes people very uncomfortable ("if we don't talk about it, it doesn't exist!") (Kingston, 2000). In recent years, class has finally made a comeback, and a growing subfield of psychology has been dedicated to the psychology of social class as culture.

Defining Social Class

Objective social class refers to the elements of wealth, education, and occupational prestige that lead to material differences between upper versus lower class individuals—differences like the neighborhoods you live in, the clubs you frequent, the schools you attend (and whether the school offers one iPad per student or one textbook per classroom), the food you eat, the activities you consider fun, and the clothes that you wear (Adler, Epel, Castellazzo, & Ickovics, 2000; Oakes & Rossi, 2003). These objective markers are highly direct signals of class and are clearly observable. In fact, people can accurately judge the education and income bracket of a complete stranger simply based on a 60-second video clip of the stranger's behavior (Ambady & Rosenthal, 1992).

Subjective social class rank, in contrast, refers to how individuals perceive themselves in relation to others in terms of education, income, and occupational status (e.g., Adler et al., 2000). The subjective nature of class is based on the idea that human hierarchies invariably exist and are almost always vertical and relational; class, in this context, is very hierarchical, and your sense of class largely depends on where you rank in relation to other people around you. Of course, objective and subjective social classes are related, and it is through observable signals of objective class that people make inferences about subjective class. However, a growing number of psychological studies have shown that subjective social class rank may be an even more powerful predictor of health outcomes than objective class (Adler et al., 2000); even apart from objective measures, subjective class can powerfully shape a person's thoughts, emotions, and behaviors (Kraus, Piff, & Keltner, 2011).

A related idea is the notion that class is also a feature of a person's identity. The term *social status identity* refers to the cultural and socialization experiences people have that shape their perceptions and interactions (Fouad & Brown, 2000). The fact that it is related to, but distinct from, a person's actual economic resources and power suggests that two people can come from the same income bracket but nevertheless hold different life experiences (Rossides, 1997).

Social Class and the Self

Self-Construal Relative to upper class individuals, lower class individuals may be more interdependent because they are necessarily more dependent on other people's resources; because upper class individuals possess more resources, they are less dependent on others and can "afford" to be more independent (Kraus & Keltner, 2009). Consistent with this idea, observational studies of lower and upper class participants revealed that the latter exhibited more socially disengaged behaviors, like checking their phones and doodling, while the former acted in more socially engaged ways—laughing, engaging in eye contact, and nodding (Kraus & Keltner, 2009).

These findings aside, other studies have shown that this interdependence in social engagement among lower class individuals may be more complex than a simple dichotomy between interdependent lower classes and independent upper classes. In a study on how working class and middle class individuals describe "the good life," Markus, Ryff, Curhan, and Palmersheim (2004) found that both classes mentioned close relationships, but the way they envisioned such relationships differed. While middle class individuals considered the ideal relationships ones where they influenced others and improved themselves, working class individuals described ideal relationships as ones where they adjust to one another, control their emotions, and avoid negative situations (Markus et al., 2004).

Consistent with these findings, other studies have found that the types of relationships working class and middle class individuals tend to have may be different. Working class communities tend to be more densely structured and dominated by family interactions; in these situations, individuals may have little choice in whom they interact with, and when they do so (Lamont, 2000). Middle class communities, on the other hand, tend to be looser and self-selected; as such, individuals can exert more choice in their interactions (Lamont, 2000).

Studies of parenting styles have further confirmed that subtle differences exist between the classes in how they see and behave in relationships. Sociological studies have shown that in U.S. contexts, there are two types of individualism: **Soft individualism** characterizes the middle and upper classes and dictates that the self is delicate and full of potential; as a result, it encourages open emotional expression, creativity, and striving to be unique (Kusserow, 1999; 2005). To achieve these ends, parents tend to be encouraging and nurturing, and give much praise; after all, the world is a safe and welcoming place where the future is full of possibilities for success and achievement (Kusserow, 1999; 2005). **Hard individualism**, on the other hand, is more characteristic of the working class and dictates that the self is tough and determined; it encourages emotional restraint, self-reliance, and perseverance, because the world is dangerous and unstable (Kusserow, 1999; 2005). As a result, parents tend to use stricter discipline styles and teasing to avoid spoiling their children and to prepare them for a future that is riddled with uncertainty and challenges (Kusserow, 1999; 2005).

Empirical studies have further confirmed these differences between the classes. Even among college students, middle class students strive for differentiating themselves from others and establishing their identities as unique; when they do so, they show more satisfaction (Stephens, Markus, & Townsend, 2007). In contrast, working class students are more likely to conform to others' behavior and are more satisfied when they do so (Stephens et al., 2007). Not surprisingly, middle class individuals are happier when given choices, whereas working class individuals are less impacted by whether or not they have choice (Snibbe & Markus, 2005). These differences even extend to the kind of music working class versus middle and upper class individuals listen to. In their comparison of the musical preferences of high-school- versus college-educated individuals— education being a key indicator of class—Snibbe and Markus (2005) found that

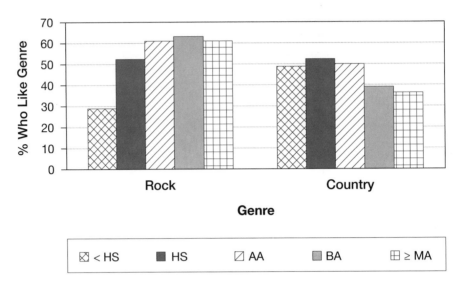

FIG. 2.1. Figure 1 from Snibbe & Markus (2005): education & music preferences

Source: Based on Snibbe, A. C., & Markus, H. R. (2005). You can't always get what you want: Educational attainment, agency, and choice. *Journal of Personality and Social Psychology, 88*(4), 703–720.

high-school-educated participants preferred country whereas college-educated participants preferred rock (see figure 2.1). Content analysis of country versus rock lyrics confirmed that, consistent with the previous evidence regarding what different classes value, country music emphasized integrity, adjustment, and resistance, whereas rock music emphasized uniqueness, control, and influence over others (Snibbe & Markus, 2005).

Interestingly, these cultural differences in soft versus hard individualism occurred within a single ethnic/racial context—in this case, White European American families (Kusserow, 2005). Consistent with these ideas, cross-national studies have shown that working class parents across the board tend to punish children more harshly than middle class parents (Kohn, 1963, as cited in Hoff, Laursen, & Tardif, 2002), and this effect remained across multiple countries, including the United States, England, France, Belgium, Greece, Portugal, Italy, Canada, and Japan (Lambert, 1983). Taken together, this suggests that in some cases, class may trump race in determining human behavior.

Specific Personality Traits Beyond self-construal, other studies have suggested that classes also differ in their likelihood of exhibiting particular personality traits, such as **narcissism**, or an inflated sense of the self that is associated with dominance, grandiosity, and high feelings of uniqueness and entitlement (Piff, 2014). Generally speaking, narcissism is associated with individualism (Foster, Campbell, & Twenge, 2003); thus, given the class differences in self-construal as individualistic versus interdependent, it is not surprising that similar class differences also exist in the personality correlates of individualism. Studies comparing upper and lower class individuals have confirmed that the former tend to score higher on measures of psychological entitlement and narcissism and behave in more narcissistic ways (i.e., looking at themselves in a

APPLYING WHAT WE KNOW: SPOTTING SOFT VERSUS HARD INDIVIDUALISM

Not all individualists are created equal, and your annual salary can make a big difference. Consider the following quotes from middle class versus working class parents describing their children and see if you can spot which ones are which.

- "I hate when they bicker. I hate it when they don't stand up for themselves. That bothers me. I have one child who whines. I don't want her to come running. I'm like, defend yourself and fight it out, get over it. It happens, this is going to happen and you don't need to turn to me every single time something bad happens." (Kusserow, 1999, p. 218)

- "You have to give them a very strong background, principles, given them meanings, values, strong values about everything, you give them principles that you have to rely on, and you draw the line for them, if they have that, they know where they're going, where they're coming from." (Kusserow, 1999, p. 218)

- "My daughter is Attila the Hun, very charming, impulsive, creative—it'll work well for her . . . she is not an amenable child, she's wonderful, empathetic, yet stubborn as can be, strong willed, then again that's what we sort of wanted." (Kusserow, 1999, p. 223)

- "I treat her like an adult too much, like telling her the truth no matter what. It gives her a certain status in the family, makes her feel like she's on an equal footing, her feelings are important as anyone else's." (Kusserow, 1999, p. 223)

The first two are from working class families in Queens, whereas the last two are from upper middle class families on the Upper East Side in Manhattan.

mirror; Piff, 2014). Other studies have shown similar results—for example, that high SES individuals see themselves in an inflated way (e.g., perceive their own empathy as higher than it actually is—Varnum, Blais, Hampton, & Brewer, 2015). However, in one study, simply reminding upper class individuals of the benefits of egalitarianism reduced these narcissistic tendencies (Piff, 2014).

You can see the same phenomena on prime-time television (or Netflix or Amazon or Hulu, for that matter). When F. Scott Fitzgerald (1926) famously said, "Let me tell you about the very rich . . . they are different from you and me. They possess and enjoy early, and it does something to them, makes them soft where we are hard, and cynical where we are trustful, in a way that, unless you were born rich, it is very difficult to understand" (p. 4), he wasn't kidding. To illustrate, find two television shows that take place in different class contexts, and compare/contrast them. Consider, for example, *Roseanne* or even cult-favorite Walter White in *Breaking Bad* (photo 2.1) as quintessential displays of working class lives versus the Hampton socialites on ABC's *Revenge* or suburbanites on *Modern Family* (photo 2.1a). Or, if reality TV is more your thing, consider Bravo's *Million Dollar Listing* (take your pick of its New York, Los Angeles, or San Francisco versions) versus, say, TLC's *Here Comes Honey Boo Boo*. Compare what they wear, how they eat, what they say, how they relate to one another, and the underlying assumptions of the worlds they perpetuate (and see Insight Box 2.1).

PHOTO 2.1. Prime-time class-focused shows: The working/middle class lives of *Breaking Bad*

Source: Photofest

PHOTO 2.1A. Prime-time class-focused shows: The upper-middle class lives of *Modern Family*

Source: Photofest

INSIGHT BOX 2.1

You Are Where You Live

They used to say, "You are what you eat," but these days, what you eat has everything to do with where you live and what class you fall into, whether you like your bread white and Wonder-esque or seven-grain and sprouted, what kinds of leafy greens you put on your sandwich (iceberg lettuce or kale), where you get your groceries (Whole Foods or—better yet—a local co-op versus Walmart), and whether or not you know what a black truffle is (and what it goes with). And it's not just what we eat but where we go to school, what we do for fun, whether we have kids and how many, what industry we work in, and the size of our house—class dictates a whole host of our behaviors.

Now, there is a quick and easy way to figure out your class and the class of everyone else, just in case you didn't already know. Demographers created a system called the Potential Rating Index of Zip Markets (PRIZM), which allows for marketers and others to figure out your class based on zip code. But it doesn't just stop there: Instead of just differentiating between working versus middle and upper class, the PRIZM system has 66 different clusters to label people, from "Money and Brains" to "Bohemian Mix" to "Young Digerati." For each cluster, you can then find a snapshot of their lifestyle— the "Pools and Patios" cluster comprises predominantly upper middle class older people without kids who "shop at Office Max" and "read USA Today" and drive Infiniti Exes, with an annual income of $71K. To find out where you live and who your neighbors are, visit the website and search for yourself:

https://segmentationsolutions.nielsen.com/mybestsegments/.

Social Class and Emotion

Felt Emotion Studies suggest that lower class individuals are more likely to experience a host of negative emotions as a function of their status, largely because of **classism**, or the idea that you can be oppressed because of your socioeconomic position and identity (e.g., Ostrove & Cole, 2003). Classist experience permeates interactions with both institutions and people and as a result can shape a broad range of everyday experiences (e.g., Langhout, Rosselli, & Feinstein, 2007; Liu, 2006). The affective or emotional consequences of classism include shame, guilt, depression, anxiety, and feelings of alienation and a lack of belongingness (Liu, 2002; Ostrove & Long, 2007). More generally, even apart from classism, low SES is associated with lower subjective well-being (Diener & Suh, 1997) and negative moods (Gallo & Matthews, 2003).

Lower class individuals also appear more susceptible to emotional contagion, or the tendency to transmit emotion from one person to another over the course of an interaction (Barsade, 2002). When Kraus, Horberg, Goetz, and Keltner (2011) recruited friends to come into the lab and tease one another, they found that the friends who were lower in social class rank were more likely to "catch" the negative emotions of their upper class friends. In other words, other people's hostile emotions—in this case, anger, contempt, and disgust—were more contagious for lower ranked individuals (Kraus, Horberg et al., 2011). Other studies have shown that it is not just negative emotions: Even positive emotions like compassion were reportedly experienced more by lower class individuals than higher class ones in daily diary studies of felt emotion (Shiota, Keltner, & John, 2006).

Empathic Accuracy Similar to the effects of culture as race discussed in the previous chapter, class also changes the kinds of emotional processes people engage in. Given that lower class individuals hold more interdependent selves that are more engaged with other people (Kraus & Keltner, 2009), it also follows that they are more accurate at reading other people's emotions. In general, research from mainstream psychology suggests that people who are highly interdependent tend to be better at reading emotion than people who are highly independent (Graziano, Habashi, Sheese, & Tobin, 2007).

Empirical evidence supports this idea. In a series of studies, Kraus, Cote and Keltner (2010) examined both objective and subjective social class and tested its relationship with **empathic accuracy,** or the ability to accurately infer what another person is thinking and feeling. For objective social class, Kraus et al. (2010) compared people with a high school versus college education; for subjective social class, they manipulated feelings of class rank by having participants imagine that they were interacting with a very high class or very low class person—someone with either the most education, money, and prestige imaginable, or the least; here the idea is that by social comparison, interacting with an extremely high class person would make a person feel lower class by contrast and interacting with an extremely low class person would make a person feel higher class. In both the objective and subjective case, being or feeling higher class led to less accuracy when participants were reading emotions on a series of photographed faces (Kraus et al., 2010). Neuroimaging studies have confirmed that even on a neural level, high SES is associated with diminished empathic response to faces expressing pain (Varnum et al., 2015).

Social Class and Cognition

Cognitive Styles Lower SES individuals tend to be more contextual: They are more vigilant of changes in their environment and more focused on what others are doing (Kraus, Piff, Mendoza-Denton, Rheinschmidt, & Keltner, 2012). The argument is that because low SES leads to increased vulnerability to external threats (including, but not limited to the criminal justice system, health problems, stigma), lower class individuals have developed highly active threat detection systems to enable them to monitor and respond to potentially aversive events in their environment (Kraus et al., 2012). In line with this idea, behavioral studies have shown that lower class individuals respond with more physiological activation to negative external cues (e.g., angry faces; Evans, Shergill, & Averbeck, 2010) and are especially sensitive to negative social cues (e.g., hostile emotions in other people; Kraus, Horberg et al., 2011).

Beyond being contextually sensitive to threat, those who reported lower subjective class rank also reported, as shown by survey studies, having less personal control over their lives (Kraus, Piff, & Keltner, 2009). Consistent with this idea, they also explained different outcomes using situational or contextual factors rather than dispositional ones, citing features of the external environment, rather than the person, as the true cause of behavior (Kraus et al., 2009). Interestingly, this means that upper class individuals attribute their wealth to themselves and their own talents, whereas lower class individuals attribute their status to their context (e.g., political systems, discrimination; Kraus et al., 2009).

A consequence of these class differences in contextualism is that upper class individuals also tend to be more essentialist and lower class individuals more social constructivist in their views of groups. **Essentialism** refers to the tendency to see group differences as inherent, stable, and unchanging; **social constructivism**, in contrast, posits that group differences are the product of changing (or at least changeable) external forces (e.g., Haslam, Rothschild, & Ernst, 2000). Studies of both U.S. and international participants (in this case, lower and upper caste Indians) found that regardless of nationality, lower class individuals were more likely to believe that class could be changed, whereas upper class individual were more likely to believe that class was an essential, unchangeable quality about a person (Kraus & Keltner, 2012; Mahalingam, 2003, 2007).

This contextualism presumably serves to help lower class individuals navigate more difficult and less stable situations that characterize their day-to-day life (Kraus et al., 2009). In other words, being lower class means that your life is often in the hands of other people—whether this be the government, your boss, or your landlord. Thus, by necessity, lower class people must be more sensitive to these external influences, because how others behave can fundamentally alter their lives; upper class individuals, in contrast, tend to be more focal and centered on the self because their resources allow them to have more individual control over their activities (Kraus et al., 2009; Piff, Kraus, Côté, Cheng, & Keltner, 2010). Perhaps not surprisingly, this difference in contextualism is even reflected in people's worldviews: While lower income individuals cite contextual factors like educational opportunities as the reason for social inequality, higher income individuals cite internal traits like talent as the reason for why some people have more than others (Kluegel & Smith, 1986).

Cognitive Complexity Individuals living in lower income neighborhoods tend to exhibit greater complexity insofar as they possess multiple—and often conflicting—cultures with different values and worldviews (Harding, 2007). Sociologists have noted that in low income neighborhoods, there tends to be a wider variety of jobs and lower levels of social control—factors that contribute to exposure to more complex ways of being (Harding, 2007). Because of this exposure, people from disadvantaged areas tend to have alternative goals (Harding, 2011). To illustrate, poor single mothers often value traditional family structures even as they themselves do not fit into those structures (Edin & Kefalas, 2005). The pattern suggests that being from lower class neighborhoods promoted more complexity and allowed these individuals to hold multiple worldviews and realities at once, even when those realities contradicted one another (i.e., aspiring for college even in a neighborhood where few make it to college).

Social Inequality

Actual Inequality in Outcomes Actual inequality fluctuates. In the 20th century alone, poverty levels showed both periods of sharp decline as well as minor fluctuations (Stone, Trisi, Sherman, & Debot, 2015). Although household incomes rose substantively between the end of the Great Depression through 1970, due to the post-WWII prosperity, these rises in standards of living did not last. Rather, the gap between the rich and the poor started to increase after 1970 and has not stopped since; even the economic growth of the 1990s and the latest 2008 recession did not do much to stop this general trend of increasing income gap (Stone et al., 2015).

Being lower class is associated with poorer academic outcomes. This is likely due to a combination of an acute deficit in resources as well as social processes, like the fact that academic settings tend to have an overrepresentation of higher class individuals (Johnson, Richeson, & Finkle, 2011). When the U.S. Department of Education released its three-decade-long study of young adults, between 1974 and 2006, it found that if your parents did not finish high school, you had a 46% chance of enrolling in college; in contrast, if your parents were college graduates themselves, that likelihood jumped to 73%, and if your parents had advanced degrees, then the likelihood was even higher: 84% (Ingels, Glennie, Lauff, & Wirt, 2012).

Class inequality is also largely confounded with race inequality, and many of the achievement gaps along racial lines can largely be explained by socioeconomic differences (Orr, 2003). When researchers looked at data on intelligence from twin studies to compare the relative role of genes versus the environment, they found that among upper class children, 72% of the variance in intelligence was due to genes, but among lower class children, only 10% of the variance in intelligence could be explained by genes (Turkheimer, Haley, Waldron, D'Onofrio, & Gottesman, 2003). Conversely, most of the variance in intellectual ability and achievement among lower class children was explained by environmental factors (Turkheimer et al., 2003).

More generally, class also shapes the psychological expectancies and behaviors that are associated with actual outcomes. For example, status identity was associated with self-efficacy when making career decisions, feelings of certainty about one's decided career, and how comfortable persons felt about their decision (Thomas & Subich, 2006). Moreover, people with high status identity were more likely to report that their career realities and expectations matched (Metz, Fouad, & Ihle-Helledy, 2009).

Responses to Inequality Perhaps one of the most ironic processes involved in the research on class and inequality is the finding that it is precisely the people who have less who tend to give more. In a way, this should not be terribly surprising, given all the previous research; after all, lower class individuals are more interpersonal, socially engaged, sensitive to the environment, and attuned to other people's feelings. Taken together, these qualities suggest a very relational and prosocial kind of person. Indeed, sociological evidence confirms that at least percentage-wise, those from lower income brackets gave proportionally more of their salary to charity than those from higher income brackets: 4.2% versus 2.7% (Independent Sector, 2002).

Psychological studies have also shown the same pattern of findings, using both subjective and objective class. In both cases, people who are of lower socioeconomic status—or made to feel that way—gave more generously to an anonymous stranger, were more likely to help someone in need, and supported more charities (Piff et al., 2010).

APPLYING WHAT WE KNOW: HOW CLASS CHANGES BEHAVIOR

Perhaps you are unconvinced that your class actually changes your behavior (I run into similar problems when trying to convince fish about the existence of water). To illustrate just how quickly and surreptitiously class can change you when you least expect it, consider setting up this social experiment (modeled after the ingenious procedures outlined by Piff, Stancato, Côté, Mendoza-Denton, & Keltner, 2012) at your next Monopoly Night:

1. Before your friends arrive, divide the Monopoly money unevenly into different envelopes, one envelope per player (or team). To make this effective, the larger the gap, the better: On the extreme end, give all the $1s to one person and all the $500s to another, and split the middle-value denominations. This will establish the social inequality that rules your game.
2. When your friends arrive, ask each person or player to randomly pick an envelope. Do not explain to them what the envelopes contain or the point of the game, because life does not afford you any explanations either.
3. Let the games begin! At this point you can just sit back and watch what happens.

When Paul Piff and his colleagues (2012) set up this rigged version of the beloved Monopoly game in a windowless lab at UC, Berkeley, it only took them about 15 minutes to catch a host of class-based changes in behavior. The rich player spreads out his arms and legs, taking up more space at the game table, as is customary when people experience power (Piff, 2013). He gets louder, smacking his game piece against the board and making all kinds of verbal jabs (Piff, 2013). He eats more pretzels (there are pretzels on the table; Piff, 2013). He doesn't look at the poor player when he does these things (Miller, 2012; Piff, 2013; Piff et al., 2012). When you set up your own social experiment in social inequality, what did you see?

INSIGHT BOX 2.2

Closing the Gap

My favorite thing about culture is this: Because it is human-made and only semistable, it can change. This relates to a broader idea in science: the naturalistic fallacy and the deterministic fallacy (Frankena, 1939; Nagel, 1960). The **naturalistic fallacy** says that what is natural is acceptable. It's a fallacy because just because something is natural doesn't make it OK (Frankena, 1939). In nature, you will see brutality, rape, violence, and all kinds of harm, and just because those things come naturally to us does not make them good or ideal or right. The **deterministic fallacy** says that because something is natural, it must happen (Nagel, 1960). But why must something happen? Humans are extraordinarily good at changing the natural; we've domesticated animals, developed agriculture, genetically modified food, used medicine to prolong our lives, and utilized technology to make the impossible possible. If we are so good at changing these other features of our existence, then surely we could change the social inequality that marks modern American life—if we wanted to.

When Bill Gates (photo 2.2), Melinda Gates, and Warren Buffett created the Giving Pledge, they challenged the richest people in the world to commit at least half of their wealth to charity. A dozen and counting have signed on. And it's not just the Gates and the Buffetts. The late Margaret Cargill left $6 billion to foundations supporting the arts and the environment, among other causes; the late Will Dietrich left $500 million to help Pennsylvania nonprofits and colleges (Voorhees, 2013). It's also the living: Paul Allen, who cofounded Microsoft, gave $373 million, and Mayor Michael Bloomberg gave $311 million (Voorhees, 2013). These examples remind us that who we are likely to be because of our socioeconomic class is not who we have to be.

PHOTO 2.2. Class doesn't always have to be associated with greed: Just ask billionaire philanthropists like Bill Gates.

Source: Photofest

Experiments confirm this. High SES participants who were shown a 46-second video clip of childhood poverty acted as prosocially as their lower SES counterparts—in this case, by helping out a partner in distress (Piff et al., 2010). Other studies show that on a group level, setting up social networks that both link the rich to the poor and desegregate the classes can reduce system inequality (Chiang, 2015).

My hope is that, by showing you these things, no matter how much money you end up making postgraduation, no matter how many figures are in your salary or letters are behind your last name, you will not forget that your social class can change you when you're not watching—but it doesn't have to. You, when all your dreams are being achieved, can also be the person to make the American dream possible for others.

Class Differences in Psychopathology

Clear class differences exist in terms of both physical and mental health. As socioeconomic status rises, health rises, and mortality decreases, along with a host of diseases from heart disease to cervical cancer (Adler et al., 1994). Likewise, rates of mental illness—including major depressive disorder, antisocial personality disorder, anxiety disorder, and substance abuse disorders—are also higher among individuals of lower socioeconomic status than among individuals of higher SES (e.g., Johnson, Cohen, Dohrenwend, Link, & Brook, 1999; Kohn, Dohrenwend, & Mirotznik, 1998). In a longitudinal study that tested the relationship of socioeconomic status and psychopathology over the course of nine years, it was found that children from a low SES background had a greater incidence of behavioral syndromes and, despite the higher incidence of mental health issues, mental health service rates were not elevated for this group (Wadsworth & Achenbach, 2005).

Classism and Well-Being
In the same way that racism negatively impacts well-being, classism also leads to poor psychological outcomes. Experiences of discrimination based on class predicts stress, depression, anxiety, and self-esteem (Langhout et al., 2007; Thompson & Subich, 2013). In an early study on class-based versus race-based discrimination, Schiller (1971) examined the outcomes of Black and White children receiving public assistance; he concluded that discrimination on the basis of class was as powerful a predictor of life outcomes as racial discrimination. More recent studies on the link between low SES and well-being has found that 13% of the effect of SES on health can be explained by perceived discrimination (Fuller-Rowell, Evans, & Ong, 2012).

Mental Health Disparities Even independent of the effects of classism, lower social class is generally associated with a host of poor mental health conditions, including higher rates of depression and other disorders, as well as substance abuse (Lorant et al., 2003; Poulton et al., 2000). Unfortunately, minority groups tend to be disproportionately in poverty, and this shows in the mental health disparities between them and Whites. Blacks and Hispanics tend to receive and use fewer mental health care services than Whites (Cook & Miranda, 2007). In the case of non-Latino Blacks and non-Latino Whites, the disparity has only increased, while between Latinos and non-Latino Whites the disparity has stayed the same (Ault-Brutus, 2012). People of color tend to access professional care less, to drop out of care more, and to be less satisfied with received sources (Carpenter-Song, Whitley, Lawson, Quimby, & Drake, 2011). The link between class and mental health also interacts with gender, at least in some cultural contexts. To illustrate, a large-scale study in Spain found that stressful economic events like unemployment appear to be especially linked to negative mental health outcomes among married, working class men, but not as much among other groups (like married, white-collar class men or women), presumably because of changes in family roles, such as the inability to be the breadwinner (Artazcoz, Benach, Borrell, & Cortès, 2011).

It's not just access but care received: Minorities receive less information, less supportive talk, and less proficient clinical performance, which affects minorities and those of lower SES in general (Cooper & Roter, 2003). There are many efforts to mitigate this diversity through programs and to increase the diversity of the field (Carpenter-Song et al., 2011). Many of the steps needed to alleviate this disparity start with psychiatrists, of whom many may not recognize the pervasiveness of racial inequality in the system or within themselves and therefore unfortunately do not attend disparity-reducing programs (Mallinger & Lamberti, 2010). What's more, the complex relationships between mental health and class, race, and gender are often not well understood. Some researchers have referred to these (class, race, gender) as a "triple threat" that can influence mental health by also shaping internal psychological processes, like the belief systems people have about their own importance relative to others (Rosenfield, 2012).

Differential Rates of Diagnoses and Efficacy To compound the problem of these mental health disparities, other studies show that low income individuals are also less likely to receive treatment, and most research on psychopathology and psychotherapy have been done on, used with, and developed for middle class individuals (Isaacs & Schroeder, 2004; Pope & Arthur, 2009).

To make matters worse, there are also practical barriers to getting effective mental health care, including but not limited to issues of access (transportation, health insurance, costs), cultural differences (language differences, stigma, cultural sensitivity), and the fear that future employers might find out about one's mental health issues (Corrigan, 2004; Kim et al., 2011; Link, Cullen, Mitrotznik, & Struening, 1992; Scheppers, Van Dongen, Dekker, Geertzen, & Dekker, 2006; Whaley & Davis, 2007). Relative to high SES individuals, low SES populations are more likely to report barriers to mental health services (Steele, Dewa, & Lee, 2007).

The limited research on working class individuals suffering from psychological disorders means that even when lower class members receive treatment, it may not be as effective. Studies on therapy outcomes found that being of lower SES was linked to less improvement after receiving therapy across a wide range of different types of therapy (including IPT, cognitive behavior therapy, and pharmacotherapy, or mediation) among people suffering from depression (Falconnier, 2009). Consistent with these findings, lower SES patients also reported that their therapists were less effective (Hillerbrand, 1988).

Moderating (Protective) Factors Nevertheless, the news is not all bleak, and low SES is not always a risk factor for illness. When Lachman and Weaver (1998) examined a large national sample of both men and women ages 25–75, they found that although low SES was linked to worse health outcomes, sense of control emerged as a powerful moderator. Specifically, low SES individuals with a high sense of control were as healthy, on average, as their high SES counterparts, suggesting that personal control can serve as a protective factor against the negative effects of class (Lachman & Weaver, 1998).

Other studies have suggested that the protective factors that may buffer young people from negative mental health outcomes, like depression, and promote positive life outcomes, like achievement, may be similar across ethnic (but not necessarily class) groups. For example, both Black and White high schoolers appeared to benefit from their parents' involvement in school in terms of their mental health and achievement; class-wise, low SES teens appeared to experience even greater benefits from parental involvement (Wang & Sheikh-Khalil, 2014). This suggests that strong, supportive families may be a potent force in protecting young people from the aforementioned risks.

Key Concepts

Objective vs. subjective social class
Soft vs. hard individualism
Narcissism
Classism
Empathic accuracy
Essentialism vs. social constructivism

References

Adler, N. E., Boyce, T., Chesney, M. A., Cohen, S., Folkman, S., Kahn, R. L., & Syme, L. S. (1994). Socioeconomic status and health: The challenge of the gradient. *American Psychologist, 49*(1), 15–24. doi:10.1037/0003-066X.49.1.15

Adler, N. E., Epel, E. S., Castellazzo, G., & Ickovics, J. R. (2000). Relationship of subjective and objective social status with psychological and physiological functioning: Preliminary data in healthy White women. *Health Psychology, 19*(6), 586–592.

Ambady, N., & Rosenthal, R. (1992). Thin slices of expressive behavior as predictors of interpersonal consequences: A meta-analysis. *Psychological Bulletin, 111*(2), 256–274. doi:10.1037/0033-2909.111.2.256

Artazcoz, L., Benach, J. Borrell, C., & Cortès, I. (2004). Unemployment and mental health: understanding the interactions among gender, family roles, and social class. *American Journal of Public Health, 94*(1), 82–88.

Artazcoz, L., Cortès, I., Borrell, C., Escribà-Agüir, V., & Cascant, L. (2011). Social inequalities in the association between partner/marital status and health among workers in Spain. *Social Science & Medicine, 72*(4), 600–607.

Ault-Brutus, A. A. (2012). Changes in racial-ethnic disparities in use and adequacy of mental health care in the United States, 1990–2003. *Psychiatric Services, 63*(6), 531–540.

Barsade, S. G. (2002). The ripple effect: Emotional contagion and its influence on group behavior. *Administrative Science Quarterly, 47*(4), 644–675. doi:10.2307/3094912

Brown, J. D., & Taylor, S. E. (1986). Affect and the processing of personal information: Evidence for mood-activated self-schemata. *Journal of Experimental Social Psychology, 22*(5), 436–452. doi:10.1016/0022-1031(86)90044-2

Carpenter-Song, E., Whitley, R., Lawson, W., Quimby, E., & Drake, R. E. (2011). Reducing disparities in mental health care: Suggestions from the Dartmouth-Howard collaboration. *Community Mental Health Journal, 47*(1), 1–13. doi:10.1007/ s10597-009-9233-4

Chiang, Y.-S. (2015). Good Samaritans in networks: An experiment on how networks influence egalitarian sharing and the evolution of inequality. *PLoS ONE, 10*(6). doi:10.1371/ journal.pone.0128777

Cook, B. L., McGuire, T., & Miranda, J. (2007). Measuring trends in mental health care disparities, 2000–2004. *Psychiatric Services, 58*(12), 1533–1540.

Cooper, L. A., Roter, D. L., Johnson, R. L., Ford, D. E., Steinwachs, D. M., & Powe, N. R. (2003). Patient-centered communication, ratings of care, and concordance of patient and physician race. *Annals of Internal Medicine, 139*(11), 907–915.

Corfield, P. J. (1991). *Language, history, and class.* Oxford, U.K.: Basil Blackwell.

Corrigan, P. (2004). How stigma interferes with mental health care. *American Psychologist, 59*(7), 614.

Diener, E., & Suh, E. (1997). Measuring quality of life: Economic, social, and subjective indicators. *Social Indicators Research, 40*(1-2), 189–216.

Domhoff, G. W. (1967). Who rules America? Englewood Cliffs, NJ: Prentice-Hall.

Edin, K., & Kefalas, M. (2011). *Promises I can keep: Why poor women put motherhood before marriage.* Oakland: University of California Press.

Evans, S., Shergill, S. S., & Averbeck, B. B. (2010). Oxytocin decreases aversion to angry faces in an associative learning task. *Neuropsychopharmacology, 35*(1), 2502–2509. doi: 10.1038/npp.2010.110

Falconnier, L. (2009). Socioeconomic status in the treatment of depression. *American Journal of Orthopsychiatry, 79*(2), 148–158.

Fitzgerald, F. S. (1926). Rich boy. In F. S. Fitzgerald (Ed.), *All the sad young men.* (pp. 3–41) New York, NY: Scribner.

Foster, J. D., Campbell, W. K., & Twenge, J. M. (2003). Individual differences in narcissism: Inflated self-views across the lifespan and around the world. *Journal of Research in Personality, 37*(6), 469–486.

Fouad, N. A., & Brown, M. T. (2000). Role of race and social class in development: Implications for counseling psychology. In S. D. Brown & R. W. Lent (Eds.), *Handbook of Counseling Psychology* (pp. 379–408). Hoboken, NJ: John Wiley & Sons Inc.

Frankena, W. K. (1939). The naturalistic fallacy. *Mind, 48*(192), 464–477.

Fuller-Rowell, T. E., Evans, G. W., & Ong, A. D. (2012). Poverty and health: The mediating role of perceived discrimination. *Psychological Science, 23*(7), 734–739.

Gallo, L. C., & Matthews, K. A. (2003). Understanding the association between socioeconomic status and physical health: Do negative emotions play a role? *Psychological Bulletin, 129*(1), 10–51.

Graziano, W. G., Habashi, M. M., Sheese, B. E., & Tobin, R. M. (2007). Agreeableness, empathy, and helping: A person × situation perspective. *Journal of Personality and Social Psychology, 93*(4), 583–599. doi:10.1037/0022-3514.93.4.583

Harding, D. J. (2007). Cultural context, sexual behavior, and romantic relationships in disadvantaged neighborhoods. *American Sociological Review, 72*(3), 341–364.

Harding, D. J. (2011). Rethinking the cultural context of schooling decisions in disadvantaged neighborhoods: From deviant subculture to cultural heterogeneity. *Sociology of Education, 84*(4), 322–339.

Haslam, N., Rothschild, L., & Ernst, D. (2000). Essentialist beliefs about social categories. *British Journal of Social Psychology, 39*(1), 113–127. doi:10.1348/014466600164363

Herzstein, D. (1969). Anthropology and racism in nineteenth century Europe. *Duquesne Review, 14*(2), 112–126.

Hillerbrand, E. (1988). The relationship between socioeconomic status and counseling variables at a university counseling center. *Journal of College Student Development, 29*(3), 250–254.

Hoff, E., Laursen, B., & Tardif, T. (2002). Socioeconomic status and parenting. In M. Borenstein (Ed.), *Handbook of Parenting Volume 2: Biology and Ecology of Parenting, 8*(2), 231–252. Mahway, NJ: Erlbaum.

Independent Sector. (2002). *Giving and volunteering in the United States.* Washington, DC: Independent Sector.

Ingels, S. J., Glennie, E., Lauff, E., & Wirt, J. G. (2012). *Trends among young adults over three decades, 1974–2006*. Retrieved from http://nces.ed.gov/pubs2012/2012345.pdf

Isaacs, S. L., & Schroeder, S. A. (2004). Class—the ignored determinant of the nation's health. *The New England Journal of Medicine*, *351*(11), 1137–1142.

Johnson, J. G., Cohen, P., Dohrenwend, B. P., Link, B. G., & Brook, J. S. (1999). A longitudinal investigation of social causation and social selection processes involved in the association between socioeconomic status and psychiatric disorders. *Journal of Abnormal Psychology*, *108*(3), 490–499. doi:10.1037/0021-843X.108.3.490

Johnson, S. E., Richeson, J. A., & Finkel, E. J. (2011). Middle class and marginal? Socioeconomic status, stigma, and self-regulation at an elite university. *Journal of Personality and Social Psychology*, *100*(5), 838–852. doi: 10.1037/a0021956

Kim, G., Loi, C. X. A., Chiriboga, D. A., Jang, Y., Parmelee, P., & Allen, R. S. (2011). Limited English proficiency as a barrier to mental health service use: A study of Latino and Asian immigrants with psychiatric disorders. *Journal of Psychiatric Research*, *45*(1), 104–110.

Kingston, P. W. (2000). *The classless society*. Stanford, CA: Stanford University Press.

Kluegel, J. R., & Smith, E. R. (1986). *Beliefs about inequality: Americans' views of what is and what ought to be*. Hawthorne, NY: Aldine De Gruyter.

Kohn, M. L. (1963). Social class and parent–child relationships: An interpretation. *American Journal of Sociology*, *68*, 471–480.

Kohn, R., Dohrenwend, B. P., & Mirotznik, J. (1998). Epidemiological findings on selected psychiatric disorders in the general population. In B. P. Dohrenwend (Ed.), *Adversity, stress, and psychopathology* (pp. 235–284). New York, NY: Oxford University Press.

Kraus, M. W., Côté, S., & Keltner, D. (2010). Social class, contextualism, and empathic accuracy. *Psychological Science*, *21*(11), 1716–1723.

Kraus, M. W., Horberg, E. J., Goetz, J. L., & Keltner, D. (2011). Social class rank, threat vigilance, and hostile reactivity. *Personality and Social Psychology Bulletin*, *37*(10), 1376–1388.

Kraus, M. W., & Keltner, D. (2009). Signs of socioeconomic status: A thin-slicing approach. *Psychological Science*, *20*(1), 99–106. doi:10.1111/j.1467-9280.2008.02251.x

Kraus, M. W., & Keltner, D. (2013). Social class rank, essentialism, and punitive judgment. *Journal of Personality and Social Psychology*, *105*(2), 247–261.

Kraus, M. W., Piff, P. K., & Keltner, D. (2009). Social class, the sense of control, and social explanation. *Journal of Personality and Social Psychology*, *97*(6), 992–1004. doi: 10.1037/a0016357

Kraus, M. W., Piff, P. K., & Keltner, D. (2011). Social class as culture: The convergence of resources and rank in the social realm. *Current Directions in Psychological Science*, *20*(4), 246–250. doi:10.1177/0963721411414654

Kraus, M. W., Piff, P. K., Mendoza-Denton, R., Rheinschmidt, M. L., & Keltner, D. (2012). Social class, solipsism, and contextualism: How the rich are different from the poor. *Psychological Review*, *119*(3), 546–572.

Kusserow, A. S. (1999). Dehomogenizing American individualism: Socializing hard and soft individualism in Manhattan and Queens. *Ethos*, *27*, 210–234.

Kusserow, A. S. (2005). The workings of class. *Stanford Social Innovation Review*, *3*(3), 38–44.

Lachman, M. E., & Weaver, S. L. (1998). The sense of control as a moderator of social class differences in health and well-being. *Journal of Personality and Social Psychology*, *74*(3), 763–773. doi:10.1037/0022-3514.74.3.763

Lambert, W. E. (1983). A multinational perspective on child-rearing values. In G. Schwartz (Ed.), *Advances in research & services for children with special needs* (pp. 42–53). Vancouver, Canada: University of British Columbia.

Lamont, M. (2000). *The dignity of working men*. New York: Russell Sage Foundation.

Langhout, R. D., Rosselli, F., & Feinstein, J. (2007). Assessing classism in academic settings. *The Review of Higher Education*, *30*(2), 145–184.

Link, B. G., Cullen, F. T., Mirotznik, J., & Struening, E. (1992). The consequences of stigma for persons with mental illness: Evidence from the social sciences. In P. J. Fink & A. Tasman (Eds.), *Stigma and mental illness* (pp. 87–96). Arlington, VA: American Psychiatric Association.

Liu, W. M. (2006). Classism is much more complex: Comment. *American Psychologist*, *61*(4), 337–338.

Lorant, V., Deliège, D., Eaton, W., Robert, A., Philippot, P., & Ansseau, M. (2003). Socioeconomic inequalities in depression: A meta-analysis. *American Journal of Epidemiology*, *157*(2), 98–112.

Mahalingam, R. (2003). Essentialism, culture, and power: Representations of social class. *Journal of Social Issues*, *59*(4), 733–749. doi:10.1046/j.0022-4537.2003.00087.x

Mahalingam, R. (2007). Essentialism, power, and the representation of social categories: A folk sociology perspective. *Human Development*, *50*(1), 300–319. doi:10.1159/000109832

Mallinger, J. B., & Lamberti, S. J. (2010). Psychiatrists' attitudes toward and awareness about racial disparities in mental health care. *Psychiatric* Services, *61*(2), 173–179.

Markus, H. R., Ryff, C. D., Curhan, K. B., & Palmersheim, K. A. (2004). In their own words: Well-being at midlife among high school-educated and college-educated adults. In O. Brim, C. Ryff, & R. Kessler (Eds.), *How healthy are we?* 273–319. Chicago, IL: University of Chicago Press.

Mendoza-Denton, R., & Mischel, W. (2007). Integrating system approaches to culture and personality: The cultural cognitive-affective processing system. In S. Kitayama & D. Cohen (Eds.), *Handbook of cultural psychology* (pp. 175–195). New York, NY: Guilford Press.

Metz, A. J., Fouad, N., & Ihle-Helledy, K. (2009). Career aspirations and expectations of college students: Demographic and labor market comparisons. *Journal of Career Assessment*, *17*(2), 155–171.

Miller, L. (2012, July 1). The money-empathy gap. *New York Magazine*. Retrieved from http://nymag.com/news/features/money-brain-2012-7/

Nagel, E. (1960). Determinism in history. *Philosophy and Phenomenological Research*, *20*(3), 291–317. doi:10.2307/2105051

Oakes, J. M., & Rossi, P. H. (2003). The measurement of SES in health research: Current practice and steps toward a new approach. *Social Science & Medicine*, *56*(4), 769–784.

Orr, A. J. (2003). Black-white differences in achievement: The importance of wealth. *Sociology of Education*, *76*(4), 281–304.

Ostrove, J. M., & Cole, E. R. (2003). Privileging class: Toward a critical psychology of social class in the context of education. *Journal of Social Issues*, *59*(4), 677–692.

Ostrove, J. M., & Long, S. M. (2007). Social class and belonging: Implications for college adjustment. *The Review of Higher Education*, *30*(4), 363–389.

Piff, P. (2013, October). *Paul Piff: Does money make you mean?* Retrieved from http://www.ted.com/talks/paul_piff_does_money_make_you_mean

Piff, P. K. (2014). Wealth and the inflated self: Class, entitlement, and narcissism. *Personality and Social Psychology Bulletin*, *40*(1), 34–43.

Piff, P. K., Kraus, M. W., Côté, S., Cheng, B. H., & Keltner, D. (2010). Having less, giving more: The influence of social class on prosociality. *Journal of Personality and Social Psychology*, *99*(5), 771–784. doi:10.1037/a0020092

Piff, P. K., Stancato, D. M., Côté, S., Mendoza-Denton, R., & Keltner, D. (2012). Higher social class predicts increased unethical behavior. *Proceedings of the National Academy of Sciences of the United States of America*, *109*(11), 4086–4091.

Pope, J. F., & Arthur, N. (2009). Socioeconomic status and class: A challenge for the practice of psychology in Canada. *Canadian Psychology/Psychologie canadienne, 50*(2), 55–65.

Poulton, R., Caspi, A., Milne, B. J., Thomson, W. M., Taylor, A., Sears, M. R., & Moffitt, T. E. (2002). Association between children's experience of socioeconomic disadvantage and adult health: A life-course study. *The Lancet, 360*(9346), 1640–1645.

Rosenfield, S. (2012). Triple jeopardy? Mental health at the intersection of gender, race, and class. *Social Science & Medicine, 74*(11), 1791–1801.

Rossides, D. W. (1997). *Social stratification: The interplay of class, race, and gender.* London, U.K.: Pearson College Division.

Roth, T. (2014, November 7). After fall of Berlin wall, German reunification came with a big price tag: Officials scrambled for a plan to annex a bankrupt state 25 years ago. *The Wall Street Journal.* Retrieved from http://www.wsj.com/articles/after-fall-of-berlin-wall- german-reunification-came-with-a-big-price-tag-1415362635

Scheppers, E., Van Dongen, E., Dekker, J., Geertzen, J., & Dekker, J. (2006). Potential barriers to the use of health services among ethnic minorities: A review. *Family Practice, 23*(3), 325–348.

Schiller, B. R. (1971). Class discrimination vs. racial discrimination. *The Review of Economics and Statistics, 53*(3), 263–269. doi:10.2307/1937970

Shiota, M. N., Keltner, D., & John, O. P. (2006). Positive emotion dispositions differentially associated with Big Five personality and attachment style. *The Journal of Positive Psychology, 1*(2), 61–71. doi:10.1080/17439760500510833

Snibbe, A. C., & Markus, H. R. (2005). You can't always get what you want: Educational attainment, agency, and choice. *Journal of Personality and Social Psychology, 88*(4), 703–720.

Steele, L., Dewa, C., & Lee, K. (2007). Socioeconomic status and self-reported barriers to mental health service use. *Canadian Journal of Psychiatry, 52*(3), 201–205.

Stephens, N. M., Markus, H. R., & Townsend, S. S. (2007). Choice as an act of meaning: The case of social class. *Journal of Personality and Social Psychology, 93*(5), 814–830.

Stone, C., Trisi, D., Sherman, A., & Debot, B. (2015). A guide to statistics on historical trends in income inequality. Center on Budget and Policy Priorities. Retrieved from https://www.cbpp.org/research/poverty-and-inequality/a-guide-to-statistics-on-historical-trends-in-income-inequality

Sutter, J. (2013). Is class the new race? CNN. Retrieved from http://www.cnn.com/2013/08/30/opinion/sutter-class-race-fast-food/index.html

Thompson, M. N., & Subich, L. M. (2006). The relation of social status to the career decision-making process. *Journal of Vocational Behavior, 69*(2), 289–301.

Thompson, M. N., & Subich, L. M. (2013). Development and exploration of the experiences with classism scale. *Journal of Career Assessment, 21*(1), 139–158.

Turkheimer, E., Haley, A., Waldron, M., D'Onofrio, B., & Gottesman, I. (2003). Socioeconomic status modifies heritability of IQ in young children. *Psychological Science, 14*(6), 623–628. doi:10.1046/j.0956-7976.2003.psci_1475.x

United States Department of Education, Office of Educational Research and Improvement. (1996). *A comparison of high school drop out rates in 1982 and 1992.* Retrieved from http://nces.ed.gov/pubs/96893.pdf

Varnum, M. E., Blais, C., Hampton, R. S., & Brewer, G. A. (2015). Social class affects neural empathic responses. *Culture and Brain, 3*(2), 122–130.

Voorhees, D. (2013). *The extraordinary book of useless information: The most fascinating facts that don't really matter.* New York, NY: TargerPerigee.

Wadsworth, M. E., & Achenbach, T. M. (2005). Explaining the link between low socioeconomic status and psychopathology: Testing two mechanisms of the social causation hypothesis. *Journal of Consulting and Clinical Psychology, 73*(6), 1146–1153. doi:10.1037/0022- 006X.73.6.1146

Wallace, M., & Jenkins, J. C. (1995). The new class, postindustrialism, and neocorporatism: Three images of social protest in the western democracies. In J. C. Jenkins & B. Klandermans, *The politics of social protest: Comparative perspectives on states and social movements* (pp. 96–137). Minneapolis: University of Minnesota Press. Retrieved from http://0-search. proquest.com.leopac.ulv.edu/docview/60037376?accountid=25355

Wang, M. T., & Sheikh-Khalil, S. (2014). Does parental involvement matter for student achievement and mental health in high school? *Child Development, 85*(2), 610–625.

Whaley, A. L., & Davis, K. E. (2007). Cultural competence and evidence-based practice in mental health services: A complementary perspective. *American Psychologist, 62*(6), 563.

CHAPTER 3

Religion

Race, ethnicity, nationality, and class are examples of ostensible forms of culture; in our growing radicalized and secular world, religion has continued to emerge as a potent force that brings people together and differentiates them in life-changing ways. This chapter discusses how religious beliefs lead to cultural milieus. It begins by exploring the obvious questions like whether subscribing to religion indeed makes you moral, or if the content of one's theology makes all the difference (it does). It then covers the domains in which religious background emerges as a strong predictor of both basic psychological processes (e.g., conceptions of agency, moral behaviors, personal control, death) as well as practical life outcomes (e.g., teen pregnancy, crime, health behaviors, economic exploitation).

Joel Osteen and Brad Pitt are two people you might know (not personally, but if you're familiar with American culture, you likely know who they are). In many ways, Joel and Brad are similar people—they come from the same country and speak the same language (which, if you read chapter 1, means that they are likely analytical and individualistic), are both male (see chapter 4) and are both rich (see what the previous chapter has to say about their health and interdependence). Yet you don't need me to tell you that they likely are nevertheless very different people, with vastly different worldviews, attitudes, beliefs, and norms. While these differences between Joel and Brad can potentially be attributable to any number of differentiating experiences in their lives, one of the most powerful predictors is their religion— and the fact that one is an evangelical Christian and the other is a self-professed atheist.

But forget televangelists and Hollywood A-listers; religion can also exert far more extenuating and poignant effects on human behavior.

To illustrate: What does photo 3.1 look like to you? I think it looks like Madonna, circa 1984, but Diane Duyser, who made this grilled cheese sandwich in 1994 and took just one bite, will tell you that it's the Virgin Mary, whose elegy is so magical that it has protected the sandwich from molding for 10 years; she sold

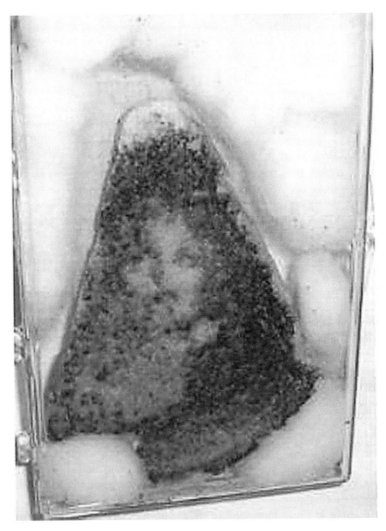

PHOTO 3.1. Religion is powerful. Just ask the person who bought this Virgin Mary grilled cheese sandwich.

Source: Getty

it on eBay to an internet casino for $28,000 ("'Virgin Mary grilled cheese' sells for $28,000," 2004).

There is Jedi-ism (Castella, 2014), a religion inspired by George Lucas's *Star Wars* (photo 3.2). But there are also doomsday cults that have led to mass suicides and mass public attacks, like when Shoko Asahara led his followers to release poison gas on a Tokyo subway in preparation for Armageddon (Juergensmeyer, 1997). There's the Inquisition and there's ISIS, but then there's also this: Jim Elliot was 29 years old when he took an 18-day boat trip from San Pedro to the jungles of Ecuador to minister to the Aucas, a historically violent native group who, up to that point, had had little contact with the rest of civilization ("Jim Elliot: No fool," n.d.).

PHOTO 3.2. *Star Wars* inspires its own religion.

Source: iStock

When Jim got there, he sent buckets of food and presents to the tribe, shared meals with them, took them on plane rides, learned their language, and then was promptly speared to death ("Jim Elliot: No fool," n.d.). His body was found in a stream five days later; he still had a gun in his pocket—one that he had refused to use on his attackers (Saint, 1996). Two years later, his widowed wife did the unthinkable: She took their little daughter and moved in with the tribe that killed her husband. When asked why, she said, "The fact that Jim loved and died for the Aucas intensifies my love for them" (Elliot, 1961, as quoted in Howard, 2015).

So what's the bottom line? The real or imagined presence of God—and other supernatural beings—can and will change people in immense ways. So if we're going to talk about culture as race and culture as social class and gender and where you live, then we must also talk about culture as religion, because what you believe has everything to do with what you do. Like race/ethnicity and class, religion is also associated with strong group affiliations, values, goals, rules, norms, ideas, and practices. Thus it is not surprising that anthropologists (e.g., Geertz, 1973) and psychologists (e.g., Cohen, 2009) have long argued that religion is itself a form of culture. Also like race/ethnicity and class, religion can be incredibly fuzzy and subject to interpretation; religious divisions have not always remained the same over time, and how we sort people into religious groups can change—theists versus polytheists; Christians versus Jews; religious versus nonreligious. Ultimately the comparisons will vary, but the message is the same: Religion matters, and what you believe has everything to do with who you are.

How Religious Are We, Really?

The short answer is: very, very religious.

The long answer is this: Religion has been around for more than 100,000 years, exists in every culture on this planet, and even in this day and age, the overwhelming majority of people subscribe to some sort of religious belief (Azar, 2010). Estimates range from 85% in terms of the world's population being religious (Pew Research Center, 2015) to upward of more than 90% of the U.S. American population being so (Newport, 2011). Just about every society on earth has supernatural beliefs, and most of the world believes in some kind of supernatural power.

In the United States, the numbers are striking: According to Gallup polls, 92% of Americans believe in God, and this percentage has stayed relatively stable over the past century (e.g., compared to 96% of Americans a half century earlier; Newport, 2011). Belief in other supernatural entities (photo 3.3) are also high: 81% of Americans believe in heaven (although only 70% believe in hell); 78% believe in angels, 70% believe in the devil (Winseman, 2004). Related research by the Pew Research Center has found that about a third of Americans report having been in touch with the dead, a quarter believe in reincarnation, one in five believe they've had contact with a ghost, and one in seven have consulted a psychic (Pew Research Center, 2009).

Across the world, the numbers are similar. When Pew's researchers did a poll on religion globally, they simply asked people everywhere, "How important is religion

PHOTO 3.3. The majority of Americans believe in supernatural beings, like angels.

Source: iStock

in your life?" Here is what they found in terms of the percentage of people who answered "very important" (Pew Research Center, 2015):

Middle East: Pakistan (98%); Palestinian territory (85%); Jordan (82%); Lebanon (57%)

Africa: Senegal (97%); Nigeria (90%); Ghana (89%); Kenya (87%); Uganda (86%); South Africa (69%)

Latin America: El Salvador (80%); Brazil (74%); Bolivia (68%); Mexico (45%), Venezuela (42%); Chile (39%); Argentina (32%)

Asia: Indonesia (94%); Philippines (86%); Malaysia (77%); South Korea (19%); Japan (10%); China (2%)

Europe: Italy (30%); Spain (22%); Germany (21%); Britain (17%); France (13%)

Thus religion does not seem to be going away anytime soon, contrary to the claims of the **secularization myth** that with the development of science and technology, religion is diminishing in importance (Stark, 1998). With the exception of (1) Europe, and (2) academia in general, there is little evidence that religion is decreasing in prominence in any other sphere (aforementioned Pew data; Mixon, Lyon, & Beaty, 2004). If anything, the persistence and rise of religion in the 21st century may be one factor that can explain the rise of religious conflicts. Religious conflict itself is as old as time. Back in the year 64 CE, Nero set Rome on fire and then said the Christians did it; afterward—and not surprisingly—many Christians were executed for their alleged arson. There's the St. Bartholomew's Day Massacre and the Crusades, the Inquisition and the Thirty Years' War. These days, things have not gotten much better:

- In the Central African Republic (CAR), the Muslim group Seleka and the mostly Christian and animist group anti-Balaka have been in war since 2012, leading to thousands of civilian deaths, countless burned villages, and a half million refugees (Cadman, 2015).
- In the Middle East, the conflict between Arabs and Jews dates back more than 3,000 years and continues to be responsible for military and civilian lives, not to mention the billions of dollars spent on military establishments and humanitarian needs (Center for Reduction of Religious-Based Conflict, 2016).
- In Iran, Baha'is, Christian converts, Sufi and Sunni Muslims, and dissident Shi'a reformers and clerics are routinely jailed for their beliefs. Similar imprisonments are also common in Uzbekistan, North Korea, and Eritrea (Morgan, 2015).
- In Pakistan, Shi'a, Christians, Hindus, Ahmadis are often the target of violent attacks because of their religious minority status (Morgan, 2015).
- The ISIS conflict is a religious war (Belz, 2014).
- Taken together, this has led the U.S. Commission on International Religious Freedom (USCIRF) to estimate that approximately 13 million people worldwide have fled religious conflicts; most of the conflicts are in Syria, Iraq, Nigeria, Central African Republic, Eritrea, Burma, and Afghanistan.

Brief History of Religion as Culture: The Protestant Work Ethic

The notion that religion can confer cultural values is not new. One of the first widely read treatises on this topic was German sociologist Max Weber's publication on the so-called **Protestant Work Ethic**, which argued that the Calvinist brand of Christian Protestantism was especially conducive to capitalism. As Weber argued, the Calvinist notion of predestination—that God himself decided who was to be saved and who wasn't, long before we lived out our lives—meant that outward signs of success could be an indication of a person's eternal fate; as a result, ensuring one's eternal destiny meant ensuring one's earthly success via hard work and resourcefulness (Weber, 2002). Since Weber's original manifesto, subsequent empirical studies have confirmed that indeed, Protestants and non-Protestants differ substantively in their attitudes toward work. Although there isn't strong evidence that Protestants are actually more successful at work—at least insofar as the economy is concerned (Cantoni, 2015), relative to non-Protestants, Protestants were found to be less happy about unemployment (van Hoorn & Maseland, 2013). This emphasis on work also has relational liabilities: As Sanchez-Burks (2002) showed, when Calvinists were put into a work context, they were less relational and less attentive to emotion; members of other religions, in contrast, did not show these effects.

Defining Religion: Culture, Religion, and Spirituality

Broadly speaking, religion, like ethnic culture and class, consists of a set of beliefs, practices, value systems, symbols, and artifacts (Cohen, 2009) that involve a sense of community, rituals, and emotions (Saroglou, 2003; Hinde, 1999). Nevertheless, religion is different from these other forms of culture, given its emphasis on supernatural entities (Ysseldyk, Matheson, & Anisman, 2010). One of the defining features of religion is its function in explaining **metaphysical** phenomena using gods, spirits, and other immaterial beings. Importantly, beliefs about these supernatural agents almost always implicate a broader set of values, inferences about origins (i.e., where or what we come from), and destinations (i.e., where we are going), and norms (Atran & Norenzayan, 2004; Paloutzian & Park, 2005; Sosis, 2006).

Interestingly, religion and ethnic culture also intersect. Religion, like every other form of culture, is not a stable, monolithic thing; rather, it changes over time and contexts. History abounds with cases where the same religion has taken on different emphases or included distinct elements as a function of its larger ethnic or national context. When European colonizers brought their religion to the New World, the emergent Christianity in places like Mexico retained many original, indigenous symbols (e.g., Kaplan, 1995). In more recent years, the popularity of different types of churches in the United States has varied as a function of economic and political vicissitudes; during economic recessions and periods of political turmoil, more people flock to authoritarian churches (McCann, 1999; Sales, 1972). Psychologists call this phenomenon the bidirectionality of religion and (national/ethnic) culture (Johnson, Hill, & Cohen, 2011).

At the same time, religion can also transcend ethnic culture. People from different nationalities and ethnic backgrounds can identify with the same religion, and in certain contexts, religion can even trump national culture—for example, in cases where an individual does not subscribe to the dominant belief system of his or her compatriots.

Finally, it is important to point out that alternatives to organized religions also exist. Namely, there are numerous versions of nontheistic worldviews, as well as individual, metaphysical belief systems that are idiosyncratic and not always shared. For example, **spirituality** can be distinguished from religion owing to its independence from traditional religious institutions, its lack of ritual structural in a communal context, and its lack of authority (Saroglou, 2003). Despite not possessing features typically associated with religion, however, spirituality nevertheless has the same emphasis on humanity's fundamental connection with the larger universe (Emmons & Paloutzian, 2003). In this sense, self-identified "religious" and "spiritual" individuals are similar in that they both believe that the inherent meaning and purpose of life involve being connected with a greater reality that is beyond the individual; among people who identify as being "spiritual" (but not "religious"), this typically involves being connected with other humans, living things, and the universe (Emmons & Paloutzian, 2003).

Religion and Emotion

Emotional Experience Generally speaking, religion is often the source of intense emotional experiences (Pruyser, 1976). While charismatic religious movements tend to emphasize strong, high arousal and positive emotions, especially during rituals (McCauley, 2001), contemplative movements tend to emphasize lower arousal emotions. Religion also tends to prescribe specific kinds of emotions in particular contexts—for example, love (or fear) toward God (depending on one's particular theological orientation), joy during service toward others, awe in response to creation, and so forth (Emmons, 2005; Silberman, 2003). The specific kinds of emotions that are often experienced in the context of religion or in response to a divine being or "ultimate" reality are often referred to as sacred emotions (Hill et al., 2000). The main types of sacred emotions are outlined below:

Gratitude refers to the emotional response a person has upon recognizing that he or she has gained something valuable, usually from another person or being (Bertocci & Millard, 1963; Emmons & McCullough, 2004). Both dispositional and state gratitude are positively correlated or linked with both spirituality and religiousness (McCullough, Kilpatrick, Emmons, & Larson, 2001; McCullough, Emmons, & Tsang, 2002), which led researchers to conclude that this positive emotion serves a crucial role in religious contexts—namely, by serving as a measure of one's own level of morality, motivating **prosocial** behaviors as a response of being grateful for being a beneficiary of other people's prosocial actions, and increasing the likelihood of these prosocial actions (McCullough et al., 2002).

Perhaps even more central to religion than gratitude are the feelings of **awe and reverence**, which refer to the sensation of being in the presence of an overpowering, mysterious, and holy majesty (Otto, 1958). More generally, awe is about being sensitive to a greatness or vastness outside the self (Keltner & Haidt, 2003; Roberts, 2003) and a need for accommodation when the present experience is something so fantastical that it can't be assimilated into one's existing understanding (Keltner & Haidt, 2003). Interestingly, existing studies suggest that awe and reference are actually not that commonly experienced in religious contexts, at least relative to other positive emotions like joy, peace, and security (Hardy, 1979).

In addition to gratitude and awe/reverence, **hope** is a religious virtue that is typically central to most of the world's faiths. In a broad psychological context, hope has long been established as important to human thriving, and the opposite of hope—e.g., phenomena like learned helplessness—can be devastating to well-being (Snyder, Sigmon, & Feldman, 2002). Consistent with this idea, researchers have proposed that hope can potentially explain the link between religion and well-being by directing people to relevant goals and enabling them to pursue those goals (Snyder et al., 2002).

Emotion Regulation Religion doesn't just promote positive feelings like gratitude, awe, and hope; it also offers to help regulate negative emotions. Eastern religious practices like Zen **meditation** have been shown to relieve a number of negative feelings, including anxiety and depression, while also promoting positive feelings, like compassion (Baer, 2003). Meditative practices are also commonly associated with the broader practice of **mindfulness**, which entails an increased attention to, and awareness of, the present. Across broad samples that included religious and irreligious individuals alike (e.g., college students, cancer patients, and Zen meditators), researchers have found that mindfulness predicts both better self-regulation and higher well-being (Brown & Ryan, 2003). This suggests that being mindful can help people be both more attuned to their own feelings and better at regulating those internal states.

In addition to changing emotions via meditation and mindfulness, religion may also promote effective emotional regulation with regard to forgiveness. Studies where participants were asked to imagine forgiving someone who had offended them revealed that those who forgave showed changes in both self-reported emotion and physiological states—they reported being less angry, sad, and likely to hold a grudge; moreover, their bodily states reflected these changes and exhibited lower sympathetic nervous system activation (Witvliet, Ludwig, & Vander Laan, 2001).

Religion and Cognition

Cognitive Predispositions for Religious Beliefs A growing body of work suggests that religious beliefs may be hardwired in our very brains and that basic cognitive processes predispose people to see the world as something that has been intentionally designed, created by a being. In seminal work by Justin Barrett (2000) at Oxford University, he found that children as young as three naturally believe in God (photo 3.4) and assume that he is immortal, with supernatural abilities. Astonishingly, kids show these tendencies even in the absence of explicit religious instruction; moreover, they are able to tell detailed, developed stories about their existence prior to their birth (Barrett, 2000).

Other studies have shown that supernatural or counterintuitive stories are ultimately the best remembered. When Atran and Norenzayan (2006) gave participants a variety of stories that ranged from the ordinary and intuitive—e.g., a cow that grazes on grass—to the slightly unusual and somewhat supernatural—e.g., a frog that curses—to the downright bizarre—e.g., a brick that squealed and blossomed—people ended up remembering the ordinary stories in the short run but remembered the supernatural, slightly counterintuitive ones in the long run, when asked about them a week later. Even when these researchers redid this same study in Mexico with Mayan villagers, they found that this different sample reacted in the

PHOTO 3.4. Research shows that even young children have intuitive beliefs in God.

Source: iStock

same way, remembering the counterintuitive, supernatural stories the best (Atran & Norenzayan, 2006). This finding further confirms that we are predisposed to remember stories with supernatural elements, and this may explain why religion can be easily transmitted and sustained over time.

Recent neural imaging work suggests that religious beliefs implicate the same areas of the brain that are used in more everyday social cognitions, like how we infer the feelings and thoughts of other people. This ability is classically known as **Theory of Mind**—or the idea that I have a mind, you have a mind, and our minds may not see the world in exactly the same way (Goldman, 2012). When researchers had people think about religious statements about God's will or his protection while in an fMRI scanner, they found that the same areas of the brain that are usually involved in theory of mind lit up during these religious thoughts (Kapogiannis et al., 2009). Similar studies have found that theory-of-mind areas of the brain are also active during prayer (Schjoedt, Stødkilde-Jørgensen, Geertz, & Roepstorff, 2009). Thus one interpretation of these findings is that our brains are "predisposed" to believe, because the same brain areas that are responsible for our deciphering the thoughts and intentions of other people may also promote our ability to infer the thoughts and intentions of a supreme being.

Religion's Impact on Cognitive and Neural Processes Not only does religion implicate basic cognitive processes but religious practices also appear to change the actual nature of the brain. To illustrate, when long-term Buddhist monks have their brain activity measured while they are meditating, their brains show better, more organized attention patterns on both fMRI scans and EEG recordings than the brains of novice meditators (Davidson & Lutz, 2008). This suggests that religious and spiritual practices like meditation can have long-term neural effects, particularly when it comes to improving attention.

The impact of religion doesn't stop at just meditation. In an interesting study devised by University of Toronto psychologist Michael Inzlicht and colleagues (2009), he found that people who endorsed a stronger belief in God were less likely to exhibit strong brain responses to mistakes that they themselves made. In their paradigm, Inzlicht et al. (2009) gave participants a classic **Stroop task**, where they had to name the color of words without reading the word itself (e.g., say "red" when they saw the word "blue" spelled out in red font); in past work, Inzlicht et al. found that when people make mistakes, the anterior cingulate cortex area of the brain exhibits a "event-related negativity" spike (ERN), that is essentially a mental alarm bell. They found that more religious people were less likely to exhibit strong ERN responses when they misread a word on the Stroop task, suggesting that they were calmer under pressure (Inzlicht et al., 2009).

Religion and Well-Being

This previous finding that religious individuals were less likely to respond neurally to their own honest mistakes is consistent with a large body of work that suggests that religion has a host of benefits for health and well-being. Studies consistently show that those who are more religious are less likely to be depressed or anxious (Plante, 2010) Although the reasons for this link are varied and not abundantly clear, one possibility is that specific religious or spiritual practices like meditation can be especially useful in curbing anxiety and depression.

Besides these mental health outcomes, religion also serves as a protective factor against a host of other maladaptive physical health behaviors, like alcohol and drug consumption (Francis, 1997), and in promoting a variety of prevention practices, from getting Pap smears and prostate screenings (Benjamins & Brown, 2004) to using seat belts and taking vitamins (Hill, Burdette, Ellison & Musick, 2006). Other studies have shown that those who frequently attend religious services are more likely to stop smoking and increase their exercise (Hill et al., 2006). Laboratory experiments have confirmed these patterns and shown that religiosity acts as a buffer against ego-depletion effects: After once exerting their self-control, religious (but not irreligious) individuals were more likely to be able to continue to self-regulate (Watterson & Giesler, 2012). This link between religiosity and self-regulation has been replicated across many studies (McCullough & Willoughby, 2009).

Even cross-cultural studies have supported this idea. Researchers in Uganda found that in a sample of over 4,000 young Christian and Muslim adults, HIV infection was more common among the less religious (among other factors, including education, whether both parents were still alive, sexual activity, number of sexual partners, condom use, and alcohol or drug use; Kagimu et al., 2012). Even when these other factors were held constant, however, religiosity—in this case, private prayer—still predicted a lower risk of HIV infection (Kagimu et al., 2012). Along related lines, studies in Brazil have found that parallel effects emerge when examining both physical and mental health outcomes: Those who considered religion to be very important were less likely to experience dementia, depression, hospitalization, and smoking (Lucchetti, Lucchetti, Peres, Moreira-Almeida, & Koenig, 2012).

Consistent with these findings, religious people also live longer. In a large-scale study with over 21,000 participants followed over eight years, Hummer, Roger, Nam, and Ellison (1999) found that people who never attended religious services had 1.87 times the risk of death compared with people who attend services more than once a week. Although the size of this effect varied as a function of type of death, the pattern was consistent across all types of death; moreover, this effect held even when holding 16 different control variables constant (Hummer et al., 1999). In the end, Hummer et al. (1999) found that this translated into a seven-year difference in life expectancy. The aforementioned differences in health are likely responsible for a portion of this religiosity effect, but religion can also work through additional mechanisms, such as increased social support.

Religion, Morality, and Prosocial Behavior

Early theories proposed that religion serves to counteract natural human selfishness (Campbell, 1975). In other words, people are naturally self-serving and prone to evil, but religion curbs this and encourages more prosocial behavior. More recent theorists like Batson (1993) have elaborated on this idea and argued that religion is particularly good at driving humans beyond the tendency to only be altruistic toward their own kin (i.e., others with whom they share genetic material) and making them more indiscriminately altruistic toward everyone. Said differently, classic models of evolution allow for kin-specific **altruism** and general selfishness to coexist. People usually serve their own interests but will occasionally self-sacrifice to help their family members, because doing so also perpetuates their own DNA. According to researchers like Batson (1993), religion took this altruism one step further by removing the kin-only requirement and motivating people to be more generally altruistic and giving toward all people.

The big question, of course, is whether this actually happens: Does religion make people good? As usual, the answer is: It depends.

Religion and Self-Reported Prosociality An abundant body of work suggests that exposing individuals to religious primes will, at minimum, increase their intentions to behave themselves. In one study, participants primed with religious objects like heaven and miracles were likely to take more pamphlets for charity with the presumed intention of distributing them (although actual distribution was never measured; Pichon, Boccato, & Saroglou, 2007). Consistent with this idea, people who self-reported as more spiritual were more likely to report valuing other people as equals (Saroglou & Galand, 2004), and people who pray and attend religious services report giving more to charity and volunteering (Brooks, 2006; Monsma, 2007).

These patterns are consistent across nations; generally speaking, believing in God and the afterlife predicts having more moral attitudes toward a variety of behaviors, including infidelity and tax evasion (Atkinson & Bourrat, 2011). Although this relationship is not always strong, meta-analysis of large numbers of international studies have shown that religiosity correlates positively with concern for others (Saroglou, Delpierre, & Dernelle, 2004).

Religion and Behavioral Prosociality Religion also has an effect on actual behavior. When Azim Shariff and Ara Norenzayan (2007) primed individuals with religious thoughts by having them unscramble statements that contained words like *divine*, *God*, and *spirit* (and compared them to a separate control group that unscrambled statements with neutral words), they found that those who were primed with religion gave more money to a stranger—in this case, an average of $2.38 more (out of a possible total of $10 that they received for being part of the study).

Other behavioral studies have relied on economic games, such as the ultimatum game or the dictator game. In the ultimatum game, one person is given a sum of money (let's say, $10) and simply has to decide how much of that amount he or she wants to keep versus share with an anonymous partner; the person deciding has to get his or her partner to agree with the decision—otherwise, they both walk away with nothing; similarly, in the dictator game, whatever the person decides becomes the outcome, and the game ends there (Camerer & Thaler, 1995). Cross-cultural studies have found that across religions, those who were religious made fairer offers to strangers than those who were not (Henrich, 2010).

Similar patterns have emerged with immoral behaviors (see Insight Box 3.1). When Randolph-Seng and Nielsen (2007) exposed participants to religious words (like *heaven*, *prayer*, *holy*, etc.) before having them complete a difficult task—one that entailed writing numbers inside small circles with their eyes closed—they found that those primed with religion were less likely to cheat, regardless of the persons' actual level of religiosity.

INSIGHT BOX 3.1

Religion and the Morality of Mentality

Religion also exerts powerful effects in less intuitive ways, like how important you think mental states are when judging the rightness of an action. Consider these two similar yet starkly divergent cases:

> Donte Stallworth of the Cleveland Browns killed Mario Reyes, 49, on March 14, 2009. He had a blood alcohol of 0.128. As a result, he spent 24 days in prison (Naqi, 2010).
> Michael Vick of the Philadelphia Eagles was released and reinstated into the NFL after being charged for dogfighting. He spent almost two years in prison ("Vick leaves federal penitentiary for Va.," 2009).

Both were NFL football players. Both lived in the same country, had the same profession, spoke the same language, had similar levels of resources, identified with the same race and gender, and broke the law. Yet Stallworth and Vick experienced vastly different punishments for their crime. Why is that?

Alternatively, consider this: What is more important, your thoughts or your behaviors? Is it OK to

- Act nice to someone (photo 3.5) but secretly hate the person?
- Think of someone else when making love to your significant other?
- Entertain thoughts about horrible things happening to your least favorite person?

PHOTO 3.5. Consider the morality of pretending to like someone you secretly detest.

Source: Photofest

As it turns out, how you answer these questions may depend largely on your religious beliefs and, in particular, whether you are Christian or Jewish. While Christians emphasize thoughts, Jews focus on actions, and this has everything to do with their theology (Cohen, Hall, Koenig, & Meador, 2005). Consider the Sermon on the Mount (Matthew 5), when Jesus famously told people that there are actually *two* sins associated with adultery: (1) for the actual act, and (2) for just thinking about it ("Anyone who looks at a woman lustfully has already committed adultery in his heart"; Matthew 5: 27–29). This suggests that from a Christian standpoint, thoughts are the moral equivalent of actions, and considering doing something is as bad as actually doing it. In contrast, Judaism emphasizes the idea that inner thoughts and feelings are less important than what you actually do; if anything, having thoughts and feelings about something and going against those thoughts and feelings is evidence that one truly values obedience to God (Cohen et al., 2005). After all, doing the thing you want and intend is easy; not doing the thing you've been entertaining in your head is much harder, and the latter is a better reflection of true dedication to God's moral code.

To test this idea, Cohen and Rozin (2001) gave Jews and Christians a series of hypothetical scenarios about a man named Mr. B. and asked them to judge his thoughts and behaviors. In one case, Cohen and Rozin (2001) have him entertain thoughts about having an affair with his colleague at work even though he is married; in another, they have him consider poisoning his professor's dog after the professor gives him a bad grade. In both cases, Protestant Christians, relative to Jews, judged Mr. B more negatively; moreover, Christians thought Mr. B should be able to control his thoughts and believed that his thoughts had greater moral significance (Cohen & Rozin, 2001).

But religion can also backfire and lead to decreased prosocial outcomes. Exposure to religious primes have been shown to increase both implicit and explicit prejudice (Johnson, Rowatt, & LaBouff, 2010). In a study with Jewish Israelis, thinking about going to synagogue led to increased support for suicide attacks against Palestinians (Ginges, Hansen, & Norenzayan, 2009). Similarly, being exposed to Bible stories in which violence was done in the name of God led participants to act more aggressively toward a total stranger—in this case, they chose to give them extraloud headphones (Bushman, Ridge, Das, Key, & Busath, 2007).

How do we make sense of these oppositional findings?

One idea is that religion, in some cases, acts as a form of ingroup, and as such, religiousness promotes both increased cooperation and **prosociality** toward ingroup members *and* increased hostility and aggression toward outgroup members (Saroglou, 2006). In other words, because people identify—often strongly—with religious groups in the same way that they identify with racial, ethnic, or class groups, they may similarly show ingroup favoritism and outgroup hostility on the basis of religion, just like they do with any other cultural group membership. Thus religious "prosociality" may be confined to ingroup members. In other words, the Golden Rule applies, but primarily to people that agree with you.

In line with this idea, religious people have been shown to be likely to help a family member or friend but not likely to help an unknown target (Saroglou, 2006), and priming people with religion led them to be more likely to help a homeless person but not a criminal foreigner (Pichon & Saroglou, 2009).

Another related idea is that religion and God are distinct ideas with divergent outcomes, and even though religion leads to "groupiness," God leads to more generalized prosociality. Evidence for this comes from a study where researchers primed different participants with either "religion" or "God" (or a control word) before having them play a Prisoner's Dilemma game that involved deciding whether or not to cooperate with a stranger (Ritter & Preston, 2010). Participants primed with "God" were more likely to cooperate with outgroup members, but those primed with "religion" were more likely to cooperate with ingroup members (Ritter & Preston, 2010). Similarly, after the swine flu outbreak of 2009, individuals who were asked whether or not they believed in God were more likely to donate money to an outgroup charity (in this case, the Mexican Red Cross), but those asked about their religion were more likely to donate to an ingroup charity (the American Red Cross; Hernandez & Preston, 2010).

Explaining Religion's Effects

Religion as a Form of Meaning-Making

Perhaps the most common way psychologists have tried to explain the prevalence of religion is to assert that religion allows people to make sense of the events that happen to them and imbue their life with meaning. On a most basic level, religion can be seen as a manifestation of basic cognitive and motivational processes (Saroglou, 2003). Individuals naturally attribute causes to events; in the process, they will establish links between different phenomena ("if I do this, then this other thing will happen"). Usually, humans will try to tie these interpretations together in a consistent kind of way that will bring meaning and coherence to their lives (Saroglou, 2003).

Although psychologists have studied many different ways that people establish meaning in their lives, religion is somewhat unique in that it focuses specifically on addressing the issue of origins and ends—that is, where we have come from and why we are here (i.e., origins), as well as where we are ultimately going and what that place will be like (i.e., ends). In this sense, religion seems to be preoccupied with both proximate causes (explaining why specific, daily events happen) as well as ultimate causes (explaining why humanity exists to experience these events in the first place; Saroglou, 2003).

Agency Detection One idea is that religion is a by-product of human agency detection mechanisms (in this context, agency detection refers to the tendency for people to perceive that events are caused by willful, intentional beings; Valdesolo & Graham, 2014). At the heart of this argument is the idea that humans have intuitions about nonphysical, theistic agents from an early age (Keleman, 2004) and this capacity is a crucial part of our daily thought processes. Moreover, this tendency for people to perceive agency was crucial for our survival over time because it allowed for predator detection—being hypervigilant allowed our ancestors to figure out if there were other entities around that might threaten their livelihood and to watch out for those beings (Atran & Norenzayan, 2004). As the argument then goes, when agency detection, an ordinary cognitive capacity, goes into overdrive (i.e., when it is activated excessively), it leads to the detection of intentionality and agency of nonmaterial, nonhuman beings, like gods and other spirits (Atran & Norenzayan, 2004; Barrett, 2000).

Terror Management Humans are unique in that we appear to be the only species that is aware of our own mortality. This, however, poses a bit of a problem, because the fear of death can be paralyzing to our superbly well-developed brains. As such, terror management theory (TMT) suggests that humans evolved coping strategies to defend themselves against their own mortality—namely, through either symbolic and literal immortality (Pyszczynski, Greenberg, Solomon, Arndt, & Schimel, 2004). Symbolic immortality involves defense of one's cultural ideologies (for a review, see Pyszczynski et al., 2004). There are many ways to do this, including psychological distancing from innocent victims, derogation of outgroups and dissimilar others, and promotion of ingroups and similar others; literal immortality, on the other hand, involves adherence to religious ideologies that endorse an afterlife (Pyszczynski et al., 2004).

TMT studies have generally found that people endorse religion more after a death prompt (e.g., Burling, 1993; Greenberg et al., 1990; Norenzayan, Dar-Nimrod, Hansen, & Proulx, 2009; Vail, Rothschild, Weise, Solomon, Pyszczynski, & Greenberg, 2010). Other studies have shown that while making someone think about his or her own death usually leads to defensiveness, this pattern doesn't emerge among people who are intrinsically religious (Jonas & Fischer, 2006). TMT researchers suggest that there might be a special link between awareness of one's own mortality and supernatural beliefs (Pyszczynski et al., 2004).

Moral Typecasting In 2009, Kurt Gray and Dan Wegner had over 1,000 online participants evaluate an eclectic array of targets on two dimensions of moral perception: agency (i.e., how much responsibility and control a person has) and experience (i.e., how much subjective experience a person has). Agency measures included questions like these: "How much blame or praise does this person deserve for his or her actions in life?" and "How much thought does this person give to behavior before acting?" (Gray & Wegner, 2009). As a measure of experience, Gray and Wegner (2009) asked participants to imagine that the target stepped on a piece of glass that cut the target's foot, and to evaluate how much pain the target would feel and how easy it would be to take advantage of the target, more generally. Targets included supernatural agents (God himself), positive and negative natural agents (Mother Teresa, Osama bin Laden), natural patients (an orphan), and neutral targets (a network administrator; Gray & Wegner, 2009). Agents are those who are primarily known for their ability to do things; patients, in contrast, are those primarily known for the ability to feel things (Gray & Wegner., 2009).

According to what Gray and Wegner (2009) called the *moral typecasting theory*, people tend to divide the world dichotomously (photo 3.6), and this also applies to moral situations. So moral agents do good or evil, whereas moral patients receive good or evil being done to them, and once you are labeled as an agent or patient, you are typecast forever in your role, which shapes all subsequent perception of who you are and what you do (Gray & Wegner, 2009). If we typecast people, we also typecast supernatural entities, and in their study, Gray

PHOTO 3.6. Moral typecasting theory says people tend to see the world dichotomously.

Source: iStock

and Wegner (2009) found that God appears to be the "ultimate" moral agent—the one entity with total agency but virtually no experience. God can do anything but is perceived to feel very little.

Why is this important? According to Gray and Wegner (2009), having an ultimate moral agent like God can be useful insofar as God can now be used to explain anything that lacks explanation. Terrible things happen in the world all the time, and in many cases, there is no obvious reason. But, if an ultimate moral agent exists, then he can always be held accountable. In support of this idea, Gray and Wegner (2009) found that across the United States, regions with greater "suffering"—mortality rates for babies, cancer diagnoses, infectious diseases, violent crime—were more likely to believe in God. When the researchers subsequently manipulated suffering in the lab by having participants read about a scenario in which a family out on a picnic either unexpectedly dies (or not) because of either human error or a freak accident of nature, people were more likely to believe in God after there is both a tragedy and no explanation (i.e., the family dies because of a freak accident of nature; Gray & Wegner, 2010).

Religion as a Source of Control A different idea is that religion is fundamentally related to control. In this case, religion and control form a curious feedback loop, because religion both appears to satisfy humans' need for control and demands increases in (self-)control.

On the one hand, religion can serve to satisfy the ostensibly fundamental need for humans to exert control over their lives. **Compensatory control** models (Gaucher, Hafer, Kay, & Davidenko, 2010; Kay, Gaucher, Napier, Callan, & Laurin, 2008; Kay, Gaucher, McGregor, & Nash, 2010; Kay, Laurin, & Shepherd, 2011; Kay, Shepherd, Blatz, Chua, & Galinsky, 2010; Laurin, Kay, & Moscovitch, 2008) says that a number of external and internal forces can trade on the same system—for example, threats to an internal force, like personal control, can lead to compensation via other external forces, like religion (e.g., Kay et al., 2008). An important part of these studies is the idea that human beings are good at trading between different psychological "currencies" or at using resources in one form (e.g., control by God) to address deficits in another form (e.g., personal control). Thus believing that God has control can protect people from an otherwise random and unpredictable world. Consistent with this idea, studies have shown that economic recessions tend to be accompanied by increases in religiosity (Sales, 1972), and laboratory studies that require participants to recall uncontrollable past events lead to increased beliefs in a controlling God (Kay et al., 2008).

On the other hand, religion also demands high levels of self-control from its constituents. Across all the major world religions, demand for mastery over one's actions (and sometimes, even one's thoughts) forms a central tenet. According to the **supernatural punishment hypothesis**, believing in a God that is always watching you allows for large-scale human control, which in turn enables cooperative societies to exist (Bering & Johnson, 2005; Johnson & Bering, 2006). This idea is related to the notion that religious practices and communities work to strengthen one's self-regulation strategies and track behavior (McCullough & Willoughby, 2009). By always having a moral audience (via God or the church), religious individuals are chronically sensitive to what is permissible or not; over time, they become more likely to self-regulate and less likely to engage in impulsive or risky behaviors (Baier & Wright, 2001; Bartkowski, Xu, & Levin, 2008; French, Eisenberg, Vaughan, Purwono, & Suryanti, 2008).

Religion as Social Support

Religion can also serve to bring people together by binding them in groups that share the same moral codes. Researchers Jesse Graham and Jonathan Haidt (2010) have argued that the reason rituals are so prevalent across the world's religions is that they allow people to publicly demonstrate their group's shared moral codes. For example, by having all members of a religious group eat a certain way (e.g., avoiding pork) or dress a certain way (e.g., saying no to tube tops, spaghetti straps, short shorts, miniskirts, and anything with spandex), they are essentially demonstrating to the rest of the world their moral codes about purity and sanctity. In doing so, this shared morality allows members of the group to live cohesively and cooperatively (Haidt & Graham, 2010).

Beyond simply forming these moral communities, religion is also related to the social support people experience in these groups. Studies show that religiosity is positively correlated with social support (Koenig et al., 1997). Religious individuals are also more trusting, especially if the target at hand is also religious (Berg, Dickhaut, & McCabe, 1995). Studies confirm this effect when the outcome is community dissolution versus survival; when Sosis (2000) compared 200 religious versus secular communities in the United States, he found that religious ones were four times as likely to survive.

Summary

If (social) psychology is all about the real or imagined presence of other people having a profound effect on a person's thoughts, feelings, and behaviors, then surely metaphysical entities are no exception; the psychology of religion, then, is about how the real or imagined presence of supernatural beings affect the way people think, feel, and act. In this sense, religion can both be seen as an alternate form of culture as well as a force that interacts with existing cultural differences, like ethnicity. In other words, religion both seems to exert effects that are independent of other forms of culture (e.g., Christians, Muslims, Buddhists, "spiritual" individuals everywhere may behave in similar ways, regardless of their ethnic culture) as well as depend on other forms of culture (e.g., churches in the United States may emphasize different ideas than churches in Mexico or East Asia do).

In addition to *how* religion changes people—how religious and irreligious people differ in their cognition, emotions, and well-being; how Christians and Jews differ in their attitudes toward mentality—theories and studies abound on *why* religion exists. The question of why is always the harder question, and the latter part of this chapter covered the major explanations psychologists have put forth in the attempt to explain why the overwhelming majority of all humans on the planet appear to believe in things that science has a hard time testing and thereby verifying. Keep in mind that the explanations offered here are only a limited set, offered from psychologists (who are overwhelmingly irreligious themselves, as is typically the case in academia); other fields will invariably have their own ideas (theologians and religious individuals will likely posit, for example, that religion exists because supernatural entities are real). Ultimately, the aim of this chapter has been to show you what some researchers believe so you can decide for yourself.

Key Concepts

Secularization myth
Protestant Work Ethic
Metaphysical
Spirituality
Gratitude, awe and reverence, hope
Meditation
Mindfulness
Theory of Mind
Stroop task
Prosociality
Compensatory control
Supernatural punishment hypothesis

References

Atkinson, Q. D., & Bourrat, P. (2011). Beliefs about God, the afterlife and morality support the role of supernatural policing in human cooperation. *Evolution and Human Behavior*, 32(1), 41–49.

Atran, S., & Norenzayan, A. (2004). Religion's evolutionary landscape: Counterintuition, commitment, compassion, communion. *Behavioral and Brain Sciences*, 27(6), 713–770.

Azar, B. (2010). A reason to believe. *Monitor on Psychology*, 41(11). Retrieved from http://www.apa.org/monitor/2010/12/believe.aspx

Barrett, J. L. (2000). Exploring the natural foundations of religion. *Trends in Cognitive Sciences*, 4(1), 29–34. doi:10.1016/S1364-6613(99)01419-9

Bartkowski, J. P., Xu, X., & Levin, M. L. (2008). Religion and child development: Evidence from the Early Childhood Longitudinal Study. *Social Science Research*, 37(1), 18–36. doi:10.1016/j.ssresearch.2007.02.001

Batson, C. D. (1983). Sociobiology and the role of religion in promoting prosocial behavior: An alternative view. *Journal of Personality and Social Psychology*, 45(6), 1380-1385.

Batson, C. D., Schoenrade, P., & Ventis, L. W. (1993). *Religion and the individual: A social-psychological perspective* (2nd ed.). New York, NY: Oxford University Press.

Belz, M. (2014, October 15). Yes, the ISIS conflict is a religious war. *World Magazine*. Retrieved from https://world.wng.org/2014/10/yes_the_isis_conflict_is_a_religious_war

Benjamins, M. R., & Brown, C. (2004). Religion and preventative health care utilization among the elderly. *Social Science & Medicine*, 58(1), 109–118. doi:10.1016/S0277-9536(03)00152-7

Berg, J., Dickhaut, J., & McCabe, K. (1995). Trust, reciprocity, and social history. *Games and Economic Behavior*, 10(1), 122–142.

Bering, J. M., & Johnson, D. D. (2005). "O Lord . . . you perceive my thoughts from afar": Recursiveness and the evolution of supernatural agency. *Journal of Cognition and Culture*, 5(1), 118–142.

Bertocci, P. A., & Millard, R. M. (1963). *Personality and the good: Psychological and ethical perspectives*. New York, NY: David McKay Company.

Brooks, A. C. (2006). Who really cares: The surprising truth about compassionate conservatism. New York, NY: Basic Books.

Brown, K. W., & Ryan, R. M. (2003). The benefits of being present: Mindfulness and its role in psychological well-being. *Journal of Personality and Social Psychology, 84*(4), 822–848. doi:10.1037/0022-3514.84.4.822

Burling, J. W. (1993). Death concerns and symbolic aspects of the self: The effects of mortality salience on status concern and religiosity. *Personality and Social Psychology Bulletin, 19*(1), 100–105.

Bushman, B. J., Ridge, R. D., Das, E., Key, C. W., & Busath, G. L. (2007). When god sanctions killing: Effect of scriptural violence on aggression. *Psychological Science, 18*(3), 204–207.

Cadman, T. (2015, July 01). Religious war in Central African Republic: Religious intolerance and violence continue to rage on in the Central African Republic. *Al Jazeera*. Retrieved from http://www.aljazeera.com/indepth/opinion/2015/06/religious-war-central-african- republic-150629104901894.html

Camerer, C., & Thaler, R. H. (1995). Anomalies: Ultimatums, dictators and manners. *The Journal of Economic Perspectives, 9*(2), 209–219.

Campbell, D. T. (1975). On the conflicts between biological and social evolution and between psychology and moral tradition. *American Psychologist, 30*(12), 1103–1126. doi: 10.1037/0003-066X.30.12.1103

Cantoni, D. (2014). The economic effects of the Protestant Reformation: Testing the Weber hypothesis in the German Lands. *Journal of the European Economic Association, 13*(4), 561–598. doi:10.1111/jeea.12117

Cantoni, D. (2015). The economic effects of the Protestant Reformation: Testing the Weber hypothesis in the German lands. *Journal of the European Economic Association, 13*(4), 561–598.

Castella, T. (2014, October 25). Have Jedi created a new "religion"? BBC News. Retrieved from http://www.bbc.com/news/magazine-29753530

Center for Reduction of Religion-Based Conflict (2016). *Hotspots-Middle East*. Retrieved from http://www.center2000.org/hotspots-middle-east/

Cohen, A. B. (2009). Many forms of culture. *American Psychologist, 64*(3), 194–204. doi: 10.1037/a0015308

Cohen, A. B. (2010). Just how many different forms of culture are there? *American Psychologist, 65*(1), 59–61. doi:10.1037/a0017793

Cohen, A. B., Hall, D. E., Koenig, H. G., & Meador, K. G. (2005). Social versus individual motivation: Implications for normative definitions of religious orientation. *Personality & Social Psychology Review: An Official Journal of the Society for Personality and Social Psychology, Inc., 9*(1), 48–61.

Cohen, A. B., & Hill, P. C. (2007). Religion as culture: Religious individualism and collectivism among American Catholics, Jews, and Protestants. *Journal of Personality, 75*(4), 709– 742. doi:10.1111/j.1467-6494.2007.00454.x

Cohen, A. B., Malka, A., Hill, E. D., Thoemmes, F., Hill, P. C., & Sundie, J. M. (2009). Race as a moderator of the relationship between religiosity and political alignment. *Personality and Social Psychology Bulletin, 35*(3), 271–282.

Cohen, A. B., & Rozin, P. (2001). Religion and the morality of mentality. *Journal of Personality & Social Psychology, 81*(4), 697–710. doi:10.1037//O022-3514.81.4.697

Davidson, R. J., & Lutz, A. (2008). Buddha's brain: Neuroplasticity and meditation. *IEEE Signal Processing Magazine, 25*(1), 176, 172–174.

Elliot, E. (1961). *The savage my kinsman*. New York, NY: Harper & Brothers.

Emmons, R. A. (2005). Emotion and religion. In R. F. Paloutzian and C. L. Park (Eds.), *Handbook of the psychology of religion* (pp. 235–252). New York, NY: Guilford Press.

Emmons, R. A., & McCullough, M. E. (Eds.). (2004). *The psychology of gratitude.* New York, NY: Oxford University Press.

Emmons, R. A., & Paloutzian, R. F. (2003). The psychology of religion. *Annual Review of Psychology, 54*(1), 377–402. doi:101146/annurev.psych.54.101601.145024

Francis, L. J. (1997). The impact of personality and religion on attitude toward substance use among 13–15 year olds. *Drug and Alcohol Dependence, 44*(2-3), 95–103. doi:10.1016/S0376-8716(96)01325-7

French, D. C., Eisenberg, N., Vaughan, J., Purwono, U., & Suryanti, T. A. (2008). Religious involvement and the social competence and adjustment of Indonesian Muslim adolescents. *Developmental Psychology, 44*(2), 597– 611. doi: 10.1037/0012-1649.44.2.597

Gaucher, D., Hafer, C. L., Kay, A. C., & Davidenko, N. (2010). Compensatory rationalizations and the resolution of everyday undeserved outcomes. *Personality and Social Psychology Bulletin, 36*(1), 109–118.

Geertz, C. (1973). *Interpretation of cultures: Selected essays.* New York, NY: Basic Books.

Ginges, J., Hansen, I., & Norenzayan, A. (2009). Religion and support for suicide attacks. *Psychological Science, 20*(2), 224–230.

Goldman, A. I. (2012). Theory of mind. *The Oxford Handbook of Philosophy of Cognitive Science,* 402-424. doi:10.1093/oxfordhb/9780195309799.013.0017

Graham, J., & Haidt, J. (2010). Beyond beliefs: Religions bind individuals into moral communities. *Personality and Social Psychology Review, 14*(1), 140–150.

Gray, K., & Wegner, D. M. (2009). Moral typecasting: Divergent perceptions of moral agents and moral patients. *Journal of Personality and Social Psychology, 96*(3), 505–520.

Gray, K., & Wegner, D. M. (2010). Blaming God for our pain: Human suffering and the divine mind. *Personality and Social Psychology Review, 14*(1), 7–16.

Greenberg, J., Pyszczynski, T., Solomon, S., Rosenblatt, A., Veeder, M., Kirkland, S., & Lyon, D. (1990). Evidence for terror management theory II: The effects of mortality salience on reactions to those who threaten or bolster the cultural worldview. *Journal of Personality and Social Psychology, 58*(2), 308–318.

Hardy, A. (1979). The spiritual nature of man: A study of contemporary religious experience. Oxford, U.K.: Clarendon Press.

Henrich, J., Ensminger, J., McElreath, R., Barr, A., Barrett, C., Bolyanatz, A., . . . Lesorogol, C. (2010). Markets, religion, community size, and the evolution of fairness and punishment. *Science, 327*(5972), 1480–1484.

Hernandez, J. I., & Preston, J. L. (2010). *Brother, can you spare a dime? How religion and god priming affect ingroup and outgroup swine flu donations differently.* Poster presented at the annual meeting of the Society for Personality and Social Psychology, Las Vegas, Nevada.

Hill, P. C. (2002). Spiritual transformation: Forming the habitual center of personal energy. *Research in the Social Scientific Study of Religion, 13*(1), 87–108.

Hill, P. C., Pargament, K. I., Wood, R. W. Jr., McCullough, M. E., Swyers, J. P., Larson, D. B., & Zinnbauer, B. J. (2000). Conceptualizing religion and spirituality: Points of commonality, points of departure. *Journal for the Theory of Social Behavior, 30*(1), 51–77. doi:10.1111/1468-5914.00119

Hill, T. D., Burdette, A. M., Ellison, C. G., & Musick, M. A. (2006). Religious attendance and the health behaviors of Texas adults. *Preventive Medicine, 42*(4), 309–312.

Hill, T. D., Burdette, A. M., Ellison, C. G., & Musick, M. A. (2006). Religious attendance and the health behaviors of Texas adults. *Preventive Medicine, 42*(4), 309–312. doi:10.1016/j.ypmed.2005.12.005

Hinde, R. A. (1999). Why Gods persist: A scientific approach to religion. London, U.K.: Routledge.

Howard, D. (2015). The Intrepid Missionary Elisabeth Elliot. *The Wall Street Journal*. Retrieved from https://www.wsj.com/articles/the-intrepid-missionary-elisabeth-elliot-1435261809

Hummer, R. A., Rogers, R. G., Nam, C. B., & Ellison, C. G. (1999). Religious involvement and US adult mortality. *Demography*, *36*(2), 273–285. doi:10.2307/2648114

Inglehart, R., & Baker, W. E. (2000). Modernization, cultural change, and the persistence of traditional values. *American Sociological Review*, *65*(1), 19–51.

Inzlicht, M., McGregor, I., Hirsh, J. B., & Nash, K. (2009). Neural markers of religious conviction. *Psychological Science*, *20*(3), 385–392.

Jim Elliot: No fool. (n.d.). Retrieved from https://www.christianity.com/church/church-his tory/church-history-for-kids/jim-elliot-no-fool-11634862.html

Johnson, D., & Bering, J. (2006). Hand of God, mind of man: Punishment and cognition in the evolution of cooperation. *Evolutionary Psychology*, *4*(1), 219–233.

Johnson, K. A., Hill, E. D., & Cohen, A. B. (2011), Integrating the study of culture and religion: Toward a psychology of worldview. *Social and Personality Psychology Compass*, *5*(3), 137–152. doi:10.1111/j.1751-9004.2010.00339.x

Johnson, M. K., Rowatt, W. C., & LaBouff, J. (2010). Priming Christian religious concepts increases racial prejudice. *Social Psychological and Personality Science*, *1*(2), 119–126. doi:10.1177/1948550609357246

Jonas, E., & Fischer, P. (2006). Terror management and religion: Evidence that intrinsic religiousness mitigates worldview defense following mortality salience. *Journal of Personality and Social Psychology*, *91*(3), 553–567. doi:10.1037/0022-3514.91.3.553

Juergensmeyer, M. (1997). Terror mandated by God. *Terrorism and Political Violence*, *9*(2), 16–23.

Kagimu, M., Guwatudde, D., Rwabukwali, C., Kaye, S., Walakira, Y., & Ainomugisha, D. (2012). Religiosity for HIV prevention in Uganda: A case study among Christian youth in Wakiso district. *African Health Sciences*, *12*(3), 282–290. doi:10.4314/ahs.v12i3.6

Kaplan, S. (Ed.). (1995). *Indigenous responses to western Christianity*. New York, NY: New York University Press.

Kapogiannis, D., Barbey, A. K., Su, M., Zamboni, G., Krueger, F., & Grafman, J. (2009). Cognitive and neural foundations of religious belief. *Proceedings of the National Academy of Sciences*, *106*(12), 4876–4881.

Kay, A. C., Gaucher, D., McGregor, I., & Nash, K. (2010). Religious conviction as compensatory control. *Personality and Social Psychology Review*, *14*(1) 37–48. doi: 10.1177/1088868309353750

Kay, A. C., Gaucher, D., Napier, J. L., Callan, M. J., & Laurin, K. (2008). God and the Government: Testing a compensatory control mechanism for the support of external systems. *Journal of Personality and Social Psychology*, *95*(1), 18–35. doi: 10.1037/0022-3514.95.1.18

Kay, A. C., Shepherd, S., Blatz, C. W., Chua, S. N., & Galinsky, A. D. (2010). For God (or) country: The hydraulic relation between government instability and belief in religious sources of control. *Journal of Personality and Social Psychology*, *99*(5), 725–739.

Kelemen, D. (2004). Are children "intuitive theists"? Reasoning about purpose and design in nature. *Psychological Science*, *15*(5), 295–301.

Keltner, D., & Haidt, J. (2003). Approaching awe: A moral, spiritual, and aesthetic emotion. *Cognition and Emotion*, *17*(2), 297–314. doi:10.1080/02699930302297

Koenig, H. G., Hays, J. C., George, L. K., Blazer, D. G., Larson, D. B., & Landerman, L. R. (1997). Modeling the cross-sectional relationships between religion, physical health, social support, and depressive symptoms. *The American Journal of Geriatric Psychiatry*, *5*(2), 131–144. doi:10.1097/00019442-199700520-00006

Laurin, K., Kay, A. C., & Moscovitch, D. A. (2008). On the belief in God: Towards an understanding of the emotional substrates of compensatory control. *Journal of Experimental Social Psychology, 44*(6), 1559–1562.

Laurin, K., Kay, A. C., & Shepherd, S. (2011). Self-stereotyping as a route to system justification. *Social Cognition, 29*(3), 360–375.

Lucchetti, G., Lucchetti, A. L. G., Peres, M. F. P., Moreira-Almeida, A., & Koenig, H. G. (2012). Religiousness, health, and depression in older adults from a Brazilian military setting. *International Scholarly Research Network Psychiatry, 1*(1), 1–7. doi: 10.5402/2012/940747

McCann, S. J. (1999). Threatening times and fluctuations in American church memberships. *Personality and Social Psychology Bulletin, 25*(3), 325–336.

McCauley, R. N. (2001). Ritual, memory, and emotion: Comparing two cognitive hypotheses. In J. Andresen (Ed.), *Religion in mind: Cognitive perspectives on religious belief, ritual, and experience* (pp. 115–140). Cambridge, U.K.: Cambridge University Press.

McCullough, M. E. (2001). Forgiveness: Who does it and how do they do it? *Current Directions in Psychological Science, 10*(6), 194–197.

McCullough, M. E., Emmons, R. A., & Tsang, J. (2002). The grateful disposition: A conceptual and empirical topography. *Journal of Personality and Social Psychology, 82*(1), 112–127. doi:10.1037//0022-3514.82.1.112

McCullough, M. E., Kilpatrick, S. D., Emmons, R. A., & Larson, D. B. (2001). Is gratitude a moral affect? *Psychological Bulletin, 127*(2), 249–266. doi: 10.1037//0033-2909.127.2.249

McCullough, M. E., & Willoughby, B. L. B. (2009). Religion, self-regulation, and self-control: Associations, explanations, and implications. *Psychological Bulletin, 135*(1), 69–93. doi: 10.1037/a0014213

Mixon, S. L., Lyon, L., & Beaty, M. (2004). Secularization and national universities: The effect of religious identity on academic reputation. *Journal of Higher Education, 75*(4), 400–419.

Monsma, S. V. (2007). Religion and philanthropic giving and volunteering: Building blocks for civic responsibility. *Interdisciplinary Journal of Research on Religion, 3*(1), 1–28.

Morgan, T. C. (2015, April 29). 13 million flee religion-linked conflicts worldwide. *Christianity Today.* Retrieved from http://www.christianitytoday.com/gleanings/2015/april/13- million-flee-religion-linked-conflicts-worldwide.html

Naqi, K. (2010, December 30). Financial agreement avoids lawsuit. ESPN. Retrieved from http://www.espn.com/nfl/news/story?id=4262751

Newport, F. (2011, June 3). More than 9 in 10 Americans continue to believe in God. Gallup. Retrieved from http://www.gallup.com/poll/147887/americans-continue-believe- god.aspx

Norenzayan, A., Dar-Nimrod, I., Hansen, I. G., & Proulx, T. (2009). Mortality salience and religion: Divergent effects on the defense of cultural worldviews for the religious and the non-religious. *European Journal of Social Psychology, 39*(1), 101–113.

Norenzayan, A., & Shariff, A. F. (2008). The origin and evolution of religious prosociality. *Science, 322*(5898), 58–62. doi:10.1126/science.1158757

Otto, R. (1958). *The idea of the holy: An inquiry into the non-rational factor in the idea of the dive and its relation to the rational* (J. W. Harvey, Trans.). New York, NY: Oxford University Press. (Original work published 1923)

Paloutzian, R. F., & Park, C. L. (Eds.) (2005). *Handbook of the psychology of religion and spirituality.* New York, NY: Guilford Press.

Pew Research Center. (2009). *Many Americans mix multiple faiths.* Retrieved from http:// www.pewforum.org/2009/12/09/many-americans-mix-multiple-faiths/#ghosts- fortunetellers-and-communicating-with-the-dead

Pew Research Center. (2015). *Religion and GDP topline.* Retrieved from http:// assets.pewresearch.org/wp-content/uploads/sites/2/2015/03/Religion-and-GDP- Topline.pdf

Pichon, I., Boccato, G., & Saroglou, V. (2007). Nonconscious influences of religion on prosociality: A priming study. *European Journal of Social Psychology, 37*(5), 1032–1045. doi:10.1002/ejsp.416

Pichon, I., & Saroglou, V. (2009). Religion and helping: Impact of target thinking styles and just-world beliefs. *Archive for the Psychology of Religion, 31*(1), 215–236. doi: 10.1163/157361209X424466

Plante, T. G. (2010). The Santa Clara Strength of Religious Faith Questionnaire: Assessing faith engagement in a brief and nondenominational manner. *Religions, 1*(1), 3–8.

Pruyser, P. W. (1976). *A dynamic psychology of religion.* New York, NY: Harper & Row.

Pyszczynski, T., Greenberg, J., Solomon, S., Arndt, J., & Schimel, J. (2004). Why do people need self-esteem? A theoretical and empirical review. *Psychological Bulletin, 130*(3), 435–468.

Randolph-Seng, B., & Nielsen, M. E. (2007). Honesty: One effect of primed religious representations. *The International Journal for the Psychology of Religion, 17*(4), 303–315. doi:10.1080/10508610701572812

Ritter, R. S., & Preston, J. L. (2010). *"And who is my neighbor?" revisited: Divergent effects of God and religion primes on cooperation with ingroup and outgroup members in the prisoner's dilemma.* Poster presented at the annual meeting of the Society for Personality and Social Psychology, Las Vegas, Nevada.

Roberts, R. C. (2003). *Emotions: An essay in aid of moral psychology.* Cambridge, U.K.: Cambridge University Press.

Rowatt, W. C., & Franklin, L. M. (2004). Research: Christian orthodoxy, religious fundamentalism, and right-wing authoritarianism as predictors of implicit racial prejudice. *The International Journal for the Psychology of Religion, 14*(2), 125–138. doi: 10.1207/s15327582ijpr1402_4

Saint, S. (1996). Did they have to die? *Christianity Today.* Retrieved from http://www.christianitytoday.com/ct/1996/september16/missionaries-did-they-have-to-die.html

Sales, S. M. (1972). Economic threat as a determinant of conversion rates to authoritarian and nonauthoritarian churches. *Journal of Personality and Social Psychology, 23*(3), 420–428. doi:10.1037/h0033157

Sanchez-Burks, J. (2002). Protestant relational ideology and (in)attention to relational cues in work settings. *Journal of Personality and Social Psychology, 83*(4), 919–929.

Saroglou, V. (2003). Psychology of religion and culture. In *Encyclopedia of life support systems.* Paris, France: UNESCO–Eolss Publishers.

Saroglou, V. (2006). Religion's role in prosocial behavior: Myth or reality? *Psychology of Religion Newsletter, 31*(2), 1–8.

Saroglou, V., Delpierre, V., & Dernelle, R. (2004). Values and religiosity: A meta-analysis of studies using Schwartz's model. *Personality and Individual Differences, 37*(4), 721–734. doi:10.1016/j.paid.2003.10.005

Saroglou, V., & Galand, P. (2004). Identities, values, and religion: A study among Muslim, other immigrant, and native Belgian young adults after the 9/11 attacks. *Identity, 4*(2), 97–132.

Saroglou, V., Pichon, I., Trompette, L., Verschueren, M., & Dernelle, R. (2005). Prosocial behavior and religion: New evidence based on projective measures and peer ratings. *Journal for the Scientific Study of Religion, 44*(3), 323–348. doi:10.1111/j. 1468-5906.2005.00289.x

Schjoedt, U., Stødkilde-Jørgensen, H., Geertz, A. W., & Roepstorff, A. (2009). Highly religious participants recruit areas of social cognition in personal prayer. *Social Cognitive and Affective Neuroscience, 4*(2), 199–207. doi:10.1093/scan/nsn050

Shariff, A. F., & Norenzayan, A. (2007). God is watching you: Priming god concepts increases prosocial behavior in an anonymous economic game. *Psychological Science, 18*(9), 803–809.

Silberman, I. (2003). Commentary: "Spiritual role modeling: The teaching of meaning systems." *The International Journal for the Psychology of Religion*, 13(3), 175–195. doi:10.1207/ S15327582IJPR1303_03

Snyder, C. R., Sigmon, D. R., & Feldman, D. B. (2002). Hope for the sacred and vice versa: Positive goal-directed thinking and religion. *Psychological Inquiry*, 13(3), 234–238.

Solomon, R. C. (1976). *The passions*. Garden City, NY: Anchor Press/Doubleday.

Sosis, R. (2000). Religion and intragroup cooperation: Preliminary results of a comparative analysis of utopian communities. *Cross-Cultural Research, 34*, 70–87.

Sosis, R. (2006). Religious behaviors, badges, and bans: Signaling theory and the evolution of religion. In P. McNamara (Ed.), *Where God and science meet: How brain and evolutionary studies alter our understanding of religion* (Vol. 1, pp. 61–86). Westport, CT: Praeger Publishers.

Stark, R. (1998). Secularization: The myth of religious decline. *Fides et Historia, 30*(2), 1–19.

Vail, K. E., Rothschild, Z. K., Weise, D. R., Solomon, S., Pyszczynski, T., & Greenberg, J. (2010). A terror management analysis of the psychological functions of religion. *Personality and Social Psychology Review, 14*(1), 84–94.

Valdesolo, P., & Graham, J. (2014). Awe, uncertainty, and agency detection. *Psychological science, 25*(1), 170–178.

van Hoorn, A., & Maseland, R. (2013). Does a Protestant work ethic exist? Evidence from the well-being effect of unemployment. *Journal of Economic Behavior & Organization, 91*(1), 1–12. doi:10.1016/j.jebo.2013.03.038

Vick leaves federal penitentiary for Va. (2009, May 21). ESPN. Retrieved from http://www.espn.com/nfl/news/story?id=4183786

"Virgin Mary grilled cheese" sells for $28,000 (2004, November 23). NBC News. Retrieved from http://www.nbcnews.com/id/6511148/ns/us_news-weird_news/t/virgin-mary-grilled-cheese-sells/

Watterson, K., & Giesler, B. R. (2012). Religiosity and self-control: When the going gets tough, the religious get self-regulating. *Psychology of Religion and Spirituality, 4*(3), 193–205. doi:10.1037/a0027644

Weber, M. (2002). *The Protestant ethic and the "spirit" of capitalism and other writings*. London, U.K.: Penguin.

Winseman, A. (2004, May 25). Eternal destinations: Americans believe in Heaven, Hell. Gallup. Retrieved from http://www.gallup.com/poll/11770/eternal-destinations-americans-believe-heaven-hell.aspx

Witvliet, C. V., Ludwig, T. E., & Vander Laan, K. L. (2001). Granting forgiveness or harboring grudges: Implications for emotion, physiology, and health. *Psychological Science, 12*(2), 117–123.

Ysseldyk, R., Matheson, K., & Anisman, H. A. (2010). Religiosity as identity: Toward an understanding of religion from a social identity perspective. *Personality and Social Psychology Review, 14*(1), 60–71.

CHAPTER 4

Gender

How different are men and women, really? Gender differences remain one of the most asked about and least understood phenomenon within social psychology, and much of this has to do with how our cultural expectations (or stereotypes) of men and women align (or misalign) with the empirical evidence. This chapter explores the literature on gender to unpack the domains in which men and women reliably and substantively differ. As this chapter will reveal, gender can also be thought of as a form of culture (Reid, 2002). This chapter will also explore recent research on the ways in which sexual orientation permeates our automatic behaviors and subconscious processes, as well as the way culture interacts with gender roles.

Back in the late '70s, a wildly popular book called *I'm Glad I'm a Boy! I'm Glad I'm a Girl!* hit bookstores and libraries everywhere. Inside, it contained clear messages about boys' and girls' differential abilities, earnings/wages, roles, prestige, power—about boys in construction but girls in the cleaning business, about boys who invent and girls who rely on what boys invent. Even though books like this one are no longer in print, you can currently find a used ("vintage") copy on Amazon.com for about $300.

Development of a Gendered Identity

Socialization

The story of gender, then, is fundamentally the story of what people believe about gender (not dissimilar to the story of race and religion). Parents of toddlers often encourage their kids to play with gender-specific toys (see photo 4.1), and they act more approving when the children do so (Caldera, Huston & O'Brien, 1989).

Along similar lines, other studies have found that even classic gender differences—for example, as concerns aggression—can be eliminated relatively easily. Although the finding that men tend to be more aggressive than women is one of the most longstanding, observed differences anchored in strong biological roots between the genders, Lightdale and Prentice (1994) found that simply making

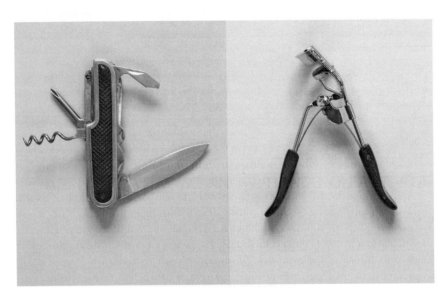

PHOTO 4.1. Gender stereotypes are everywhere.

Source: iStock

people feel deindividuated could remove this difference entirely. In their case, they had male and female participants play a video game under conditions where their identity was known and salient (i.e., the individuation condition) versus not (i.e., the deindividuation condition); they found that under conditions of deindividuation, men and women behaved equally aggressively (Lightdale & Prentice, 1994).

Sociocognitive Development

The story, though, is not as simple as mere parental socialization. Most three-year-olds can accurately identify another child's sex (Egan & Perry, 2001). Not surprisingly, knowledge of gender comes with preferences concerning gender: When little girls are asked to indicate their favorite toys, they tend to list dolls, stuffed animals, and educational activities, but when little boys are asked about their favorites, in contrast, they tend to list manipulative toys, vehicles, and action figures as their favorites (e.g., Cherney & London, 2006).

These gender differences, if anything, seem to increase with age. As children outgrow toys, other gendered products come in, like TV programs. Preferences for masculine and feminine television programming emerge in children and become stronger over time. This means that adults have even more gaps between what men and women watch than children do (Cherney & London, 2006).

These emergent gender beliefs also have long-term consequences. When Levy, Sadovsky, and Troseth (2000) asked children to predict their future happiness levels if they chose different occupations, they found that stereotypical ideas about gender largely influenced these predictions. Boys expected to be happier in stereotypically male-dominated fields (e.g., mechanic; airplane pilot) and girls expected to be happier in female-dominated ones (e.g., clothing designer; secretary).

Internal Environments

Although the focus of this chapter (and this book) is on socially contracted cultural phenomena, it is still important to acknowledge the role of internal biological and physical factors, particularly in the context of gender development. Biological sex differences exist at the level of genes, neurotransmitters, hormones, brain structures, and brain functions/circuits (Zahn-Waxler, Crick, Shirtcliff, & Woods, 2006). Prenatal exposure to testosterone can account for a variety of biological, physical, and psychological differences—for example, those related to disinhibition, empathy, sociality, maturation, and stress (Zahn-Waxler, Shirtcliff, & Marceau, 2008). Sex differences also emerge in terms of brain function and size: Not only are boys' brains about 10 times larger in volume overall, but differences also emerge in terms of the relative size of different structures, including the amygdala and the hippocampus (Durston et al., 2001). Over the course of development, the time line for brain growth also varies between boys and girls; for girls, the frontal cortex, the site of judgment and decision-making, develops faster than for boys (Zahn-Waxler et al., 2008).

External Environments

External cues also matter. Media are an obvious and major source of gender socialization, especially for teenage girls. In a study on the most widely covered topics among magazines geared toward female adolescents, researchers found that the most popular features centered around physical appearance, including fashion and beauty (Willemsen, 1998). In addition, there was also a strong focus on how to appeal to the opposite gender; in contrast, for men, the focus was on feature articles regarding a wide range of topics, like celebrities, hobbies, and sex (Willemsen, 1998).

Defining Gender versus Sex

Like race, culture, and ethnicity, "gender" and "sex" have also been used interchangeably, but they reflect distinct concepts. **Sex** refers to biological characteristics, whereas **gender** refers to the social, cultural, and other psychological features that are typically associated with being male or female (Wester & Trepal, 2008, and see Insight Box 4.1). Despite these distinctions, when scholars

---

INSIGHT BOX 4.1

Men's Problems; Women's Problems

Back in the 1990s, a self-proclaimed relationship counselor by the name of John Gray released a ridiculously popular book titled *Men Are from Mars, Women Are from Venus*. His message was so well received that it spawned a one-man, off-Broadway play, a number of sequels, and a coveted spot on *USA Today*'s Best-Selling Books list after selling more than nine million copies (McClurg, 2013). In it, he argues that marital happiness requires understanding the differences between men and women in terms of how we communicate and what we need. The basic concept was both simple and wildly accepted: Men and women are so different that it's essentially like being from two different planets.

Gray focused on gender differences—for example, how women complain about problems because they want validation, while men complain about problems because they are looking for solutions. It didn't matter that the author received his training from a discredited and now defunct (i.e., nonexistent) school that was shut down by the California Board of Education ("John Gray's Life Story," n.d.). His narrative of gender was compelling, and people believed him.

Lest you think this is a 1990s phenomenon that has since become outdated, go and watch the viral "Nail in the Head" YouTube video (https://www.youtube.com/watch?v=-4EDhdAHrOg) that has spawned over 14 million views. As you'll see, this relatively recent YouTube sensation endorses virtually the same ideas about the nature of men versus women endorsed by Gray himself two decades prior, and before him, the author of *I'm Glad I'm a Boy! I'm Glad I'm a Girl!*. The problem with these messages is that although they imply a model of gender differences—where men and women are overwhelmingly distinct—the actual science suggests that, if anything, men and women are more alike than anything else (photo 4.2, and see the section "How Different Are Men and Women, Really?").

PHOTO 4.2. Men versus women: really that different?

Source: iStock

discuss **sexual identity**, they typically refer to a process that involves both gender and sex—one that can start with recognition of sexual norms based on one's sex, followed by a more elaborate process of coming to terms with how that fits or does not fit with other experiences and preferences (Howard, 2000); these ultimately can result in identifying oneself as, for example, heterosexual, lesbian, gay, or bisexual, to name several. **Gender identity**, on the other hand, typically refers to the self-schemas people adopt that are based on perceptions of femaleness and maleness (Howard, 2000). In other words, gender identity can change and doesn't necessarily need to match a person's biological sex; gender expression, in turn, is about how the person decides to express and communicate his or her gender with the outside world (Aleshire, 2016).

Additional gender terms also exist to more accurately capture the nuances of gender identity. **Cisgender** is the term used when a person's gender identity and expression are identical to his or her biological gender, or the gender assigned at birth (Aleshire, 2016). This is the most common type of gender identity (Tate, Ledbetter, & Youssef, 2013). **Transgender** is used to describe those whose birth gender and current gender identity are not one and the same; similarly **genderqueer** is the term used to refer to those who prefer to move beyond existing gender categories (Tate et al., 2012).

Beyond gender terms, there are also various types of sexual orientations, including **bisexual** (i.e., attracted to both sexes); **asexual** (attracted to neither sex); **gay** or **lesbian** (i.e., attracted to the same sex); and **pansexual** (i.e., when a person's attraction is not limited by the person's biological sex, gender, or identity; Aleshire, 2016). Research on individuals attracted to the same sex have often relied on neurohormonal theories of sexual orientation, or the idea that differences in brain structures drive differential preferences for the sex of one's mate (Ellis & Ames, 1987; for a review, see Bailey, Gaulin, Agyei, & Gladue, 1994); other research has also shown that sexual orientation predicts different levels of sex hormones (i.e., testosterone, estradiol, progesterone; Juster et al., 2016), which can have complex effects on mating preferences (Bailey et al., 1994).

APPLYING WHAT WE KNOW: GENDERED TOYS

Get together with several other people and have everyone shop online for a (hypothetical) child who is celebrating his or her fifth birthday. Half of you should shop for a girl and the other half for a boy (photo 4.3); for consistency, everyone should choose a toy in a predetermined range (e.g., $10–20). Afterward, compare your answers. Then respond to and discuss the following:

• What influenced your decision to pick the toy you chose?

• What toys did you play with as a child, and how did this influence your choice?

• Was your choice influenced by your parents, the media, or other sources?

PHOTO 4.3. Decision-making about gifts for a children's birthday: a classic gender dilemma?

Source: iStock

How Different Are Men and Women, Really?

The short answer is: not that different. Based on decades of evidence, a meta-analysis by Hyde (1990) on psychological gender differences found that the majority of studies found nonexistent (30%) to small gender differences (48%). Only a small minority of studies found moderate (15%) or large differences (8%) between men and women (Hyde, 1990). As always, though, the answer still largely depends on the domain at hand. Below, gender differences (or the lack thereof) in different areas are outlined.

Gender Differences in Cognition

Men and Math When I was in college, my roommate, Vania, once bought a tank top with the simple logo: "I'm too pretty to do math." It was pink and stretchy and she never dared wear it in public, perhaps for fear of backlash. Still, that sentiment reflects one of the most longstanding and often stereotyped disparities between men and women that centers on one particular type of cognitive ability: the ability to do things with numbers. The assumption held privately in the hearts of many— and reflected very publicly in the gender distribution of many real classes—is the notion that math is a gendered thing, something men are more likely to be good at than women.

The evidence suggests otherwise. A meta-analysis by Hyde (1990) of 100 studies of math performance, based on data collected on more than three million participants across three decades, revealed no major differences between men and women in math performance. In elementary and middle school, the pattern went counter to expectation, with girls being slightly better at computation; it was only starting in high school that boys showed a slight edge in problem solving (Hyde, 1990). If anything, gender differences that were found decreased over the years, suggesting that whatever gender differences do exist when it comes to math have little to do with any underlying fixed or biological differences between being male versus being female (Hyde, 1990).

Women and Verbal Ability

If the stereotype is that men are better at math, then the converse stereotype is that women are better at verbal ability. If men are known for their exceptional ability to do mysterious things with numbers, then women are equally known for their exceptional capacity to talk at will, constantly, and without fail. Yet the evidence for this purported female exceptionalism when it comes to all things verbal is also lacking. A different meta-analysis on gender and verbal ability revealed that women's advantage over men was slight even when looking at various forms of verbal ability (Hyde & Linn, 1988). Whether in reading comprehension or speech or vocabulary, any distinctions between men and women were small at best (Hyde & Linn, 1988).

Gender Difference in Emotion As with cognition, common assumptions about gender differences between men and women in emotional matters abound. Women are often touted as more "emotional" than men, and this is one of the strongest, most prevalent gender stereotypes that exist (Timmers, Fischer, & Manstead, 2003)—so much so that it has been labeled a "master stereotype" (Shields, 2003, as cited in Evers, Fischer, & Manstead, 2011). Regardless of a person's gender, age, or cultural ethnic background, it appears that people everywhere hold the assumption that women are more emotional than men (Hess, Blairy, & Peck, 2000).

Although conventional wisdom rarely gets into the specifics of what this greater emotionality looks like or means (emotional as in more facially expressive, more bodily and nonverbal, more intense in subjective experience, more physiologically reactive, or better regulators of their feelings?), the science has accumulated quite specific evidence for the particular ways in which men and women differ.

Expressivity In terms of **emotional expressiveness**, the evidence is pretty clear: Relative to men, women are more likely to outwardly display what they are feeling on the inside. Women say they are more expressive themselves (Gross & John, 1995), are more accurate at communicating their feelings (Wagner, Buck, & Winterbotham, 1993), exhibit greater EMG (i.e., electromyography, which measures electrical signals of the brain) responses (Lang, Greenwald, Bradley, & Hamm, 1993), and smile and gesture more (Barr & Kleck, 1995). This gender difference also appears to be diffuse and is widespread across different types of emotion—regardless of whether you are looking at sadness or happiness, fear or disgust, surprise or anger, women consistently tend to be more expressive (for review, see Kring & Gordon, 1998).

Experience This difference in expressiveness begs a deeper question: Do men and women differ in how they display feelings because of actual differences in what they feel inside, and if so, how much? On this topic of **emotional experience** the evidence is far more mixed (in other words, we don't really know). Some studies suggest that women not only express more but also experience more emotion (e.g., Gross & Levenson, 1993); other studies find that no differences in experienced emotion exist between men and women (e.g., Cupchik & Poulos, 1984; Kring & Gordon, 1998).

Differences in experience among boys and girls are clearer. Relative to boys, girls seem to be more likely to experience other people's feelings and feel remorse after they've done something wrong (McClure, 2000; Zahn-Waxler et al., 2006). At the same time, they also experience more fear, anxiety, guilt, shame, and sadness (Else-Quest, Hyde, Goldsmith, & Van Hulle, 2006).

Regulation Related to emotional experience is the question of **emotion regulation**, or how people calibrate and change their emotional response. Relative to men, women are more likely to dwell or ruminate on their feelings, focusing on their internal states and engaging in passive responses to them; men, on the other hand, are more likely to suppress or avoid undesirable feelings (Tamres et al., 2002; Nolen-Hoeksema, 2011). Meta-analysis of more than 2,000 participants has shown that women consistently report higher levels of **rumination** in the face of distress, and this pattern emerges for both adolescents and adults (Tamres, Janicki, & Helgeson, 2002). Laboratory studies have only confirmed these self-reported differences: When male and female students, made to feel sad, were given a choice between a task that involved focusing on their feelings versus not doing so, women overwhelmingly opted for the emotion-focused task; only half of the men chose similarly (Butler & Nolen-Hoeksema, 1994).

Other studies have found that women are more likely to engage in other emotion-regulation strategies beyond just rumination. They like to do wishful thinking, seek social support, and turn to religion in the face of distress. Interestingly, women also reported using effective regulation techniques like reappraisal, problem-focused coping, and distraction; in fact, there was not a single emotion-regulation strategy that men reported using more than women did (Tamres et al., 2002).

The same emotion-regulation strategy may also look different for males and females. Take **social support**, for example. When women seek the company of others to cope with distress, it's typically in the form of emotional support through verbal self-disclosure (Nolen-Hoeksema, 2012). In contrast, when men seek social support, they tend to engage in shared activities, a difference that emerges in childhood (Zarbatany, McDougall, & Hymel, 2000). This type of invisible and practical support—that is, support that is given when the people involved are not consciously aware of it—appears to benefit men more than women (Bolger & Amarel, 2007; Howland & Simpson, 2010).

Perception and Accuracy If women are more expressive, experience their emotions more strongly, and regulate their emotions more, then does this mean they are also better at perceiving the emotions of other people? Here the evidence is mixed. From an early age, girls do pay more attention to emotions and appear to understand them better (Zahn-Waxler et al., 2008). They report being more concerned about, and aware of, other people's feelings (McClure, 2000) as well as more impacted by what other people are feeling (Fritz & Helgeson, 1998).

Some studies have suggested that this concern for others' feelings leads to greater accuracy in perceiving emotions in others — a phenomenon known as **empathic accuracy**. Klein and Hodges (2001) found evidence of gender differences in empathic accuracy between men and women, with women being more accurate at detecting a stranger's feelings than men were. They inferred that this was primarily driven by differences in motivation (rather than ability), so in a follow-up study, they gave participants monetary incentives—people could earn up to eight dollars if they were accurate at guessing the target's feelings. Money increased accuracy for both men and women, thereby eliminating the gender difference. Other studies, however, have found no gender differences (e.g., Ma-Kellams & Blascovich, 2013), so the evidence remains mixed as to whether gender truly predicts greater accuracy in detecting others' feelings.

Physiology Finally, there is the issue of whether men and women differ in terms of their **physiological reactions** to emotion. Once again, the findings are mixed. Some data suggest that women, by virtue of their expressiveness, are more likely to externalize their emotion and experience less internal changes, whereas men, who are not likely to rely on external displays, are more likely to internalize and thereby undergo greater bodily changes (Buck, Miller, & Caul, 1974). Other studies suggest that this difference depends on the type of emotion at hand—Kring and Gordon (1998), for example, found that men reacted more strongly physiologically to fear (in this case, they exhibited greater skin conductance reactivity). Other studies have found no sex differences at all (Kelly, Tyrka, Anderson, Price, & Carpenter, 2008; Vrana & Rollock, 2002).

Recent studies in neuroimaging have tried to clarify these mixed results but have revealed more inconsistent findings. Some studies have found that men exhibit greater amygdala activity than women did (Hamann, Herman, Nolan, & Wallen, 2004; Schienle, Schafer, Stark, Walter, & Vaitl, 2005)—the amygdala being part of the fast, emotional, limbic structure in the center of your brain—whereas other studies have failed to find this difference (Wager, Phan, Liberzon, & Taylor, 2003). Still other studies have found that men show less brain activity in response to emotional situations than women, with less activity in areas like the amygdala, the prefrontal cortex (which is involved in emotion regulation), and the ventral striatum (which is involved in reward processing; McRae, Ochsner, Mauss, Gabrieli, & Gross, 2008).

Gender Differences in Psychopathology

When it comes to psychopathology, gender differences between men and women are relatively clear: Women are more likely than men to be diagnosed with a variety of disorders.

Feeling (Mood) Disorders

Women are prone to higher rates of most feeling disorders. Gender differences in the "common cold" of feeling disorders—that is, depression—start to emerge in adolescence. Depression is rare in childhood and with little difference in frequency between boys and girls; by the teenage years, however, girls are two to three times more likely to be diagnosed with depression than boys (Zahn-Waxler et al., 2006). However, other studies suggest that this relationship may be moderated by other factors, like age and other risk factors. For example, rates of depression appear to be somewhat different over time, but more so for boys than girls (Twenge & Nolen-Hoeksema, 2002).

Beyond these differences in unipolar depression (Kessler, Merikangas, & Wang, 2007), women are also more likely to exhibit every anxiety disorder except obsessive-compulsive disorder, or OCD (e.g., generalized anxiety disorder, panic disorder, etc.; McLean & Anderson, 2009). Anxiety disorders typically peak during the teenage years but may emerge earlier on; yet, irrespective of the time line, they are more common in teenage girls than boys (Zahn-Waxler, Shirtcliff, & Marceau, 2008).

Personality Disorders Women are also more likely to be diagnosed with borderline personality disorder (Lenzenweger, 2008). Antisocial disorders, in contrast, are more common in boys than girls (Zahn-Waxler et al., 2008). However, some research suggests that men and women with personality disorders might exhibit their disorders differently; consistent with this idea, studies show that men with borderline personality disorder tend also to exhibit drug-dependent and narcissistic tendencies (in addition to being more likely to be antisocial), whereas women tend to exhibit more links with trauma and PTSD (for review, see Johnson et al., 2003). Other research suggests that gender stereotypes may also play a role in the diagnostic process (Nehls, 1998).

Eating Disorders, Substance Abuse Disorders, and Risky Behaviors Women are more likely to have eating disorders (Striegel-Moore, Seeley, & Lewinsohn, 2003). Recent work by Chao, Grilo, and Sinha (2016) found, for example, that the link between having food cravings and exhibiting eating disorders was stronger for women than for men; moreover, women were more likely to crave sugary foods, especially if they were overweight.

Men, in contrast, are more likely to be diagnosed with disorders related to alcohol abuse (Keyes, Grant, & Hasin, 2008). This is largely consistent with the finding that men are more likely to engage in risky behaviors in a variety of contexts, including recreational and health/safety ones (Harris, Jenkins, & Glaser, 2006). However, more recent studies have found that, among women, abusing drugs was more linked to antisocial behaviors relative to men (Schulz, Murphy, & Verona, 2016).

Behavioral and Developmental Disorders A variety of behavioral and developmental disorders are more common among males, especially teenage males. These include antisocial behaviors, autism, developmental language disorders, attention deficit hyperactivity disorders, and dyslexia (Rutter, Caspi, & Moffitt, 2003; see also Zahn-Waxler et al., 2008). In other words, among children, boys are more likely to be diagnosed with a disorder than girls; these disorders primarily center around behavior, language, attention, reading, and sociality.

Conduct disorders (CD) are characterized by repeat breaking of social norms and inattention to other people's rights (American Psychiatric Association, 2013). People with CD tend to be aggressive toward others (people and animals) and likely to engage in nonnormative behaviors like stealing, lying, and property destruction. Personality-wise, they tend to be more impulsive, hostile, and less empathic. Males are more likely to have CD than females (Maughan, Rowe, Messer, Goodman, & Meltzer, 2004), although the rates for females are substantial (Keenan, Loeber, & Green, 1999). Other studies have suggested that despite the gender differences in prevalence, the patterns of association (e.g., between CD and other maladaptive behaviors or disorders) are similar across men and women (Marmorstein & Iacono, 2003).

Explanations There are a variety of reasons why males and females experience differential likelihoods of being diagnosed with different mental illness. Broadly speaking, these may relate to

- different levels of the same environmental risk factors
- susceptibility to different environmental risk factors
- underlying biological or genetic differences
- unique gene-environment interactions (Zahn-Waxler et al., 2008).

As an illustrative example, women who have been exposed to violence are especially likely to develop mood disorders (e.g., depression, anxiety; Walsh, Keyes, Koenen, & Hasin, 2015). Furthermore, they are also more likely to develop substance abuse issues, a phenomenon that is typically more common among men (Walsh et al., 2015). One explanation suggests that the reason mood disorders are more prevalent among women whereas antisocial disorder and substance abuse are more common among men is that women might be more likely to internalize their problems, whereas men are more prone to externalize them (Eaton et al., 2012). Along similar lines, others have argued that even when faced with the same disorder (e.g., depression), men are more likely to take an active stance to cope with their symptoms (e.g., trying to distract themselves) whereas women are more likely to take a passive stance (e.g., ruminating); these differences in response can, in turn, exacerbate the depression for women but alleviate the state for men (Nolen-Hoeksema, 1987).

Social forces also matter. Parenting studies have found that coercive, cold mothers and disruptive family life tend to be linked to more aggressive and behaviorally problematic boys but less aggressive girls (Cole, Teti, & Zahn-Waxler, 2003; Davies & Windle, 1997; and McFadyen-Ketchum et al., 1996, as cited by Zahn-Waxler et al., 2008). To further amplify this difference, teenage girls are more responsive to parenting attempts to correct nonnormative behaviors (Griffin et al., 2000; see also Zahn-Waxler et al., 2008). When women become parents themselves, other studies suggest that they are especially prone to experience stress associated with parenting, more so than men (Simon, 1992). These differences in vulnerability to stress from parenting, in turn, can explain why women experience higher levels of psychological distress than men do (Simon, 1992).

Beyond family life, societal pressures may also play a role. A classic explanation for why women are depressed more often than men is the notion of the

gender-intensification hypothesis, which says that female stereotypes create women that are dependent, highly emotional, passive, helpless, and sacrificial, which, taken together, produces a perfect cocktail for depression (Hill & Lynch, 1983; see also Zahn-Waxler et al., 2008). Consistent with this idea, studies have shown that teenage girls report experiencing more challenges associated with adolescence than boys do, and this accounts for differences in depression (Petersen, Sarigiani, & Kennedy, 1991). However, more recent work has not found evidence for this idea; it has shown instead that teenage boys and girls show similar levels of masculinity (e.g., Priess, Lindberg, & Hyde, 2009).

Another idea that has come out of these patterns is that gender differences in emotion regulation may account for these differences in feeling disorders. Mediation analyses testing the underlying mechanisms behind these group differences based on data from a large community sample found that gender differences in rumination explained why women were more likely to be depressed than men (Nolen-Hoeksema & Aldao, 2011). In other words, women dwell and ruminate on their problems more often than men do, and this explains their higher rates of depression.

At the same time, other emotion-regulation strategies that men rely on appear to explain their greater incidence of alcohol-related disorders. Namely, the fact that men are more likely to rely on alcohol as a coping strategy can explain why men experience more alcohol problems than women do (Nolen-Hoeskema & Aldao, 2011).

Beyond these psychosocial forces, genetic and biological factors may play a role. Given that gender differences in anxiety tend to emerge early (i.e., in childhood and adolescence), it is possible that biological factors may play an important role in their emergence. To this end, efforts to use psychosocial factors to account for gender differences in anxiety disorders have not been consistently successful—even when holding a host of psychosocial factors constant (e.g., as related to stress, self-esteem, coping, social support, health, etc.), gender differences still persisted (Lewinsohn, Gotlib, Lewinsohn, Seeley, & Allen, 1998). This suggests that social and psychological factors may not be able to fully explain gender differences in psychopathologies like anxiety disorder.

Finally, **comorbidity** may also play a crucial role. As with mental illness more generally, having one disorder puts a person at a greater risk of having another. Thus one possibility is that depression and anxiety are especially likely to co-occur, but apparently only among females (Lewinsohn, Zinbarg, Seeley, Lewinsohn, & Sack, 1997; see also Zahn-Waxler et al., 2008). If so, then the greater likelihood of women getting depression may simply be the by-product of women's greater likelihood of experiencing anxiety. Moreover, relative to men, women with anxiety disorders are also more likely to be diagnosed with not just depression, but other anxiety disorders and bulimia (McLean, Asnaani, Litz, & Hofmann, 2011). Other related studies have shown that women (but not men) with OCD are also more likely to exhibit panic disorder (Lensi et al., 1996). These comorbidity trends have been documented in young women as well: Antisocial and aggressive girls tend to be depressed, attention-deficient, hyperactive, anxious, and prone to substance abuse and somatization as well (Loeber & Keenan, 1994; see also Zahn-Waxler et al., 2008). In other words, when women have disorders, they tend to have them in multiples.

Gender Differences in Life Outcomes and Achievement

The question of gender differences in life outcomes and achievement is a matter of whether you want the good news or the bad news.

The good news is this: Women today have opportunities that were unknown to women in previous eras of human history. The percentage of females in fields previously dominated by men—like medicine, business, and law—are much higher than they were 20 years ago (U.S. Bureau of Labor Statistics, 2015).

The bad news is much more complex. To this day, at least in the United States, women tend to earn less money than men for the same work; as of 2016, females were still being paid 77 cents for the male dollar (U.S. Bureau of Labor Statistics, 2015).

Outside the United States and other Western contexts, prospects for women are often worse, and relative to boys, teenage girls have far fewer educational and occupational opportunities. Not only are girls less likely than boys to go to a secondary school but they hold lower literacy rates, are less representative in governments worldwide (holding approximately only 22% of seats in parliaments), and have higher rates of unemployment (World Bank, 2015).

Female Advantage in Grades First, a disclaimer: Ability and outcomes are not identical. Aforementioned tests of cognitive ability have largely found a small but reliable pattern of male advantage in math and female advantage in verbal ability. In these studies, ability is usually measured by cognitive tests or standardized national test scores. Outcomes, on the other hand, refer to results—grades, diplomas, jobs, salaries. In a perfectly rational world, abilities and outcomes would be highly, if not perfectly, correlated. By now, though, you don't need me to tell you that we don't live in such a world.

If female ability reflects higher aptitude with all things verbal and male ability reflects a higher aptitude with all things math, then the ironic outcome is this: Females almost always do better when it comes to educational outcomes—namely, grades. A recent meta-analysis by Voyer and Voyer (2004) of over 300 samples revealed a consistent and stable tendency for girls and women to get higher grades than boys and men. The largest difference was in language classes and the smallest difference was in math; moreover, most of these differences emerged in middle and high school; by the time students reached graduate school, this female advantage disappeared (Voyer & Voyer, 2004) (photo 4.4). These effects stayed stable over time and were replicated in non-U.S. samples, although the size of the difference was somewhat smaller in Scandinavian countries (relative to the United States; Voyer & Voyer, 2014). Other studies have found that countries with more gender equality generally tend to exhibit smaller gender differences in performance, at least when it comes to commonly stereotyped domains like math (Else-Quest et al., 2010).

This female advantage even extends to college. In the United States, more women than men have been getting college degrees (Bauman, 2016), and this trend started back at the middle of the century (Charles & Luoh, 2003). Outside the United States, this difference is most pronounced among highly developed countries (i.e., countries with at least median-level incomes). Worldwide, this pattern really started to emerge among these nations by the 1970s (Becker, Hubbard, & Murphy, 2010). In these relatively developed countries—that is, nations that

PHOTO 4.4. A female advantage in school appears to extend through secondary school and college but end afterward.

Source: iStock

are members of OECD, or the Organization for Economic Cooperation and Development—women make up about 58% of the incoming class of college students (OECD, 2015). Not only are they more likely to enroll but they also make up the majority of the graduating class (with the only exceptions being Japan and Germany, where the gender balance is equal—50% of graduates are men; Flabbi, 2011).

These findings fly in the face of long-held stereotypes about men and women being good at different things (i.e., math and science)—given that, at least when it comes to grades, women appear to be better overall. Although these gender differences were still on the small side, they nevertheless debunk common ideas about females struggling in math classes. Furthermore, given that these findings are not new—researchers like Kimball have found these effects since the late 1980s—they beg the question of why common knowledge has been so slow to catch up with the empirical evidence.

It is also interesting to consider how these patterns fit in with what we've long known about various aspects of stereotypes. When a person from a stereotyped group becomes aware of (or reminded of) the stereotype, this awareness will often impact the person's performance—a phenomenon classically known as **stereotype threat** (Steele & Aronson, 1995). For example, in the context of gender, this would mean that a female who has to indicate her gender at the beginning of a math test would not perform to the best of her ability. Being reminded of her gender would also remind her of the negative stereotypes about women and math (Spencer, Steele, & Quinn, 1999). In the "original" version of the stereotype threat phenomenon, performance is usually hurt by this knowledge of a (negative) stereotype (Steele & Aronson, 1995). In the context of gender and grades, kids as young as four to seven years old apparently hold the belief that adults consider girls to be better students; having this negative stereotype against them, in turn, made boys perform worse, at least in domains like reading and writing (Hartley & Sutton, 2013). Studies have also found that the opposite phenomenon can also occur—that is, **stereotype lift**, when a group member performs better because of a positive stereotype that applies to him or her (Walton & Cohen, 2003).

Disparities in Higher Education and Beyond Even though more women are attending and graduating from college than men, the kind of college majors they choose and the careers they end up in are not identical. Studies of data from developed countries show that women consistently are congregating in fields related to humanities and health, whereas men constitute the majority in the sciences (Flabbi, 2011). In terms of how well they end up doing in these majors, grades are rather hard to compare across countries (different countries use different scoring systems, with distinct distributions), but overall, there is a slight tendency for women to do better than men, with the exception being Japan and the U.K. (where women do worse), and Italy, the Netherlands, and Estonia (where women do substantially better; Flabbi, 2011).

The gaps only get bigger after college graduation. This same data set of developed countries shows that not all college degrees result in a job after graduation, and about 4% of men are out of the labor force or unemployed versus 2.5 times that percentage, 10%, for women (Flabbi, 2011). Although the precise differences vary by country, the pattern is identical: More women than men in every country end up doing nothing (at least in the workplace) with their college degree. In addition to the likelihood of having a job, even among the employed, there is a consistent difference: Women everywhere earn less than men. Sometimes it's 18.5% less (in Portugal) and other times it's 3% less (in Belgium), but for every country, the pattern is once again identical, with the advantage going to men (Flabbi, 2011). Moreover, these differences in earning can't be explained by men and women going into different fields (Flabbi, 2011).

Beyond pay and employment status, what kind of jobs do women versus men end up in? Apparently the answer is simple: Women become teachers; men become professionals. If you majored in the humanities and you're female, you have an overwhelming likelihood of becoming a teacher—70% of women do so, compared to 50% of men (Flabbi, 2011). If you majored in the sciences and you're male, you're likely to become a professional in your field—55% of men do so, relative to only 33% of women (Flabbi, 2011).

The Good News The great thing about culture is that it's dynamic: You're not stuck with it. As you change, so does your culture. Gender equality is a moral imperative, but a moral imperative with economic benefits. Theoretically and abstractly, it's about fairness and equality; practically, it's about increasing well-being and prosperity.

A report by OECD cites lack of access to childcare, penalties for career disruptions due to child-rearing, and the gender gap in terms of who does the housework as primary reasons why the gains women have made in education have not translated to equality in the workforce. Sure, women are going to school and doing well, but a college degree and a perfect transcript matter little if they are soon stuck doing the majority of the dishes or single-handedly caring for children, or if their employers fail to promote them after they've taken an extended leave of absence for giving birth or caring for aging parents. At the same time, they're more likely to work part-time (which pays less) in addition to doing unpaid work (again: dishes, children); they're also less likely to become entrepreneurs (OECD, 2012).

But here is the good news: Increasing women's participation in the workforce could benefit everyone involved. In a recent McKinsey report, narrowing the gender gap by doing things like increasing paid parental leave for both men and women, providing more childcare options, and supporting care for elderly or disabled family members would increase the number of women who could be in the labor market and help families with work-life balance (Sahadi, 2016). Ultimately this would boost the U.S. economy by upward of $2.1 trillion in GDP (Sahadi, 2016). Far from a dream of a utopian future, it's a picture of what equality looks like—with benefits.

Key Concepts

Sex vs. gender
Sexual vs. gender identity
Cisgender, transgender, genderqueer
Bisexual, asexual, gay, lesbian, pansexual
Emotional expressiveness vs. experience
Emotion regulation
Rumination
Social support
Empathic accuracy
Physiological reactions (to emotion)
Gender-intensification hypothesis
Comorbidity
Stereotype threat vs. lift

References

Aleshire, M. E. (2016). Sexual orientation, gender identity, and gender expression: What are they? *The Journal for Nurse Practitioners*, 12(7), e329–e330. doi:10.1016/j.nurpra.2016.03.016

American Psychiatric Association (2013). "Conduct Disorder." Retrieved from https://www.psychiatry.org/File%20Library/Psychiatrists/Practice/DSM/APA_DSM-5-Conduct-Disorder.pdf

Bailey, J. M., Gaulin, S., Agyei, Y., & Gladue, B. A. (1994). Effects of gender and sexual orientation on evolutionarily relevant aspects of human mating psychology. *Journal of Personality and Social Psychology, 66*(6), 1081–1093.

Barr, C. L., & Kleck, R. E. (1995). Self-other perception of the intensity of facial expressions of emotion: Do we know what we show? *Journal of Personality and Social Psychology, 68* (4), 608–618. doi:10.1037/0022-3514.68.4.608

Bauman, K. (2016). College completion by cohort, age and gender, 1967–2015. U.S. Census Bureau. Retrieved from https://www.census.gov/content/dam/Census/library/working-papers/2016/demo/SEHSD-WP2016-04.pdf

Becker, G. S., Hubbard, W. H., & Murphy, K. M. (2010). Explaining the worldwide boom in higher education of women. *Journal of Human Capital, 4*(3), 203–241.

Bolger, N., & Amarel, D. (2007). Effects of social support visibility on adjustment to stress: Experimental evidence. *Journal of Personality and Social Psychology, 92*(3), 458–475. doi:10.1037/0022-3514.92.3.458

Buck, R., Miller, R. E., & Caul, W. F. (1974). Sex, personality and physiological variables in the communication of affect via facial expression. *Journal of Personality and Social Psychology, 30*(4), 587–96. doi:10.1037/h0037041

Butler, L. D., & Nolen-Hoeksema, S. (1994). Gender differences in responses to depressed mood in a college sample. *Sex Roles, 30*(5-6), 331–346. doi:10.1007/BF01420597

Caldera, Y. M., Huston, A. C., & O'Brien, M. (1989). Social interactions and play patterns of parents and toddlers with feminine, masculine, and neutral toys. *Child Development*, 70–76.

Callis, A. S. (2014). Bisexual, pansexual, queer: Non-binary identities and the sexual borderlands. *Sexualities, 17*(1-2), 63–80. doi:10.1177/1363460713511094

Chao, A. M., Grilo, C. M., & Sinha, R. (2016). Food cravings, binge eating, and eating disorder psychopathology: Exploring the moderating roles of gender and race. *Eating Behaviors, 21*, 41–47. Retrieved from http://doi.org/10.1016/j.eatbeh.2015.12.007

Charles, K. K., & Luoh, M. C. (2003). Gender differences in completed schooling. *Review of Economics and Statistics, 85*(3), 559–577.

Cherney, I. D., & London, K. (2006). Gender-linked differences in the toys, television shows, computer games, and outdoor activities of 5- to 13-year-old-children. *Sex Roles, 54*(9- 10), 717–726. doi:10.1007/s11199-006-9037-8

Cole, P. M, Teti, L. O., & Zahn-Waxler, C. (2003). Mutual emotion regulation and the stability of conduct problems between preschool and early school age. *Development and Psychopathology, 15*(1), 1–18. doi:10.1017/S0954579403000014

Cupchik, G. C., & Poulos, C. X. (1984). Judgments of emotional intensity in self and others: The effects of stimulus, context, sex, and expressivity. *Journal of Personality and Social Psychology, 46*(2), 431–439. doi:10.1037/0022-3514.46.2.431

Cyranowski, J. M., Frank, E., Young, E., & Shear, M. K. (2000). Adolescent onset of the gender difference in lifetime rates of major depression: A theoretical model. *Archives of General Psychiatry, 57*(1), 21–27.

Davies, P. T., & Windle, M. (1997). Gender-specific pathways between maternal depressive symptoms, family discord, and adolescent adjustment. *Developmental Psychology, 33*(4), 657–668. doi:10.1037/0012-1649.33.4.657

Durston, S., Pol, H. E. H., Casey, B. J., Giedd, J. N., Buitelaar, J. K., & Van Engeland, H. (2001). Anatomical MRI of the developing human brain: What have we learned? *Journal of the American Academy of Child & Adolescent Psychiatry, 40*(9), 1012–1020.

Eaton, N. R., Keyes, K. M., Krueger, R. F., Balsis, S., Skodol, A. E., Markon, K. E., . . . Hasin, D. S. (2012). An invariant dimensional liability model of gender differences in mental disorder prevalence: Evidence from a national sample. *Journal of Abnormal Psychology, 121*(1), 282–288. doi:1 0.1037/a0024780

Egan, S. K., & Perry, D. G. (2001). Gender identity: A multidimensional analysis with implications for psychosocial adjustment. *Developmental Psychology*, *37*(4), 451–463.

Ellis, L., & Ames, M. A. (1987). Neurohormonal functioning and sexual orientation: A theory of homosexuality–heterosexuality. *Psychological Bulletin*, *101*(2), 233–258.

Else-Quest, N. M., Hyde, J., Goldsmith, H. H., & Van Hulle, C. A. (2006). Gender differences in temperament: A meta-analysis. *Psychological Bulletin*, *132*(1), 33–72. doi: 10.1037/0033- 2909.132.1.33

Else-Quest, N. M., Hyde, J. S., & Linn, M. C. (2010). Cross-national patterns of gender differences in mathematics: A meta-analysis. *Psychological Bulletin*, *136*(1), 103–127. doi:10.1037/a0018053

Evers, C., Fischer, A. H., & Manstead, A. S. (2011). Gender and emotion regulation: A social appraisal perspective on anger. In Nyklíček, I., Vingerhoets, A., & Zeelenberg, M. (Eds.), *Emotion regulation and well-being* (pp. 211–222). New York, NY: Springer.

Flabbi, L. (2011). Gender differences in education, career choices, and labor market outcomes on a sample of OECD countries. World Development Report 2012. Retrieved from: http://siteresources.worldbank.org/INTWDR2012/Resources/7778105-1299699968583/7786210-1322671773271/flabi-educ-segregation-and-labor-market-outcomes-REFLEX-march12-2011.pdf

Fritz, H. L., & Helgeson, V. S. (1998). Distinctions of unmitigated communion from communion: Self-neglect and overinvolvement with others. *Journal of Personality and Social Psychology*, *75*(1), 121–140. doi:10.1037/0022-3514.75.1.121

Griffin, K. W., Botvin, G. J., Scheier, L. M., Diaz, T., & Miller, N. L. (2000). Parenting practices as predictors of substance use, delinquency, and aggression among urban minority youth: Moderating effects of family structure and gender. *Psychology of Addictive Behaviors*, *14*(2), 174–184. doi:10.1037/0893-164X.14.2.174

Gross, J. J., & John, O. P. (1995). Facets of emotional expressivity: Three self report factors and their correlates. *Personality and Individual Differences*, *19*(4), 555–568. doi: 10.1016/0191-8869(95)00055-B

Gross, J. J., & Levenson, R. W. (1993). Emotional suppression: Physiology, self report, and expressive behavior. *Journal of Personality and Social Psychology*, *64*(6), 970–986. doi:10.1037/0022-3514.64.6.970

Hamann, S., Herman, R. A., Nolan, C. L., & Wallen, K. (2004). Men and women differ in amygdala response to visual sexual stimuli. *Nature Neuroscience*, *7*(4), 411–416.

Harris, C. R., Jenkins, M., & Glaser, D. (2006). Gender differences in risk assessment: Why do women take fewer risks than men? *Judgment and Decision Making*, *1*(1), 48–63.

Hartley, B. L., & Sutton, R. M. (2013). A stereotype threat account of boys' academic underachievement. *Child Development*, *84*(5), 1716–1733. doi:10.1111/cdev.12079

Hess, U., Blairy, S., & Kleck, R. E. (2000). The influence of facial emotion displays, gender, and ethnicity on judgments of dominance and affiliation. *Journal of Nonverbal Behavior*, *24*(4), 265–283.

Hill, J. P., & Lynch, M. E. (1983). The intensification of gender-related role expectations during early adolescence. In J. Brooks-Gunn & A. Peresen (Eds.), *Girls at puberty: Biological and psychosocial perspectives* (pp. 201–28). New York: Plenum.

Howard, J. A. (2000). Social psychology of identities. *Annual Review of Sociology*, 367–393.

Howland, M., & Simpson, J. A. (2010). Getting in under the radar: A dyadic view of invisible support. *Psychological Science*, *21*(12), 1878–1885. doi: 10.1177/0956797610388817

Hyde, J. S. (1990). Meta-analysis and the psychology of gender differences. *Signs*, *16*(1), 55–73. doi:10.1086/494645

Hyde, J. S. (2005). The Gender Similarities Hypothesis. *American Psychologist*, *60*(6), 581–592. doi:10.1037/0003-066X.60.6.581

Hyde, J. S., & Linn, M. C. (1988). Gender differences in verbal ability: A meta-analysis. *Psychological Bulletin*, *104*(1), 53–69.

John Gray's life story. (n.d.). Retrieved from http://www.marsvenus.com/john-grays-life-story.htm

Johnson, D. M., Shea, M. T., Yen, S., Battle, C. L., Zlotnick, C., Sanislow, C. A., . . . Gunderson, J. G. (2003). Gender differences in borderline personality disorder: Findings from the Collaborative Longitudinal Personality Disorders Study. *Comprehensive Psychiatry*, *44*(4), 284–292.

Juster, R. P., Almeida, D., Cardoso, C., Raymond, C., Johnson, P. J., Pfaus, J. G., . . . Lupien, S. J. (2016). Gonads and strife: Sex hormones vary according to sexual orientation for women and stress indices for both sexes. *Psychoneuroendocrinology*, *72*, 119–130.

Keenan, K., Loeber, R., & Green, S. (1999). Conduct disorder in girls: A review of the literature. *Clinical Child and Family Psychology Review*, *2*(1), 3–19.

Kelly, M. M., Tyrka, A. R., Anderson, G. M., Price, L. H., & Carpenter, L. L. (2008). Sex differences in emotional and physiological responses to the Trier Social Stress Test. *Journal of Behavior Therapy and Experimental Psychiatry*, *39*(1), 87–98.

Kessler, R. C., Merikangas, K. R., & Wang, P. S. (2007). Prevalence, comorbidity, and service utilization for mood disorders in the United States at the beginning of the twenty-first century. *Annual Review of Clinical Psychology*, *3*, 137–158. doi: 10.1146/annurev.clinpsy.3.022806.091444

Keyes, K. M., Grant, B. F., & Hasin, D. S. (2008). Evidence for a closing gender gap in alcohol use, abuse, and dependence in the United States population. *Drug & Alcohol Dependence*, *93*(1), 21–29.

Klein, K. J., & Hodges, S. D. (2001). Gender differences, motivation, and empathic accuracy: When it pays to understand. *Personality and Social Psychology Bulletin*, *27*(6), 720–730.

Kring, A. M., & Gordon, A. H. (1998). Sex differences in emotion: expression, experience, and physiology. *Journal of Personality and Social Psychology*, *74*(3), 686–703.

Lang, P. J., Greenwald, M. K., Bradley, M. M., & Hamm, A. O. (1993). Looking at pictures: Affective, facial, visceral and behavioral reactions. *Psychophysiology*, *30*(3), 261–273. doi:10.1111/1469-8986.ep11656928

Lensi, P., Cassano, G. B., Correddu, G., Ravagli, S., Kunovac, J. L., & Akiskal, H. S. (1996). Obsessive-compulsive disorder. Familial-developmental history, symptomatology, comorbidity and course with special reference to gender-related differences. *The British Journal of Psychiatry*, *169*(1), 101–107.

Lenzenweger, M. F. (2008). Epidemiology of personality disorders. *Psychiatric Clinics of North America*, *31*(3), 395–403. doi:10.1016/j.psc.2008.03.003

Levy, G. D., Sadovsky, A. L., & Troseth, G. L. (2000). Aspects of young children's perceptions of gender-typed occupations. *Sex Roles*, *42*(11-12), 993–1006.

Lewinsohn, P. M., Gotlib, I. H., Lewinsohn, M., Seeley, J. R., & Allen, N. B. (1998). Gender differences in anxiety disorders and anxiety symptoms in adolescents. *Journal of Abnormal Psychology*, *107*(1), 109–117.

Lewinsohn, P. M., Zinbarg, R., Seeley, J. R., Lewinsohn, M., & Sack, W. H. (1997). Lifetime comorbidity among anxiety disorders and between anxiety disorders and other mental disorders in adolescents. *Journal of Anxiety Disorders*, *11*(4), 377–394. doi:10.1016/S0887-6185(97)00017-0

Lightdale, J. R., & Prentice, D. A. (1994). Rethinking sex differences in aggression: Aggressive behavior in the absence of social roles. *Personality and Social Psychology Bulletin*, *20*(1), 34–44. doi:10.1177/0146167294201003

Loeber, R., & Keenan, K. (1994). The interaction between conduct disorder and its comorbid conditions: Effects of age and gender. *Clinical Psychology Review*, *14*(6), 497–523. doi:10.1016/0272-7358(94)90015-9

Ma-Kellams, C., & Blascovich, J. (2013). The ironic effect of financial incentive on empathic accuracy. *Journal of Experimental Social Psychology, 49*(1), 65–71.

Marmorstein, N. R., & Iacono, W. G. (2003). Major depression and conduct disorder in a twin sample: Gender, functioning, and risk for future psychopathology. *Journal of the American Academy of Child & Adolescent Psychiatry, 42*(2), 225–233.

Maughan, B., Rowe, R., Messer, J., Goodman, R., & Meltzer, H. (2004). Conduct disorder and oppositional defiant disorder in a national sample: Developmental epidemiology. *Journal of Child Psychology and Psychiatry, 45*(3), 609–621.

McClurg, J. (2013). John Gray looks back at *Men Are from Mars. USA Today.* Retrieved from https://www.usatoday.com/story/life/books/2013/10/30/men-are-from-mars-women-are-from- venus/3297375/

McLean, C. P., & Anderson, E. R. (2009). Brave men and timid women? A review of the gender differences in fear and anxiety. *Clinical Psychology Review, 29*(6), 496–505.

McLean, C. P., Asnaani, A., Litz, B. T., & Hofmann, S. G. (2011). Gender differences in anxiety disorders: Prevalence, course of illness, comorbidity and burden of illness. *Journal of Psychiatric Research, 45*(8), 1027–1035.

McRae, K., Ochsner, K. N., Mauss, I. B., Gabrieli, J. J., & Gross, J. J. (2008). Gender differences in emotion regulation: An fMRI study of cognitive reappraisal. *Group Processes & Intergroup Relations, 11*(2), 143–162.

Nehls, N. (1998). Borderline personality disorder: Gender stereotypes, stigma, and limited system of care. *Issues in Mental Health Nursing, 19*(2), 97–112.

Nolen-Hoeksema, S. (1987). Sex differences in unipolar depression: Evidence and theory. *Psychological Bulletin, 101*(2), 259–282.

Nolen-Hoeksema, S. (2012). Emotion regulation and psychopathology: The role of gender. *Annual Review of Clinical Psychology, 8*, 161–187.

Nolen-Hoeksema, S., & Aldao, A. (2011). Gender and age differences in emotion regulation strategies and their relationship to depressive symptoms. *Personality and Individual Differences, 51*(6), 704–708.

Nolen-Hoeksema, S., & Girgus, J. S. (1994). Emergence of gender differences in depression during adolescence. *Psychological Bulletin, 115*(3), 424–443.

OECD. (2012). *Closing the Gender Gap.* Retrieved from https://www.oecd.org/gender/Executive%20Summary.pdf

OECD (2015). *Gender gap in education.* Retrieved from http://www.oecd.org/gender/data/gender-gap-in-education.htm

Petersen, A. C., Sarigiani, P. A., & Kennedy, R. E. (1991). Adolescent depression: Why more girls? *Journal of Youth and Adolescence, 20*(2), 247–271.

Priess, H. A., Lindberg, S. M., & Hyde, J. S. (2009). Adolescent Gender-Role Identity and Mental Health: Gender Intensification Revisited. *Child Development, 80*(5), 1531–1544.

Reid, P. T. (2002). Multicultural psychology: Bringing together gender and ethnicity. *Cultural Diversity and Ethnic Minority Psychology, 8*(2), 103–114.

Rutter, M., Caspi, A., & Moffitt, T. E. (2003). Using sex differences in psychopathology to study causal mechanisms: Unifying issues and research strategies. *Journal of Child Psychology and Psychiatry, 44*(8), 1092–1115.

Sahadi, J. (2016, April 7). Closing the gender gap could grow the economy by 2.1 trillion. CNN Money. Retrieved from http://money.cnn.com/2016/04/07/pf/gender-gap-women-work/index.html

Schienle, A., Schäfer, A., Stark, R., Walter, B., & Vaitl, D. (2005). Gender differences in the processing of disgust-and fear-inducing pictures: an fMRI study. *Neuroreport, 16*(3), 277–280.

Schulz, N., Murphy, B., & Verona, E. (2016). Gender differences in psychopathy links to drug use. *Law and Human Behavior*, *40*(2), 159–168. doi:10.1037/lhb0000165

Simon, R. W. (1992). Parental role strains, salience of parental identity and gender differences in psychological distress. *Journal of Health and Social Behavior*, *33*(1), 25–35.

Spencer, S. J., Steele, C. M., & Quinn, D. M. (1999). Stereotype threat and women's math performance. *Journal of Experimental Social Psychology*, *35*(1), 4–28.

Steele, C. M., & Aronson, J. (1995). Stereotype threat and the intellectual test performance of African Americans. *Journal of Personality and Social Psychology*, *69*(5), 797–811. doi:10.1037/0022-3514.69.5.797

Striegel-Moore, R., Seeley, J. R., & Lewinsohn, P. M. (2003). Psychosocial adjustment in young adulthood of women who experienced an eating disorder during adolescence. *Journal of the American Academy of Child & Adolescent Psychiatry*, *42*(5), 587–593. doi: 10.1097/01.CHI.0000046838.90931.44

Tamres, L. K., Janicki, D., & Helgeson, V. S. (2002). Sex differences in coping behavior: A meta-analytic review and an examination of relative coping. *Personality and Social Psychology Review*, *6*(1), 2–30. doi:10.1207/S15327957PSPR0601_1

Tate, C. C., Bettergarcia, J. N., & Brent, L. M. (2015). Re-assessing the role of gender-related cognitions for self-esteem: The importance of gender typicality for cisgender adults. *Sex Roles*, *72*(5-6), 221–236. doi:10.1007/s11199-015-0458-0

Tate, C. C., Ledbetter, J. N., & Youssef, C. P. (2013). A two-question method for assessing gender categories in the social and medical sciences. *Journal of Sex Research*, *50*(8), 767–776.

Timmers, M., Fischer, A., & Manstead, A. (2003). Ability versus vulnerability: Beliefs about men's and women's emotional behaviour. *Cognition & Emotion*, *17*(1), 41–63.

Trepal, H. C., Wester, K. L., & Shuler, M. (2008). Counselors'-in-training perceptions of gendered behavior. *The Family Journal*, *16*(2), 147–154.

Twenge, J. M., & Nolen-Hoeksema, S. (2002). Age, gender, race, socioeconomic status, and birth cohort difference on the children's depression inventory: A meta-analysis. *Journal of Abnormal Psychology*, *111*(4), 578–588.

U.S. Bureau of Labor Statistics. (2015). *Highlights of women's earnings in 2014*. Retrieved from http://www.bls.gov/opub/reports/womens-earnings/archive/highlights-of-womens-earnings-in-2014.pdf

Voyer, D., & Voyer, S. D. (2014) Gender differences in scholastic achievement: A meta-analysis. *Psychological Bulletin*, *140*(4), 1174–1204. doi:10.1037/a0036620

Vrana, S. R., & Rollock, D. (2002). The role of ethnicity, gender, emotional content, and contextual differences in physiological, expressive, and self-reported emotional responses to imagery. *Cognition & Emotion*, *16*(1), 165–192.

Wager, T. D., Phan, K. L., Liberzon, I., & Taylor, S. F. (2003). Valence, gender, and lateralization of functional brain anatomy in emotion: a meta-analysis of findings from neuroimaging. *Neuroimage*, *19*(3), 513–531.

Wagner, H. L., Buck, R., & Winterbotham, M. (1993). Communication of specific emotions: Gender differences in sending accuracy and communication measures. *Journal of Nonverbal Behavior*, *17*(1), 29–52. doi:10.1007/BF00987007

Walsh, K., Keyes, M. K., Koenen, C. K., & Hasin, D. (2015). Lifetime prevalence of gender-based violence in US women: Associations with mood/anxiety and substance abuse disorders. *Journal of Psychiatric Research*, *62*, 7–13. doi:10.1016/j.jpsychires 2015.01.002

Walton, G. M., & Cohen, G. L. (2003). Stereotype lift. *Journal of Experimental Social Psychology*, *39*(5), 456–467.

Willemson, M. T., (1998). Widening the gender gap: Teenage magazines for boys and girls. *Sex Roles, 38*(9-10), 851–861. doi:10.1023/A:1018881316340

World Bank. (2015). *Gender*. Retrieved from http://data.worldbank.org/topic/gender

Zahn-Waxler, C., Crick, N., Shirtcliff, E. A., & Woods, K. (2006). The origins and development of psychopathology in females and males. In D. Cicchetti, D. J. Cohen, D. Cicchetti, D. J. Cohen (Eds.), *Developmental psychopathology: Theory and method* (2nd ed. Vol. 1, pp. 76–138). Hoboken, NJ: John Wiley & Sons Inc.

Zahn-Waxler, C., Shirtcliff, E. A., & Marceau, K. (2008). Disorders of childhood and adolescence: Gender and psychopathology. *Annual Review of Clinical Psychology, 4*, 275–303. doi:10.1146/annurev.clinpsy.3.022806.091358

Zarbatany, L., McDougall, P., & Hymel, S. (2000). Gender-differentiated experience in the peer culture: Links to intimacy in preadolescence. *Social Development, 9*(1), 62–79. doi: 10.1111/1467-9507.00111

CHAPTER 5

Region

The single most challenging thing about coming up with a science of human beings is that humans are incredibly complex; even within the same "culture," there is substantive variation. The psychology of regional culture is a prime example of this effect. As this chapter will demonstrate, key differences exist between (1) the American North and the American South (i.e., in terms of social norms concerning aggression), (2) Japan's northern frontier and the rest of Japan (i.e., in terms of self-construal), and, more broadly, (3) city-dwellers and those who live in more rural areas (i.e., also in terms of self-construal). These cases of regional cultural differences highlight the importance of within—and not just between—cultural variation.

Regional Variation in the United States: A Tale of Three Cities

At 70 years old, Ralph Wald likely considered himself a lucky man. He was a retired army lieutenant colonel living in Florida with his 41-year-old wife, Johnna—that is, until March 10, 2013 (Jamison, 2013).

That night, a little after midnight, Ralph awoke from his sleep, meandered into his living room, and found his wife Johnna having sex with a man by the name of Walter Conley (Jamison, 2013). At this point, Ralph did the only thing a Florida man could do after finding his wife, who was "half his age," sleeping with a younger man. Without disturbing the scene, Wald slipped back into his bedroom, grabbed a .38 revolver, and returned to the living room, where he shot Conley in the stomach and head, killing him instantly (Jamison, 2013).

Now, the crazy part of the story is not the fact that a man killed his cheating wife's lover—that has happened many times before. Nor is the crazy part that a 70-year-old could get a woman half his age to marry him. The crazy part is not even that a married woman would decide to have sex with her lover in her living room while her husband was home. The most astounding part came during the trial.

First, Ralph and Johnna made up (Jamison, 2013). Second, during the trial itself, Joe, the defense attorney, said that his client was the kind of man that made America great (Jamison, 2013). Now, why is a man who murders his wife's lover the kind of person that makes America great?

Most surprising of all? It took Tampa jurors only two hours to return a "not guilty" verdict (Jamison, 2013).

The bigger question is: Why would this kind of ruling, in this kind of case, not happen in LA or Chicago or Manhattan?

Javier Bahena from Chicago stabbed his ex-wife to death with a screwdriver while she was in the hospital because of her cheating ways; afterwards, he was sentenced to 45 years (Sobol & Houde, 2015).

Steven Whittingham of Brooklyn was also found guilty of murder when he stabbed both his wife and his wife's lover to death after finding them naked and midcoitus in a parked car (Carrega-Woodby, 2015).

What were the differences in these cases?

The long answer will likely involve a protracted discussion about gender, race, the criminal justice system, the morality of mentality, insanity, self-defense, rights, and the like. The short answer is the topic of this chapter: region.

In some ways, the American South is like a different country compared to the American North. History itself suggests this: A little more than a century ago, the South (photo 5.1) wanted to be its own country, tried quite hard to secede from the North, and paid dearly when its desires were not granted.

If you want to understand the South, you could do what I did in elementary school, before the days of Google—that is, look it up in the encyclopedia. If you find

PHOTO 5.1. The American South

Source: iStock

the *New Encyclopedia of Southern Culture* (Griffin, Hargis, & Wilson, 2012), you will find that a substantive portion of the book is devoted to the issue of violence. The experts on Southern culture—Griffin et al. (2012)—repeatedly return to the idea that violence is a fundamental part of the South and has been since the birth of this nation, whether in the form of "personal violence" (i.e., to "defend their masculine honor" [p. 89]), "mob violence" in the context of ethnic conflict (p. 169), or "political violence" in regard to activism (p. 233), to name a few.

Historical examples of cultural practices in the South embody this emphasis on violence. Included are feuds (i.e., conflicts), duels (arranged battles to settle issues usually involving honor), lynchings (i.e., hangings; see also Alexandre, 2008), bushwhackings (i.e., sudden attacks), whupping (i.e., corporal punishment), and the game, "purring"—that is, a game that entails holding your opponent by the shoulder and kicking him or her in the shins; for reviews, see Dizard, Muth, & Andrews (1999); Nisbett & Cohen (1999); Vandello & Cohen (2004); Wilson & Ferris (1999).

Regional Variation in Homicides

Perhaps the most paradigmatic example of violence is homicide. About 12,000 to 13,000 Americans die in homicides every year ("Crime in the U.S.," 2013). Given that the majority of homicides are committed by a person that the victim knows (historical data suggests that only about 18% of murders are committed by strangers; Fox & Pierce, 1987, p. 57), the cause of the crime may likely have involved some interpersonal conflict (Cohen, Nisbett, Bowdle, & Schwarz, 1996). According to a historical breakdown of all the potential circumstances leading up to a homicide, 31% involved some "other" argument that did not fall under any of the typical categories of causes (e.g., robbery, alcohol, narcotics, gambling, money, gang violence, etc.; Fox & Pierce, 1987, p. 58).

The fact of the matter is that many murders are done by ordinary people put in circumstances that motivate them to take an extraordinary measure of violence (Daly & Wilson, 1988, as cited in Cohen et al., 1996). When they do this, they are participating in a **culture of honor**, where even small fights reflect conflicts where a person's reputation and social status are at stake (Cohen et al., 1996; Nisbett, 1993). Parts of the United States have this culture of honor norm, and most of them are in the American South (Cohen et al., 1996; Hayes & Lee, 2005; Nisbett, 1993; Vandello, Cohen, & Ransom, 2008).

How do we know? Actual homicide rates are telling. Analysis of numbers of homicides revealed that, relative to the rest of America (i.e., the West, Northwest, and Midwest), the American South consistently had the highest homicide rates over time (Grosjean, 2014). To give a specific example, South Carolina is consistently one of the top 10 states in the nation in terms of homicide by domestic violence, with an average number of 33 women murdered each year because of partner violence (Farber & Miller-Cribbs, 2014). Moreover, Southern White men are more than twice as likely to carry a gun than their Northern counterparts, and Southern White women are more than six times as likely to carry, compared to their Northern counterparts (Felson & Pare, 2010). These practices are also reinforced by gun control laws (photo 5.2), which support the mentality that people should be self-reliant with regard to the ability to protect and provide (Copes, Kovandzic, Miller, & Williamson, 2014).

PHOTO 5.2. Gun control vs gun rights: a key American regional difference

Source: iStock

Homicide alone (within the context of culture), however, isn't incredibly telling, because violence generally can be used for a variety of reasons. Maybe you're just protecting your own back; maybe you are trying to teach people a lesson; maybe you are responding to an insult. Thus it's more helpful to look at the precise content of laws that govern what happens after a homicide is committed. There is random homicide, when a person kills a stranger for no apparent reason, perhaps by virtue of a stray bullet (Sherman, Steele, Laufersweiler, Hoffer, & Julian, 1989); there is instrumental homicide, when a person kills another to obtain something of practical value—money, jewelry, or goods (Miethe & Drass, 1999). Finally, there is the most variable kind of homicide—the kind of homicide that restores a person's honor, saves face, and enhances one's social status, or is expressive (e.g., Miethe & Drass, 1999; Papachristos, 2009).

To understand this last type of violence—violence in the name of honor, local laws offer a clue. For a long time in Southern history, it was impossible to be convicted of murder in certain contexts. In Florida, for example, their 2016 statutes outline what they deem "justifiable use of force"—if you have reason to believe that your body or your property is being threatened, then you are allowed to use deadly force. There is also the "true man rule"—the idea that you should stand your ground in the event of an attack, even if it means killing the other person (Copes et al., 2014). All this is consistent with the broader observation that legal perspectives in the South appear to condone the use of violence across a variety of contexts, including in punishment, domestic violence, and national defense (Borg, 1997; Copes et al., 2014). In some cases, even the use of an insult was argued to constitute a threat that warranted self-defense and assault (for review, see "Homicide, Self-Defense, Effect of Insulting, and

Opprobrious Words," 1926). In other words, in certain contexts, you could legally kill someone for offending you and not recanting the person's offense. Until 1970, similar laws protected men who killed their wife's lover—as long as he caught them "in flagrante delicto"—that is, in the act—then technically, it was not a crime (Reed, 1981, as cited in Cohen & Nisbett, 1994). In both of these cases, the type of violence being condoned is **honor-restorative.** Whether you are punching someone who called your mother fat or shooting the man sharing your marital bed or stabbing a mouthy stranger at a bar for insulting your good name, you are essentially engaging in violence to restore your social status.

The History of the South

The origin story of the United States goes something like this: The Calvinists settled in the American North and the Cavaliers in the South (Woodard, 2013). With them, they brought two very different cultures: In the North, the Calvinists followed a culture of laws (e.g., Woodard, 2013). Because people lived in densely populated cities, they were forced to establish laws; in doing so, individuals no longer could defend themselves but instead relied on authority and law enforcement to do it for them. If someone wrongs you, you don't wrong them back; you report them. In contrast, the South was much less populated, and the frontier allowed the Cavaliers to bring their culture of honor (Cohen, Nisbett, Bowdle, & Schwarz, 1996). Without the infrastructure of laws and the people to enforce them, a person's reputation for violence was the only thing that prevented others from taking advantage of him or her (for reviews, see Cohen & Nisbett, 1994; Cohen et al., 1996; Dawson, 1978; Nisbett, 1994).

Other historic and economic reasons further promoted this culture of honor. Unlike the North, the South largely had a herding economy (Cohen, 1996). Given that herding involved the maintenance and protection of cattle that, given their mobile nature, could be easily stolen, herdsmen had to be able to use force to protect themselves and their property; as a result, herding societies generally tended to be more prone toward lawlessness, instability, violence, and clan rule, in Europe as in the United States (Cohen, 1996). For herders to maintain their livelihood, they had to reattribute any time there were threats to themselves or their property, especially since police officers were either nonexistent or too far away (Vandello et al., 2008).

This culture of honor has persisted in the South. National surveys show that Southerners are more likely to approve of using violence to defend oneself, respond to an offensive remark, and to discipline children (Cohen & Nisbett, 1994). Although Southerners did not endorse more violence in general, they were more likely to support violence in these particular contexts where honor and reputation were at stake (Cohen & Nisbett, 1994). Not surprisingly, these attitudes are also reflected in modern laws that rule the South—including gun control laws (or the lack thereof) and stand-your-ground laws relating to self-defense (Cohen, 1996).

The Filing Cabinet Study

In 1996, Cohen et al. recruited 42 Northern and 41 Southern white, male participants to complete the single, most often cited study in the psychology of region. At the start of the study, participants were asked to complete a short questionnaire that asked basic demographic information and were told to place it on a table at the end of a long, narrow hallway filled with filing cabinets that left little room to walk (Cohen et al., 1996).

Cohen et al. (1996) hired a confederate to wait in this hallway and walk toward the unsuspecting participant; as the two passed, the confederate would purposely bump into him and call him "'asshole'" under his breath. When the participant arrived at the table on the other end of the hallway, another experimenter gave him an additional questionnaire—one that assessed his response to what had just happened (Cohen et al., 1996).

Northerners were primarily amused. Looking at self-reports, two out of three Northerners reported experiencing more amusement than anger; Southerners, in contrast, had the opposite reaction—the overwhelming majority of them (85%) were more angry than amused (Cohen et al., 1996).

In a follow-up study, Cohen et al. (1996) assessed the participants' hormonal responses. Of particular interest were **cortisol**, the classic stress hormone, and **testosterone**, the hormone behind aggression. In both cases, Northerners exhibited little hormonal response to the manipulation, whereas Southerners reacted very strongly, showing significant spikes in both hormones after being insulted (Cohen et al., 1996).

In another follow-up study, Cohen et al. (1996) looked at a behavioral measure—namely, how participants responded in a game of "chicken." In this version of the game, they hired a large, burly confederate to wait in the same hallway and walk toward the participants when they were presumably "leaving" the study. Given the nature of the hallway, physics says that the two men could not squeeze past each other at the same time; one had to give way to the other (Cohen et al., 1996). The big question is: Who gives way? For Northerners, being insulted earlier in the study made them extra polite—when the confederate was over eight feet away, they moved to one side and waited for the other person to pass; Southerners, in contrast, were more likely to stand their ground after being insulted and waited for the last possible moment to give way (Cohen et al., 1996).

Finally, Cohen et al. (1996) looked to see if Southerners (but not Northerners) would apply their newly found aggression to a subsequent social interaction. After the initial insult, they had these participants interact with another male experimenter: First, they shook hands; afterward, the participants rated their impression of the experimenter's masculinity (Cohen et al., 1996). The male experimenter rated Southern men's handshakes as more firm after they had been insulted (compared to the control condition, when there was no insult hurled); Northern men's handshakes did not change (Cohen et al., 1996). Southern men also came away with very different impressions of the male experimenter. They did not differ from Northerners in the control condition, but after being insulted—particularly in public—they saw the other male experimenter as less masculine (Cohen et al., 1996).

The Job Letter Study

These differences between Northern and Southern men didn't just appear in the lab. Cohen and Nisbett (1997) went further and did a naturalistic experiment where they sent letters to employers in the U.S. North and South, requesting a job application. In the cover letter, the fictional applicant admitted that he had committed a felony: In one case, it was a car theft; in another, manslaughter (Cohen & Nisbett, 1997).

In both conditions, Cohen and Nisbett (1997) had the letter writer explain the reasons for his crime and provided both justification and remorse: In the case of the car theft, he explained that, despite knowing that it was wrong, he had a family to support and stealing expensive cars offered a way to pay the bills; in the case of manslaughter, he explained that a person confronted him at a bar and told everyone present that he was sleeping with the letter writer's fiancée—in response, the two took it outside, and the supposed cuckold killed the braggart with a blow to the head with a pipe (Cohen & Nisbett, 1997).

Relative to Northern employers, Southern ones were more likely to respond to the manslaughter convict—the man who had killed in the name of honor (Cohen & Nisbett, 1997). When they did, Cohen and Nisbett (1997) found that they were likely to use a warm tone and indicate that jobs were available. To rule out the possibility that Southern companies were more lax about criminal records more generally, Cohen and Nisbett (1997) also analyzed responses to the car theft letter; no differences between region emerged there.

For additional insights on regional differences, see Insight Box 5.1.

INSIGHT BOX 5.1

The Southern Paradox

For a brief period of my life, I lived in Texas before moving out to California. When I did, I quickly noticed cultural differences between the two states. For one, I found that Californian men were more rude and were more likely to check you out very obviously when you are walking down the street, making no effort whatsoever to hide what they are doing. I never remembered that happening in Texas, perhaps because, if men did that there, they had a relatively high likelihood of being punched in the face. For another, I noticed that people honked their horns in California. You drive on the freeway and people will, on occasion, give you the finger or yell at you from their window. Again, I never saw that happen in Texas, presumably because if they did, they might be inciting murder. In other words, Texans—and Southerners in general—seem, in many ways, much nicer and more polite than the rest of the country.

This brings up a riddle for you: Consider all the findings discussed in this chapter on the South's culture of violence and honor. Now think about what people normally associate with the South.

If you're like most people, the list varies, but it usually invariably involves some mention of:

- Southern hospitality
- Southern food
- Southern belles

The underlying theme that ties all three of these common associations with the South is the idea of being friendly, polite, and warm—Southern hospitality is known around the country as the response you get when you are welcomed into a Southerner's home. You see it in living rooms, but you also see it on the road and in interactions between strangers. Southern food is something they typically offer you when they welcome you into their house and Southern belles are beauties who practice this hospitality and cooking to near perfection.

The paradox, then, is this: If Southern culture promotes such strict rules for politeness, then how can we reconcile this with the Southern tendency toward violence?

The resolution involves understanding that politeness and violence go hand-in-hand. If anything, Southern politeness probably evolved as a response to the culture of honor.

Regional Variation in Japan: The Case of the "Northern Frontier"

The United States is not the only country to have documented regional variation in our basic psychological processes. Take, for example, the case of Japan.

Back in 2006, three American psychologists paired up with two psychologists from Hokkaido University in Japan to test an unexpected idea: whether some Japanese looked more psychologically like Americans than other Japanese (Kitayama, Ishii, Imada, Takemura, & Ramaswamy, 2006). They recruited students from Hokkaido, one of Japan's northern islands, students from other parts of Japan, and U.S. students and gave these participants an array of surveys—asking them about the kinds of emotions they reported feeling, whether they were prone to **cognitive dissonance** effects, and whether they explained others' behaviors via their stable traits rather than the situation (i.e., the **fundamental attribution error**; Kitayama et al., 2006).

Across all measures, Kitayama and his colleagues (2006) found a common pattern: Japanese from Hokkaido were much more similar to U.S. Americans than fellow Japanese. Feelings-wise, they were most happy when fulfilling their own goals (in contrast to other Japanese, who were most happy when they got along well with others; Kitayama et al., 2006). In terms of cognitive dissonance, the Hokkaido residents also behaved like Americans, showing an aversion to realizing that their thoughts and beliefs do not match up—in this case, when they had to pick a CD they did not like very much originally (Kitayama et al., 2006). Other Japanese, in contrast, only showed these dissonance effects when they were made to feel like other people were watching them, suggesting that they were concerned with their public self, whereas Americans and Hokkaido residents were concerned with their private self (Kitayama et al., 2006). Finally, in terms of attributions, participants from Hokkaido and the United States were once again very similar, both showing a tendency to blame the person for their (hypothetical) actions rather than blame the situation (Kitayama et al., 2006).

What explained these patterns? Here Kitayama and his colleagues (2006) put forth a **voluntary settlement hypothesis**. In a nutshell, this says that people who willingly leave their homeland to pursue a new and uncertain life on the frontier are a special group—if they are willing to leave everything behind for a chance at a potentially more glorious future, then they are likely highly independent, comfortable with risk, and preoccupied with freedom (Kitayama et al., 2006). Citing evidence about the difficulties involved in breaking new ground in a previously uninhabited land—a place with no infrastructure, prefabricated housing, or criminal justice system—Kitayama et al. (2006) argued that people living in frontiers needed to be highly self-reliant and focused on their own goals in order to survive; over time, this special group of people likely formed their own culture of independence.

The United States, of course, is a perfect illustration of this pattern. When a motley mix of Europeans left the motherland to cross the dangerous seas for a new home they had invested in sight unseen, they presumably brought with them a spirit of individualistic pursuit that, over time, became the basis of American individualism. As it turns out, Hokkaido is a parallel example of this same phenomenon. Here Kitayama et al. (2006) cite the unique history of the island, which, up until the mid-1800s, was a vast wilderness enjoyed only by the local indigenous residents,

not unlike pre-Columbus America. Then the Japanese government recruited unemployed samurai warriors to go set up camp there (Kitayama et al., 2006). They did
what Columbus and other explorers did—they drove out the locals, built a new
society from scratch, and set the stage for others to follow; over time, the island
of Hokkaido grew just like the United States grew (Kitayama et al., 2006). Now,
although Hokkaido (photo 5.3) is still ostensibly fully Japanese—it's inhabited by
ethnic Japanese who speak the language and belong to the same government—it
nevertheless shows strong traces of its independent roots (Kitayama et al., 2006).

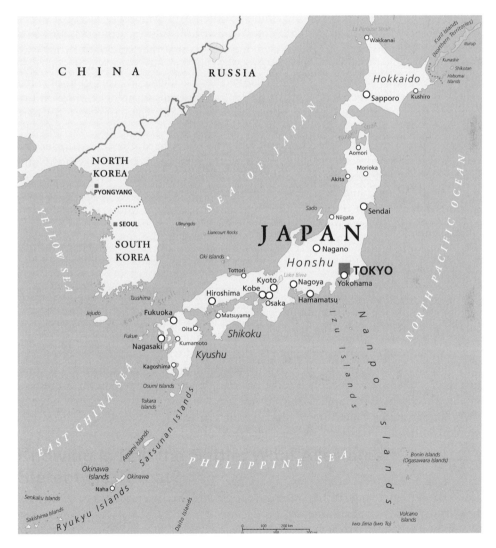

PHOTO 5.3. Hokkaido, Japan: The case for within-culture differences

Source: iStock

Global Regional Variation: The Urban versus Rural Difference

The United States and Japan are not the only places with stark regional variation in basic psychological processes. One often discussed difference is between people who live in cities versus people who in the countryside—that is, the urban versus rural distinction.

Differences in Helping

Perhaps the most longstanding and often cited difference between people who live in cities and people who live in the country is their average level of nicety. It's been widely observed that, in places like New York or Los Angeles, strangers don't nod or wave to one another; the best you can hope for is that they stay out of your way. In small towns between those two metropolises, in contrast, people will smile, say hello, maybe even invite you in for tea. Anecdotal evidence for this kind of difference abounds. When George Vaillant (2012), a Harvard psychologist, took on one of the biggest longitudinal studies of modern science—one spanning seven decades, following a class of Harvard men from college until the day they died—he noticed a striking pattern over the years. Longitudinal studies are hard; they take forever and require tracking people down all over the world sometimes. In the Harvard Grant Study, Vaillant followed the participants throughout their adult lives and noticed the same trend over and over: People in New York rarely invited him to eat and, instead, opted to meet in their offices, whereas those in the Midwest would invite him home and talk over a meal (Vaillant, 2012).

This question of whether city and country folk were truly different in how prosocially they behaved was a topic of much study in the 1970s and '80s, and a great number of experiments came out of testing whether urban individuals were less likely to help than their rural counterparts were. A meta-analysis of 65 datasets containing over 14,000 participants revealed that yes, in fact, the anecdotes and stereotype in this case rang true: Overall, helping is less likely to happen in cities than in the countryside (Steblay, 1987). The kinds of helping behaviors Steblay (1987) tested varied: Some were serious, like helping a child who was lost or a person that was injured; others were trivial, like providing change or telling someone the time, and many others were in between, like returning a letter dropped on the ground or giving directions. Geographic origin of the studies also varied—although most of them were from the United States, studies from Canada, Israel, Turkey, and Australia were also included—but across contexts, the pattern remained the same: Helping was much more likely to happen in a rural context than an urban one (Steblay, 1987; and see photo 5.4). Subsequent studies have shown that this pattern is especially true among older adults; among younger adults, people who live in cities typically receive help from friends, whereas people who live in rural areas typically get help from family members (Amato, 1993).

Why might this be? Steblay (1987) suggested that Stanley Milgram might've been onto something when he said that the stresses of city living might make the average city dweller more likely to ignore anything that is outside the domain of personal concern—in other words, city folk cannot afford to attend to strangers

PHOTO 5.4. Cross-culturally, helping appears more likely in rural contexts than in urban ones.

Source: iStock

because they simply have too many demands at hand within their stressful external environment (Milgram, 1970). When they do help, they help friends, most likely because their family members are likely to live farther away (Amato, 1993).

Differences in Psychopathology

Urban-rural differences in stress level don't simply implicate helping; they also are important in studies on psychopathology. As shown in chapter 1, at the core of understanding the origins and causes of illness is the diathesis-stress model, or the idea that most disorders are a combination of diathesis (an underlying vulnerability, often genetic or biological) and a stressor (an external factor like loss or threat; Zuckerman, 1999). If living in the city is a major cause of stress, then it logically follows that city dwellers are more likely to experience mental disorders relative to those who live in the country.

A meta-analysis of survey studies on this rural-urban difference in psychopathology confirmed that, as expected, people who lived in cities were more likely to experience a variety of psychological disorders—namely, mood disorders, like depression and bipolar disorder, and anxiety disorders, like phobia, panic disorder, and generalized anxiety disorder (Peen, Schoevers, Beekman, & Dekker, 2010). Interestingly, Peen et al. (2010) found that no differences emerged when it came to substance-related disorders. A number of different countries across Europe were included in the sample, along with the United States and South Korea; moreover, the differences in prevalence rates were substantial—a difference of 38% overall, with stronger effects for mood than anxiety disorders (Peen et al., 2010). Since then, additional studies have further confirmed that this difference between rural and urban is strong—when Stickley, Koyanagi, Roberts, and McKee (2015) looked at psychological distress across nine different countries in Eastern Europe and Russia (i.e., countries that were part of the former Soviet Union), they found that, once again, urbanites reported more psychological distress than rural dwellers.

Other research has suggested that this urban-rural distinction is especially pronounced when it comes to one particular type of disorder—schizophrenia. Although the causes for this thought disorder vary, city dwelling has consistently emerged as one of the risk factors; consistent with the previous studies, the assumption has largely been that this is potentially due, at least in part, to the increased exposure to stress (Lederbogen, Haddad, & Meyer-Lindenberg, 2013). Neuroimaging studies have even shown that people currently living in a city were likely to have increased activity in the parts of the brain that were responsible for regulating the amygdala, negative emotion, and stress (Lederbogen et al., 2011).

The exception to this rule seems to be with autism spectrum disorder—existing studies have shown that people living in rural places are more likely to have ASD than those living in cities (Kiani, Tyrer, Hodgson, Berkin, & Bhaumik, 2013).

Global Regional Variation: The Role of Environmental Threats

Beyond the urban-rural distinction, recent studies have shown that certain universal patterns exist in terms of global regional variation. The basic idea is this: All over the world, certain ecological conditions make some psychological processes more adaptive and, therefore, more likely than others. This again goes back to the idea that culture is not magic; it always comes from somewhere. Part of the answer to where that "somewhere" is has to do with threats to humans and how we as a species reacted.

If you're a human being, there are likely many things that threaten your existence. On the one hand, there are the obvious, visible, large threats—lions, tigers, bears, earthquakes, meteors, and natural disasters. On the other hand, there are the tiny, invisible, hard to see threats— bacteria, parasites, and pathogens.

Big Threats: Lions, Tigers, and Bears, Oh My!

One idea that has emerged from evolutionary theorists is this: Different ancestral environments likely had different ecologies that supported different kinds of fauna and flora, and not all fauna and flora (fauna more than flora) are equally dangerous to humans. To illustrate, say you are a caveman (photo 5.5) and you live in a world where your primary source of food is large, speedy animals like leopards, cheetahs, lions, and tigers. These creatures are big, difficult to catch, and extremely fast, so your success at hunting down your own dinner is largely variable—there is no guarantee. As such, if it weren't for your nice neighbors who are willing to share their leopard on days when you can't manage to catch your own, you would surely die a slow, painful death, one skipped meal at a time—unless, of course, you and your neighbors agreed upon a shared social system for sharing your food. Given that you are a caveman, you also don't have access to refrigeration or other forms

PHOTO 5.5. Imagining life as a caveman can explain important cultural differences.

Source: iStock

of long-term food preservation, so in the event of a big kill, sharing is also in the successful hunter's best interest, because otherwise large amounts of meat will go to waste, uneaten (for a discussion of these ideas, see Sterelny, 2007).

(In an alternate universe where your main source of food is, say, vegetables, or small, furry animals, like gerbils, then these ecological pressures would not apply, because vegetables and gerbils are presumably easier to catch and less likely to eat you back).

These scenarios are not just mental exercises; they actually have been demonstrated among modern hunter-gatherer groups. When Hillard Kapland and Kim Hill (1985) went to the lowlands of Paraguay to observe the food-sharing habits of the Ache—a group that is unique in that they rely on both agriculture and foraging for their calories—they found that vegetation (palms, oranges, etc.) were shared far less often than meat (deer, monkey, armadillo).

Other researchers have taken this one step further and used these ancestral patterns to explain current-day **within-cultural variation**. In ancient times, the greatest dangers to humans and their dinner were wild, meaty animals. In modern times, our threats are more varied and can include other forms of resources—retirement money, insurance, the cost of a college degree, or the price of rent. As in ancient times, some people struggle more with these modern threats than others—namely, people with fewer resources are more at risk than people with more resources. Another way to say this is that class differences exist and are our modern-day equivalent of ecological threat. Working class individuals, like ancient hunter-gatherers who lived and dined on large animals, live in a more uncertain world where things are not always guaranteed. Upper-middle class individuals are more akin to gatherers or farmers who enjoy a certain level of predictability in their resources. If this is the case, then working class individuals should also be more prone to sharing, and develop stronger **egalitarian norms**, because their livelihood depends on it more (Kameda, Takezawa, & Hastie, 2005).

Evidence for this link between environmental uncertainty, sharing norms, and egalitarianism have emerged within the same cultural context. When Kameda and colleagues (2005) asked college students across Japan what their attitudes were toward how resources should be divided, they found that different colleges had divergent ideas about whether equality or merit should drive the allocation process; in the end, less prestigious schools with more working class students were more likely to be in favor of egalitarian norms.

Small (but Just as Dangerous) Threats: Pathogens

Pathogens and Egalitarianism Large animals, of course, are not the only danger to modern or ancestral humans. For as long as we have been around, tiny, sometimes invisible threats have also existed—bacteria, parasites, and other kinds of pathogens. As a threat, pathogens are dangerous because they cause disease, disability, and often—at least in the ancient world—death. Typhus could kill you; leprosy could socially isolate you for life; malaria and tuberculosis could make you bedridden.

Like animals, the prevalence of different pathogens also varies across the globe: Not all regions of the world have the same levels of diseases, and some areas have more diseases in general. When Fincher and his colleagues (Fincher, Thornhill, Murray, & Schaller, 2008) examined variation in pathogen levels across the world, they found that individualistic countries tended to have fewer pathogens than collectivistic ones. Why might that be?

Fincher et al.'s (2008) argument goes something like this: If you live in a part of the world where infectious diseases are more common, then this should make you generally cautious when interacting with other people, because other people could kill you and not know it. A handshake, a cough, or a sexual encounter could all spell your demise when a pathogen from a stranger makes its way into your own system. This general wariness of other people, especially other people you do not know well or are unfamiliar with, might turn into a dampened likelihood of wanting to interact with certain kinds of people—namely, foreigners, outgroup members, or anyone who deviates from the norm (Fincher et al., 2008). As Fincher et al. (2008) argued, this is characteristic of collectivists, who value conforming to group rules, following traditions, maintaining the status quo, and avoiding foreigners. By having these stronger norms, they can protect themselves from pathogens via their lower amounts of interaction with people outside their ingroup and reliance on stricter practices (e.g., about how to prepare food a certain way so as to prevent the spread of disease; Fincher et al., 2008).

Pathogens and Mating Preferences Infection and disease don't just impact our preferences regarding how we prepare our meat before eating it and whether we have a love-hate relationship with foreigners. Other studies also suggest that pathogens impact our dating and mating behavior. In the context of reproduction, this idea seems simple enough; generally speaking, we prefer to be with healthy people rather than unhealthy people. The reasons are clear: Healthy partners are less likely to pass diseases to any children that come out of the relationship and are more likely to live long enough to help raise said children.

How then, can we tell who is healthy and who is not? Some diseases (like leprosy) are obvious; others, less so. So, according to evolutionary psychologists like Gangestad and Buss (1993), humans have evolved a quick and dirty system to tell the difference: physical attractiveness. Legions of studies have now shown that people who are more physically appealing tend to be healthy on a variety of domains—women with smaller waists and bigger hips are more fertile (Zaadstra et al., 1993) and less likely to get some cancers (Adebamowo et al., 2003); the link between male physical attractiveness and health appears to be less reliable and consistent (Weeden & Sabini, 2005).

When Gangestad, Haselton, and Buss (2006) analyzed the data from a large-scale international mating study that Buss collected in 1989, they found evidence that the level of parasites found in a country has a strong bearing on mating preferences in the country. One of the strongest effects that Gangestad et al. (2006) found was that places with more parasites placed more emphasis on the importance of physical attractiveness relative to places with fewer parasites, and this effect applied for both men and women, although the size of the effect was somewhat larger for women (see also Gangestad & Buss, 1993). At the same time, people who were more susceptible to parasites were also more likely to value other mate qualities that might offer protection from parasites—namely, health, intelligence, education, and youth (for men choosing women; Gangestad et al., 2006). People who are healthier and younger are more able to defend themselves against pathogens, and high levels of achievement might be a signal that a person is strong and capable (Gangestad et al., 2006).

The Broader Case for Evoked Culture

Both of the above examples of pathogens predicting reliable differences between people are examples of a broader idea called **evoked culture**, or the idea that ecological differences between different parts of the world gave rise to cultural differences (Tooby & Cosmides, 1992). In other words, the actual physical environments people reside in gave rise to the psychological environments inside their own heads—that is, values and norms. Distinct ecologies mean that people faced different kinds of threats and demands, and those threats and demands—whether they were in the form of large meat or small parasites—shaped the way people behave; over time, these commonly "evoked" behaviors converged to produce what we now call culture (Tooby & Cosmides, 1992).

Key Concepts

Culture of honor
Honor-restorative (and other types of violence)
Cortisol and testosterone

Cognitive dissonance
Fundamental attribution error
Voluntary settlement hypothesis
Within-cultural variation
Egalitarian norms
Evoked culture

References

2016 Florida Statutes (2016). Retrieved from www.leg.state.fl.us/statutes/index.cfm?App_mode=Display_Statute&Search_String=&URL=0700-0799/0776/Sections/0776.013.htm

Adebanowo, C., Ogundiran, T., Adenipekun, A., Oyesegun, R., Campbell, O., Akang, E., . . . Olopade, O. (2003). Waist-hip ratio and breast cancer risk in urbanized Nigerian women. *Breast Cancer Research, 5*(2), 18–24.

Alexandre, S. (2008). Out on a limb: The spatial politics of lynching photography. *Mississippi Quarterly, 62*(1-2), 71–112.

Amato, P. R. (1993). Urban-rural differences in helping friends and family members. *Social Psychology Quarterly, 56*(4), 249–262.

Anderson, E. (1994). The code of the streets. *The Atlantic Monthly, 5,* 81–94.

Borg, M. J. (1997). The southern subculture of punitiveness? Regional variation in support for capital punishment. *Journal of Research in Crime and Delinquency, 34*(1), 25–45.

Carrega-Woodby, C. (2015, November 2). Brooklyn man gets 25 years to life for fatal stabbing of wife and her lover. *Daily News.* Retrieved from http://www.nydailynews.com/new-york/nyc-crime/brooklyn-man-25-years-life-fatal-stabbings-article-1.2421166

Cohen, D. (1996.) Law, social policy, and violence: The impact of regional cultures. *Journal of Personality and Social Psychology, 70*(5), 961–978.

Cohen, D., & Nisbett, R. E. (1994). Self-protection and the culture of honor: Explaining Southern violence. *Society for Personality and Social Psychology, 20*(5), 551–567.

Cohen, D., & Nisbett, R. E. (1995). Field experiments examining the culture of honor: The role of institutions in perpetuating norms. *Social Psychology Bulletin, 23*(11), 1188–1199.

Cohen, D., Nisbett, R. E., Bowdle, B. F., & Schwarz, N. (1996). Insult, aggression, and the southern culture of honor: An "experimental ethnography." *Journal of Personality and Social Psychology, 70*(5), 945–960.

Copes, H., Kovandzic, T. V., Miller, J. M., & Williamson, L. (2014). The lost cause? Examining the southern culture of honor through defensive gun use. *Crime and Delinquency, 60*(3), 356–378. Retrieved from http://0-search.proquest.com.leopac.ulv.edu/docview/1511434687?accountid=25355

Crime in the U.S. (2013). FBI. Retrieved from https://ucr.fbi.gov/crime-in-the-u.s/2013/crime-in-the-u.s.-2013/offenses-known-to-law-enforcement/expanded-homicide/expanded_homicide_data_table_8_murder_victims_by_weapon_2009-2013.xls

Daly, M., & Wilson, M. (1988). *Homicide.* Hawthorne, NY: Aldine de Gruyter.

Dawson, J. C. (1978). The Puritan and the Cavalier: The South's perception of contrasting traditions. *The Journal of Southern History, 44*(4), 597–614.

Dizard, J. E., Muth, R., & Andrews, S. P. (Eds.). (1999). *Guns in America: A historical reader.* New York: New York University Press.

Farber, N., & Miller-Cribbs, J. E. (2014). Violence in the lives of rural, southern, and poor white women. *Violence Against Women, 20*(5), 517–538.

Felson, R. B., & Pare, P. (2010). Gun cultures or honor cultures? Explaining regional and race differences in weapon carrying. *Social Forces, 88*(3), 1357–1378. Retrieved from http://0-search.proquest.com.leopac.ulv.edu/docview/366312972?accountid=25355

Fincher, C. L., Thornhill, R., Murray, D. R., & Schaller, M. (2008). Pathogen prevalence predicts human cross-cultural variability in individualism/collectivism. *Proceedings of the Royal Society of London B: Biological Sciences, 275*(1640), 1279–1285.

Fischer, D. H. (1989). *Albion's seed: Four British folkways in America.* New York, NY: Oxford University Press.

Fox, J. A., & Pierce, G. L. (1987). *Uniform Crime Reports [United States]: Supplementary Homicide Reports, 1976-1983.* Inter-university Consortium for Political and Social Research.

Griffin, L. J., Hargis, P. G., & Wilson, C. R. (Eds.). (2012). *The New Encyclopedia of Southern Culture* (Volume 20: *Social Class*). Chapel Hill: University of North Carolina Press.

Gangestad, S., & Buss, D. (1993). Pathogen prevalence and human mate preferences. *Ethology and sociobiology, 14*(2), 89–96.

Gangestad, S. W., Haselton, M. G., & Buss, D. M. (2006). Evolutionary foundations of cultural variation: Evoked culture and mate preferences. *Psychological Inquiry, 17*(2), 75–95.

Gilmore, D. D. (1990). *Manhood in the making: Cultural concepts of masculinity.* New Haven, CT: Yale University Press.

Grosjean, P. (2014). A history of violence: The culture of honor and homicide in the U.S. south. *Journal of the European Economic Association, 12*(5), 1285–1316.

Hayes, T. C., & Lee, M. R. (2005). The southern culture of honor and violent attitudes. *Sociological Spectrum, 25*(5), 593–617.

"Homicide. Self-defense. Effect of insulting and opprobrious words." (1926). *Virginia Law Review,* 602–604.

Jamison, P. (2013, May 30). Jury acquits Brandon man in killing of wife's lover. *Tampa Bay Times.* Retrieved from http://www.tampabay.com/news/courts/criminal/brandon-defendant-accused-of-murdering-wifes-lover-to-testify/2123822

Kameda, T., Takezawa, M., & Hastie, R. (2005). Where do social norms come from? The example of communal sharing. *Current Directions in Psychological Science, 14*(6), 331–334.

Kaplan, H., & Hill, K. (1985). Food sharing among ache foragers: Tests of explanatory hypotheses. *Current Anthropology, 26*(2), 223–246.

Kiani, R., Tyrer, F., Hodgson, A., Berkin, N., & Bhaumik, S. (2013). Urban–rural differences in the nature and prevalence of mental ill-health in adults with intellectual disabilities. *Journal of Intellectual Disability Research, 57*(2), 119–127.

Kitayama, S., Ishii, K., Imada, T., Takemura, K., & Ramaswamy, J. (2006). Voluntary settlement and the spirit of independence: Evidence from Japan's "northern frontier." *Journal of Personality and Social Psychology, 91*(3), 369–384.

Lederbogen, F., Haddad, L., & Meyer-Lindenberg, A. (2013). Urban social stress–risk factor for mental disorders: The case of schizophrenia. *Environmental Pollution, 183,* 2–6.

Lederbogen, F., Kirsch, P., Haddad, L., Streit, F., Tost, H., Schuch, P., . . . Meyer-Lindenberg, A. (2011). City living and urban upbringing affect neural social stress processing in humans. *Nature, 474*(7352), 498–501.

McCall, N. (1994). *Makes me wanna holler: A young black man in America.* New York, NY: Random House.

McWhiney, G. (1988). *Cracker culture: Celtic ways in the Old South.* Tuscaloosa: University of Alabama Press.

Miethe, T. D., & Drass, K. A. (1999). Exploring the social context of instrumental and expressive homicides: An application of qualitative comparative analysis. *Journal of Quantitative Criminology, 15*(1), 1–21.

Milgram, S. (1970). The experience of living in cities. *Science, 167*(3924), 1461–1468.

Nisbett, R. E. (1993). Violence and U.S. regional culture. *American Psychologist, 48*(4), 441–449.

Nisbett, R. E., & Cohen, D. (1999). Violence and honor in the Southern United States. In J. E. Dizard, R. M. Muth, & S. P. Andrews (Eds.), *Guns in America: A reader* (pp. 264–274). New York: New York University Press.

Papachristos, A. V. (2009). Murder by structure: Dominance relations and the social structure of gang homicide. *American Journal of Sociology, 115*(1), 74–128.

Peen, J., Schoevers, R. A., Beekman, A. T., & Dekker, J. (2010). The current status of urban-rural differences in psychiatric disorders. *Acta Psychiatrica Scandinavica, 121*(2), 84–93.

Peristiany, J. G. (Ed.). (1965). *Honour and shame: The values of Mediterranean society.* London, U.K.: Weidenfeld & Nicolson.

Pitt-Rivers, J. (1968). Honor. In D. Sills (Ed.), *International encyclopedia of the social sciences* (pp. 509–510). New York, NY: Macmillan.

Sherman, L. W., Steele, L., Laufersweiler, D., Hoffer, N., & Julian, S. A. (1989). Stray bullets and "mushrooms": Random shootings of bystanders in four cities, 1977–1988. *Journal of Quantitative Criminology, 5*(4), 297–316.

Sobol, R. R., & Houde, G. (2015, March 23). Estranged husband charged with murder in hospital stabbing. *Chicago Tribune.* Retrieved from http://www.chicagotribune.com/news/local/breaking/chi-elk-grove-hospital-stabbing-20150322-story.html

Steblay, N. M. (1987). Helping behavior in rural and urban environments: A meta-analysis. *Psychological Bulletin, 102*(3), 346–356.

Sterelny, K. (2007). Social intelligence, human intelligence and niche construction. *Philosophical Transactions of the Royal Society of London B: Biological Sciences, 362*(1480), 719–730.

Stickley, A., Koyanagi, A., Roberts, B., & McKee, M. (2015). Urban-rural differences in psychological distress in nine countries of the former Soviet Union. *Journal of Affective Disorders, 178,* 142–148.

Tooby, J., & Cosmides, L. (1992). The psychological foundations of culture. In J. Barkow, L. Cosmoses & J. Tooby (Eds.), *The adapted mind: Evolutionary psychology and the generation of culture.* Oxford, U.K.: Oxford University Press.

Vaillant, G. E. (2012). *Triumphs of experience: The men of the Harvard Grant Study.* Cambridge, MA: Belknap Press.

Vandello, J. A., & Cohen, D. (2004). When believing is seeing: Sustaining norms of violence in cultures of honor. In M. Schaller & C. Crandall (Eds.), The psychological foundations of culture (pp. 281–304). Mahwah, NJ: Erlbaum.

Vandello, J. A., Cohen, D., & Ransom, S. (2008). U.S. southern and northern differences in perceptions of norms about aggression: Mechanisms for the perpetuation of a culture of honor. *Journal of Cross-Cultural Psychology, 39*(2), 162. Retrieved from http://0-search.proquest.com.leopac.ulv.edu/docview/230090139?accountid=25355

Weeden, J., & Sabini, J. (2005). Physical attractiveness and health in Western societies: A review. *Psychological Bulletin, 13*(5), 636–653.

Wolfgang, M. E., & Ferracuti, F. (1967). *The subculture of violence.* London, U.K.: Tavistock.

Woodard, C. (2013). Up in Arms. *Tufts Magazine.* Retrieved from http://emerald.tufts.edu/alumni/magazine/fall2013/features/up-in-arms.html

Zaadstra, B., Seidell, J. C., Van Noord, P. A., te Velde, E. R., Habbema, J. D., Vrieswijk, B., & Karbaat, J. (1993). Fat and female fecundity: Prospective study of effect of body fat distribution on conception rates. *British Medical Journal, 306,* 484–487.

Zuckerman, M. (1999). Diathesis-stress models. In M. Zuckerman (Ed.), Vulnerability to psychopathology: A biosocial model (pp. 3–23). Washington, DC: American Psychological Association.

CHAPTER 6

Human Universals

The study of cultural differences would not be complete without the acknowledgment that human universals also exist; culture changes many things but certainly not everything. This chapter will cover core mental characteristics and processes that are shared by people everywhere. It will begin by presenting a conceptual framework for understanding universality and highlight four different levels of universals (from nonuniversals to attributes that are accessible by everyone to the same degree and used in the same way). It will then present concrete examples of psychological processes that fall within each category of universality (e.g., on the one end, the mere exposure effect is one example of the highest form of universality; on the other end, numerical thinking and statistical reasoning is an example of a phenomenon that is highly culture-specific and that does not exist in certain cultural contexts). As the last chapter in part 1, this chapter will highlight a central but often overlooked thesis in the study of culture and psychology: The goal of cross-cultural studies is *not* to always find cultural differences but, rather, to highlight the precise ways that human beings are similar and different in order to better understand our inherent complexity.

A Reasonable (but Wrong) Conclusion

Up to this point, if you've been paying attention to the previous chapters in the textbook, you would've realized that we have focused exclusively on cultural differences. We've discussed culture as race/ethnicity, comparing European Americans with Latino/as, Asians, African Americans, and Native Americans; and culture as social class, gender, religion, and region. In doing so, you might've walked away with the perfectly reasonable assumption that everyone is always different all the time and that there is little we have in common. And that would be only half true (and therefore wrong).

The reality is this: Group differences are a part of many efforts to understand human behavior. As a result, in cross-cultural psychology, we will say things like "Japanese people have lower self-esteem than European-Americans," or "Southern men are more prone to violence when insulted." In other fields of psychology, they will say things like "people with GAD have irrational beliefs and fears that cause them anxiety" or "the relationships people have with their parents or caregivers will shape the relationships they have for the rest of their lives" or "athletes can choke under pressure." In still other fields (outside of psychology entirely), they will say things like "free trade promotes the global economy" or "the Northern Hemisphere is colder than the Southern Hemisphere."

At the same time, **within-group heterogeneity** is also a basic reality to consider. The statements in the previous paragraph were all generalizations—meaning that they describe how, on average, one group might be different from another, but they do not imply that everyone within a given group is going to act a certain way. This assumption of the heterogenous group is a given across just about every discipline that studies human group differences, and psychology—including cultural psychology—is no different. Where we get into trouble is when we make additional assumptions about cultural differences.

Culture versus Stereotypes

It's an easy accusation to say at the end of a course on culture that the study of cultural differences is no different than a long, illustrious set of stereotypes. If you arrive at that conclusion (and you wouldn't be the first), you would be making the implicit (but erroneous) assumption that cultural differences are stable over time, and somehow based on underlying genetic or biological distinctions between groups, and not changeable. In actuality, cultural differences are only semistable, interactive with genes, and prone to change over time (Norenzayan & Heine, 2005; Heine & Norenzayan, 2006).

The American poet Mark van Doren said something very insightful when he noticed that "there are two statements about human beings that are true: that all human beings are alike, and that all are different. On those two facts all human wisdom is founded" (van Doren, as cited in Klempe & Smith, 2016, p. 29).

The trick, then, is to reconcile and clarify these two dual realities and figure out how we can both be exceedingly similar and yet totally different. The problem is that these two sets of statements reflect larger assumptions in the field of psychology: Mainstream psychology is based on the underlying notion that there are general patterns of human nature that should be relatively universal, stable, and independent of the situation or context, whereas cultural psychology is founded on the alternate reality that humans are fundamentally diverse and dependent on the context. The assumption here is that there are, in a sense, many forms of human nature out there that are culturally bound. While people who study culture do not deny that there are certain processes or phenomena that are indeed universal, they tend to think that culture is incredibly interesting and that all the fun is really in the "noise" of human variability.

The Same, but Different

One way to grapple with the paradox of human nature is to use an analogy you might be familiar with: the Mac versus the PC (photo 6.1). If you've seen any of the ads Apple has created in the past or Apple's general "lifestyle" branding, you should know the general contention Mac users like to put out there—that Macs constitute a fundamentally different animal of a computer than PCs, one that is infinitely more streamlined, efficient, hip, and overall "cool." On a more basic level though, we all know that Macs and PCs are comprised of the same general components, one of the most important of which is the processor. In the same way, we can think of the psyche in the same way. Human nature is essentially the computer processor—we are all "hardwired", so to speak, with a certain set of capacities that allows us to process information, respond to the world around us, and so forth. At the same time, we also have culture-specific tendencies that arbitrate how we behave in a variety of specific situations.

The reason we have a whole field (and textbook) dedicated to the study of these differences is that for the longest time, psychologists have been assuming that they are studying a single, unified human nature but not realizing that in fact, they might have been studying a very particular human nature: the nature of **WEIRD** people (Western, Educated, Industrialized, Rich, Democratic; Henrich, Heine, & Norenzayan, 2010). This raises the question of whether everything we think we know about human nature might apply only to rich, extensively schooled individualists with high self-esteem, or whether some of the things we've learned also apply to the rest of the world.

PHOTO. 6.1. Macs versus PCs, and the paradox of human nature: same, but different

Source: iStock

What does this all mean? Three possibilities exist; all of them are true:

1. Culture doesn't matter.
2. Culture does matter, but not that much.
3. Culture matters and changes everything.

Levels of Universality

To understand how all three of these possibilities could be true, it's useful to consider an analogy that Steve Heine and Ara Norenzayan—two premier cultural psychologists—had put forth back in 2005: Consider that most of the things our brains can do can be called mental "tools"; our brain, therefore, is simply a mental toolbox with different devices we can use to fix, create, and change the world around us. In some cases, everyone might have the same tools in their toolbox. For example, just about every handyman and housewife on the planet likely has a hammer; in this case, a hammer is considered the most universal of universals—everyone has access to it, it works the same way no matter who you are (i.e., for nailing nails), and it is always there when you need it. Norenzayan and Heine (2005) call this type of tool—mental or otherwise—an **accessibility universal**, the most universal of universals. Other terms for this type of universals exist—for example, Daniel Brown's notion of absolute universals—and additional examples include language, emotions, ingroup bias, and reciprocity (Brown, 2004).

Say, alternatively, that you live in a world where you have a hammer, but it's at the very bottom of your toolbox. Technically, you can still use it when you want to, but it would be hard to get to; it wouldn't be the first tool you reach for. Still, you use the hammer in the same way as everyone else. In this case, Heine and Norenzayan (2005) refer to the hammer as a **functional universal**. There are additional tools that are not only easily accessible but used for entirely different purposes. So if you were to use your hammer as a paperweight or a weapon (instead of a device for nailing nails), then it would become an **existential universal** (Heine & Norenzayan, 2005). Finally, if you didn't have a hammer at all, then a hammer would become a **nonuniversal**, something that not everyone had (Heine & Norenzayan, 2005).

Examples of Accessibility Universals

Accessibility universals are typically what most people think of when they say the word, "universal." Not only does everyone have this tool but they use it the same way as everyone else and can use it with equal ease (Heine & Norenzayan, 2005). Heine and Norenzayan (2005) offer up numeracy, social facilitation, and the mere exposure effect as paradigms of accessibility universals. With numeracy, it appears that every society on the planet has some capacity for quantifying things—they don't all rely on the same arabic numeric system, but they have some concept of "number"—even if the only numbers are "one," "two," and "many" (i.e., in the case of the Piraha tribe in the Amazon; Gordon, 2004). Another concept that seems to replicate consistently across populations is "social loafing," the idea that people try less hard when they are working in a group (Karau & Williams, 1993).

Perhaps the most widely studied example of an accessibility universal is the mere exposure effect (photo 6.2), the idea that we like things that are familiar to us. In 1992, Richard Moreland and Scott Beach decided to do an interesting experiment on a psychology class: They picked out a large class—it had a little under 200 kids—in a spacious, fan-shaped lecture hall at the University of Pittsburgh. They also hired four women—all college-age, normal-looking women—to either show up or not show up to class throughout the quarter (Moreland & Beach, 1992). The first woman was told to not show up at all; the second was asked to show up for just five classes; the third was told to go to 10 classes, and the fourth was told to attend 15 classes (Moreland & Beach, 1992). Each woman was also given specific instructions to simply walk into the classroom before class started, sit somewhere near the front row, stay through the entire class, and ignore anyone who tried to talk to her (Moreland & Beach, 1992).

At the end of the quarter, Moreland and Beach (1992) put up photographs of each of these four hired women and asked the psychology class to consider and rate each woman. Had they seen her before? How much did they like her, want to spend time with her, be her friend? How much did they think they had in common with her?

Moreland and Beach (1992) found that most people did not recognize any of the women at all—only a handful reported having seen any of them before. The more interesting finding, however, was that the students reported a greater liking for the women who showed up more often (Moreland & Beach, 1992). In other words, even though they didn't recognize these four women, they liked the ones that came to class more. The one who attended 15 times received the highest ratings, the one who attended 10 times received the second highest, the one who attended five times the third, and the one who didn't come to class at all had the lowest ratings (Moreland & Beach, 1992). Without any kind of recognition, these students had a feeling that they would like, want to spend time with, befriend, and have much in common with the women they had greater exposure to compared to the women they had less exposure to (Moreland & Beach, 1992).

This same experiment has been done dozens of times over, using everything from different people to Chinese characters to flavored drinks. Time after time, the pattern is clear: We like things we've seen or experienced before, even without us knowing that we've seen them. In fact, we like things the most if we've "seen" them before but don't remember that we've seen them. It's so universal that even chickens (Zajonc, Reimer, & Hausser, 1973) and crickets (Harrison & Fisicaro, 1974) appear to show this effect.

Examples of Functional Universals

A functional universal is like an accessibility universal with one difference: Not everyone can use it readily; it comes more easily or more often to some than to others (Heine & Norenzayan, 2005). To illustrate this idea, consider two film renditions (photos 6.3 and 6.4) of Jane Austen's wildly popular novel, *Pride and Prejudice*. In a 2005 remake of this classic tale, Keira Knightley plays the protagonist and must decide whether or not to accept an exceedingly dry marriage proposal in England. In a different, Bollywood version (aptly named *Bride & Prejudice*), Aishwarya Rai Bachchan finds herself in the exact same dilemma, but in an Indian-American community. In both cases, the issue is the same: Do I marry someone that I'm not attracted to? Although in the movie the

PHOTO 6.2. Accessibility universal: so universal that a chicken would show it (in this case, the mere exposure effect)

Source: iStock

plot remains the same, in "real life" the outcomes may vary across cultures as functions of the norms that govern society. In some cultures, there may be strong social norms that emphasize important qualities other than attraction; in a culture like the United States, being attracted to your mate may be of the utmost importance. Attraction is universal, but whether you act on that attraction is a different matter.

As one more example of this idea, consider the previous topic of physical attractiveness and pathogen prevalence. As discussed in the last chapter, everyone likes physically attractive people, but some environments make it so that beauty is especially important. These are environments in which pathogen prevalence is high, and beauty becomes a useful proxy for the ability to avoid pathogens (Gangestad & Buss, 1993). Along a related vein, other research has shown that in areas of the world where overall health is poor, women exhibit especially strong preferences for masculine men, presumably because markers of masculinity in males are often predictors of overall health (DeBruine, Jones, Crawford, Welling, & Little, 2010).

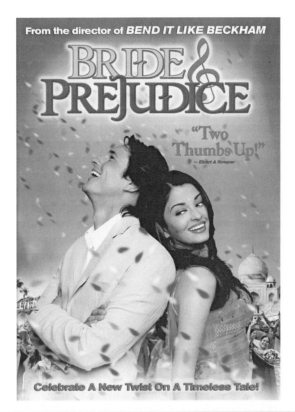

PHOTOS 6.3 AND 6.4. *Bride & Prejudice* versus *Pride & Prejudice*: A matter of functional universals?

Source: Photofest

Examples of Existential Universals

Existential universals are tools that get used differently across cultures, and don't get used at the same rate or frequency everywhere (Norenzayan & Heine, 2005). You and I both have hammers at home, but I use mine primarily for opening young Thai coconuts (that are very hard to crack otherwise), and this on regular occasions (once or twice a month); I imagine you use yours for a different purpose (say, nailing up family photos) and with a different frequency (say, once every few years).

Psychologically speaking, Heine and Norenzayan (2005) cite reasoning as a prime example of an existential universal. Everyone reasons, but not everyone reasons in the same way; East Asians are holistic and intuitive, whereas European Americans are linear and rule-based (e.g., Peng & Nisbett, 1999). It's not that West Asians can't use rules or that European Americans have no idea what intuition is; it's just that on average, the two groups typically opt for different reasoning strategies, and as a result, the likelihood that one group will use a rule (or an intuitive judgment) to make a decision will vary from the other group (Heine & Norenzayan, 2005).

Examples of Nonuniversals

Nonuniversals are fairly self-explanatory; they appear in some cultures but not others. For example, as we discussed in chapter 1, there are certain types of culturally bound disorders, like amok or *dhat*, that are only found in some contexts but not in others. A phobia about your penis shrinking may be found in Southeast Asia or Africa but has rarely been documented in the United States (Yap, 1965).

Summary

Thus, taken together, the evidence for these different levels of universality confirm that all three aforementioned possibilities are true. When it comes to things like quantification, liking things we see often (i.e., the mere exposure effect)—in these cases, culture has no bearing and does not matter; these are fairly universal. In other cases, like who gives you butterflies in your stomach and what you do with those butterflies, culture does change things but only somewhat; these effects are secondary. Finally, in still other cases, like how you reason about the world around you, culture can potentially change everything.

Psychological Universals in the Four Fs: Fighting/ Fleeing, Flirting, and Feeding

Here's the thing: Human beings carry DNA, the basic units of our genetic makeup. And as Dan Gilbert (2012a) once put it, your genes have an agenda for you: They want to make it to the next generation. To do this, they had to make you, build you out of protein and light. The problem is, you don't last forever; you break down over time. But here's the good news: If your genes made you the way they intended, then it doesn't matter if you wear out, because even if you do, you will have built mini-yous to carry on your legacy and your genes (Gilbert, 2012a).

If this story is true, then it naturally follows that all genes everywhere pro-grammed certain basic instincts into all people—certain nonnegotiables that most humans on this planet follow. And so far, the data suggest that these "deal breakers" exist; there are basic psychological universals that rule human nature, and they have to do with the basic duties our genetic material called us to do: to eat and thereby sustain ourselves, to defend ourselves (so we don't die too early, before we've had the chance to procreate), and to mate and thereby pass on our genes.

Fighting and Fleeing

Let's talk about our basic instincts of **fight or flight**—two possible responses people have to defend themselves when threatened. The fact that human beings have been known to aggress is a bit of an understatement; since the beginning of humankind, we have attacked other animals (and other humans included). The question then is: Why do we aggress?

One basic, ostensibly universal idea is the link between pain and aggression, which suggests that in a state of pain, animals will attack (for review, see Berkowitz, 1993). It's not a bad idea either: If you feel pain and you don't necessarily know what is causing your pain, then a good idea would be to attack whatever is nearby, because chances are, it's something close to you that is hurting you (Gilbert, 2012b). We see this phenomenon throughout the animal kingdom, and human beings are no exception. A related phenomenon is the observed link between heat and vio-lence—for example, the fact that violent crime increases in the summer months. Presumably this occurs because unless you live in coastal California or some other highly temperate part of the world, extreme heat is a common source of pain in the summer, and when people are in pain, they are more likely to lash out at others (even though in this case, other people usually have little to do with the heat; Anderson, Anderson, Dorr, DeNeve, & Flanagan, 2000). Experiments show that manipulating the temperature in a laboratory study can lead participants to give strangers more intense electrical shocks when the room feels hot (Baron & Bell, 1976).

Besides heat and pain, one additional commonly observed universal trend when it comes to aggression is gender: Everywhere, men are more violent than women. Lab studies show that this is directly related to testosterone, which has been consis-tently linked to many different forms of aggression; generally speaking, people (men and women alike) who have higher levels of baseline testosterone or who are given injections of testosterone are more likely to behave aggressively (Book, Starzyk, & Quinsey, 2001).

Flirting (and What Comes After)

Fighting to defend yourself is but one of your multiple duties, but fighting alone will not get your genes into the next generation. You also need to flirt or, at min-imum, do the things that typically come after flirting. Unless you mate with other members of your species, your genes will have little chance of getting into the next generation. Although there is immense diversity in how and when people have sex—some will sleep with one person, others will sleep with one million people (consider Genghis Khan, who slept with so many women that 0.5% of the world's population is related to him; Zerjal, 2003). Some like sleeping with women, others prefer men, and some will never sleep with anyone at all. Despite this diversity, averages still exist, and on average, people like sleeping with people of the opposite gender. Thus our focus will be on heterosexual mating patterns in the context of reproduction.

Choosing a Mate

How people mate has certain universal patterns. For one, there is consistent variability in terms of **selectivity**, or who is more demanding in terms of whom they are willing to mate with. The **parental investment model** explains why all across the world, one group of people is more selective than another: women (e.g., see Kendrick, Sadalla, Groth, & Trost, 1990). The reasons for this consistent gender difference are both biological and social. Biologically speaking, the parental investment model suggests that women have a bigger investment at stake when it comes to producing children (for a review, see Kendrick et al., 1990). Women have relatively few eggs compared to men's seemingly unlimited sperm, and not only that, eggs are calorically much more expensive than sperm because of their enormous relative size (Gilbert, 2012a). The time involved in fertilizing said eggs also is vastly different than the time involved in releasing sperm. For a man, it's an investment of one minute or 12 minutes or, if you're really lucky, maybe 20 minutes. For a woman, it's an investment of 10 months at the minimum (40 weeks gestation; see also Finkel & Eastwick, 2009) and more often than not, much longer, because breastfeeding is a natural form of birth control (albeit not a foolproof one). So fertilization costs a man less than an hour but costs a woman years of her life (see photo 6.5). Finally, there is the actual physical cost of having a child: For a man, the work is done postfertilization; for a woman, labor remains the number one cause of mortality for young women in many parts of the world (Mayor, 2004). There are social costs too—a sexually active, unattached man who has sex rarely has elicited much of a societal reaction over the course of human history, but a sexually active, unattached woman who has sex has more often than not been the target of scrutiny, debate, barter, ostracism, stoning, or slut-shaming (Jackson & Cram, 2003).

Given this immense differential in costs involved in the act of mating, it's no surprise that women tend to be highly selective in terms of whom they sleep with, because generally things that are free or cheap elicit little thought but things that are expensive elicit much more. How long does it take for you to accept a free sample of chocolate at See's Candy or jump on a futon posted on the "Free" section of craigslist? (A couple of seconds?) In contrast, how long does it take to pick a college, a spouse, a car, or a house—hours, weeks, months, and sometimes, years? Expensive things necessarily take more time and effort to decide on, and when it comes to mating, things are much more expensive for women than for men. Consistent with this idea, many laboratory studies have confirmed this link between gender and selectivity. In speed dating, on college campuses, and online, men consistently appear less picky than women: They were less likely to say yes when they had a relatively large group of partners to choose from (Fisman, Iyengar, Kamenica, & Simonson, 2006), were more likely to say yes to sex after being propositioned by a moderately attractive confederate (Clark & Hatfield, 1989), and had a greater probability of sending an email after viewing a profile (Hitsch, Hortaçsu, & Ariely, 2010).

PHOTO 6.5. Women: The more selective gender (according to parental investment theory)

Source: iStock

The act of selecting a mate is no accident either, and universally, there are things that nearly everyone finds more attractive than not.

Familiarity and Similarity Consider two depictions (photo 6.6) of one of the most beloved paintings in the world, the Mona Lisa.

Which one do you like better? If you're like most fans, you prefer the photo on the left. But if you ask the actual Mona Lisa, she would most likely say the photo on the right, because people generally like the mirror image of themselves; after all, it's the version of themselves they see the most often. This reflects a broader phenomenon of referring the familiar, which we've already discussed—the **mere exposure effect** (Zajonc, 1968). This effect is so universal that it doesn't just happen in mating and with humans, it appears to happen across romantic and platonic contexts alike and with various animals, too (recall that even bugs and chickens prefer things they've seen before; Harrison & Fisicaro, 1974; Zajonc, et al., 1973).

Related to familiarity is the appeal of similarity. Generally speaking, people prefer those who share their same values, beliefs, and traits. A whole host of evidence is consistent with this idea. In 1990, psychologist David Buss at the University of Michigan, Ann Arbor, had a crazy idea: He thought it'd be interesting to go all over the world and ask people what turned them on. What was it about a woman that makes a man go, "I want that one"? What was it about a man that makes a woman say, "Take me now" (or alternatively, decide "He's gonna be the father of my children")? So he started the International Mate Selection Project (Buss et al., 1990). Contacting 49 fellow researchers from 33 countries, on six different continents and five islands, he asked 9,474 people from Zambia to Taiwan, Norway to Venezuela, what they looked for in a significant other (Buss et al., 1990). Buss et al. (1990) found all kinds of people—men and women, Californians and Arab-Palestinians, yuppies and peasants, Christians and Muslims and every religion in between, majority groups and minorities, from the South African Zulu to the Santa Catarina Brazilians, city-slickers who inhabited well-known metropolises like Shanghai, Tel-Aviv, and Rio de Janeiro to folk who lived in less well-known locales like Kunmings and Ahmadabad. To these people Buss and his research team asked all kinds of questions, from "How many kids would you like?" to "How important is it that your man (or woman) is neat?" He went on to ask about whether culinary skills or a college degree, virgin status or artistic ability—not to mention a host of other possible traits—mattered in a mate (Buss et al., 1990).

In the end, people didn't necessarily rate specific similarities (i.e., in education, religion, and political orientation) as particularly high relative to other qualities (discussed below). But having (presumably similar) desires for home and children emerged as important (at least based on average ratings collapsed across the board,

PHOTO 6.6. The more attractive Mona Lisa?

Source: iStock

it emerged in the top 10 for both men and women; Buss et al., 1990). Buss subsequently went on to conclude that generally speaking, having a partner who is compatible in the goals they want to accomplish and the values they find most important is one of the most important mating strategies that exist (Buss, 2007).

Physical Attractiveness Lesson #1: We are shallower than we think, and this appears to be universally true. At the University of Alberta in Edmonton, Canada, a certain sociologist by the name of Dr. Andrew Harrell likes to study shopping carts. For the past two decades, he's been hanging out at supermarkets and watching the things that would happen when people pushed them around or when children climbed on top of them, or when parents left them temporarily to search for a particular version of Hamburger Helper (Murray, 2005). If you and he were at a cocktail party and you asked him what he did for a living, he'd likely tell you he works on accident analysis and prevention. And that'd be true.

But Harrell would be but far too modest if he left it at just that, because in fact he does so much more. He also studies the beautiful—and ugly—children around those shopping carts. Or more precisely, he studies the parents of these hot and not-so-hot kids. In doing so, he upsets a lot of people.

Harrell upsets them because on one fine Canadian day, he got a team of observers to go to 14 different supermarkets and follow people who had children between the ages of two and five (Murray, 2005). The researchers followed these parents for 10 minutes each; during that fraction of an hour, they wrote down how attractive their kids were, whether they were buckled into the cart, and how often and how far children wandered away from the cart before their parents took notice (Murray, 2005).

The part that frustrated people was not the fact that random strangers were following them around while they were trying to get their week's shopping done. In fact, if those parents who were followed knew that they were being watched, they probably would have acted very differently from the way they did. And how they behaved was precisely what got everyone all riled up.

Harrell and his observers found, very simply, that the prettier children got treated better by their own parents. Overall, of all the children they watched, 1.2% of the ugliest ones were buckled in with a seat belt on the cart compared to more than 10 times that many—13%—of the cutest ones (Murray, 2005). The nice-looking kids also received more attention from their parents, and far fewer of them were allowed to wander more than 10 feet away from the shopping cart, compared to the not-so-nice-looking ones (Murray, 2005).

The difference became all the greater when they were simply looking at fathers. Among all the men observed, not a single one buckled his child in when the child was ugly, whereas 12.5% did when the child was beautiful (Bakalar, 2005). Mothers, on average, were slightly better—with a rate of 4% buckling in not-cute kids and 13% with cute kids—but not by much (Bakalar, 2005).

Lest you think that this shallowness is purely a Canadian phenomenon, consider this: A multinational study of the effects of physical attractiveness across the globe found that men across countries consistently preferred women with large eyes, small noses, and full lips (Jones et al., 1995). Additional meta-analyses have also confirmed that there is largely cross-cultural and cross-age agreement about who is physically appealing and who isn't (Langlois et al., 2000).

Lesson #2: Our universal shallowness takes on specific forms. Contrary to popular belief (even really smart guys like Charles Darwin thought this, when he declared that there was no such thing as "universal standards of beauty"; Darwin, 1874, as cited in Mazur, 1986), beauty is almost never solely in the eye of the beholder; rather, beauty appears to be inherent in the object beheld—meaning that everyone seems to agree on what is beautiful and what isn't. All across this planet, people have this strange, pervasive idea about what is beautiful. Part of it has to do with the way our faces and bodies are arranged, which is likely one of the critical features that differentiated beautiful babies from ugly ones in the aforementioned shopping carts. It's all about **bilateral symmetry** (e.g., Grammer & Thornhill, 1994). If you cut a face in half (digitally) and the right side matches up with the left, then you are bilaterally symmetrical (photo 6.7), and this makes for a beautiful face. You can do this at home with any photographed face taken straight on: Copy the left side of the face, reverse it (i.e., the mirror image), and paste it; do the same for the right side of the face, and compare the three versions you've created—the original face, the left-symmetrical and the right-symmetrical. (If they look the same, then congratulations! You're symmetrical).

There is also good reason for valuing symmetry: It's a good indicator of how many pathogens you were exposed to in your mother's womb, and how currently susceptible you are to disease (Singh, 2002). Like mere exposure, this effect is so universal that we've even observed it in other species. Macaques, for example, prefer to mate with other symmetrical members of their species (Beck, Pinsk, & Kastner, 2005).

It's not just faces; bodies also matter. Here what we find physically attractive depends on gender. For women, the ideal universal body shape is the classic "hour-glass" figure, whose defining characteristics are the small waist and large hips. This shape is so universally sought after that a mathematical formula has been named to capture it: the **Waist-to-Hip ratio** (or **WHR**); ideally, a WHR of around 0.7 is everyone's favorite (Singh, 1993).

Here, it's important to distinguish WHR from a related but nonuniversal index of attractiveness, **Body Mass Index** (or **BMI**). **BMI** varies by country and region; it's also changed over history and time. We used to like our women porkier, then we preferred them skinny, and the tide continues to change—even in the last several decades within the United States, the average size of models in magazines has fluctuated (Singh, 1993). Even when you ask different men at the same time what they prefer, answers about BMI will differ—older men, on average, tend to like heavier women, whereas younger men tend to prefer thinner ones (Singh, 1993). But even though BMI changes, WHR remains stable; young or old, American or not, men consistently like the 0.7 ratio. Even blind men choose mannequins with a 0.7 ratio (Karremans, Frankenhuis, & Arons, 2010).

But what is so magical about 0.7? Studies show that like symmetry, a 0.7 WHR is also an indicator of health and fertility. Women with 0.7 WHRs ovulate more regularly (making it easier to become pregnant) and have higher levels of estrogen (for review, see Singh, 2002). They are less prone to get a variety of diseases (Singh, 2002), including cardiovascular diseases (Dalton et al., 2003) and diabetes (Vazquez, Duval, Jacobs, & Silventoinen, 2007). Not surprisingly, higher WHR is a better predictor of death than high BMI (Price, Uauy, Breeze, Bulpitt, & Fletcher, 2006).

PHOTO 6.7. Beyoncé's bilateral symmetry

Source: Photofest

Beyond WHR, there are additional gender-specific indices of physical attractiveness. For women, those primarily have to do with youth; features like large eyes and large foreheads are also commonly desired, because who has big foreheads and humongous eyes? Babies! And women who resemble babies by virtue of their youthfulness are considered more beautiful for the same reasons that have to do with WHR and symmetry—health and fertility. Younger women tend to be healthier, and more likely to be able to conceive. (Fertility peaks at in the early twenties and goes downhill from there; Dunson, Colombo, & Baird, 2002).

Resources We don't just value beauty; we also like resources. This is particularly true when it comes to men, for which resources appears to be a universal index of appeal. Historically, it's easy to see why this might be the case: If patriarchy has been the norm for millennia, then having access to resources required having access to them through men. Recent studies have shown, though, that even in relatively gender-equal societies like ours and even among wealthy women, women *still* prefer men with resources (Fales et al., 2016). If anything, rich women want men even richer than themselves (Fales et al., 2016). This observation isn't new; popular culture abounds with intuitions about the importance of a man's resources for a woman evaluating his mate appeal:

> Now I ain't sayin' she a gold digger / But . . . —Kanye West, "Gold Digger"

Kanye may have not been calling her a gold digger (not explicitly, at least, in that particular line), but one baby Louis Vuitton, one Serena-like ass, and four kids later, he advises, "holla, 'we want prenup / WE WANT PRENUP.'" And rightfully so, perhaps.

Consider the aforementioned international mating study by David Buss (1989). Across all countries, the biggest difference between the sexes was how much (1) good financial prospects and (2) good looks (as mentioned before) mattered. Overall, women valued earning capacity and all the things associated with this dough-making ability—ambition, industriousness, stability, maturity, social status, education, intelligence, and a college degree—far more than men. Men, in contrast, considered physical attractiveness far more important than women did (Buss, 1989).

Kindness and Love Lest you think that humanity is invariably more shallow than you thought possible, consider this: What's on the inside also matters. Character traits like kindness and understanding are on the top of the list of what people everywhere look for when choosing someone to spend their lives with. When David Buss asked men and women from 37 different cultures what was important to them in choosing a life partner, individuals unanimously declared that kindness was one of their top three criteria—not a single group ranked it lower than third (Buss, 2008). In a few cases, men and women differed: Sometimes, men cared about kindness more than women (e.g., Japan, Taiwan) and other times, women cared more than men (e.g., Nigeria, Israel, France), but in all the other cultures, both men and women agreed on its utmost importance (Buss, 2008).

Related to kindness, Buss also found other internal features that people everywhere found important. For example, mutual love and attraction consistently were also rated very highly; in the Americas, Eastern and Western Europe, and much of Southeast Asia and the Middle East, they consistently ranked in the top three in importance; only in China and a few African countries like Nigeria and South Africa did it rank lower, ranging from number four to number eight (Buss, 1989). Other highly rated qualities across the board included intelligence, exciting personality, dependability, and emotional stability (Buss, 1989).

Feeding: Universal Patterns in BMI?

The previous findings have suggested that BMI is *not* a universal; it varies too much over time and between countries. But this variability might belie a deeper underlying universality in terms of *why* people prefer certain BMIs, and when they do so. Consider this finding: South African Zulus prefer women with higher BMIs than Brits, but British Zulus and Brits of African descent both prefer women with relatively low BMIs (Tovée, Swami, & Furnham, 2006). It might be because of British *Vogue*, or it might be because of something deeper: the link between body size, poverty, hunger, and health.

Consider one of the cultural examples of places where men prefer larger women: South Africa. Given the challenges South Africans face in terms of access to resources, economic opportunities, and adequate medical care, then in a place like that, higher BMI might be a relatively good index of wealth (Tovée et al., 2006). If being larger means having access to resources, then it is precisely the places where resources are lacking that especially tend to emphasize large body size as an appealing mate quality (for review, see Swami & Tovée, 2006).

BMI in these contexts is also reflective of health. In the South African example, illnesses like diarrhea and tuberculosis are real public health issues that plague a substantive portion of the population, and one of the side effects of these common illnesses is weight loss (Tovée et al., 2006). Thus, once again, having a high BMI becomes a signal in one's favor, because it indicates that the person is unlikely to be dying from a parasitic or contagious disease (for review, see Swami & Tovée, 2006).

To test this theory empirically, British psychologists Viren Swami and Martin Tovée (2006) decided to do a brilliant and simple study. Between 6:00 and 7:00 p.m. on a somewhat random school day in London, Swami and Tovée (2006) stationed two tables outside their U.K. university's dining hall, one at the entrance and one at the exit, and stopped every man that walked by; upon stopping them, the psychologists first asked how hungry the men were. As expected, the guys entering the dining commons were way hungrier than the ones leaving, but that, however, was not the point; the point came with what they gave to each man after he admitted his hunger pains (or lack thereof; Swami & Tovée, 2006). To each, Swami and Tovée (2006) had experimenters hand a booklet of full-body images of 50 real women: Of the 50 women, there were 10 starving-African-child types, 10 who were thin but not quite anorexic, 10 average, 10 rather chunky, and 10 full-on obese. Each wore an identical, utterly unforgiving outfit of gray leotards and tights (science can be cruel at times), and to protect their anonymity—as well as to avoid the persuasive effects of faces—each had their facial features blurred (Swami & Tovée, 2006).

The two groups of men—the hungry ones entering the dining hall and the full ones leaving—were simply asked to rate how attractive they found each woman (Swami & Tovée, 2006). Afterward, Swami and Tovée (2006) went back to their labs, plugged in each man's response into their computers, and found that the hungry guys liked their women chunkier than the full ones. While for both groups of men there was a clear preference for women closer to the average body size than either extreme—both the too fat and the too thin—there was also a clear difference in optimal curviness, with the empty-stomached males finding the well-insulated women more attractive than the full ones (Swami & Tovée, 2006).

Apart from offering hope to those of us with more of ourselves to love—literally— Swami and Tovée's (2006) finding also explains a good deal about the strange changes we've seen in society's idealization of women's bodies over the history of humankind. If you've ever walked through an art museum and peered, slightly amazed or confused, at the life-sized portraits of naked female bathers with their fair share of rolls, handles, and jiggle, and later that day you opened a *Cosmo* and found a photo of Kate Moss, as waif-like as ever, then you know what I'm referring to. It seems that for the first 1,800 years or so of modern human history, fat women were "it." If Ruben's *The Three Graces* or Renoir's *The Bathers* portraits were the closest thing the 19th century had to *Playboy*, then certainly most of our incumbent "girls next door" would need to put on one or two (or fifty) pounds to compete. Come the 1920s, and the American flapper image causes a temporary cutback in desired female bodily baggage, but with the iconic fame of Marilyn Monroe in the 1950s, curves are in again. (The rest of the world, in the meantime, doesn't appear to change their mind as much about what they want.) But since Marilyn's untimely death, things have pretty much headed downhill in terms of desirable female body weight, and the 2010s are certainly no exception.

Even nowadays, though, there is still a good deal of variability in terms of what men—and women themselves—want. Go anywhere in the continent of Africa and chances are no man will look twice at you if you're one of those 5'11", 115-pound types. And even within a country such as Great Britain or Malaysia, scientists have found that the rich tend to prefer the skinnier while the poor tend to prefer the fatter (Swami & Tovée, 2007). Taken together, it all points to the overarching idea that *desire* is fundamentally a function of *availability*: When food is scarce (as was the case for the vast majority of time in human history), we want the fat girls because there're not that many around, and the ones that are can survive the famines and aren't deprived. But when food is abundant—as we increasingly find in this country—then thin is in, because thin is now so devastatingly hard to attain: When was the last time you heard of a famine in the United States? And what's more, thin is a luxury; it means you have the means to eat well and get a trainer (or at least a membership to 24 Hour Fitness) and have the spare change to buy magazines and books that tell you what to put in your mouth if you want to achieve the Mary-Kate Olsen look.

Morality Universals

Back in 2002, the United Kingdom's premier tabloid magazine, *The Sun*, came out with the year's most startling allegation: Jean Curtis was shocked and appalled to find her husband, Ian Curtis, penetrating her Sunday lunch—in this case, a frozen chicken. A dismayed Jean promptly files for divorce while Ian protests that she told the story all wrong (according to him, it wasn't his wife that caught him doing the nasty with the frozen chicken but a neighbor who allegedly caught him in the deed and ended up telling on him to his wife—because that changes everything; "Wife caught husband having sex with frozen chicken," 2002).

Surprisingly or not, when a group of psychologists presented this kind of scenario (minus the details about any wife, upset or not) to a group of Philadelphia residents and Brazilians, most people agreed that yes, it is indeed wrong to have sex with a frozen chicken and then try to cook and eat it afterward (Haidt, Koller, & Dias, 1993).[1] Despite all the differences Philadelphians may have with Brazilians— from their culinary uses for chicken to the amount of fabric contained in their swimsuits—almost everyone tended to come together on this basic fact of life: It's morally reprehensible to violate frozen meat (Haidt et al., 1993).

Now this consensus in and of itself is not terribly shocking—that is, until you sit still for a minute and ask yourself why exactly it is wrong to have sex with a frozen chicken. After all, the chicken is frozen and dead and thereby indifferent to

---

[1] The only exception to this finding: High socioeconomic status residents from Philly tended to find nothing wrong with the scenario (Haidt, Koller, & Dias, 1993).

anyone's sexual advances, however ludicrous. The man paid for the chicken, surely, so what is it to anyone else what he does to his own groceries?

Who then is the victim in this scenario?

As long as the man does the deed in the privacy of his own home, who is about to suffer for his sexual idiosyncrasies? In other words, when you consider the scenario from a purely rational standpoint, you very quickly realize that there is absolutely nothing technically wrong with having sex with a frozen chicken after all. As long as it's a single man doing it in his own home using his own money to pay for the chicken, there is no victim and no harm. But still, something feels awry with this picture.

Alternatively, consider this story: Julie and Mark are siblings who decide to go on a summer trip to France, where they find a cabin to stay in by the beach (Haidt, 2001). One night, they decide it'd be fun to have sex with one another—it'd be a new experience for both of them (Haidt, 2001). Julie is on birth control, and Mark uses a condom just to be extra safe; moreover, although they both enjoy it, they decide not to do it again and keep their special night together a secret (Haidt, 2001).

What's wrong—if anything—with that?

Once again, if you're like most people, you're probably rather appalled right about now. The idea of a brother and sister doing it at a beachside French cabin is not exactly your idea of a romantic love story or even an acceptable one-night-stand story at that. Still, like the story with the frozen chicken, the same questions arise: Who is the victim here, and who is being harmed? Assuming that Julie and Mark are both consenting adults, what's wrong with a man and a woman, with no alternative commitments, having safe sex once with no possibility of repercussions and no reported emotional damage?

Such scenarios also extend beyond the realm of sex—consider, again alternatively, a woman who finds an old, raggedy [American] flag in her closet and decides to clean her toilet with it, or a family whose dog is hit by a car and, after grieving for their pet, decides to have him for dinner (Haidt et al., 1993). In all such cases, no victim can be found, and no harm can be pointed to. Yet still, something feels vaguely (or intensely) wrong with each one. How come?

Scenarios like the ones above have led recent moral psychologists to conclude that our human notions of right and wrong have little to do with what is rational (Haidt, 2001). After all, rationality would tell you that a man is allowed to do what he wants with a frozen chicken he buys himself, and two consenting adults can have any kind of sex they please as long as they're not hurting or implicating anyone else. Yet the majority of people in the world appear to throw their rationality out the door when they declare, with great conviction and little doubt, that eating a piece of meat you've recently penetrated is surely wrong, as is two siblings doing it in a beachside cabin. It appears then, that it is not our rationality at work when we decide what is right versus wrong but something entirely oblivious to reason: our intuition. This idea is at the core of the **Social Intuitionist Model** of morality, which says that morality is fundamentally intuitive, social, and about more than just harm or fairness (Haidt, 2001). In other words, our notions of what is good, right, and appropriate (versus bad, wrong, and inappropriate) have little to do with our mind's ability to reason about the world; instead, it has everything to do with what our gut tells us about how we feel (Haidt, 2001). We can't necessarily put our finger on it, but something inside us jumps up in protest when we encounter something disgusting or reprehensible or terribly out of place. We may not be able to tell you why, but we know for sure that it is true. Goodness and badness, rightness and wrongness, then, are not so much about reasoning but rather about feeling. We know because we feel. That's not to say that we, as rational human beings, haven't come up with all kinds of ways to rationalize what we feel, particularly when we have to explain ourselves to other people. And that is precisely why our sense of right and wrong seems to have the illusion of rationality—because so much time is spent justifying why we think what is right is right and what is wrong is wrong. In actuality though, our feeling came first, and reasoning only came about as an afterthought, a contraption we've devised to show others that we're not crazy (Haidt, 2001).

At this point though, you might be wondering why it is, if our morality is so intuitive, so natural, so something we're born with rather than something we arrive at, that people can disagree so intensely sometimes on what is right and wrong? After all, you don't have to look much farther beyond gay rights, abortion, illegal immigrants, and war to realize that normal, everyday Americans profoundly disagree on some of the things they consider acceptable or not. If morality is truly a matter of "gut feelings," then why do our guts differ so much?

To answer this question, all we have to do is look at something else we humans are all born with but yet differs drastically across people: language. As a species we have the unique ability to communicate through words and speech, syntax and metaphor. Indeed, developmental psychologists have long noted that our human capacity for language is something encoded in our very genes (for review, see Davies, 2003). As babies we are born ready for language, and as nearly all parents can attest to, children learn language at astonishing rates—rates that can only be explained by some innate, biological program that sets us up for language acquisition quickly, easily, almost effortlessly. Yet despite our universal capacity to speak and listen, (grown) people differ drastically in the kinds of sounds that they use and can recognize within language. The Chinese word for *fish*, or "yüe" (spelled phonetically), for example, is one sound that most nonnative-Chinese speakers cannot recognize, much less pronounce. Yet when you examine young children, you find that across cultures, kids are able to distinguish between far more sounds used in different languages (phonemes) than their adult counterparts. With age and learning, however, children very quickly loose this capacity to make and distinguish the sounds that are not commonly used within their own languages. Thus it appears that we selectively "lose" our capacity for things that don't get used.

The same thing apparently applies to morality as well. We may be born with all kinds of moral intuitions about what is inherently right or wrong, but with time, learning, and acculturation, we very quickly learn to emphasize certain intuitions over others and lose sense of some intuitions entirely. Among certain cultures, for example, there is a very keen sense of "the sacred." These are the things that have special significance, usually of a divine nature, that need to be treated with special attention and care—even if they seem to the unsuspecting outsider to be very ordinary at face value (cases in point: cows; virginity; Saturdays). Yet to the average

American, our sense of the sacred is pretty rusty, if not nonexistent. Apart from perhaps a handful of truly devout religious folk, most people—regardless of their official religious affiliation—have little conviction about the specialness of the Sabbath, or what the sanctity of marriage truly means for the way they talk to their spouse when no one is watching. As Americans, though, we do have a very sharp sense of "the fair." It's been the reason that we kicked out the British, launched the Civil War, and started every movement (for women, for Blacks, for gays, etc.) in our history. Unlike most other countries, we have a particularly strong obsession with dividing up our pies in equal shares (though we still fail quite often), but when we don't, there is usually a class-action lawsuit somewhere around the corner. Ultimately, then, though we may be born with a universal sense of right and wrong—about "the fair," "the sacred," and a host of other moral intuitions—we gradually learn from the world around us to give certain intuitions up and retain others. Nevertheless, at the end of the day, some things—like eating a frozen chicken you've bonked—still strike mostly everyone as at least a tad wrong.

Moral psychologists formulated these ideas into the **moral foundations theory**, which states that there are universal moral "building blocks" that every culture has; every society on the planet has norms and values, and people are born with the innate capacity to learn them (Graham et al., 2012). These blocks they call "moral foundations," and which foundations get emphasized depends on the cultural context; these foundations include harm/care, fairness, loyalty, authority, and sanctity (Graham et al., 2012). Thus, according to Graham et al. (2012), moral foundations theory says that these building blocks are universal, but culture dictates what ultimately emerges from these basic units.

Religious Universals

Related to morality is the issue of religion, given that religion often has much to say about the many lines between right and wrong. As with other forms of culture, religions also share many similarities across religious groups. Similar arguments have also been made about the nature of the universals in religion. Researchers like Saroglou (2011) have argued that in the same way that there are five universal dimensions underlying morality (Haidt, 2001; Graham et al., 2012), there are also universal dimensions underlying religion—namely, the **"Big Four" Religious Dimensions** having to do with beliefs, bonds, behavior, and belonging. Beliefs have to do with cognitive ideas about the nature of humans' relationship with the larger universe—a feature that is part of most world religions (Saroglou, 2011). Belonging centers on promoting community and group cohesion (Saroglou, 2011); it's consistent with the organized, communal nature of religion and the finding that generally speaking, collectivistic cultures are also more religious (Sagy, Orr, & Bar-On, 1999). Bonds deal with using rituals (like prayer) to promote specific religious emotions (like awe; Saroglou, 2011). Finally, behaviors are about following particular rules and guidelines, similar to the moral codes discussed previously (Saroglou, 2011). Ultimately, then, culture will change the content and importance of these dimensions, but all religions contain some version of them (Saroglou, 2011).

Despite variations in the specific content and importance of these dimensions between different world religions, nearly all major religious traditions share commonalities in personality structures and values.

Universal Correlates between Religiosity and Individual Differences

Human beings are walking, talking pentaracts—five-dimensional entities. Psychologists disagree about many things, but on the topic of personality there is almost universal agreement that all human beings fall somewhere along a five-dimensional space known classically as the **Big Five Model of Personality** (Pervin & John, 1999). These five dimensions of personality include openness to experience (i.e., are you exploratory and spontaneous?), conscientiousness (i.e., are you reliable and consistent?), extraversion (i.e., do you prefer a high degree of arousal and are you energized by the presence of other people?), agreeableness (i.e., are you easy to get along with?), and neuroticism (i.e., are you prone to negative emotions?), commonly referred to as OCEAN (Pervin & John, 1999). Reviews of studies on personality and religiosity have consistently found that religious people everywhere tend to share the share the same personality profile: They are highly agreeable and very conscientious (Saroglou, 2002). Interestingly, religiosity's link to openness and neuroticism is more nuanced (see Saroglou, 2002, for review). This relationship between religion and personality appears to exist cross-culturally and across different religious traditions (Saroglou, 2002). In other words, when it comes to personality, whether you are religious (or not) matters more than the precise content of your religion.

Personality is not the only individual difference that is related to religion, however. An additional, well-studied distinction is that between men and women. Overall, women are more likely to be religious than men, and this difference cannot be explained by social roles, secularization, or division of labor; across cultures and societies, the religious tend to be female (Stark, 2002).

Universal Links between Religiosity and Values

In addition to individual differences, religion also appears to be correlated with specific kinds of values. Values themselves have certain universal structures—Schwartz (1992) argued that there are 10 value types that exist across cultures, and cultures agree on the general content and motivational nature of these. Others have gone on to argue that these values also vary consistently across religions. For example, studies on Christians, Jews, and Muslims have found that in a meta-analysis of data from 15 countries, religious individuals placed higher value on tradition, conformity, and benevolence and lower value on hedonism, stimulation, and self-direction relative to nonreligious individuals (Saroglou, Delpierre, & Dernelle, 2004). Still, other studies have not found strong evidence that religion or spirituality is universally linked to a specific value profile (Schwartz, 1992).

Key Concepts

Within-group heterogeneity
WEIRD
Levels of universality: accessible, functional, existential, nonuniversal
Fight or flight
Selectivity
Parental investment model
Mere exposure effect
Bilateral symmetry
Waist-to-Hip ratio (or WHR) vs. Body Mass Index (or BMI)
Social Intuitionist Model
Moral foundations theory
"Big Four" Religious Dimensions
Big Five Model of Personality

References

Anderson, C. A., Anderson, K. B., Dorr, N., DeNeve, K. M., & Flanagan, M. (2000). Temperature and aggression. *Advances in experimental social psychology, 32*, 63–133.

Bakalar, N. (2005). Ugly children may get parental short shrift. *The New York Times*. Retrieved from http://www.nytimes.com/2005/05/03/health/ugly-children-may-get-parental-short-shrift.html?mtrref=www.google.com

Baron, R. A., & Bell, P. A. (1976). Aggression and heat: The influence of ambient temperature, negative affect, and a cooling drink on physical aggression. *Journal of Personality and Social Psychology, 33*(3), 245–255.

Beck, D. M., Pinsk, M. A., & Kastner, S. (2005). Symmetry perception in humans and macaques. *Trends in Cognitive Sciences, 9*(9), 405–406.

Berkowitz, L. (1993). Pain and aggression: Some findings and implications. *Motivation and emotion, 17*(3), 277–293.

Book, A. S., Starzyk, K. B., & Quinsey, V. L. (2001). The relationship between testosterone and aggression: A meta-analysis. *Aggression and Violent Behavior, 6*(6), 579–599.

Brown, D. E. (2004). Human universals, human nature & human culture. *Daedalus, 133*(4), 47–54.

Buss, D. M. (1989). Sex differences in human mate preferences: Evolutionary hypotheses tested in 37 cultures. *Behavioral and Brain Sciences, 12*(1), 1–14.

Buss, D. M. (2007). The evolution of human mating. *Acta Psychologica Sinica, 39*(3), 502–512.

Buss, D. M. (2008). The evolution of desire. New York, NY: Basic Books.

Buss, D. M., Abbott, M., Angleitner, A., Asherian, A., Biaggio, A., Blanco-Villasenor, A., . . . Ekehammar, B. (1990). International preferences in selecting mates: A study of 37 cultures. *Journal of Cross-Cultural Psychology, 21*(1), 5–47.

Clark, R. D., & Hatfield, E. (1989). Gender differences in receptivity to sexual offers. *Journal of Psychology & Human Sexuality, 2*(1), 39–55.

Dalton, M., Cameron, A. J., Zimmet, P. Z., Shaw, J. E., Jolley, D., Dunstan, D. W., & Welborn, T. A. (2003). Waist circumference, waist–hip ratio and body mass index and their correlation with cardiovascular disease risk factors in Australian adults. *Journal of Internal Medicine, 254*(6), 555–563.

Darwin, C. (1874). *The descent of man*. New York, NY: Prometheus Books.

Davies, A. (2003). *Nativism*. London, U.K.: Blackwell Publishing.

DeBruine, L. M., Jones, B. C., Crawford, J. R., Welling, L. L., & Little, A. C. (2010). The health of a nation predicts their mate preferences: Cross-cultural variation in women's preferences for masculinized male faces. *Proceedings of the Royal Society of London B: Biological Sciences, 277*(1692), 2405–2410.

Dunson, D. B., Colombo, B., & Baird, D. D. (2002). Changes with age in the level and duration of fertility in the menstrual cycle. *Human reproduction, 17*(5), 1399–1403.

Fales, M. R., Frederick, D. A., Garcia, J. R., Gildersleeve, K. A., Haselton, M. G., & Fisher, H. E. (2016). Mating markets and bargaining hands: Mate preferences for attractiveness and resources in two national US studies. *Personality and Individual Differences, 88*, 78–87.

Finkel, E. J., & Eastwick, P. W. (2009). Arbitrary social norms influence sex differences in romantic selectivity. *Psychological Science, 20*(10), 1290–1295.

Fisman, R., Iyengar, S. S., Kamenica, E., & Simonson, I. (2006). Gender differences in mate selection: Evidence from a speed dating experiment. *The Quarterly Journal of Economics, 121*(2), 673–697.

Fisman, R., Iyengar, S. S., Kamenica, E., & Simonson, I. (2008). Racial preferences in dating. *The Review of Economic Studies, 75*(1), 117–132.

Gangestad, S. W., & Buss, D. M. (1993). Pathogen prevalence and human mate preferences. *Ethology and sociobiology, 14*(2), 89–96.

Gilbert, D. (2012a). Reproduction. Retrieved from Harvard University course, Science of Living Systems.

Gilbert, D. (2012b). Survival. Retrieved from Harvard University course, Science of Living Systems.

Gordon, P. (2004). Numerical cognition without words: Evidence from Amazonia. *Science, 306*(5695), 496–499.

Graham, J., Haidt, J., Koleva, S., Motyl, M., Iyer, R., Wojcik, S. P., & Ditto, P. H. (2013). Moral foundations theory: The pragmatic validity of moral pluralism. In *Advances in experimental social psychology* (Vol. 47, pp. 55–130). Cambridge, MA: Academic Press.

Grammer, K., & Thornhill, R. (1994). Human (Homo sapiens) facial attractiveness and sexual selection: The role of symmetry and averageness. *Journal of Comparative Psychology, 108*(3), 233–242.

Haidt, J. (2001). The emotional dog and its rational tail: A social intuitionist approach to moral judgment. *Psychological Review, 108*(4), 814–834.

Haidt, J., Koller, S. H., & Dias, M. G. (1993). Affect, culture, and morality, or is it wrong to eat your dog? *Journal of Personality and Social Psychology, 65*(4), 613–628.

Harrison, A. A., & Fisicaro, S. A. (1974). Stimulus familiarity and alley illumination as determinants of approach response latencies of house crickets. *Perceptual and Motor Skills, 39*, 147–152.

Heine, S. J., & Norenzayan, A. (2006). Toward a psychological science for a cultural species. *Perspectives on Psychological Science, 1*(3), 251–269.

Henrich, J., Heine, S. J., & Norenzayan, A. (2010). Most people are not WEIRD. *Nature, 466*(7302), 29.

Hitsch, J. H., Hortaçsu, A., & Ariely, D. (2010). Matching and sorting in online dating. *The American Economic Review, 100*(1), 130–163.

Jackson, S. M., & Cram, F. (2003). Disrupting the sexual double standard: Young women's talk about heterosexuality. *British Journal of Social Psychology, 42*(1), 113–127.

Jones, D., Brace, C. L., Jankowiak, W., Laland, K. N., Musselman, L. E., Langlois, J. H., . . . Symons, D. (1995). Sexual selection, physical attractiveness, and facial neoteny: Cross-cultural evidence and implications [and comments and reply]. *Current Anthropology, 36*(5), 723–748.

Karau, S. J., & Williams, K. D. (1993). Social loafing: A meta-analytic review and theoretical integration. *Journal of Personality and Social Psychology, 65*(4), 681–706.

Karremans, J. C., Frankenhuis, W. E., & Arons, S. (2010). Blind men prefer a low waist-to-hip ratio. *Evolution and Human Behavior, 31*(3), 182–186.

Kenrick, D. T., Sadalla, E. K., Groth, G., & Trost, M. R. (1990). Evolution, traits, and the stages of human courtship: Qualifying the parental investment model. *Journal of personality, 58*(1), 97–116.

Klempe, S. H., & Smith, R. (Eds.). (2016). *Centrality of History for Theory Construction in Psychology* (Vol. 14). Berlin, Germany: Springer.

Langlois, J. H., Kalakanis, L., Rubenstein, A. J., Larson, A., Hallam, M., & Smoot, M. (2000). Maxims or myths of beauty? A meta-analytic and theoretical review. *Psychological Bulletin, 126*, 390–423.

Man bonks frozen chicken. (2002). *The Sun.* Retrieved from https://www.thesun.co.uk/article/0,,2-2002391829,00.html

Mayor, S. (2004). Pregnancy and childbirth are leading causes of death in teenage girls in developing countries. *British Medical Journal, 328*(7449), 1152.

Mazur, A. (1986). US trends in feminine beauty and overadaptation. *Journal of Sex Research, 22*(3), 281–303.

Moreland, R. L., & Beach, S. R. (1992). Exposure effects in the classroom: The development of affinity among students. *Journal of Experimental Social Psychology, 28*(3), 255–276.

Murray, T. (2005). Are ugly kids less loved? Retrieved from https://sites.ualberta.ca/~publicas/folio/42/16/05.html

Norenzayan, A., & Heine, S. J. (2005). Psychological universals: What are they and how can we know? *Psychological Bulletin, 131*(5), 763–784.

Peng, K., & Nisbett, R. E. (1999). Culture, dialectics, and reasoning about contradiction. *American Psychologist, 54*(9), 741–754.

Pervin, L. A., & John, O. P. (1999). *Handbook of personality: Theory and research.* New York, NY: Guilford Press.

Price, G. M., Uauy, R., Breeze, E., Bulpitt, C. J., & Fletcher, A. E. (2006). Weight, shape, and mortality risk in older persons: Elevated waist-hip ratio, not high body mass index, is associated with a greater risk of death. *The American Journal of Clinical Nutrition, 84*(2), 449–460.

Sagy, S., Orr, E., & Bar-On, D. (1999). Individualism and collectivism in Israeli society: Comparing religious and secular high-school students. *Human Relations, 52*(3), 327–348.

Saroglou, V. (2002). Religion and the five factors of personality: A meta-analytic review. *Personality and Individual Differences, 32*(1), 15–25.

Saroglou, V. (2011). Believing, bonding, behaving, and belonging: The big four religious dimensions and cultural variation. *Journal of Cross-Cultural Psychology, 42*(8), 1320–1340.

Saroglou, V., & Cohen, A. B. (2013). Cultural and cross-cultural psychology of religion. In R. F. Paloutzian & C. Park (Eds.), *Handbook of the psychology and religion and spirituality* (2nd ed., pp. 330–354). New York, NY: Guilford Press.

Saroglou, V., Delpierre, V., & Dernelle, R. (2004). Values and religiosity: A meta-analysis of studies using Schwartz's model. *Personality and Individual Differences, 37*(4), 721–734.

Schwartz, S. H. (1992). Universals in the content and structure of values: Theoretical advances and empirical tests in 20 countries. *Advances in Experimental Social Psychology, 25,* 1–65.

Singh, D. (2002). Female mate value at a glance: Relationship of waist-to-hip ratio to health, fecundity and attractiveness. *Neuroendocrinology Letters, 23*(Suppl. 4), 81–91.

Singh, D., Dixson, B. J., Jessop, T. S., Morgan, B., & Dixson, A. F. 2010. Cross-cultural consensus for waist-to-hip ratio and women's attractiveness. *Evolution and Human Behavior, 31*, 176–181.

Stark, R. T. (2002). Physiology and faith: Addressing the "universal" gender difference in religious commitment. *Journal for the Scientific Study of Religion, 41(3)*, 495–507.

Swami, V., & Tovée, M. J. (2006). Does hunger influence judgments of female physical attractiveness? *British Journal of Psychology, 97(3)*, 353–363.

Swami, V., & Tovée, M. J. (2007). The relative contribution of profile body shape and weight to judgements of women's physical attractiveness in Britain and Malaysia. *Body Image, 4(4)*, 391–396.

Tovée, M. J., Swami, V., Furnham, A., & Mangalparsad, R. (2006). Changing perceptions of attractiveness as observers are exposed to a different culture. *Evolution and Human behavior, 27(6)*, 443–456.

Vazquez, G., Duval, S., Jacobs, D. R., & Silventoinen, K. (2007). Comparison of body mass index, waist circumference, and waist/hip ratio in predicting incident diabetes: A meta-analysis. *Epidemiologic Reviews, 29(1)*, 115–128.

Wife caught husband having sex with frozen chicken. (2002). Retrieved from http://www.shortnews.com/start.cfm?id=24763

Yap, P. M. (1965). Koro—a culture-bound depersonalization syndrome. *The British Journal of Psychiatry, 111(470)*, 43–50.

Zajonc, R. B. (1968). Attitudinal effects of mere exposure. *Journal of Personality and Social Psychology, 9(2, pt. 2)*, 1–27.

Zajonc, R. B., Reimer, D. J., & Hausser, D. (1973). Imprinting and the development of object preference in chicks by mere repeated exposure. *Journal of Comparative and Physiological Psychology, 83(3)*, 434–440.

Zerjal, T. (2003). The genetic legacy of the Mongols. *The American Journal of Human Genetics, 72(3)*, 717–721.

CHAPTER 7

Intergroup Conflict
Stereotypes, Prejudice, and Discrimination

The first chapter of Part 2 will begin by highlighting how cultural differentiation (i.e., the processes outlined in Part 1) and stereotyping are based on the same underlying processes—in this case, categorization of people into different groups—but can lead to drastically different outcomes. This chapter will discuss how both negative and positive stereotypes can produce systematic and detrimental effects, including stereotype threat, prejudice, and discrimination. This chapter will also highlight the distinction between traditional notions of racism versus modern racism, implicit versus explicit racial attitudes, and the implications racism has for real-world behavior, such as police shootings, personnel selection, and mating.

Otrar, Kazakhstan, 1218: A Mongol and his entourage arrive in the city to greet Shah Ala ad-Din Muhammad, then ruler of Khwarezmid Empire; they come in the name of Genghis Khan, their fearless leader, to inquire about the recent killing spree of Mongolian merchants in the area (Islam, 2016). Things do not go well; Genghis finds this out soon enough and sends his troops to destroy the entire city and invade greater Central Asia (Islam, 2016). Today, Otrar is a ghost town ("Ancient city of Otrar," n.d.).

Jaffa, Syria, early 1799: A short Frenchman with a little-man complex takes 13,000 French soldiers into the city and sticks bayonets through each of the 2,000 Turkish soldiers there who are trying to surrender (afterward, he goes on to kill all their wives and children); he went by the name of Napoleon (Peterson, 1995).

People's Republic of China, 1949–1953: A librarian issues a policy to kill at least one landlord in every village in China a la public execution, and two to five million landlords, business owners, revolutionaries, intellectuals, and farmers die or disappear during his first political campaign; his name was Mao (Strauss & Southerl, 1994).

Location undisclosed, 2004: A bearded, graying man shoots a home video. On it, he talks about the 1982 invasion of Lebanon and mourns the killing of women and children among the 15,000 Arabs that were killed and many more injured; he goes on to say that he is responsible for the September 11 attacks on the Manhattan Twin Towers ("Full transcript of bin Laden's speech," 2004). He called himself Osama.

Syria, 2016: There are the Sunnis and the Shias, the pro-Assad and the rebels, jihadists, and other sectarian groups. As of this writing, a quarter million Syrians have died over the conflict and more than 11 million have become refugees (BBC News, 2016).

All of the above examples were cases of intergroup conflict, and each yielded devastating, history-shifting consequences. Thus you can't really talk about cultural differences without making at least some mention of the fact that yes, cultural conflict is often part of the equation. And you don't even need me and my stories of war criminals and young men gone bad, terribly bad, to notice that conflict due to cultural, racial, ethnic, or religious reasons is A Pretty Big Deal last time you checked. Maybe it's not as big a deal as it used to be, but still, for much of human history—and particularly that of the past few centuries, it seems—these group differences have instigated all kinds of quibbles and wars and genocides. Real or not, group differences have nevertheless been the reason Hitler gave his comrades when he explained why they were going after brunettes and not blondes, the rationale Mao gave his compatriots when he told them why they were going to turn inward for revolution and throw out all things White and Western.

The common story about the problem of groups goes a little something like this: A particular group of people doesn't like another group of people because it's "different." As a result, they end up doing terrible things to each other, like call each other names; kill one another; refuse to associate, marry, live next to, go to school with, or share a drinking fountain with one another; and the like. If you're lucky, both groups just get away with associating with their own kind and spending as little time with the other group as possible, while secretly holding their ideas about what "those" people are like. If you're not so lucky, they end up stoning, burning, and generally annihilating each other.

Now, I am not here to discount group differences. I'm certainly not one to say that groups don't matter, or that we in the 21st century have somehow learned to get over it (we haven't). What I will argue is that the story is simply not as simple as it seems.

Consider this: Recently, a middle school election in San Francisco became a controversy of national proportions when the school principal announced that she would not be revealing the winners of the school election because the elected candidates were not "diverse enough" (Cestone, 2015). Everett Middle School is in the Mission District of a progressive, liberal, racially diverse, and relatively well-to-do city (the housing market in San Francisco is one of the most expensive in the country, rivaled only by Manhattan). Yet despite this social milieu, parents, students, and administrators could not apparently agree on the best course of action for a usually straightforward affair—choosing a student body president and other elected officials. Apparently, despite the school's large Latino/a and African American population (65%), the top elected spots all went to White and Asian students ("Student election kerfuffle," 2015). This is an example of intergroup conflict in an unusual but modern way: We want to be fair; we want to treat everyone equally; sometimes, though, the solutions remain murky and hotly contested.

The fact that intergroup conflict remains even as diversity and egalitarian attitudes become more and more the norm highlights a basic, underlying reality about the nature of stereotypes: On a fundamental level, stereotyping is largely a cognitive by-product of important and unavoidable processes all humans engage in—categorization. Categorization (photo 7.1) is what happens when you effectively put a "label" on an object and identify it as a member of a group or category; you then use that group membership to make (general) inferences about the object and what it is like (Taylor, 1981). Without categorization and generalization, you would not begin to be able to function, because we categorize and generalize all the time about virtually everything we encounter—be it breakfast items or neighbors or household goods or strangers. The problem is that when we use these processes too often or too indiscriminately, we're engaging in stereotyping, or using group membership to make generalizations about an individual member of that group (see Ashmore & Del Boca, 1981; Taylor, 1981).

Stereotypes versus Prejudice versus Discrimination

You don't need me to tell you that stereotypes are problematic; you don't even need to look farther back than the last 100 years of society to recall all the ills brought on by stereotypes, prejudice, and discrimination—from exclusionary policies and tactics to keep certain groups out to segregation and hate crimes. Nevertheless, it's important to distinguish between these three phenomena, because stereotypes, prejudice, and discrimination are not synonymous.

PHOTO 7.1. Categorization forms the basis for stereotyping.

Stereotypes are typically cognitive in nature; they refer to the specific judgments you make about a person based on what group he or she appears to belong to (Dovidio, Hewstone, Glick, & Esses, 2010). You can have stereotypes about the intelligence of blondes or the mathematical abilities of Asians or the athletic abilities of African Americans or about the monetary practices of the Irish or the childbearing practices of Catholics, for that matter. Prejudices are affective or emotional; they have to do with the negative attitudes you have toward a person or a group because of the stereotypes you believe about them (Dovidio et al., 2010). So if you consider blondes to be less than ideal students and you like them less because of it, then you are both stereotyping and experiencing prejudice. Discrimination is primarily behavioral; it occurs when you act in ways that disadvantage a person or group because of group membership (for a review, see also Dovidio, Brigham, Johnson, & Gaertner, 1996). So if you choose not to pick a class member for a group project because of the person's hair color, you are engaging in discrimination.

Although all three of these phenomena are related, it's important to distinguish between them because some of them are more avoidable than others, a topic we will elaborate on below.

The Automatic Nature of Stereotypes and Prejudice

Let's start with the bad news: Stereotypes are unavoidable; they are one feature of intergroup relations that we will likely never be rid of, because they reflect a cognitive process built into our very brains. Studies on the illusory correlation suggest that people seem to inevitably associate minority groups with negative behaviors because both represent statistically rare events, and we associate like with like (Hamilton & Gifford, 1976). Several decades of work on the Implicit Association Test (IAT) have found that after giving millions of people a computerized categorization task involving the use of different keys to represent different groups (e.g., different races, ages, religions, sexualities, etc.) and different words (e.g., good, bad), the conclusion is abundantly clear: Everyone holds stereotypes, at least unconsciously (Greenwald, McGhee, & Schwartz, 1998). For example, people routinely are faster to pair Whites, butterflies, and young people with good than to pair African Americans, bugs, and elderly people with good (Greenwald et al., 1998). The difference is a matter of seconds, but the effects suggest that when we have little control over our behavior in a reaction-time task that demands us to tap keys on a keyboard as quickly as possible, our unconscious minds take over—and our unconscious is incredibly stereotypical and prejudiced.

Interestingly, these effects don't disappear when members of the stereotyped group are doing the IAT. African Americans, it appears, also are faster to associate European Americans with good and African Americans with bad; although their effects are not as pronounced as those of European American participants, the pattern is nevertheless the same (Greenwald et al., 1998). This suggests that part of the reason stereotypes and prejudice are so ingrained and ostensibly intractable is that we are all too often exposed to the same associations all around us—in the news, on the TV, and in movies. And even when we don't mean to stereotype or show prejudice, our brains can't help but notice the number of times a Black male is committing a fictional crime on the screen compared to the number of times a White male is doing so. Over the course of a lifetime, these patterns form and contribute to stereotypes and prejudices based on skin color.

The IAT is not without its critics, however. Some have argued that the IAT is more about societal associations than personal prejudices and that even the staunchest proponents of African American rights would "fail" the IAT and show anti-Black sentiment (e.g., see Hal Arkes and Phil Tetlock's 2004 article, "Would Jesse Jackson Fail the IAT?"). Even so, additional studies have further confirmed that regardless of whether our IAT effects are societal or personal in nature, the outcomes are devastating. When Black and White participants come into the lab to play a video game containing Black and White targets holding guns or household objects, everyone tends to make the same mistakes: They fail to shoot armed White targets and accidentally shoot unarmed Black targets (Correll, Park, Judd, & Wittenbrink, 2002).

The Self-Confirming Nature of Stereotypes

If the automatic nature of stereotypes is responsible for some of their most devastating effects—leading to errors not just in the aforementioned shooter studies but also in recent (and not so recent) tragedies involving cases of police shooting unarmed Black targets—then the self-confirming nature of stereotypes is likely responsible for the fact that stereotypes, once they exist, are incredibly hard to get rid of.

Stereotype Threat and Lift

One of the oldest and most studied phenomena involving stereotypes is stereotype threat. Claude Steele and Joshua Aronson first discovered this effect in 1995, when they gave African American and European American college students an achievement test akin to the SAT; half of the participants were asked to indicate their race and the other half were not. In an alternative version, Steele and Aronson (1995) told half of the participants that the test was diagnostic of their ability whereas the other half were told it simply measured "problem solving." When participants weren't reminded of their race—or when the participants thought the test was not diagnostic of their ability—race had no bearing on the outcomes; Black and White students performed equally well, as you would expect for college students who made it into the same competitive university (Steele & Aronson, 1995). But when race was made salient or the test was alleged to be diagnostic, stereotypes became a reality and Black students underperformed compared to their White counterparts (Steele & Aronson, 1995).

Numerous studies on stereotype threat have followed this seminal study, and we now know that the effect doesn't just happen with African Americans in achievement contexts. It also happens with

- Women and math (Spencer, Steele, & Quinn, 1999)
- Men and social sensitivity (Koenig & Eagly, 2005)

- Students from low socioeconomic backgrounds and intellectual underperformance (Croizet, 1998).
- Minorities and women and academic underperformance (Aronson, Quinn, & Spencer, 1998).
- Blacks and Whites and athletic performance (Stone, Lynch, Sjomeling, & Darley, 1999).

Interestingly, the reverse pattern happens when the stereotype is positive—a phenomenon known as stereotype lift (i.e., when you perform better in a positively stereotyped domain; Shih, Pittinsky, & Trahan, 2006). Think about it—for every group that is subject to a negative stereotype, there is also a different group that, relatively speaking, is subject to the positive version of the same stereotype. If women are supposedly bad at math, then men are supposedly good at math; if men are supposedly bad at being emotionally attuned, then women are supposedly good at it. Consistent with this idea, studies have shown that reminding people of a positive stereotype that applies to their group can also help performance. Take the example of Asian women, who are subject to two divergent stereotypes when it comes to their math abilities. Remind them of their Asian-ness and they do worse on a math test; remind them of their gender and they do better (Shih et al., 2006; and also see photo 7.2).

PHOTO 7.2. Whether an Asian woman experiences stereotype threat or lift when taking a math test depends largely on whether you remind her of her gender or ethnicity.

Source: iStock

Collective Threat

These aforementioned effects don't just happen at the individual level; they can even happen when you are watching another member of your group find himself or herself in a stereotypical situation. Researchers have labeled this **collective threat** (Cohen & Garcia, 2005). In 2005, Geoffrey Cohen and Julio Garcia recruited Black college students to come into the lab and complete a study; when they showed up, half of them saw a fellow Black student about to take a SAT-like test measuring verbal ability (the other half saw a fellow Black student do a nonthreatening task—namely, completing a series of verbal puzzles). Most notably, the participants themselves did not have to take the test and were not being evaluated at all, but still, Black participants showed lower self-esteem after watching a member of their group cast in a stereotype-threat situation (Cohen & Garcia, 2005). Not only that, but when asked about their qualities and interests, these participants avoided picking stereotypically "Black" ones (e.g., basketball, working out, or rap); when given the chance to sit next to the other Black student, they sat farther away (Cohen & Garcia, 2005). When Cohen and Garcia (2005) later replicated this same experimental setup with women watching a fellow woman do a math test, the same effects emerged. Interestingly, they specifically recruited math and engineering majors—essentially, women who should be used to defying the stereotype that math is a field that men are better at—and they still found evidence of collective threat (Cohen & Garcia, 2005).

Prejudice and Discrimination

Stereotypes are but one feature that mars intergroup relations. Although they are, by definition, cognitive constructs we hold in our minds, the previously mentioned studies on stereotype threat, lift, and collective threat suggest that they can nevertheless exert powerful and harmful effects on very real outcomes. Speaking of outcomes, stereotypes are also prone to leading to two other forms of problematic intergroup contact—prejudice and discrimination. Unlike stereotypes, these take on more affective and behavioral manifestations.

Microaggressions

Jerry Seinfeld—having long retired from starring in his long-running, cult-following of a sitcom named after himself—produces his own online show. He calls it, *Comedians in Cars Getting Coffee*; not surprisingly, it involves exactly what the title implies. One day, he invited a South African comic by the name of Trevor Noah to have coffee with him; Noah had recently acquired the highly coveted gig of host of *The Daily Show*, a news program on Comedy Central. The two comics discussed many things, but at one point, they got onto the topic of soccer, which Jerry called "your football."

Why is this important? The comment was no doubt harmless and not intended to offend, but as Noah himself pointed out, it's a bit patronizing to refer to soccer as "your" football when considering the reality that worldwide, far more people play and watch that sport than American football. Thus, as he argued, soccer really should be referred to as "the" football.

This is somewhat of a superficial example, but it reflects a broader phenomenon we call **microaggressions**—ostensibly small comments or actions that appear trivial to the person committing them but not to the person they are directed at (Sue, 2010). Instead, these seemingly "little things" tend to elicit anger, irritation, hurt, and racial tension (Williams, 2000). Microaggressions can happen to a variety of groups and are not exclusively about race; in addition to people of color, we find that women, immigrants, and people from underrepresented sexual identities (i.e., LGBTQ individuals) are often the target of them (Sue, 2010). Like more overt forms of racism, microaggressions also send highly negative messages and often lead to poor outcomes when it comes to performance and mental health (Sue, 2010).

Examples of microaggressions abound. When a photographer at a New York university asked her classmates to write down the kinds of microaggressive comments they've personally received, they had no shortage of examples (see https://www.buzzfeed.com/hnigatu/racial-microaggressions-you-hear-on-a-daily-basis).

Whether it's someone marveling at your English skills or giving you a compliment-jab ("Wow, you're really [insert positive trait here] for a [insert negatively stereotyped group here]") the underlying sentiments appear to be the same. Microaggressions undermine people's identities and achievements. According to Sue, Bucceri, Lin, Nadal, and Torino (2009), they can take on the form of micro assaults, or explicitly prejudicial and discriminatory statements (e.g., using derogatory racial slurs), micro insults, which often sound like compliments but actually imply that the person being targeted belongs to an inferior group (e.g., telling a woman that she can really throw, for a girl), and micro invalidations, which minimize or ignore a group's experiences (e.g., by telling someone that you "don't see race").

Despite the label "micro," microaggressions are still harmful. Alvin Poussaint calls them "death by a thousand nicks" (Jones, 2000). While some may think that they reflect innocent statements that mean no harm, others like Sue et al. (2009) contend that if anything, microaggressions may be even more harmful than explicit, conventional racism.

Racism Comes in Many Flavors: Implicit versus Explicit Prejudice

Before the IAT and microaggressions, there were self-reported measures of explicit racism. Contrary to implicit prejudice—which is involuntary, fast, and subconscious—explicit prejudice was the opposite—voluntary and deliberate; this distinction is consistent with the larger literature on attitudes more broadly, which also distinguishes between attitudes we hold implicitly versus explicitly (for review, see Dovidio, Kawakami, & Beach, 2008). You may not be aware of, or have much control over, your response on the IAT, but you are fully cognizant of how you rate other groups on explicit measures, which typically take the form of a survey or questionnaire.

Because of these differences, it's not surprising that how people respond on implicit versus explicit racism measures often diverge. For example, Dovidio, Kawakami, and Gaertner (2002) brought White students into the lab and had them interact with either another White person or a Black one. Beforehand, Dovidio et al. (2002) gave both implicit and explicit measures of racism: For the implicit measure, they had participants view subliminally, on a computer screen, a series of Black and White faces that were followed by positive and negative words; implicit prejudice was operationalized by reaction time to the word after seeing the face. If you were slower to respond to positive words after seeing a Black face, for example, this implied prejudice against Blacks. For the explicit measure, they completed the Attitudes Toward Blacks Scale (Brigham, 1993). Afterward, when Dovidio et al. (2010) had participants interact in the lab with a Black or White partner and rate their own behavior as well as be rated by coders, they found that not only were the implicit and explicit measures not significantly related to one another but they also predicted different outcomes: While the implicit measure predicted participants' nonverbal behavior, the explicit measure predicted their verbal behavior. In other words, what they said they felt about Blacks reflected how they talked to a Black person, but what their reaction time suggested about their subconscious racial attitudes was reflected in their body language (Dovidio et al., 2002).

Implicit and explicit prejudice—though not identical—nevertheless are related. A subsequent meta-analysis by Hofman, Gawronski, Le, and Schmitt (2005) found that after examining 126 studies that included both types of prejudice measures, the overall correlation between the two was 0.24—suggesting that the relationship between implicit and explicit prejudice is small, but the two are not entirely dissociate. Hofman et al. (2005) examined a variety of explicit self-reports, including different types of scales, semantic differential ratings, thermometers, and other kinds of ratings. Furthermore, the researchers also found that a variety of additional factors impact the strength of the association between the IAT and explicit prejudice measures (Hofman et al., 2005). For example, although social desirability did not influence the link, factors like how spontaneous the self-reported measure was or how closely the object of the self-report and IAT aligned were both important in predicting the strength of the relationship (Hofman et al., 2005).

Implications

Police Shootings Recent media coverage of tragic police shootings and movements like Black Lives Matter have made questions of racial bias in police shooting a matter of public conscience (photo 7.3), but even before Michael Brown and Freddie Gray, there was Amadou Diallo, Abner Louima, and Rodney King. Amadou Diallo was the Guinea immigrant shot 41 times by four undercover New York police officers when he was sitting on his porch (Cooper, 1999). He thought he was being robbed by four White men in plainclothes and reached in his pocket to retrieve his wallet—they thought he was reaching for a gun (Cooper, 1999). His story has since been widely disseminated thanks to books like Malcom Gladwell's best-selling *Blink*. Three years prior, in 1996, Abner Louima was tortured by a NYPD officer in a precinct bathroom (Fried, 1999). Before that, there was Rodney King, whose videotaped beating by the LAPD (and its subsequent acquittal) incited days of rioting (Adams, 2016).

In 2002, a group of psychologists headed by Joshua Correll started a series of studies that tried to unpack and explain this pattern of racial bias in these all too real life-and-death contexts. In their seminal study, they designed a video game where the premise was simple: Shoot the bad guys; don't shoot the good guys. In

PHOTO 7.3. Movements like Black Lives Matter have brought longstanding issues of implicit racism into the public eye.

Source: iStock

this case, bad guys were targets with guns; good guys were targets with household objects (Correll et al., 2002). The manipulation Correll et al. (2002) designed was a matter of race—some of the targets were White; others were Black. What they found confirmed suspicions: People tended to make mistakes with both kinds of targets, but the nature of the mistake was asymmetrical. White targets carrying guns were mistakenly not shot; Black targets not carrying guns were mistakenly shot (Correll et al., 2002). This effect replicated across multiple studies involving undergraduates as participants and continued to emerge when they looked at Black and White community members—everyone appeared to be making the same types of mistakes (Correll et al., 2002).

Correll and his colleagues went further. In a follow-up study, Correll, Park, Judd, & Wittenbrink (2007), compared trained police officers and community members on the same task and found both good and bad news. The bad news was that when it came to reaction times, everyone appeared biased—that is, both community members and police acted faster when the target was consistent with stereotypes than when the target wasn't (i.e., they took longer to react to an armed White target or an unarmed Black target; Correll et al., 2007). The good news was that police officers performed better than community members: Not only were they less trigger-happy but they were more accurate; relative to community members, police officers set a higher standard for deciding to shoot a Black target (everyone set a high standard for shooting a White target; Correll et al., 2007). Furthermore, they found that training improved accuracy among college students (Correll et al., 2007).

Additional studies have shown that context also matters. Reading newspaper stories about Black criminals exacerbated biases in shooting (Correll et al., 2007), suggesting that cultural exposure is part of both the problem and the potential solution. If we want to change our subconscious biases, we need to change what our brains are exposed to, what we see. Interestingly, in yet another follow-up series of studies, Sadler, Correll, Park, and Judd (2012) examined how racial biases played out when other groups were taken into account—namely, Latinos and Asians. Sadler et al. (2012) found that among college students, the only bias was against Black targets in terms of reaction time. With police officers, their reaction-time measures appeared biased in more nuanced ways—that is, showing more bias against Latinos than White or Asians and more bias against Whites than Asians (Sadler et al., 2012). In terms of accuracy, there was an unexpected pattern: Both samples were more accurate with Black and Latino targets than White and Asian ones (Sadler et al., 2012).

Personnel Selection Not all studies suggest that that the implicit racial bias on the IAT is a reliable predictor of discrimination, however. When Blanton, Jaccard, Klick, Mellers, Mitchell, & Tetlock (2009) reanalyzed the findings from Ziegert and Hanges's (2005) study, they found that the predictive power of the IAT was quite small and fragile—in other words, simply knowing a person's IAT score did not allow you to reliably predict whether the person would show racial bias in a hypothetical management situation. In the original study, Ziegert and Hanges (2005) found that IAT scores predicted whether a person would discriminate against a Black candidate under conditions that condoned racial bias—that is, when told the majority of people in an organization was White. Blanton et al. (2009) also reanalyzed data from a related study on the IAT and discrimination—one by McConnell and Leibold (2001), which did not examine personnel selection in particular but, rather, looked at interpersonal interactions with White versus Black experimenters. Similarly, the authors also found the IAT to be an unreliable predictor of actual discrimination; if anything, participants who showed more implicit anti-Black prejudice on the IAT actually acted more positively toward the Black experimenter (Blanton et al., 2009).

In a subsequent meta-analysis, Oswald, Mitchell, Blanton, Jaccard, and Tetlock (2013) examined the link between IAT scores and a host of discriminatory outcomes, including microaggressions, explicit judgments across a variety of contexts (like academic ability), and even support for public policies and political candidates. They concluded based on their analysis that the IAT emerged as a weak predictor of discrimination (Oswald et al., 2013). In addition, based on the studies included in their analysis, the IAT exhibited a relatively low correlation with explicit measures; the only exception was in the context of fMRI studies, where IAT scores exhibited stronger correlations with brain activity (Oswald et al., 2013).

Mating Less studied is prejudice in the context of mating. Although there might be relatively limited numbers of lab studies on how prejudice plays a role in dating and romantic contexts, recent online survey data suggest that in matters of the heart, race remains a big deal. When Facebook's dating app, Are You Interested? (AYI), asked their users to scan the profiles of other users and indicate their level of romantic interest, they found systematic patterns of favoritism: Asian women were routinely preferred by all groups of men except, ironically, men from their own group (i.e., Asian men did not favor Asian women, but everyone else did); White men were preferred by all groups of women with the exception of Black women (King, 2013). Of course, universal gender differences were also replicated, and men were more interested in women than women were in men (King, 2013).

Data from the online dating platform OKCupid revealed a similar pattern. When Christian Rudder—OKCupid's mathematician founder—analyzed five years' worth of data from millions of users in 2014, he also found consistent differences by race (Rudder, 2014). In this case, Asian men and Black women consistently got the shaft: Asian men were unfavored by all groups except Asian women (who, although they rated Asian men positively, also rated White men even more so); Black women were also unfavored by all groups (Rudder, 2014). Over time, racial preferences did not attenuate, and if anything, appeared to strengthen (Rudder, 2014). Rudder went on to cover these findings and more in his book *Dataclysm*.

Positive Stereotypes: Fact or Illusion?

Thus far we have focused almost exclusively on negative stereotypes. However, stereotypes, by definition, are not necessarily negative. If a stereotype is simply a generalized belief about members of a group, then this belief could be about a favorable or unfavorable attribute. Indeed, for every negative stereotype about one group, there is likely a complementary positive stereotype about another group. But are positive stereotypes truly beneficial?

Some of the most commonly studied cases of positive stereotypes include: Asians and math (Shih, Pittinsky, & Ambady, 1999), women and verbal ability (Shih et al., 2006), and African Americans and athleticism (Stone, Perry, & Darley, 1997; Stone et al., 1999). Not surprisingly, in all these studies, researchers have shown that being reminded of the positive stereotype associated with your group can improve your performance in that domain—essentially, the stereotype lifts phenomenon discussed earlier. A meta-analysis of this tendency revealed that overall, groups who are not subject to negative stereotypes end up doing better under conditions where they are reminded of a negative stereotype that applies to someone else (Walton & Cohen, 2003). In other words, people seem to benefit from the negative stereotypes suffered by other people, and as long as the stereotype doesn't apply to your group, you actually end up doing better when you are reminded of it.

The story, though, is almost never as straightforward as it seems. Athletes talk about "**choking**," or doing worse, not better, when expectations about their performance are high, presumably because such expectations increase their pressure to perform and heighten their anxiety about failure. The same phenomenon can apply at the group level. For example, when Asians or males were reminded about the positive stereotypes surrounding their group in terms of mathematical ability, they reported being more distracted and ended up doing worse on a math test (Cheryan & Bodenhausen, 2000; Rosenthal & Crisp, 2007).

Choking under the pressure of high expectations is not the only liability that accompanies positive stereotypes. Another idea is that positive stereotypes almost never occur in a vacuum; rather, positive and negative stereotypes go hand in hand. For every positive stereotype that benefits a group, there is almost always a negative stereotype that harms that same group. For example, although Asians are often touted as the "model minority" that benefits from positive stereotypes surrounding their math skills, educational prowess, and lack of criminality, numerous studies have shown that there are also plenty of negative stereotypes about Asians' inferior personality and social skills. They may be smart and well-behaved, but they are also deemed to be socially awkward, cold, and likely to take advantage of a situation (e.g., Cuddy et al., 2007). This tendency for negative stereotypes to accompany positive stereotypes led some researchers to coin the term *envious prejudice* in the context of Asian Americans, based on the idea that the very positive stereotypes that are applied to them ultimately lead to jealousy, which leads to the endorsement of negative stereotypes (Cuddy et al., 2007; Ho & Jackson, 2001; Lin, Kwan, Cheung, & Fiske, 2005).

Choking and envious prejudice are part of a larger, more systematic problem with positive stereotypes—namely, groups who are positively stereotyped still experience discrimination, but these barriers are often ignored or denied (Suzuki, 2002). To illustrate, work by Espenshade and Radford (2009; as cited by Nieli, 2010) found that the standards for Asian applicants to competitive colleges were far higher than those for other races in terms of SAT scores; back when the test was scored to a maximum of 1600, Asians needed a score of 1550, whereas White applicants needed a score of 1410 and African American applicants needed a score of 1100. Since then, others have observed that while the number of Asian students in top University of California schools—which adopt a race-blind system and are public—have steadily increased over time, the percentage at private Ivy League schools has remained the same, suggesting a quota system that makes it harder for Asians to get in (Unz, 2013). This has been shown in empirical studies too, which have been used to argue for a shifting standards model that suggests that people use different standards for judging members of different groups and that the standard is typically based on within-group norms—that is, individuals are judged against other members of their race or gender (Biernat, 1995). Others have argued that positive stereotypes also severely limit the chance for Asians to have opportunities in nonacademic contexts—for example, in the arts and in professional sports (Wong & Halgin, 2006; Sue & Okazaki, 2009) or in television (Taylor & Stern, 1997).

Knowing Is Half the Battle: What Alleviates Stereotype Threat?

Still, there is hope. Stereotypes and prejudices abound, but interventions are possible. One idea is to use education as a means of combating stereotype threat. To this end, in 2015, three psychologists from the University of Arizona—Michael Johns, Toni Schmader, and Andy Martens—recruited female undergraduates for a stereotype threat study, but with a twist: In one condition, they told the women about the effects of stereotype threat. In the other two conditions, they induced stereotype threat by describing the test the women were about to take as either a math test or a problem-solving one (Johns, Schmader, & Martens, 2005). Specifically, they warned women that they might feel anxious during the test and that if they did, this was likely the result of negative stereotypes but had little to do with their actual abilities (Johns et al., 2005). They found that learning about the effects of stereotype threat protected the women from the typical stereotype threat effects—in that condition, they performed no worse than when they were in the problem-solving condition (Johns et al., 2005).

Still, awareness alone may not always suffice, and not all knowledge is created equal. In a different study, Pinel, Warner, and Chua (2005) measured something they called **stigma consciousness,** or how aware college students were of the stigmas associated with race. When testing this at a predominantly White college, they found that being aware of stigmas actually predicted worse outcomes, not better ones. Among men, those who were part of stigmatized groups (in this case, African Americans and Latinos) performed worse in terms of GPA as a function of being more aware of racial stigmas (Pinel et al., 2005). Among women, stigmatized participants experienced lower self-esteem when they were more aware of stigma (Pinel et al., 2005). This suggests that mere awareness is not enough; educational interventions explaining the psychological effects of stereotypes may be necessary to alleviate those effects.

Beyond education, other interventions have also been tested. When it comes to changing implicit attitudes, past studies have shown that exposing individuals to positive examples of a stereotyped group can undermine subconscious prejudice. When Wittenbrink, Judd, and Park (2001) showed White participants a movie clip of a Black family BBQ, they found that this exposure of African Americans interacting in a positive context lead to decreased reaction time biases on the IAT. Other studies have taken this one step further and suggested that purposely conditioning people to associate stigmatized groups with positive words can also work. By using an evaluative conditioning paradigm, Olson and Fazio (2006) paired Black faces with positive words (and White faces with negative words) repeatedly; afterward, they found that individuals who went through such conditioning showed more positive implicit attitudes toward Black faces.

Summary

In this world you will have trouble. Having read this chapter, you will hopefully know by now that stereotypes are built into our very being, our brains were designed to categorize the social world, and moreover, our brains were designed to make mistakes about those categories. Once you have stereotypes ingrained, things like prejudice, discrimination, and microaggressions are only a stone's throw away; both news stories and laboratory studies abound with examples of how certain groups are systematically disadvantaged in dating, employment, and the criminal justice system, just to name a few. But what I hope you also learned was that the story of stereotypes and discrimination is not so clear-cut and simple as you might think; it is not a simple matter of one group having negative ideas about another group. Rather, stereotypes are almost always shared. Moreover, both positive and negative stereotypes come with serious liabilities. But this brings up the good news: Because they are socially constructed and culturally perpetuated, we have a hand in their existence and get to change the way we construct the realities we're exposed to.

Key Concepts

Stereotypes vs. prejudice vs. discrimination
Implicit Association Test
Collective threat
Microaggressions
Choking
Envious prejudice
Stigma consciousness

References

Adams, C. (2016, March 3). March 3, 1991: Rodney King beating caught on video. Retrieved November 2, 2016, from http://www.cbsnews.com/news/march-3rd-1991-rodney-king-lapd-beating-caught-on-video/

Ancient city of Otrar. (n.d.). Retrieved from http://www.travelokazakhstan.com/destinations/ancient-city-of-otrar/#.WkgdJGU0l-U

Arkes, H., & Tetlock, P. (2004). Attributions of Implicit Prejudice, or "Would Jesse Jackson 'Fail' the Implicit Association Test?" *Psychological Inquiry*, *15*(4), 257–278. Retrieved from http://www.jstor.org/stable/20447239

Aronson, J., Quinn, D. M., & Spencer, S. J. (1998). Stereotype threat and the academic underperformance of minorities and women. *Prejudice*, 83–103. doi:10.1016/b978-012679130-3/50039-9

Ashmore, R. D., & Del Boca, F. K. (1981). Conceptual approaches to stereotypes and stereotyping. In D. L. Hamilton (Ed.), *Cognitive processes in stereotyping and intergroup behavior* (pp. 1–35). Hillsdale, NJ: Erlbaum.

BBC News. (2016, March 11). Syria: The story of the conflict. Retrieved from http://www.bbc.com/news/world-middle-east-26116868

Belkin, D. (2016). Asian-American groups seek investigation into Ivy League admissions. Retrieved from http://www.wsj.com/articles/asian-american-groups-seek-investigation-into-ivy-league-admissions-1464026150

Biernat, M. (1995). The shifting standards model: Implications of stereotype accuracy for social judgment. In Y.-T. Lee, L. J. Jussim, & C. R. McCauley (Eds.), *Stereotype accuracy: Toward appreciating group differences* (pp. 87–114). Washington, DC: American Psychological Association.

Blanton, H., Jaccard, J., Klick, J., Mellers, B., Mitchell, G., & Tetlock, P. E. (2009). Strong claims and weak evidence: Reassessing the predictive validity of the IAT. *Journal of Applied Psychology*, *94*(3), 567–582.

Brigham, J. C. (1993). College students' racial attitudes. *Journal of Applied Social Psychology*, *23*(23), 1933–1967.

Cestone, V. (2015, October 16). Video: San Francisco middle school refuses to tell winners of election, students say principal believes winners are not diverse enough. Retrieved from http://kron4.com/2015/10/16/video-san-francisco-middle-school-refuses-to-tell-winners-of-election-students-say-principal-believes-winners-are-not-diverse-enough/

Cheryan, S., & Bodenhausen, G. V. (2000). When positive stereotypes threaten intellectual performance: The psychological hazards of "model minority" status. *Psychological Science, 11*(5), 399–402.

Cohen, G. L., & Garcia, J. (2005). "I am us": Negative stereotypes as collective threats. *Journal of Personality and Social Psychology, 89*(4), 566–582.

Cooper, M. (1999, February). Officers in Bronx fire 41 shots, and an unarmed man is . . . . *The New York Times.* Retrieved November 2, 2016, from http://www.nytimes.com/1999/02/05/nyregion/officers-in-bronx-fire-41-shots-and-an-unarmed-man-is-killed.html

Correll, J., Park, B., Judd, C. M., & Wittenbrink, B. (2002). The police officer's dilemma: Using ethnicity to disambiguate potentially threatening individuals. *Journal of Personality and Social Psychology, 83*(6), 1314–1329.

Correll, J., Park, B., Judd, C. M., Wittenbrink, B., Sadler, M. S., & Keesee, T. (2007). Across the thin blue line: Police officers and racial bias in the decision to shoot. *Journal of Personality and Social Psychology, 92*(6), 1006–1023.

Croizet, J. C., & Claire, T. (1998). Extending the concept of stereotype threat to social class: The intellectual underperformance of students from low socioeconomic backgrounds. *Personality and Social Psychology Bulletin, 24*(6), 588–594.

Dovidio, J. F., Brigham, J. C., Johnson, B. T., & Gaertner, S. L. (1996). Stereotyping, prejudice, and discrimination: Another look. In C. N. Macrae, C. Stangor, & M. Hewstone (Eds.), *Stereotypes and stereotyping* (pp. 276–319). New York, NY: Guilford Press.

Dovidio, J. F., Hewstone, M., Glick, P., & Esses, V. M. (2010). Prejudice, stereotyping and discrimination: Theoretical and empirical overview. In *The SAGE handbook of prejudice, stereotyping and discrimination* (pp. 3–29). London, U.K.: Sage Publications.

Dovidio, J. F., Kawakami, K., & Beach, K. R. (2008). Implicit and explicit attitudes: Examination of the relationship between measures of intergroup bias. In R. Brown & S. Gaertner (Eds.), *Blackwell handbook of social psychology: Intergroup processes* (pp. 175–197). Malden, MA: Blackwell.

Dovidio, J. F., Kawakami, K., & Gaertner, S. L. (2002). Implicit and explicit prejudice and interracial interaction. *Journal of Personality and Social Psychology, 82*(1), 62.

Espenshade, T. J., & Radford, A. W. (2009). *No longer separate, not yet equal: Race and class in elite college admission and campus life.* Princeton, NJ: Princeton University Press.

Fried, J. P. (1999, May 7). In Louima's first day on stand, he tells of brutal police assault. *The New York Times.* Retrieved from http://www.nytimes.com/1999/05/07/nyregion/in-louima-s-first-day-on-stand-he-tells-of-brutal-police-assault.html

Full transcript of bin Laden's speech (2004). Retrieved from http://www.aljazeera.com/archive/2004/11/200849163336457223.html

Greenwald, A. G., McGhee, D. E., & Schwartz, J. L. (1998). Measuring individual differences in implicit cognition: The implicit association test. *Journal of Personality and Social Psychology, 74*(6), 1464–1480. doi:10.1037/0022-3514.74.6.1464

Hamilton, D. L., & Gifford, R. K. (1976). Illusory correlation in interpersonal perception: A cognitive basis of stereotypic judgments. *Journal of Experimental Social Psychology, 12*(4), 392-407. doi:10.1016/s0022-1031(76)80006-6

Ho, C., & Jackson, J. W. (2001). Attitude toward Asian Americans: Theory and measurement. *Journal of Applied Social Psychology, 31*(8), 1553–1581.

Hofmann, W., Gawronski, B., Gschwendner, T., Le, H., & Schmitt, M. (2005). A meta-analysis on the correlation between the Implicit Association Test and explicit self-report measures. *Personality and Social Psychology Bulletin, 31*(10), 1369–1385.

Islam, A. (2016). The Mongol invasions of Central Asia. *International Journal of Social Science and Humanity, 6*(4), 315–319.

Johns, M., Schmader, T., & Martens, A. (2005). Knowing is half the battle: Teaching stereotype threat as a means of improving women's math performance. *Psychological Science*, 16(3), 175–179.

Jones, V., E. (2000). "It's the Little Things" explores racial misunderstandings. *Chicago Tribune*. Retrieved October 11, 2016, from http://articles.chicagotribune.com/2000-10-09/features/0010090113_1_whites-lena-williams-integral

King, R. (2013). The uncomfortable racial preferences revealed by online dating. Retrieved from http://qz.com/149342/the-uncomfortable-racial-preferences-revealed-by-online-dating/

Koenig, A. M., & Eagly, A. H. (2005). Stereotype threat in men on a test of social sensitivity. *Sex Roles*, 52(7-8), 489–496. doi:10.1007/s11199-005-3714-x

Lin, M. H., Kwan, V. S., Cheung, A., & Fiske, S. T. (2005). Stereotype content model explains prejudice for an envied outgroup: Scale of anti-Asian American stereotypes. *Personality and Social Psychology Bulletin*, 31(1), 34–47.

McConnell, A. R., & Leibold, J. M. (2001). Relations among the Implicit Association Test, discriminatory behavior, and explicit measures of racial attitudes. *Journal of Experimental Social Psychology*, 37(5), 435–442.

Nieli, R. (2010). How diversity punishes Asians, poor Whites, and lots of others. Minding the Campus. Retrieved from https://www.princeton.edu/~tje/files/Pub_Minding%20the%20campus%20combined%20files.pdf

Olson, M. A., & Fazio, R. H. (2006). Reducing automatically activated racial prejudice through implicit evaluative conditioning. *Personality and Social Psychology Bulletin*, 32(4), 421–433.

Oswald, F. L., Mitchell, G., Blanton, H., Jaccard, J., & Tetlock, P. E. (2013). Predicting ethnic and racial discrimination: A meta-analysis of IAT criterion studies. *Journal of Personality and Social Psychology*, 105(2), 171–192.

Peterson, R. K. D. (1995). Insects, disease, and military history: The Napoleonic campaigns and historical perception. *American Entomologist*, 41, 147–160.

Pinel, E. C., Warner, L. R., & Chua, P. P. (2005). Getting there is only half the battle: Stigma consciousness and maintaining diversity in higher education. *Journal of Social Issues*, 61(3), 481–506.

Rosenthal, H. E., & Crisp, R. J. (2007). Choking under pressure: When an additional positive stereotype affects performance for domain identified male mathematics students. *European Journal of Psychology of Education*, 22(3), 317–326.

Rudder, C. (2014). Race & attraction, 2009–2014. *OKCupid*. Retrieved fromhttp://blog.okcupid.com/index.php/race-attraction-2009-2014/

Sadler, M. S., Correll, J., Park, B., & Judd, C. M. (2012). The world is not Black and White: Racial bias in the decision to shoot in a multiethnic context. *Journal of Social Issues*, 68(2), 286–313.

Shih, M., Pittinsky, T. L., & Ambady, N. (1999). Stereotype susceptibility: Identity salience and shifts in quantitative performance. *Psychological Science*, 10(1), 80–83.

Shih, M., Pittinsky, T. L., & Trahan, A. (2006). *Domain-specific effects of stereotypes on performance: Self and Identity*, 5(1), 1–14.

Spencer, S. J., Steele, C. M., & Quinn, D. M. (1999). Stereotype threat and women's math performance. *Journal of experimental social psychology*, 35(1), 4–28.

Steele, C. M., & Aronson, J. (1995, November). Stereotype threat and the intellectual test performance of African Americans. *Journal of Personality and Social Psychology*, 69(5), 797–811. doi:10.1037/0022-3514.69.5.797

Stone, J., Lynch, C. I., Sjomeling, M., & Darley, J. M. (1999). Stereotype threat effects on Black and White athletic performance. *Journal of Personality and Social Psychology*, 77(6), 1213–1227. doi:10.1037//0022-3514.77.6.1213

Stone, J., Perry, W., & Darley, J. M. (1997). "White Men Can't Jump": Evidence for the perceptual confirmation of racial stereotypes following a basketball game. *Basic and Applied Social Psychology, 19*(3), 291–306.

Strauss, V., & Southerl, D. (1994). How many died? New numbers suggest far higher numbers for the victims of Mao Zhe Dong. *Washington Post*. Retrieved from https://www.washingtonpost.com/archive/politics/1994/07/17/how-many-died-new-evidence-suggests-far-higher-numbers-for-the-victims-of-mao-zedongs-era/01044df5-03dd-49f4-a453-a033c5287bce/?utm_term=.b356b3d36077

Student election kerfuffle at Bay Area middle school creates discussion about teaching democracy. (2015). SCPR. Retrieved fromhttp://www.scpr.org/programs/airtalk/2015/10/23/44949/student-election-kerfuffle-at-bay-area-middle-scho/

Sue, D. W. (2010). *Microaggressions in everyday life: Race, gender, and sexual orientation*. Hoboken, NJ: Wiley.

Sue, D. W., Bucceri, J., Lin, A. I., Nadal, K. L., & Torino, G. C. (2009, August). Racial microaggressions and the Asian American experience. *Asian American Journal of Psychology, S*(1), 88–101. doi:10.1037/1948-1985.s.1.88

Sue, S., & Okazaki, S. (2009). Asian-American educational achievements: A phenomenon in search of an explanation. *Asian American Journal of Psychology, S(1)*, 45–55.

Suzuki, B. H. (2002). Revisiting the model minority stereotype: Implications for student affairs practice and higher education. *New directions for Student Services, 2002*(97), 21–32.

Taylor, C. R., & Stern, B. B. (1997). Asian-Americans: Television advertising and the "model minority" stereotype. *Journal of Advertising, 26*(2), 47–61. doi:10.1080/00913367.1997.10673522

Taylor, S. E. (1981). A categorization approach to stereotyping. In D. L. Hamilton (Ed.), *Cognitive processes in stereotyping and intergroup behavior* (pp. 83–114). New York, NY: Psychology Press.

Unz, R. (2013). Statistics indicate an Ivy League Asian quota. *The New York Times*. Retrieved from http://www.nytimes.com/roomfordebate/2012/12/19/fears-of-an-asian-quota-in-the-ivy-league/statistics-indicate-an-ivy-league-asian-quota

Walton, G. M., & Cohen, G. L. (2003). Stereotype lift. *Journal of Experimental Social Psychology, 39*(5), 456–467.

Williams, L. (2002). *It's the little things: Everyday interactions that anger, annoy, and divide the races*. Orlando, FL: Houghton Mifflin Harcourt.

Wittenbrink, B., Judd, C. M., & Park, B. (2001). Spontaneous prejudice in context: Variability in automatically activated attitudes. *Journal of Personality and Social Psychology, 81*(5), 815–827.

Wong, F., & Halgin, R. (2006). The "model minority": Bane or blessing for Asian Americans? *Journal of Multicultural Counseling and Development, 34*(1), 38–49.

Ziegert, J. C., & Hanges, P. J. (2005). Employment discrimination: The role of implicit attitudes, motivation, and a climate for racial bias. *Journal of Applied Psychology, 90*(3), 553–562.

CHAPTER 8

Ingroup Derogation and Self-Stereotyping

The year is 1954. Marilyn Monroe had just married Joe DiMaggio, the Vietnam War was about to start, McCarthyism was haunting liberals (and not-so liberals) all over America, and the Civil Rights movement was about to officially launch. Segregation, which had been flung in full force across the country, suddenly came to a hot apex in court when thirteen parents in Topeka, Kansas, decided to file a class-action lawsuit against their board of education. The complaint was loud and clear: Why did third-grader Linda Brown have to walk six blocks every day only to take a bus to a black school a mile away from there, while another, White, school was right there, seven blocks down the street (Patterson & Freehling, 2001)?

The case was long, the debate heated, and the arguments many, but one enduring piece that came from the *Brown v. Board of Education* trial—apart from its monumental ruling—was what happened when it read the social psychological findings provided by Kenneth Clark and his colleagues. Among these was a famous study by two practicing psychologists from Harlem who did a little-known experiment back in the 1940s with Black school kids and baby dolls (Patterson & Freehling, 2001). Their findings—which startled the court and played a critical role in pushing the unanimous ruling—started an enduring and long debate over the sticky problem of race, stereotyping, and who is to blame.

Nearly a decade prior, in 1947, Kenneth and Mamie Clark had gone to Clarendon, South Carolina, to ask Black schoolgirls about what kinds of dolls they liked. They brought with them a plastic Black baby doll and a White baby doll—each wearing the exact same pinned diaper, each made from the same shiny old-school vinyl material, but one tinted black and the other tinted white (Clark & Clark, 1947). Clark and Clark (1947) found a group of six- to nine-year-old Black children, showed them the two dolls, and asked them a simple question: Which one would you like? Most of the Black kids—three out of four in fact—preferred the White dolls (Clark & Clark, 1947; and see photo 8.1).

Now in 1954, these findings shocked the Supreme Court into ruling that there was something deeply wrong with segregation—a segregation that made little Black girls not want to play with dolls that looked like them (Patterson & Freehling,

PHOTO 8.1. Clark and Clark (1947) found that Black girls didn't want to play with dolls that looked like them.

Source: iStock

2001). And if Clark and Clark's pivotal study was the end of the story, then that would've been just that—a clear case of a historical faux pas that has since been dealt with. The problem was—and still is—that Clark and Clark was only the first of its kind. Now, more than half a century later, we still have this little known problem regarding the sticky issue of race—not so much about White people and Black people and Asians and Latinos not getting along, but more about what Blacks and Asians and Latinos think about themselves—and others like them—in their own heart of hearts.

It turns out that Black schoolgirls from South Carolina in the 1940s weren't the only people who had a problem with themselves—or at least, with things that looked like them. When the same experiment was done by Kiri Davis, a 16-year old from New York City, some six decades later in 2005, she found the exact same effect: Once again, three out of four Black kids would rather play with a White doll than a Black one (Davis, 2005).

The Story of Race, Revisited

The story we unpacked in the previous chapter was mainly about certain groups exhibiting negative views, feelings, and behaviors about other groups. As this chapter will highlight, however, that story is just not as simple as it seems. The classic Clark and Clark (1947) study may have been the first psychological study on a phenomenon we will subsequently refer to as **ingroup derogation**—a counter-intuitive tendency for group members to take on an "anti-us" approach or endorse attitudes and beliefs that run counter to their own group's best interests—but it surely wasn't the last.

Ingroup Derogation among Racial Minorities

Black kids in America were not the only sample to show this peculiar trend of disliking their own racial group. Asian schoolchildren in Scotland, when shown pictures of novel Scottish and fellow Asian children, said nicer things about the Scottish ones (Jahoda, Thompson, & Bhatt, 1972). And it's not just about the children either—Black and Latino college students routinely endorse the same stereo-types about their own groups (about themselves being lazy, violent, underachieving, and the like) that White college students endorse (Jost & Banaji, 1994). More recently, both Latino and Asian American college students at UCLA reported pre-ferring to interact with (hypothetical) White partners more than partners who were members of their own ethnic groups (Jost, Pelham, & Carvallo, 2002).

Similar effects have emerged with other ethnic minorities in countries outside the United States. Hewstone and Ward (1985) examined Chinese nationals living in Malaysia; in this context, Chinese were the ethnic minorities in a country where Malays were the majority. Once more, they found that Chinese routinely dero-gated their own group members: When asked to explain the positive or negative behaviors of hypothetical Chinese and Malay targets (e.g., a vendor cheats you on a purchase or was generous to you), Chinese attributed the negative behavior of Chinese targets to their internal dispositions (i.e., explained that a Chinese vendor cheated you on a purchase because he was a deceitful person) but attributed the same negative behavior of Malay targets to the situation (the Malay vendor cheated you on a purchase because there was something wrong with his scales; Hewstone & Ward, 1985). A parallel pattern emerged when Hewstone and Ward (1985) looked at positive behaviors: Chinese participants discounted the positive actions of Chinese targets and attributed positive behavior to the situation, whereas they did not do so when the target was Malay. Malay participants, in contrast, showed the more typical pattern of favoring their own ingroup members over outgroup members (Hewstone & Ward, 1985).

More recent research has suggested that this type of race-based ingroup der-ogation is generally more prevalent among collectivist cultures and less prevalent among individualist cultures (Cuddy et al., 2009; for more information about the definitions of individualism and collectivism, see chapter 1). In a study of racial attitudes across 10 nations, Cuddy and colleagues (2009) found that more collec-tivistic countries were more likely to endorse stereotypes about their own groups relative to more individualist countries.

Ingroup Derogation among Low-Status Groups

This strange effect—of minority groups being "racist" against themselves, against their own best interests—is so powerful that it extends even beyond race. State-school kids will routinely have a better view of private-university kids than of themselves (Jost, Pelham, & Carvallo, 2002). Despite all the different possible factors that determine whether a high school graduate ends up at San Jose State or Stanford—social, economical, or otherwise—Jost et al. (2002) found that San Jose State students will readily endorse the view of Stanford students as better, harder working, smarter, and more ambitious than themselves automatically and nonconsciously—that is, on a reaction-time measure used to measure subconscious associations, the Implicit Association Test, or IAT (Greenwald, McGhee, & Schwartz, 1998). On the IAT, San Jose State students were faster to associate both positive, academic-related words like "ambitious" and "intelligent" *and* positive, affective words like "warmth" and "glory" with Stanford than with San Jose. Stanford students, in contrast, were quick to associate all the positive words with themselves (Jost et al., 2002).

Similar findings emerged among low-status nurses. In nursing, as in life, there is a clear hierarchy that differentiates those who have skills and experience (and therefore status) from those who do not; these status differentials are widely accepted by those who practice nursing and are reflected in the names assigned to its members. State Enrolled Nurses (SENs) are on the low-status end, whereas State Registered Nurses (SRNs) are on the high-status end (Skevington, 1981). In Skevington's (1981) study of SENs' and SRNs' perceptions of themselves and the other group of nurses, *both* groups agreed that SRNs possessed better, more positive attributes than SENs. In other words, the low-status nurses (SENs) rated their own group lower and the outgroup, SRNs, higher on a host of positive attributes; they deemed SRNs as more superior, educated, intelligent, ambitious, academic, responsible, competitive, organized, confident, and more aware of their place (Skevington, 1981).

In 2013, Sheryl Sandberg became a household name when, in addition to being the COO of the world's reigning social media network (Facebook), she released a TED Talk and then a national best-selling book on the merits of women "leaning in" (photo 8.2). In a nutshell, she tackled the longstanding issue of the gender divide in leadership positions across the country and in nearly every major sector within government and industry by simply calling ladies everywhere to try harder—to vie for a seat at the table, do difficult things with a smile on their face, and risk putting everything on the line for the things that they want (Sandberg, 2013). What she did not acknowledge—and may not have known—was that many studies going back all the way to the 1970s have found that women routinely support the idea that they deserve less money for doing the exact same work that men do (Callahan-Levy & Messé, 1979; Major, 1994; Major, McFarlin, & Gagnon, 1984). How are women supposed to "lean in" if they believe they don't deserve to be rewarded for their efforts?

In a study by Jost (1997), participants of both genders rated the quality of their own work and how much they should be paid for it on a 1–15 scale; the higher the rating, the better the quality and pay. Men significantly rated their own work as better quality and deserving of more pay than women did (Jost, 1997).

Lest you think that all these effects of ingroup derogation among low-status groups are idiosyncratic to these specific groups—women, state-school students, and nurses—let me tell you about one more study that will demonstrate that even just making you *think* your group is low status will make you more likely to put down your own group. In an experiment, Jost and Burgess (2000) led students at

PHOTO 8.2. Sheryl Sandberg may want you to lean in, but what about self-stereotyping?

Source: Alamy

the University of Maryland to believe that alumni from their school were either more or less successful than were alumni from the University of Virginia. The two schools were longstanding rivals, and in this particular case, Jost and Burgess (2000) made the Maryland students believe that they were the lower status group; afterward, they assessed ratings of each school. Simply believing that their alumni were less advantaged led University of Maryland students to ingroup derogate (Jost & Burgess, 2000).

Self-Stereotyping among Advantaged Groups

In fact, this trend is so strong that it doesn't even limit itself to disadvantaged groups. When Monica Biernat, Theresa Vescio, and Michelle Green (1996) asked University of Florida sorority women and fraternity men what they thought about sorority women and frat men, they were shocked that these members of the Greek system— a generally elite group occupying the "popular" end of the social strata—actually endorsed the same negative stereotypes that everyone else had about them. Sorority girls agreed that sorority girls tended to be snotty, slutty, spoiled, and shallow; frat guys agreed that frat guys tended to be cocky, obnoxious, dumb, and irresponsible (Biernat et al., 1996). This type of behavior is commonly referred to as **self-stereotyping,** or the phenomenon of a person subscribing to the same stereotypes about his or her own group as others do (Biernat et al., 1996).

Explaining Ingroup Derogation and Self-Stereotyping

Sociological Factors and System Justification

You might have noticed that the majority of the above examples of ingroup derogation nearly all occurred with minority and typically "disadvantaged" group members (with the exception of sorority and fraternity members). As a result, many of the original explanations have relied on sociological factors like high nationalism or cultural oppression by dominant groups (Fine & Bowers, 1984; Hewstone & Ward, 1985; Mlicki & Ellemers, 1996).

These ideas have been formally modeled in the theory of **system justification** (Jost & Burgess, 2000), which says that minority group members in particular will believe negative views about their group in order to justify the status quo (namely, their group's occupation of an inferior place in society) and in doing so, feed their need to believe in a just, predictable world. Following this logic, system justification theory argues that ingroup derogation primarily occurs for traits that relate to social standing or status (e.g., ambition, intelligence) but not traits that don't (e.g., honesty; Jost & Burgess, 2000; Skevington, 1981).

Another way to think about system justification is to consider the idea that most people walk around with this deep-rooted belief that Life Is Fair. Now, you've probably been told once or twice that life actually isn't fair at all, but even so, if I were to question you about what you really think in your heart of hearts, you'd probably report some sense that things happen for a reason and that people ultimately do—or at least should—get what they deserve. After all, this sense of Fairness is what drives karma (what goes around comes around), heaven (God: "Vengeance is mine"), the criminal justice system (lock away bad guys), democracy (hey, let's vote on it), the PTA (may the best mommy rule), and most likely every other major idea or institution we routinely subscribe to. If I didn't know better, I'd think it'd be part of our DNA.

The problem emerges, however, when we apply our popular notion of life being fair to a reality that—truth be told—is all too often not fair at all. In reality, people get born into privilege or disadvantage, get judged by the way they look and other characteristics beyond their control, get things they do not necessarily deserve, and don't get things they do deserve. In reality, we don't get to choose the socioeconomic status our parents have or the color of our skin (beyond a sunburn or nice tan), the shape of our eyes, or the general ideas others will have about us because of those statuses and colors and shapes. So what then do we do when our notions of Fairness go up against our experience of Reality?

It turns out that in the battle between What Should Be (i.e., Fair) and What Actually Is (i.e., Not-So-Fair), the former ends up being the one to budge. After all, it's easier to change what we think than to go out and actually change the world. The result? The Way Things Are becomes The Way Things Should Be. If being Black in America makes you underprivileged (unless your name is Barack, Denzel, or Kobe), then being Black in America *should* make you underprivileged. If Black women don't routinely don the cover pages of *Sports Illustrated* swimsuit issues (not since that one time Tyra Banks made it on, followed nearly a decade later by Beyonce), then Black women *shouldn't* be on the cover. They must not be desirable enough or pretty enough—in which case, why would anyone pick a Black doll over a White one? Likewise, if being Asian means being an inscrutable bad driver who is only really good at math (according to stereotypes), then that means Asians must be cold or nerdy or a social liability—in which case, why wouldn't anyone have a hard time saying nice things about them? And, if being part of the Greek systems renders you as either promiscuous or mean (take your pick) in the minds of every other Hollywood movie or pop culture subscriber, then who is to say that the truth is anything else?

In other words, the "problem of race" is no longer—and indeed, never was—simply an issue of one group of people holding stereotypes against and showing prejudice toward another group. It never was a one-lane road marked by bigots on one end and innocent victims on the other. It has always been more complicated—more twisted—than that. The problem with race—or any other kind of label we like to stick on people, for that matter—is really the problem that arises when people start believing things because that is the way things are. At the end of the day, the issue is not so much what White people think about Black people, but rather: what Black people think about themselves when no one is asking. What do Asians make of dragon ladies and math geeks in the privacy of their own hearts? What do sorority girls and frat guys see when they peer at themselves in the mirror?

Attitudes toward the Self and Thinking Styles

An alternative, nonsociological explanation for ingroup derogation suggests that ingroup attitudes reflect more general attitudes toward the self. Some researchers have observed that generally speaking, many instances of ingroup derogation occur among members of **collectivistic cultures** who, on average, are less self-enhancing than those from **individualistic cultures**; if collectivistic are more self-derogating, then their self-attitudes may extend to close group members (Cuddy et al., 2009; Spencer, Williams, & Peng, 2010).

A related idea is the notion that collectivistic cultures like those of East Asia are also more **dialectical**: They view the self and the world as more holistic, changeable, and inconsistent than members of nondialectical cultures do (Spencer-Rodgers & Peng, 2004). One consequence of this dialectical thinking style is that East Asians in particular show more ambivalence and contradiction in their attitudes overall; not only do they not strive to see the self in a positive light as North Americans typically do (Heine & Hamamura, 2007) but they are not as bothered by negative self-views. Self-esteem in that cultural context has little to do with psychological adjustment (Heine, Lehman, Markus, & Kitayama, 1999). If this is true of the self, and the self is a natural extension of one's social group, then the same may apply to how East Asians consider their ingroups. Thus another explanation for ingroup derogation—at least among East Asians—is that the Eastern dialectical way of thinking about the world makes it more likely and appropriate to think negative thoughts—and not just positive ones—about your own group (Ma-Kellams, Spencer-Rodgers, & Peng, 2011).

Ingroup Derogation versus Self-Stereotyping

Why are there so many Black men in pro basketball?

The most obvious answer is: because White men can't jump. And while this explanation may suffice to explain the dynamics of the NBA, you can't really use the same line of logic to explicate the racial makeup of, say, tennis or golf or base-ball—all professional sports characterized by a striking lack of Black players. Unless you want to sound like the next spokesperson for the KKK, you can't really simply explain those stats by saying that Black men must not be able to swing their arms correctly. Assuming that there are no racial differences in the kind of sports we're genetically programmed to play, why is the world of professional sports so clearly segregated?

In fact, all it takes is a simple look around any field—be it the world of pro basketball or Hollywood or engineers—to notice that virtually every occupation out there is heavily segregated in one way or another. And the segregating factor is not always race either; often it's gender or age. Why are there so few male counselors, nurses, or schoolteachers? Why are there so few Asians in sports, acting, and music? You can also ask the flip side of the question: Why are there so many men in engineering, computer science, and every other "hard" science? Why are there so many Asians in math and biology?

At this point, any theories about innate biological differences between genders or races in terms of our ability to do math problems or bounce balls or recite particularly convincing Shakespearean monologues have long been debunked. Most—if not all—scientists will tell you that no racial or gender group has a monopoly on one particular talent or ability. Despite all appearances, Black people aren't born with some special knack for layups, Asians don't come into the world solving calculus proofs, and White men aren't genetically endowed with secret How to Be a CEO information. What happens, then, somewhere between the ages of 0 and 30-ish that magically and oh-so-predictably places each group into its respective calling, its particular lots in life?

Take, for example, the case of women and math. In an influential review by Maccoby and Jacklin (1974) that looked at elementary and middle school records of math performance for boys and girls, the two groups appeared exactly the same. If anything, girls actually do slightly better in math class than boys (Maccoby & Jacklin, 1974). Starting in high school though, the trend starts to reverse: Boys not only take more advanced math and science classes than girls do but they also tend to do better on standardized tests (Maccoby & Jacklin, 1974). Since then, others have found in recent years that girls and boys do equally well in math at all grade levels, but a gender gap still persists at the highest levels of math (e.g., in math-centric PhD programs; Hyde & Mertz, 2009).

Clearly, then, this is not a matter of girls entering the world with an innate handicap for complex mathematical thinking. If they can navigate through counting, fractions, multiplication, and even pre-algebra with as much—if not more—ease than boys, then there is little to suggest that there is some natural, from-birth gender difference when it comes to the world of numbers. What happens, though, at the higher levels of math that suddenly renders girls unable to perform at the same rate as their male counterparts? Why do they abruptly start underperforming boys in graduate programs?

Mathematical ability, as it turns out, is not as stable as one might assume. It turns out that there are simple ways to manipulate a person's performance on any given math task. You can make females perform better (or worse) on a math test by simple asking them one simple question at the beginning of the test:

What gender are you? Male Female (pick one)

In the late 1990s, Spencer, Steele, and Quinn (1999) recruited a group of female University of Michigan college students to take a difficult GRE (Graduate Record Exam) math test. In particular, only a select group of highly math-talented women were recruited; the women had to have taken at least one college-level calculus course, in which their grade had to be a B or higher (Spencer et al., 1999). In addition, they had to perform above the 85th percentile on the SAT or ACT and, when you asked them about their mathematical abilities, they had to report that it was important to be good at math and that math was one of their strong points (Spencer et al., 1999). In other words, only women who were good at math and knew it were allowed in.

Before the women were given the math test, however, half of them were asked to indicate their gender while the other half were not; everyone subsequently took the test, and their scores were calculated and compared to a similar group of University of Michigan male college students' GRE math scores (who also met the same selection criteria; Spencer et al., 1999). Spencer et al. (1999) discovered an interesting pattern: The women who simply took the test without being asked to write down their gender did just as well as the men. The women who were asked to indicate their gender, however, performed significantly worse (Spencer et al., 1999).

Evidently there was something strange and damaging about indicating one's gender for these highly select women. The mere act of being reminded that they were female hurt their performance even though, by all external standards, they should have been fully capable to perform, and perform well. This phenomenon may be, in parallel terms, very similar to what happens when a single solitary White guy shows up in a court of all Black basketball players. What goes on in the head of someone like that? What is he thinking? Or more importantly, what is he afraid of?

The problem with race ultimately is—at least in part—a problem of the questions that haunt our own heads when no one is paying attention. The average GRE test proctor may not be paying attention, nor the average NBA game-goer, but the woman taking the test? She knows. The White player on the court? He knows as well.

She knows that she is female. He knows that he is White. They both know that their all-too-obvious identities have brought them a lifetime of experience, a lifetime of expectations and treatments that are all too predictable. Neither of them can help but be aware of the stereotypes that apply to their gender, their race, precisely in the area, the domain, they care most about. She may know she is smart and good at math, but she also knows that as a woman, she is on the counterstereotypical side. He may know that he can do a seamless layup and a powerful three-pointer, but as a White man, he is one of the few of his kind who supposedly fall under that category. Ultimately, then, both of them are all too afraid that if they fail now, they will only be affirming the stereotypes they worked so hard to disconfirm. And it is precisely that fear, that anxiety, that ironically poses their downfall and is the reason that so many otherwise competent individuals underperform when it matters the most.

So the race question we started this chapter with is not really about race at all, but about belief. Whether you are talking about what happens when a racial minority or low-status group (or a sorority woman) considers its own group to be inferior (as in the case of ingroup derogation), or you are reminding someone that he or she belongs to a group other people have stereotypes about, thereby leading the person, ironically, to affirm those very same stereotypes (as in the case of stereotype threat), both phenomena center on the beliefs groups have about themselves and the consequences of those beliefs. The real title of these last two chapters should have been "The Problem of Belief," because after all, what you believe may be the single most powerful thing about you. Neither your neighborhood palm reader with all her prophesies nor stereotypes with all their stipulations would have any power at all if it were not for the simple fact that they are believed (see Insight Box 8.1). They are subscribed to, acted upon, and ultimately, endorsed as if they were true. And in the end, unless we do otherwise, they become exactly what we expect them to be.

INSIGHT BOX 8.1

The Big Picture—Cultural Psychology in Context

"I'd ask you to sit down, but you're not going to anyway. And don't worry about the vase," the Oracle says in her calm, ironically soothing voice.

"What vase?" asks Neo, looking around. As he turns, he knocks over the [previously unseen] vase on the counter next to him. "I'm so sorry. . .," he tells her, somewhat sheepishly.

"Don't worry about it," the Oracle tells him again.

"How did you know?"

In classic Oracle fashion, she ignores his question and answers. "What's really going to bake your noodle later on is: Would you still have broken it if I hadn't said anything?"

The Matrix, 1999 (photo 8.3)

PHOTO 8.3. Neo in *The Matrix*: What you believe may be one of the most powerful things about you.

Source: Photofest

Speaking of belief, as a psychologist, I still get asked a lot whether I can read people's minds. They are usually somewhat disappointed by my answer, but I think it's because they're posing the wrong question. What they should really be asking is whether I can predict the future. In which case, the answer would be

"Yes, as a matter of fact, I can."

Ingroup derogation, in some ways, can be conceptualized as an extension of a well-established broader phenomenon in psychology called the **self-fulfilling prophecy**. It doesn't take an old philosopher to figure out what it means: You make a prediction, and the simple fact that you believe it to be real/true/forthcoming makes it so. Hollywood has toyed with this idea in a few well-known movies— *The Matrix* being one—but in reality, these kinds of things don't happen just to trenchcoat-clothed men named Neo. Scary, thrilling, or unbelievable, I'll let you decide. . .

Once upon a time there was an old story about a married couple—an average-looking (but most likely rich, as chapter 2 will tell you) man and a beautiful woman who were in a terrible car accident. The accident was so horrendous, in fact, that it permanently destroyed the man's eyes and crushed the face of the woman. They both survived, but the ordeal left the husband blind and the woman deformed. Afterward, whenever they would meet somebody new, the man would say,

"And here's my wife—isn't she beautiful?" because that was that he always had said and because he, being blind, didn't know that his wife's once beautiful face was now but a clearly reconstructed attempt at looking human. The stranger—now acquaintance—would uncomfortably mumble either an indecipherable answer or concede, haltingly, "Yes," out of pity for the couple. And because no one dared to break it to the man that his wife was no longer beautiful, he continued to live contented but deceived, proudly basking in the beauty that no longer was.

That's the end of the story, as far as I have heard. I never really understood the point of it. Was it a sweet example of oblivion's bliss or a sadly ironic tale of self-deception? Either way, one thing the tellers of this tale forgot to mention was how the wife, the once beautiful woman, reacted to all this. Did she know she was deformed? And if she knew—and she must've known—did she care, since her husband still thought her the most beautiful thing in the world?

Leave it to a trio of psychologists to bring this story into the lab, mess with it a little, and show us the surprisingly prophetic power of belief:

In the Laboratory for Research in Social Relations tucked away inside University of Minnesota's historic campus, three professors by the names of Mark Snyder, Elizabeth Tanke, and Ellen Berscheid recruited 51 men and women—all strangers to one another—to participate in a study on (presumably) getting acquainted (Snyder, Tanke, & Berscheid, 1977). To ensure that none of the men would see the women and vice versa, the experimenters had the two groups enter the building via separate corridors and into different rooms; once inside, they told each person that there were going to be paired up with a "partner" in another room and have an opportunity to get to know this person via telephone (Snyder et al., 1977). Before anyone was allowed to start talking, though, Snyder and his colleagues (1977) included an important task: Each individual had to fill out a brief biographical questionnaire about their major and their high school that would be given to their partner prior to the phone call in order to help facilitate the conversation.

Then things got a little tricky. To the men, Snyder et al. (1977) had the experimenters say that, along with the questionnaire, they were also going to receive a Polaroid photo of their conversation partner as well, because people have said that "they feel more comfortable having a mental picture of the person they're talking to." They went on to take snapshots of each of the male participants, gathered their questionnaires, and ostensibly left the room to hand these get-to-know-you materials to their partners in the room next door (Snyder et al., 1977). The women, in contrast, were given no such instructions about any photographs (i.e., no Polaroids were taken of them, nor were they to receive any snapshots of their partners); they simply filled out their brief biographical surveys and waited to receive the same completed questionnaires from the person they were about to talk to (Snyder et al., 1977).

When the experimenters came back, they handed to the men the biographical profile of one of the women in the other room, along with the picture of either a highly attractive or a highly unattractive female; to each of the women, they simply handed out the biographical profile of one of the men from the other room, with no picture attached (Snyder et al., 1977). In actuality, Snyder et al. (1977) ensured that the photos the men received were not of their real conversation partner, but rather random beautiful and unattractive people on campus the experimenters had taken photos of earlier that week. The phone conversations went on as planned, and both the men and the women completed additional surveys about how they felt and their impression of their partner before as well as after the call; unbeknown to them, every conversation was also tape recorded (Snyder et al., 1977).

What do you think happened?

You probably don't need a psychology experiment to tell you that the men who received a photo of a beautiful woman expected her to be more friendly, funny, and sociable; those who had gotten the ugly photo anticipated that she would be more serious and socially awkward (Snyder et al., 1977). Surprise, surprise: Men, it turns out, like beautiful women.

What you do need a scientific study to tell you is how these men's expectations—indeed, prophecies—of their female counterparts changed the very nature, character, and personality of the women themselves. I had told you, two paragraphs ago, that the phone conversations between each set of partners were recorded. In fact, they weren't simply recorded; Snyder et al. (1977) also had a panel of judges listen and rate the two individuals having each conversation on a variety of traits and characteristics, from confidence to enjoyment, intelligence to enthusiasm. What they found shook us all.

The women who were talking to men who randomly received the beautiful Polaroid were more outgoing, confident, at ease, warm, and sociable than those who were talking with men who received the ugly one (Snyder et al., 1977). Keep in mind that neither the men nor the women ever saw their conversation partner in person (everything occurred via phone) and there were no actual differences in attractiveness between these two groups of women—those who got paired with men who received beautiful photographs and those who were paired with the men who received homely ones. Nor were there any differences in character or personality before the phone conversation—individuals were randomly assigned to conversation partners, so the females who got paired with men who thought they were attractive were no different than those who got paired with men who believed that they were unattractive. Yet Snyder et al. (1977) demonstrated how a simple handing out of Polaroids, which led to an equally simple belief—however fabricated and untrue—fundamentally altered the nature of the social interaction that occurred between these sets of strangers. Not only that, but this same belief held by one person also changed the very kind of person that emerged on the other end, by the end of the conversation. His belief became prophetic, and his prophecy became true. In matters of people, that's often what prophecies do: They fulfill themselves (Snyder et al., 1977).

On the surface, all this seems a little too good to be true at best, and terrifying at worst. How, one has to ask, do beliefs come to exert so much power?

In an effort to explain the unsettling prophetic power of these men's expectations on these women's personality, our three professors, Snyder, Tanke, and Berscheid (1977), went back and looked at what the judges said about the men during the phone conversations. As Snyder et al. (1977) found, those who had thought they were talking to a beautiful woman presented themselves in a very different way than those who thought they were talking to a not-so-beautiful one. As you may have already guessed, the guys who had gotten the "hot" picture acted more bold, interesting, independent, warm, friendly, funny, and socially skilled than the guys who had gotten the "not" picture. It's no surprise, then, that the women they were speaking to also came out differently on the other end: They were interacting with a different kind of man (Snyder et al., 1977).

Perhaps this is the most unsettling part of self-fulfilling prophecies. In the simple act of believing something—in essence, creating a prophecy—we can profoundly change the nature of our world. In the case of the phone study, the men's expectations about their partner's looks drastically altered the very way their female counterpart presented herself. What we do not often realize is that our beliefs don't simply fulfill themselves and leave us unscathed; indeed, they change us, too. Thus in Snyder et al.'s (1977) study, these men's expectations about their partner's attractiveness not only changed her but changed themselves as well. The line, then, between "belief" and "prophecy" may be but an arbitrary delineation in the sand, or perhaps even an invisible one, a line that speaks more to our need to explain the universe (and ourselves) in reasonable, predictable, clear-cut terms than an accurate reflection of the actual state of affairs in the world.

So going back to our original story about the couple who survived the horrible car accident: The self-fulfilling prophecy would tell us that the blind husband, by virtue of his own however deceived and wrong belief that his once pretty but now deformed wife was still beautiful, must've treated her as such. And in being treated as if she was beautiful, she would also become warm, social, and outgoing. In a sense the man's once prophetic lie would've become true: Despite her crushed, reconstructed face, the woman would become, in a sense, beautiful as well, just as her husband believed. Just as he predicted.

And if to believe is, in essence, to prophesize, then this says a thing or two about your lot in life, how your relationships—be they romantic, platonic, familial, professional—are going, who you are, and who others are when they're around you.

In the movie *The Wedding Date*, Debra Messing's character's dad tells her, "Every woman has exactly the love life she wants." Now I'm not one to endorse romantic comedies, particularly when it comes to relationship advice, but I think in this case, the old man was onto something. If we were to each take apart our lives, break down our huge, buzzing, chaotic mess of people and relational dynamics and situations and values and upbringings, hopes and baggage and dreams and expectations, into small, chewable pieces—little kernels, if you will, of startling, isolated truth—we just might very well find that we are fulfilling our own self-made prophecies. Indeed, we are each living exactly the life we thought we would.

This is not to say that our day-to-day prophecies are ever all that dramatic or explicitly put out there, in the same way as the Oracle's mention of the vase or Oedipus's encounter at Delphi or Macbeth and his three witches. Rather, I have a hunch that most of our prophecies are silent utterances in the inner chambers of our soul—little, ordinary beliefs about the way people are, or how you look, or perhaps what your own value is—many of which may be based on the groups you belong to and those you interact with (or don't). And because you believe, you can't help but act in line with your belief. After all, everyone thinks they're right, and if they didn't think so, they would change their mind.[1] So in acting in line with your beliefs about the world and other people and yourself, you are essentially inviting the rest of reality to respond accordingly. When they do—when people treat you exactly as you teach them to or when you search out confirmation for the precise expectations you've been holding all along—then you become all the more convinced that things were the way you thought. You were right, see. And thereby we go about constructing our own destinies.

---

[1] I think the originator of this quote was Anne Lamott.

Key Concepts

Ingroup derogation
Self-stereotyping
System justification
Collectivistic vs. individualistic cultures
Dialectical self

APPLYING WHAT WE KNOW: HANDS-ON ACTIVITIES

1. To what extent can you observe ingroup derogation and self-stereotyping in popular cultural products and other daily artifacts? Find cultural products that contain attitudes, beliefs, or ideas about a specific cultural group that is produced by members of that cultural group, and content-analyze how these groups portray themselves. Possible cultural products include: (a) a television show or movie for a targeted audience by that target audience; (b) a magazine or newspaper; (c) a memoir or novel; (d) a website, blog, tweet, or other social media post.

2. Take an IAT where the target stimuli is a cultural group that you identify with (http://implicit.harvard.edu). Prior to taking the IAT, *predict* your IAT score. For example, if you're a woman taking the gender and science IAT, predict the extent to which you are likely to associate men more with science or women more with science. Then, take the actual IAT and record your IAT score. Reflect on the extent to which your prediction and results align, or fail to align, and discuss why.

3. One of the central tenets of system justification is that people will routinely endorse policies, attitudes, and behaviors that run counter to their own interests because the need to justify the larger system is a stronger drive than the need to improve one's own lot in life. Can you think of examples in recent history that reflect this tendency? (For example, consider how people vote. Do we always vote based on self-interest?)

References

Biernat, M., Vescio, T. K., & Green, M. L. (1996). Selective self-stereotyping. *Journal of Personality and Social Psychology, 71*(6), 1194–1209.

Callahan-Levy, C. M., & Messe, L. A. (1979). Sex differences in the allocation of pay. *Journal of Personality and Social Psychology, 37*(3), 433–446.

Cuddy, A. J., Fiske, S. T., Kwan, V. S., Glick, P., Demoulin, S., Levens, J., . . . Ziegler, R. (2009). Stereotype content model across cultures: Towards universal similarities and some differences. *British Journal of Social Psychology, 48,* 1–33.

Davis, K. (2005). *A Girl Like Me.* Reelworks Teen Filmmaking. Retrieved from http://www.reelworks.org/videos/a-girl-like-me-2/

Fine, M., & Bowers, C. (1984). Racial identity: The effects of social history and gender. *Journal of Applied Social Psychology, 13,* 136–146.

Greenwald, A., McGhee, D., & Schwartz, J. (1998). Measuring individual differences in implicit cognition: The Implicit Association Test. *Journal of Personality and Social Psychology, 74*, 1464–1480.

Heine, S. J., & Hamamura, T. (2007). In search of East Asian self-enhancement. *Personality and Social Psychology Review, 11*, 4–27.

Heine, S. J., Lehman, D., Markus, H., & Kitayama, S. (1999). Is there a universal need for positive self-regard? *Psychological Bulletin, 106*, 766–794.

Hewstone, M., & Ward, C. (1985). Ethnocentrism and causal attribution in Southeast Asia. *Journal of Personality and Social Psychology, 48*, 614–623.

Hyde, J. S., & Mertz, J. E. (2009). Gender, culture, and mathematics performance. *Proceedings of the National Academy of Sciences, 106*(22), 8801–8807.

Jahoda, G., Thompson, S., & Bhatt, S. (1972). Ethnic identity and preferences among Asian immigrant children in Glasgow. *European Journal of Social Psychology, 2*, 19–32.

Jost, J. T. (1997). An experimental replication of the depressed-entitlement effect among women. *Psychology of Women Quarterly, 21*(3), 387–393.

Jost, J. T., & Banaji, M. (1994). The role of stereotyping in system justification and the production of false consciousness. *British Journal of Social Psychology, 33*, 1–27.

Jost, J. T., & Burgess, D. (2000). Attitudinal ambivalence and the conflict between group and system justification motives in low status groups. *Journal of Personality and Social Psychology, 26*, 293–305.

Jost, J. T., Pelham, B. W., & Carvallo, M. R. (2002). Non-conscious forms of system justification: Implicit and behavioral preferences for higher status groups. *Journal of Experimental Social Psychology, 38*(6), 586–602.

Kenneth, B., & Clark, M. P. (1947). Racial identification and preference in Negro children. Retrieved from https://i2.cdn.turner.com/cnn/2010/images/05/13/doll.study.1947.pdf

Ma-Kellams, C., Spencer-Rodgers, J., & Peng, K. (2011). I am against us? Unpacking cultural differences in ingroup favoritism via dialecticism. *Personality and Social Psychology Bulletin, 37*(1), 15–27.

Maccoby, E., & Jacklin, C. (1974). *The psychology of sex differences.* Stanford, CA: Stanford University Press.

Major, B. (1994). From social inequality to personal entitlement: The role of social comparisons, legitimacy appraisals, and group membership. *Advances in Experimental Social Psychology, 26*, 293–355.

Major, B., McFarlin, D. B., & Gagnon, D. (1984). Overworked and underpaid: On the nature of gender differences in personal entitlement. *Journal of Personality and Social Psychology, 47*(6), 1399–1412.

Mlicki, P. P., & Ellemers, N. (1996). Being different or being better? National stereotypes and identifications of Polish and Dutch students. *European Journal of Social Psychology, 26*, 97–114.

Patterson, J. T., & Freehling, W. W. (2001). *Brown v. Board of Education: A civil rights milestone and its troubled legacy.* New York, NY: Oxford University Press.

Sandberg, S. (2013). *Lean in: Women, work, and the will to lead.* New York, NY: Random House.

Skevington, S. (1981). Intergroup relations and nursing. *European Journal of Social Psychology, 11*, 43–59.

Snyder, M., Tanke, E. D., & Berscheid, E. (1977). Social perception and interpersonal behavior: On the self-fulfilling nature of social stereotypes. *Journal of Personality and Social Psychology, 35*(9), 655–666.

Spencer, S. J., Steele, C. M., & Quinn, D. M. (1999). Stereotype threat and women's math performance. *Journal of Experimental Social Psychology, 35*(1), 4–28.

Spencer-Rodgers, J., & Peng, K. (2004). The dialectical self: Contradiction, change, and holism in the East Asian self-concept. In R. M. Sorrentino, D. Cohen, J. M. Olson, & M. P. Zanna (Eds.), *Culture and social behavior: The Ontario Symposium* (pp. 227–249). Mahwah, NJ: Erlbaum.

Spencer-Rodgers, J., Williams, M. J., & Peng, K. (2010). Cultural differences in expectations of change and tolerance for contradiction: A decade of empirical research. *Personality and Social Psychology Review, 14*, 296–312.

CHAPTER 9

Identity and Acculturation

This chapter will begin by covering how cultural identities develop, with an initial focus on racial minority identity development and outcomes associated with ethnic identification (e.g., as related to self-esteem and academic performance). It will then discuss the process of shifting between multiple identities, including frame-switching and biculturalism. This chapter will also include discussion of immigration and identify threat. Finally, the chapter will end with the process of acculturation.

What Are You? (I Mean, Where Are You From?)

Photo 9.1 is a picture of a man that you know.

You may or may not remember the election of 2008, but even in the summer months leading up that momentous occasion, Barack Obama's campaign continued to face questions about his identity. There were the unsurprising concerns about whether his Blackness was going to deter voters (Weisberg, 2008); there was the wild accusation surrounding the national origins of his birth certificate (Hollyfield, 2008). But there were also reports that he was **passing**—that is, claiming to be a member of a racial group that he did not truly belong to (Mendible, 2012). The renowned African American actor, Morgan Freeman, during an interview with National Public Radio, remarked, "America's first black president hasn't arisen yet. He's not America's first black president—he's America's first mixed-race president" (NPR Staff, 2012). What Morgan and others were essentially suggesting was that President Obama's self-proclaimed identity as a Black man was somehow less than veridical because half of his ancestors were White and therefore not enslaved; it also suggested that a person could not both be "Black" and "mixed-race."

PHOTO 9.1. Obama's family photo underscores persistent questions of race and identity.

Source: Getty

Even President Obama himself admits to struggling with questions of racial identity. In subsequent biographies of the president, stories have abounded with instances where he felt like he had to intentionally strive to fit in with different racial groups (for a review, see Coates, 2016; Maraniss, 2012). Among Black students, he was deemed an "Oreo" (Maraniss, 2012)—in other words, Black on the outside; White on the inside. He even admits to adopting the nickname "Barry" as a way of protecting himself against the complications of having to explain the origins of "Barack" (Maraniss, 2012).

Examples like this suggest that identity is everywhere yet is fluid, complicated, and often problematic. The rest of this chapter aims to unpack some of the complexities inherent in identity and the psychological repercussions of identifying one way or another.

Defining Identity, Because It's Complicated

The History of Race

The term **race** has been used for a long time and has been the source of many erroneous assumptions about the nature of people and the groups they belong to. Historically, it was most often used to describe and distinguish one portion of the human population from another based on presumable biological features; the method used in this categorization has been based on superficial physical features like skin tone, hair color, eye color or shape, skull shape, and the like (Banton, 1987).

These days, scientists largely agree that most of the physical features historically relied on by people to differentiate the races are based on responses to regional ecological variation (e.g., to different climates from different parts of the world). When you look at different "races" at the genetic level, you find that in fact, they are quite similar, and between-group variation is comparable to within-group variation (Witherspoon et al., 2007). In other words, there is very weak biological evidence for the existence of "race."

If race isn't biologically real, then why do we still talk about it and study it? Here it's important to remember that psychology is about the real *or imagined* presence of others (e.g., see Anderson & Godfrey, 1987). That means that psychologists will study unicorns along with horses—as long as we live in a world where people believe in unicorns. By the same token, we continue to refer to race and talk about it because regardless of the science, everyday people continue to believe in race, continue to use race as a way to divide people and make judgments about them. Race remains an important part of culture and society, and race is still something we judge based on highly superficial characteristics. Thus if it's psychologically real—and all the evidence suggests that it is—then it is still important to acknowledge and study.

Race versus Ethnicity/Culture versus Nationality

Despite the shaky biological justification for the existence of race, race is still commonly used and commonly confused with other constructs. Often people use race indiscriminately to refer to any group membership, even ones that are not based on visible physical qualities. The most common source of confusion is using race to mean ethnicity or culture, which technically refers to nonbiological distinctions between groups (Betancourt & López, 1993). Unlike race, ethnicity and culture are fundamentally socially constructed and shared. **Ethnicity** usually involves a shared ancestry, including common language, tradition, religion, and region (Phinney, 1996). **Culture** is more broad and refers to a shared system of values, beliefs, norms, and practices that people pass down from one generation to another (Triandis, 2002). **Nationality** is more specific and refers often to citizenship or the region that a person comes from (Betancourt & López, 1993); as a result, it usually involves attitudes about the said country (Phinney & Devich-Navarro, 1997).

Having different terms may give the impression that these distinctions are clear-cut; in reality, they are far from it. Take, for example, the case of ethnicity. Historically, ethnicity in the United States included a category labeled "Hispanic," which was meant to denote a single group that encompassed a variety of people, including those from Spain, Central America, the Caribbean, and Latin America. Since then, many have taken issue with this ethnic label and argued that these different subgroups are quite different and do not identify themselves the same; for example, many "Hispanics" do not actually trace their lineage back to Spain but, instead, have ancestry from indigenous American populations (Comas-Díaz, 2001).

Having an Identity, Because Identification Matters

Once upon a time, human beings lived in tiny, homogenous societies—groups, really—where they hunted and gathered food while trying not to get killed by nature: animals larger than them and other groups they did not know. Under such conditions, identity was a moot issue; humans had no time to think too long or hard about how they fit in with the social forces around them, and truth be told, there weren't that many social forces around them. Over the course of civilization, these groups got bigger and their functions became more stable and complex, but still, identity hardly mattered, because for much of human history identities were given at birth. You were born a certain way, with a certain configuration of physical traits and family lineage that automatically and unquestioningly put you into categories that few people ever questioned. These days, however, identity is everywhere, dynamic, and hotly contested, because we have both the resources and freedom to consider them more seriously than we did before. Thus there are now numerous forms of identity that people can take on—including, but not limited to, those based on race/nationality/ethnicity, gender, SES, religion (i.e., all the forms of culture we have already covered), as well as others we have not (e.g., age, political orientation, sexual orientation, disability, etc.; Howard, 2000). This chapter will focus exclusively on race/nationality/ethnicity as identity because it is one of the most commonly cited and most studied forms of identity within psychology. Like the protagonist (Derek) in *Zoolander* who gazed upon his own reflection and asked, "Who am I?" to the Narcissus before him (who perished over a minor ontological glitch in determining his own identity when he gazed upon his face in a pool), modern humans are very much concerned about all the variable selves we can be.

One of the classic psychological theories that addressed this question of how people see themselves and the role that social group membership plays in this process is **Social Identity Theory**, or SIT, which posited that the groups people belong to play a central role in their self-views (Tajfel & Turner, 1986). As a paradigmatic illustration of this phenomenon, Tajfel (1970) designed the minimal group paradigm, which used arbitrary, ostensibly meaningless criteria to divide people into groups, and watched to see how these group memberships dictated people's subsequent behavior. Sometimes it was a matter of dividing people into those who preferred one abstract painter over another; other times it involved estimating dots on a page and grouping people into over- and underestimators (Tajfel, Billig, Bundy, & Flament, 1971). Still other times it was a totally random process of heads versus tails (Billig & Tajfel, 1973). Regardless of the strategy, the phenomenon was the same: People favored those in their group over those from a different group, even if the groups themselves were meaningless (Billig & Tajfel, 1973; Tajfel et al., 1971).

At first glance, this stubborn desire to be part of, and support, a group formed by trivial standards may seem silly, but other subsequent research has shown that a strong sense of group identification can offer compelling psychological benefits. Among minorities in the United States, there is consistent evidence to suggest that high levels of **ethnic identification** act as a psychological buffer against many of the perils of discrimination. While discrimination is harmful for well-being—leading to worse grades, negative self-views, behavioral problems, and poor mental health outcomes—having a strong sense of connection to one's ethnic group reduced these negative effects (Wong, Eccles, & Sameroff, 2003). This phenomenon has been shown with African Americans (e.g., Wong et al., 2003) and Latino/a-Americans (Umaña-Taylor & Updegraff, 2007), and other studies have suggested that the positive psychological effects of ethnic identification generally applies across groups, including not just Blacks and Latinos but also Whites, Native Americans, and Asians (Martinez & Dukes, 1997).

These positive effects of ethnic identification on well-being notwithstanding, more recent work suggests that liabilities are also present. In his study on ethnic identification and stereotype boost/lift among Asians and Latinos, Brian Armenta (2010) found that identification helped the former but hurt the latter on a math test. Namely, highly identified Asians experienced more stereotype boost (and did better on the math test) but highly identified Latinos experienced more stereotype threat (and did worse on the math test; Armenta, 2010). This suggests that whether ethnic identification is a benefit (or not) may depend on the domain at hand and the stereotypes that are applied to the ethnic group.

Changing Identity, Because Identity Is Fluid

Matters of identity become even more complicated when you realize that identity is not stable but rather highly dynamic and prone to change. One common form of identity change is through immigration, or moving from one cultural context to another. This can result in a **bicultural identity**, or a combination of two identities—your original identity and the new identity you're being exposed to (for a review, see Nguyen & Benet-Martínez, 2007). That said, there are multiple approaches to and levels of bicultural identity, outlined below.

Acculturation refers to the first step, when people adopt a new culture and update their value systems to include their host culture and their origin culture (for a review, see Berry, Phinney, Sam, & Vedder, 2006). Acculturation, however, is not the only option in response to intercultural contact. Alternative strategies include **separation**, which is when you avoid taking on the new culture and actively strive to maintain the origin culture, or **marginalization**, which is when both the new and origin culture are avoided altogether (Berry et al., 2006).

Back in 2006, when Berry et al. conducted a large-scale study of bicultural youth across 13 different countries (the United States, Canada, Western European nations, Australia, and New Zealand), they asked these first- and second-generation individuals about their acculturation strategies (e.g., whether they tried to integrate, assimilate, separate, or marginalize), identity, behaviors, family relationships, experiences with discrimination. Berry et al. also gave the youths various measures of psychological adaptation, including how happy they were with themselves and their lives. Berry et al. (2006) found that on average, most of the teenage participants were more likely to endorse integration than to identify strongly with one culture or another (or no culture at all), indicating that they were highly involved with both their original ethnic culture as well as the culture of the new nation that they had immigrated to; they reported that they interacted with members from both groups and were comfortable in both cultural contexts.

When Berry et al. (2006) looked at well-being outcomes, they found that on average, integration was associated with more positive outcomes, including less discrimination, higher self-esteem and life satisfaction, fewer behavioral problems, and better school adjustment. Interestingly, when they compared the well-being of these bicultural teenagers with their peers who did not come from immigrant backgrounds, they found no differences, suggesting that immigration alone does not appear to negatively impact adjustment (Berry et al., 2006). Some researchers have deemed this finding the **immigrant paradox**, which centers on the idea that despite the challenges of adjusting to a new culture, immigrants appear to do as well as their nonimmigrant counterparts (Berry et al., 2006; Nguyen, 2006). Although the data on the relationship between acculturation and outcomes are mixed, some work suggests that it may depend on the specific outcome at hand. For example, research on Latino/a Americans have found that when it comes to drugs, diet, and birth outcomes, being acculturated seems to exert a negative effect, but when it comes to utilization of health care services, acculturation has a positive effect (Lara, Gamboa, Kahramanian, Morales, & Bautista, 2005). More recent meta-analysis has suggested that if anything, biculturalism is positively correlated with psychological and sociocultural adjustment (Nguyen & Benet-Martínez, 2012).

Consistent with these findings, additional studies have shown that the process of acculturation is not a unidimensional phenomenon whereby identifying with one's origin culture and new host culture are mutually exclusive or inversely related. In other words, culture is not a zero-sum game, where gains in one context must be accompanied by losses in another. In contrast, acculturation appears to be a more bidirectional phenomenon, where identifying with one's original culture and new host culture are relatively independent processes that can be dissociated (see Nguyen & Benet-Martínez, 2007, for a recent review). As an empirical test of this idea, Ryder, Alden, and Paulhus (2000) looked at how various immigrant groups identified with their origin culture, their new "mainstream" culture, and the relationship between the two. Consistently across samples—including of Chinese, Southeast Asian, and various other groups of immigrants (e.g., Indians, Arabs)—they found that identifying with one's origin culture was moderately negatively associated with identifying with one's host culture, and this relationship disappears altogether after the first generation (Ryder et al., 2000).

In contrast to acculturation, **assimilation** typically occurs farther down the road and refers to the process of wholly identifying with the (new) host culture and losing the origin culture (Berry & Sam, 1997). Individuals who assimilate do not want to keep their original culture and aim to interact almost exclusively with their new host culture. Which immigrant groups adopt acculturation or assimilation approaches varies, as does generational status—in other words, different groups are differentially likely to pursue assimilation, and first- versus second-generation individuals may also differ in their likelihood of pursuing assimilation (for review, see Berry & Sam, 1997).

Bicultural identity integration is somewhat of a middle ground and refers to the process of creating a new, superordinate identity that is distinct from both the origin culture and the host culture (Benet-Martínez, Leu, Lee & Morris, 2002). To illustrate, Asian Americans, Latino/a Americans, and African Americans may look different from their ancestors from Asia, Latin-America, and Africa, as well as from European Americans. Thus they've created a new culture that is derived from those two identities but is also different from them. They tend to see their two identities as compatible, are more likely to have friends from their new host culture, and are more adjusted (Benet-Martínez et al., 2002; Chen, Benet-Martínez, & Bond, 2007; Mok, Morris, Benet-Martínez, & Karakitapoğlu-Ayugün, 2007).

Once a bicultural identity is established, a person can often move between the two identities. In their classic study on this process—called **frame-switching**—Hong, Chiu, and Kung (1997) primed Hong Kong Chinese with images of either Chinese or Western icons—pagodas versus the White House, for example. Hong et al.'s (1997) idea was straightforward: Exposing people to iconic images of one culture or another would momentarily cause them to identify more with the culture that they've just been shown. Consistent with this prediction, they found that participants were more likely to endorse values that matched the images—that is, they supported traditional Chinese values more after seeing Chinese images and Western values more after seeing North American images (Hong et al., 1997). In addition, they also made attributions that corresponded with the primed culture when responding to the underwater fish scene (see chapter 1 for review), making more internal attributions when exposed to the Western primes but making more external attributions when exposed to the Chinese primes (Hong et al., 1997). Other studies have shown that people who are high on bicultural identity integration are especially likely to frame-switch (Benet-Martínez et al., 2002).

Not All Immigrant Experiences Are Created Equal

Differences in approaches to biculturalism constitute just one nuance; additional distinctions can be made as a function of the type of immigrant and of a host of other factors, including individual differences (e.g., age, gender), the country being immigrated to, and the country being emigrated from.

Type of immigrant varies; you could move to another country by choice or by necessity—something that distinguishes **voluntary immigrants** from **refugees** and **asylum seekers**: While the former typically move because of a job or a relationship, the latter two categories move out of necessity (Berry, 2006). Refugees are typically displaced individuals who are set up to move through government arrangements, whereas asylum seekers move because of the threat of persecution (Berry, 2006). There is also a fourth category—**sojourners**—who move temporarily, with the intention of returning to their origin country (Berry, 2006). Not only do these categories of immigrants have different motivations for their relocation but they are also likely to be received differently once they've arrived. In particular, refugees and asylum seekers may be seen negatively because of their need and subject as a result to more discrimination (Louis, Duck, Terry, Schuller, & Lalonde, 2007).

Origin of immigrant also matters, and not all ethnic groups are treated equally, as the previous chapters on stereotypes and prejudice have mentioned. For example, in a study of European immigrants, a comparison of Arabs, Somalis, Turks, Russians, Estonians, Finnish, and Vietnamese found that Arabs, Somalis, and Turks reported experiencing more discrimination than the other groups (Liebkind & Jasinkaja-Lahti, 2000). In that same study, they also found that *individual differences* matter, too—namely, men reported more discrimination than women across all seven groups (Liebkind & Jasinkaja-Lahti, 2000). Interestingly and against expectation, men nevertheless also reported less psychological stress despite their greater exposure to discrimination (Liebkind & Jaskinkaja-Lahti, 2000). This raises questions about the consistency and reliability of the link between discrimination and well-being among immigrant groups, although it's important to note that other studies have found that discrimination did predict poor health outcomes. For example, among Latino/a, Black, and Southeast Asian immigrants, greater discrimination was linked to more smoking and drinking (Tran, Lee, & Burgess, 2010). Similarly, other individual differences related to age and length of time spent in the host country can also make a difference. In the aforementioned European study, some cultural groups (e.g., Arabs and Russians) reported experiencing more discrimination the more time they spent in their host country (Liebkind & Jaskinkaja-Lahti, 2000) whereas other studies suggest that recent immigrants should be more likely the target of discrimination because of the likelihood that they are less familiar with the host country's language and practices (Yoo, Gee, & Takeuchi, 2009). As a related point, age can also be a factor, as younger immigrants might find it easier to adapt to a new culture than older ones who have more ingrained cultural practices (Schwartz, Unger, Zamboanga, & Szapocznik, 2010).

Finally, *context of host country* can also play a major role. In the United States, the immigrant experience is likely very different if you settle in a major cosmopolitan city that boasts a high degree of diversity—especially diversity that includes members of your origin culture (e.g., New York, Los Angeles, and particular ethnic enclaves in other cities)—than in other settings (and see Insight Box 9.1). Having access and exposure to one's origin culture in the context of one's new host culture can promote retention of the former's values and identity (see Schwartz et al., 2010 for a discussion of differences a host country can make in determining acculturation outcomes).

INSIGHT BOX 9.1

Attitudes toward Immigrants

It doesn't take a presidential election to realize that immigration remains a controversial political topic about which individuals and groups feel very strongly. Almost everyone has an opinion on immigration, and differences in opinion remain one of the most divisive issues across party lines (Hawley, 2011). But where do these attitudes toward immigrants come from?

One idea is that opposition to immigration and naturalization may stem from the real or imagined threat posed by immigrants. Realistic threats center around economic opportunities and political power that immigrants may gain, whereas symbolic threats center around differences in worldview (Stephan & Stephan, 2000). Said differently, people may feel threatened by immigrants because of the jobs and votes these individuals acquire, or simply because they believe different things, which threatens the validity of mainstream beliefs.

When researchers tested the potency of both types of threats across 21 different European countries, they found that realistic threat was a stronger drive of negative attitudes toward immigrants—specifically, prejudice against them and opposition to immigration policies that would allow more of such individuals to move to Europe (Pereira, Vala, & Costa-Lopes, 2010). Symbolic threat also played a role but was more predictive of opposition to naturalization, or allowing immigrants to become citizens after arrival (Pereira et al., 2010). Consistent with these findings, economists have found similar patterns when analyzing attitudes toward immigration across nations (including the United States, Canada, Japan, European countries, and the Philippines): In rich countries, highly skilled labor show more positive attitudes toward immigrants, but in poor countries, highly skilled labor show more negative attitudes toward immigrants (Mayda, 2006). This suggests that in contexts where immigrants do not pose a realistic threat against jobs (e.g., in a wealthy country, among people who are highly employable), people tend to favor them, but in contexts where immigrants might realistically be vying for the same opportunities as the individuals already there (e.g., in low GDP countries, among people who are highly skilled but may not enjoy high levels of economic opportunity), attitudes tend to be much more negative.

Unpacking Minority Group Identities, Because Identity Is Socially Constructed

Special attention to minority identities can be useful because even though all identities are socially constructed, those who identify with underrepresented or disadvantaged groups might face unique psychological challenges, outlined below.

The "Acting White" Effect

The previous two chapters covered some of the challenges that individuals of color may face in everyday life, spanning a gamut of issues that range from stereotype threat and microaggressions to overt discrimination, as well as the more complicated issues of ingroup derogation. Related to these is a little-known phenomenon called the **acting White effect**, reflecting the idea that in some communities of color, striving for goals related to education or related forms of achievement is considered to be an attempt to abandon one's own group and become part of the dominant majority group (Fryer, 2006). Essentially, getting As and aspiring to goals like college can be seen as disloyal and disingenuous; as a result, non-White individuals may get made fun of when they attempt to achieve these goals. Their popularity suffers, as does their sense of social belonging (Fryer, 2006). Moreover, it's not just in their heads—the data suggest that actual social inclusion and status drops for Black and Latino/a students who achieve very high GPAs—the inflection point varies, but it emerges somewhere around a 3.5 for the former and 2.5 for the latter (Fryer, 2006). This suggests that identity can be profoundly problematic: Even if a person doesn't want to actively change his or her own identity, others' perception of the legitimacy of the person's identity can change as a function of his or her achievements and how those achievements are construed. Thus non-White students may face a double barrier—one from the stereotypes that mainstream society holds about their group and the accompanying stereotype threat that comes with it and the other from the pressures stemming from their own group members when they neglect to act in ways consistent with their supposed group identity.

Identity Threat

Taken together, the previous findings suggest that minority group members may experience threats to their identity (see Insight Box 9.2). Because of the negative stereotypes associated with belonging to a historically disadvantaged group, these individuals may find that identifying with their ingroup poses problems—psychological and otherwise. As a result, there are typically three types of responses to this type of threat: disidentification, internalization, and collective action.

Disidentification is essentially what it sounds like—it refers to the process of separating the self from the ingroup (Steele, 1997). In the aforementioned studies on stereotype threat (e.g., by Steele, 1997), this has taken form in behaviors like distancing the self from domains that are typically associated with the ingroup—for example, when a Black student professes a dislike for basketball and jazz after being reminded of the stereotypes associated with African Americans in academic performance contexts. According to existing research, this process of disidentification comes with benefits and liabilities: On the one hand, disidentifying with a negatively stereotyped group can protect self-esteem; on the other hand, this same process also—ironically—hurts actual success in the stereotyped domain (Cokley, 2002; Steele, 1997). Thus the individual may feel better about himself or herself but still end up doing poorly in school—presumably because having a strong system of social support (that often comes from being part of a group) can be instrumental to success in school and other contexts (Steele, 1997). Furthermore, disidentification can also be problematic because it does little to combat the existing inequalities and stereotypes that motivated it in the first place (Steele, 1997).

Instead of disidentification, alternative responses are possible and potentially more adaptive. Two examples of alternative reactions to identity threat are (1) having role models and other people to guide someone through challenging situations involving their identity and (2) learning about the malleability of intelligence (Steele, 1997). In both cases, rather than dissociating the self from the group that is linked to the threat, the response is more geared toward resolving the psychological roots of the problem while preserving belonging in the group (Steele, 1997).

Internalization is an alternative but equally problematic response to identity threat; it happens when a member of a group accepts the group's disadvantaged position and endorses the very stereotypes leveraged against it (Steele, 1997). However, internalization doesn't always happen with members of disadvantaged groups, and some groups are less likely to engage in this than others. For example, previous research has found that Blacks are relatively unlikely to engage in internalization, and rather, tend to reject the negative stereotypes about their group (Schuman, Steeh, Bobo, & Krysan, 1997). Instead, they are more likely to perceive that the disadvantages faced by their group are the direct product of existing systems of discrimination inequality (Schumann et al., 1997)—which leads us to our third option, collective action.

Collective action is likely the most adaptive of these three responses to identity threat and involves group members banding together to actively change the systems that are producing identity threats in the first place. This response is more common among people who strongly identify with their group (people who do not strongly identify with their group are more likely to engage in disidentification; Doosje & Ellemers, 1997). While low identifiers are more likely to leave the group when the group is threatened, high identifiers show strong commitment to the group even in the face of threat (Ellemers, Spears, & Doosje, 1997).

INSIGHT BOX 9.2

The Many Forms of Identity Threat

The problematic nature of identity isn't something specific to minority group members. Anyone can experience identity threat, whether it centers on race or any other type of group membership that we've covered so far, including gender, class, religion, and the like. Even within race, identity can be complicated. Take the example of Rachel Dolezal (photo 9.2), whose identity became national news when she resigned from her leadership position in the National Association for the Advancement of Colored People precisely because of the issues surrounding her racial identity.

PHOTO 9.2. Rachel Dolezal brings up new questions about the fluidity of racial identity.

Source: Alamy

Growing up, Rachel ostensibly appeared to be a White girl from the Midwest—with blonde hair, fair skin, and blue eyes. Over the course of her adolescent and adult life, issues of race and identity became an ever increasingly pressing question: When she was in high school, her parents adopted four Black babies; in college, she became aware of social justice and racial reconciliation causes; upon graduation, she married a Black man and enrolled in the historically black Howard University (Johnson, Perez-Peña, & Eligon, 2015). During her time in graduate school, she reportedly faced discrimination—namely, she was denied for financial aid—because she was White (Johnson et al., 2015). In the following years, her appearance began to change; her complexion appeared to darken and her hair styling evolved, as did her self-reported identity (Johnson et al., 2015). When she worked as a human rights coordinator, she self-identified as an African American woman; she also taught and advised in African studies programs in colleges (Johnson et al., 2015).

When questions of her racial identity came under national scrutiny, Rachel remained staunch about her ability to choose her race, despite stepping down from her post as president of the NAACP chapter in Spokane, Washington (Johnson et al., 2015). Still, she continued to face accusations that she was putting on "blackface," misappropriating a racial identity and experience that was not rightfully hers, deceiving people, and using her change in racial identity for ulterior motives—namely, to get ahead in the activist organizations she worked in (Johnson et al., 2015; Perez-Peña, 2015). Nevertheless, she also has supporters, who liken her experience with being **transracial** as similar to the experience of transgendered individuals (Lee, 2015). Others treat it as a private matter, separating her admirable record of political activism from her personal identity issues (e.g., on the NAACP's own statement about their former chapter president).

Rachel's case is also not all that unique. Many observers deem her experience as another case of **passing**, or when an individual from one group portrays himself or herself as a member of a different group. Historically, passing was something that happened to Black Americans who, by virtue of their lighter complexion, were seen as White—a phenomenon with major repercussions in an era when slavery and bans on interracial marriage were still in place. There have also been cases of "reverse passing," or when White individuals come off as people of color (Sharpstein, 2015). In both cases, controversies like Rachel's and the others that have come before her beg us to question more severely our definitions of race and identity and the process by which we appear to assign people to these categorizes, sometimes without their consent. If DNA analyses suggest that a substantial percentage of Americans who think (and appear) White actually have African Americans in their lineage (Bryc, Durand, Macpherson, Reich, & Mountain, 2015), then this only further blurs the lines between Whiteness and Blackness and the potential for permeability between the two.

Key Concepts

Passing
Ethnicity vs. culture vs. nationality
Social Identity Theory
Ethnic identification
Bicultural identity
Acculturation, separation, marginalization
Immigrant paradox
Assimilation and bicultural identity integration
Frame-switching
Voluntary immigrants, refugees, asylum seekers, and sojourners
Acting White effect
Disidentification vs. internalization vs. collective action

References

Anderson, C. A., & Godfrey, S. S. (1987). Thoughts about actions: The effects of specificity and availability of imagined behavioral scripts on expectations about oneself and others. *Social Cognition*, 5(3), 238–258.

Armenta, B. E. (2010). Stereotype boost and stereotype threat effects: The moderating role of ethnic identification. *Cultural Diversity and Ethnic Minority Psychology*, 16(1), 94–98.

Banton, M. (1987). The classification of races in Europe and North America: 1700–1850. *International Social Science Journal*, 39(111), 45–60.

Benet-Martínez, V., & Haritatos, J. (2005). Bicultural identity integration (BII): Components and psychosocial antecedents. *Journal of Personality*, 73(4), 1015–1050. doi:10.1111/j.1467-6494.2005.00337.x

Benet-Martínez, V., Leu, J., Lee, F., & Morris, M. (2002). Negotiating biculturalism: Cultural frame switching in biculturals with oppositional versus compatible cultural identities. *Journal of Cross-Cultural Psychology*, 33(5), 492–516. doi:10.1177/0022022102033005005

Berry, J. W. (2006). Contexts of acculturation. In D. L. Sam & J. W. Berry (Eds.), *Cambridge Handbook of acculturation psychology* (pp. 27–42). New York, NY: Cambridge University Press.

Berry, J. W., Phinney, J. S., Sam, D. L., & Vedder, P. (2006). Immigrant youth: Acculturation, identity, and adaptation. *Applied Psychology: An International Review*, 55(3), 303–332. doi:10.1111/j.1464-0597.2006.00256.x

Berry, J. W., & Sam, D. L. (1997). Acculturation and adaptation. In *Handbook of cross-cultural psychology*, 3(2), 291–326.

Betancourt, H., & López, S. R. (1993). The study of culture, ethnicity, and race in American psychology. *American Psychologist*, 48(6), 629–637. doi:10.1037/0003-066X.48.6.629

Billig, M., & Tajfel, H. (1973). Social categorization and similarity in intergroup behaviour. *European Journal of Social Psychology*, 3(1), 27–52.

Bryc, K., Durand, E. Y., Macpherson, J. M., Reich, D., & Mountain, J. L. (2015). The genetic ancestry of African Americans, Latinos, and European Americans across the United States. *The American Journal of Human Genetics*, 96(1), 37–53.

Coates, T. (2016, December 22). "It's what we do more than what we say": Obama on race, identity, and the way forward. *The Atlantic*. Retrieved from https://www.theatlantic.com/politics/archive/2016/12/ta-nehisi-coates-obama-transcript-iii/511475/

Cokley, K. O. (2002). Ethnicity, gender and academic self-concept: A preliminary examination of academic disidentification and implications for psychologists. *Cultural Diversity and Ethnic Minority Psychology*, 8(4), 378–388.

Comas-Díaz, L. (2001). Hispanics, Latinos, or Americanos: The evolution of identity. *Cultural Diversity and Ethnic Minority Psychology*, 7(2), 115–120. doi:10.1037/1099-9809.7.2.115

Doosje, B. & Ellemers, N. (1997). Stereotyping under threat: The role of group identification. In R. Spears, P. J. Oakes, N. Ellemers, & S. A. Haslam (Eds.), *The social psychology of stereotyping and group life* (pp. 257–272). Cambridge, MA: Blackwell Publishers.

Ellemers, N., Spears, R., & Doosje, B. (1997). Sticking together or falling apart: In-group identification as a psychological determinant of group commitment versus individual mobility. *Journal of Personality and Social Psychology*, 72(3), 617–626.

Fryer, G. R. (2006). "Acting white." *EducationNext*. 6(1). Retrieved from http://educationnext.org/actingwhite/

Hawley, G. (2011). Political threat and immigration: Party identification, demographic context, and immigration policy preference. *Social Science Quarterly*, 92(2), 404–422. doi:10.1111/j.1540-6237.2011.00775.x

Hollyfield, Amy. (2008, June 27). Obama's birth certificate: Final chapter. Politifact. Retrieved from http://www.politifact.com/truth-o-meter/article/2008/jun/27/obamas-birth-certificate-part-ii/

Hong, Y. Y., Morris, M. W., Chiu, C. Y., & Benet-Martinez, V. (2000). Multicultural minds: A dynamic constructivist approach to culture and cognition. *American Psychologist*, *55*(7), 709.

Howard, J. A. (2000). Social psychology of identities. *Annual review of sociology*, *26*, 367–393. doi:10.1146/annurev.soc.26.1.367

Johnson, K., Pérez-Peña, R., & Eligon, J. (2015, June 16). Rachel Dolezal, in center of storm, is defiant: "I identify as black." *The New York Times*. Retrieved from http://www.nytimes.com/2015/06/17/us/rachel-dolezal-nbc-today-show.html?_r=0

Lara, M., Gamboa, C., Kahramanian, M. I., Morales, L. S., & Bautista, D. H. (2005). Acculturation and Latino health in the United States: A review of the literature and its sociopolitical context. *Annual Review of Public Health*, *26*, 367–397. doi:10.1146/annurev.publhealth.26.021304.144615

Lee, E. (2015, June 16). Raven-Symone supports Rachel Dolezal amidst NAACP resignation: "I love her." *Us Weekly*. Retrieved from http://www.usmagazine.com/celebrity-news/news/raven-symone-supports-rachel-dolezal-amidst-naacp-scandal-love-her-2015166

Liebkind, K., & Jasinskaja-Lahti, I. (2000). The influence of experiences of discrimination on psychological stress: A comparison of seven immigrant groups. *Journal of Community & Applied Social Psychology*, *10*(1), 1–16.

Louis, W. R., Duck, J. M., Terry, D. J., Schuller, R. A., & Lalonde, R. A. (2007). Why do citizens want to keep refugees out? Threats, fairness, and hostile norms in the treatment of asylum seekers. *European Journal of Social Psychology*, *37*(1), 53–73. doi:10.1002/ejsp.329

Maraniss, D. (2012). *Barack Obama: The story*. New York, NY: Simon & Schuster.

Martinez, R. O., & Dukes, R. L. (1997). The effects of ethnic identity, ethnicity, and gender on adolescent well-being. *Journal of Youth and Adolescence*, *26*(5), 503–516. doi:10.1023/A:1024525821078

Mayda, A. M. (2006). Who is against immigration? A cross-country investigation of individual attitudes toward immigrants. *The Review of Economics and Statistics*, *88*(3), 510–530.

Mendible, M. (2012). The politics of race and class in the age of Obama. *Revue de recherche en civilisation américaine*. Retrieved from http://journals.openedition.org/rrca/489

Mok, A., Morris, M., Benet-Martínez, V., & Karakitapoğlu-Aygün, Z. (2007). EmbracingAmerican culture: Structures of social identity and social networks among first-generation biculturals. *Journal of Cross-Cultural Psychology*, *38*(5), 629–635. doi:10.1177/0022022107305243

NAACP. (2015, June 12). NAACP statement on Rachel Dolezal. Retrieved from http://www.naacp.org/latest/naacp-statement-on-rachel-dolezal/

Nguyen, A. M. D., & Benet-Martínez, V. (2007). Biculturalism unpacked: Components, measurement, individual differences, and outcomes. *Social and Personality Psychology Compass*, *1*(1), 101–114. doi:10.1111/j.1751-9004.2007.00029.x

Nguyen, A. M. D., & Benet-Martínez, V. (2012). Biculturalism and adjustment: A meta-analysis. *Journal of Cross-Cultural Psychology*, *44*(1), 122–159. doi:10.1177/0022022111435097

NPR Staff. (2012, July 3). Morgan Freeman: No black president for U.S. yet. *Tell Me More @ NPR Podcast*. http://www.npr.org/2012/07/05/156212527/morgan-freeman-no-black-president-for-u-s-yet

Pérez-Peña, R. (2015, June 15). Rachel Dolezal leaves NAACP post as past discrimination suit is revealed. *The New York Times.* Retrieved from http://www.nytimes.com/2015/06/16/us/rachel-dolezal-quits-naacp-in-spokane.html?_r=0

Phinney, J. S. (1996). Understanding ethnic diversity: The role of ethnic identity. *American Behavioral Scientist, 40*(2), 143–152.

Phinney, J. S., & Devich-Navarro, M. (1997). Variations in bicultural identification among African American and Mexican American adolescents. *Journal of Research on Adolescence, 7*(1), 3–32. doi:10.1207/s15327795jra0701_2

Ryder, A. G., Alden, L. E., & Paulhus, D. L. (2000). Is acculturation unidimensional or bidimensional? A head-to-head comparison in the prediction of personality, self-identity, and adjustment. *Journal of Personality and Social Psychology, 79*(1), 49–65. doi:10.1037/0022-3514.79.1.49

Schuman, H., Steeh, C., Bobo, L., Krysan, M. (1997). *Racial attitudes in America: Trends and interpretations.* Cambridge, MA: Harvard University Press.

Sharpstein, D. J. (2015, June 15). Rachel Dolezal's passing isn't so unusual. *The New York Times.* Retrieved from http://www.nytimes.com/2015/06/25/magazine/rachel-dolezals-passing-isnt-so-unusual.html

Steele, C. M. (1997). A threat in the air: How stereotypes shape intellectual identity and performance. *American Psychologist, 52*(6), 613–629. doi:10.1037/0003-066X.52.6.613

Stephan, W. G., & Stephan, C. W. (2000). An integrated threat theory of prejudice. In S. Oskamp (Ed.), *Reducing prejudice and discrimination* (pp. 23–45). Mahwah, NJ: Erlbaum.

Tajfel, H. (1970). Experiments in intergroup discrimination. *Scientific American, 223*(5), 96–103.

Tajfel, H., Billig, M. G., Bundy, R. P., & Flament, C. (1971). Social categorization and intergroup behaviour. *European Journal of Social Psychology, 1*(2), 149–178. doi:10.1002/ejsp.2420010202

Tajfel, H., & Turner, J. C. (1986). The social identity theory of intergroup behavior. In S. Worchel & W. G. Austin (Eds.), *Psychology of intergroup relations* (pp. 7–24). Chicago: Nelson-Hall.

Tran, A. T., Lee, R. M., & Burgess, D. J. (2010). Perceived discrimination and substance use in Hispanic/Latino, African-born Black, and Southeast Asian immigrants. *Cultural Diversity and Ethnic Minority Psychology, 16*(2), 226–236. doi:10.1037/a0016344

Triandis, H. C. (2002). Subjective culture. *Online Readings in Psychology and Culture, 2*(2). Retrieved from https://doi.org/10.9707/2307-0919.1021

Umaña-Taylor, A. J., & Updegraff, K. A. (2007). Latino adolescents' mental health: Exploring the interrelations among discrimination, ethnic identity, cultural orientation, self-esteem, and depressive symptoms. *Journal of Adolescence, 30*(4), 549–567. doi:10.1016/j.adolescence.2006.08.002

Weisberg, J. (2008, August 23). If Obama loses. *Slate.* Retrieved from http://www.slate.com/articles/news_and_politics/the_big_idea/2008/08/if_obama_loses.html

Witherspoon, D. J., Wooding, S., Rogers, A. R., Marchani, E. E., Watkins, W. S., Batzer, M. A., & Jorde, L. B. (2007). Genetic similarities within and between human populations. *Genetics, 176*(1), 351–359.

Wong, C. A., Eccles, J. S., & Sameroff, A. (2003). The influence of ethnic discrimination and ethnic identification on African American adolescents' school and socioemotional adjustment. *Journal of Personality, 71*(6), 1197–1232. doi:10.1111/1467-6494.7106012

Yoo, H. C., Gee, G. C., Takeuchi, D. (2009). Discrimination and health among Asian American immigrants: Disentangling racial from language discrimination. *Social Science & Medicine, 68*(4), 726–732. doi:10.1016/j.socscimed.2008.11.013

CHAPTER 10

Navigating Diversity
Multiculturalism versus Culture-Blindness

Understanding the dual realities that (1) human nature is diverse and (2) as a species, we have a long and illustrious history of cultural conflict, we are led to the logical next question: How do we deal with our diversity? One approach is to adopt a culture-blind mentality and assume that on a fundamental level, people are all the same insofar as we all share some deep underlying nature. The alternative approach is multiculturalism, which aims to highlight (and appreciate) differences between groups. This chapter covers the assumptions and empirically-documented outcomes associated with both ideologies.

The previous chapter begs this urgent question: What does diversity do to our attitudes? Like all changes that happen to people and societies, pushback or reactance is almost inevitable; few revolutions occur without the shedding of blood and tears, metaphorical or otherwise. As the United States and the rest of the world become more globalized, as people increasingly have to meet individuals different from them and travel to lands foreign to their ancestors, what does this mean for our psyche? How will our values, beliefs, and institutions change as a result?

Racism without Racists? Multiple Approaches to Diversity

These days, racists don't (usually) walk around in pointy hoods with burning crosses and swastika cupcakes. Since losing the fight for people's hearts during the civil rights movement, the Ku Klux Klan appeared to largely go into hibernation—that is, until recently. As debates over a new rise in U.S. nationalism took center stage in many of the debates leading up to the 2016 presidential election, many Klan members thought that perhaps a revival in the KKK was brewing (Associated Press, 2016). Joining the KKK nowadays is as easy as an online membership form and confirmation of one's White, Christian status; members meet in conventions and local chapter meetings (Associated Press, 2016).

This, of course, represents an extreme response to diversity and one that is still relatively rare. Much more common are colorblindness or multiculturalism (see below), as well as related models based on mere exposure: the contact hypothesis, and developments in the jigsaw classroom. Each of these approaches is outlined below.

Colorblindness

The **colorblind ideology** is behind the common phrase, "I don't see color," usually followed by a statement about how the person "only sees people." The premise for this approach is that group membership doesn't matter; the reasoning is that if we act as if groups do not exist, then we can create a society where group divides no longer exist. Some have argued that this approach dates all the way back to the civil rights movement, when leaders like Martin Luther King Jr. made statements that arguably could be construed to sound like an endorsement of colorblindness: "I have a dream that my four little children will one day live in a nation where they will not be judged by the color of their skin, but by the content of their character" (see "MLK's 'content of character' quote inspires debate," 2013).

Colorblind ideology has also been endorsed by numerous conservative pundits. For example, William Bennett, the U.S. secretary of education under President Reagan, stated, "For supposedly noble reasons—including the wish to instill ethnic and racial pride, universities are drawing more and more attention to race. Increasingly we've gone from putting a premium on being color-blind to putting a premium on being color conscious" (Bennett, 1994).

Others have taken a more critical approach to the notion of colorblindness. In the movie *To Wong Foo Thanks for Everything, Julie Newmar*, Noxeema Jackson declares, "I'm not Martin Luther King. I don't need a dream. I have a plan" (Brown & Kidron, 1995).

The argument is that colorblindness ignores the cold, hard reality that race does make a difference in determining people's opportunities and outcomes and that adopting an approach that ignores color (when we live in a society where color does matter) is negligent at best and counterproductive at worst.

Research also suggests that telling people to be colorblind is an ineffective strategy that might, ironically, lead to increased stereotypes—a phenomenon known as the "**stereotype rebound effect**" (Macrae, Bodenhausen, Milne, & Jetten, 1994). In a lab demonstration by Macrae et al. (1994), participants were shown a picture of a skinhead and asked to describe his typical day; in one condition, they were purposely told to ignore stereotypes (i.e., similar to the colorblind approach) while in another, they were not given any particular direction. Afterward, all participants were given a second picture of a (different) skinhead, and once again they had to describe this person's average day. Researchers found that being told to suppress their stereotypes actually led participants to be more stereotypical, not less, when describing the second skinhead (Macrae et al., 1994).

Multiculturalism

A second, alternative, option is multiculturalism, which promises to not ignore color but, rather, take color into account when structuring society. Often, multiculturalism involves assimilating different groups to promote social cohesion and reduce prejudice. Multiculturalism itself has been debated in recent years, and at least two different versions of it exist. There is the classic notion of **melting pot** assimilation, where all groups in a society take on each other's cultures, practices, and traditions in order to create a new, higher order culture that represents a blend of all the existing subcultures (Hirschman, 1983). Although this idea of the United States as a melting pot had been widely accepted in past years, in recent times, people have cast doubt on this image, noting that majority groups do not always embrace immigrant cultures, and individual cultures tend to lose their distinctiveness in the process (for a review on America as a melting pot society, see Hirschman, 1983).

An alternative to the melting pot model is the idea of the "**salad bowl**" or "**cultural mosaic**" multiculturalism (figure 10.1), which encourages cultural groups to retain their unique practices and customs while living in harmony with other groups ("'Melting Pot' America," 2006). In contrast to the melting pot—where individual groups lose their unique, defining attributes—salad bowl multiculturalism aims to preserve each group's qualities and yet still produce a cohesive, unified outcome ("'Melting Pot' America," 2006). Still others have argued that these different models of multiculturalism are not mutually exclusive and that you can have both versions at work. For example, researchers like Bachmann (2006) argued that at least when it comes to diversity in the workplace, you can have both melting pot and salad bowl approaches—for example, by enforcing a strict assimilationist approach when it comes to assigning group tasks, but a more lenient, accommodative approach when it comes to how people behave socially.

Psychological Consequences of Colorblindness versus Multiculturalism

Regardless of which approach to diversity you take, one thing is clear: How you see and react to cultural differences will powerfully shape your social interactions,

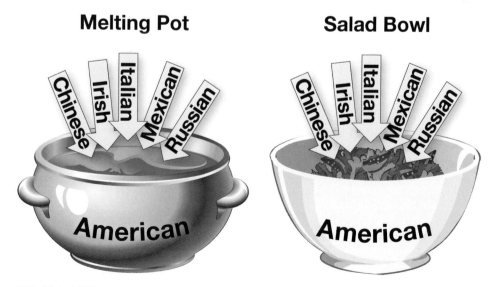

FIG. 10.1. Melting pot versus salad bowl multiculturalism

especially those interactions with other groups. Not surprisingly, many studies have been done on the effects of colorblind versus multicultural ideologies on intergroup relations. As it turns out, there are benefits and liabilities to both approaches.

In a seminal study, psychologists recruited a group of White students and assigned them to either a colorblind or multicultural ideology (Wolsko, Park, Judd, & Wittenbrink, 2000). In the former, they told participants that everyone was created equal and emphasized people's individuality; in the latter, they emphasized diversity between people and the need to recognize different groups' positive and negative qualities (Wolsko et al., 2000). Afterward, all participants rated Blacks and Whites on a variety of traits, some stereotypical and some not, indicating their guess as to the percentage of people from each race that exhibited said trait; they also rated how warmly (or coldly) they felt about members of each group (Wolsko et al., 2000). Wolsko and his colleagues (2000) found that those who were in the multiculturalism condition saw the outgroup—Black Americans—in more stereotypical ways relative to those in the colorblind group. Importantly, this increase in stereotyping happened for both positive and negative traits, suggesting a generalized tendency to see people as members of their group (rather than a tendency to show targeted prejudice against the out group; Wolsko et al., 2000). In follow-up studies, Wolsko et al. (2000) also found that not only were people who were told to think with a multicultural ideology more stereotypical but they were also more accurate in their stereotypes. Take, for example, the stereotype surrounding race and employment. Here the researchers asked participants to guess the percentage of unemployed Blacks and Whites in the United States, and they compared the guesses against U.S. Census data (Wolsko et al., 2000). They found that those in the multiculturalism condition were more likely to stereotype Blacks as more likely to be unemployed but also were more accurate in their estimates of Black versus White unemployment rates (Wolsko et al., 2000). When these same researchers did a third study, where they looked at the effect of colorblindness versus multiculturalism on how Whites perceived Latinos, they found a similar pattern of results, with multiculturalism leading to greater reliance on group membership cues when making judgments about individuals from other groups (Wolsko et al, 2000).

Other studies have shown similar effects among Black Americans. When a group of researchers at the University of Nebraska compared the effects of colorblindness versus multiculturalism on Blacks and Whites, they also found that multiculturalism was associated with increased stereotyping (Ryan, Hunt, Weible, Peterson, & Casas, 2007). Interestingly, they found that although Blacks who endorsed multiculturalism were more likely to stereotype (compared to Blacks who endorsed colorblindness), the reverse was true for Whites—that is, colorblind Whites were more likely to stereotype than Whites who endorsed multiculturalism (Ryan et al., 2007). This latter finding diverges from what Wolsko et al. (2000) found, which suggests that the link between ideology and stereotyping may not always be consistent or stable across groups.

Who Is Colorblind? Who Is Multicultural?

Moreover, Ryan et al. (2007) also found cultural differences in ideology: Colorblindness was more popular among Whites, whereas multiculturalism was more widely endorsed among Blacks. Among members of both cultural groups, those who endorsed multiculturalism were less ethnocentric than those who were colorblind (Ryan et al., 2007). This latter finding is particularly ironic: The whole premise of colorblindness purports to not see race or ethnicity yet it leads to people being more strongly aligned with their own ethnicity.

Nevertheless, it's easy to see why majority group members are motivated to not see race. After all, given both the historical and current tensions surrounding race, dominant group members may be particularly sensitive to appearing racist and thus may aim to be colorblind in order to avoid such accusations. Lab studies have confirmed that White participants who were especially sensitive to looking unprejudiced acted in more colorblind ways (Apfelbaum, Sommers, & Norton, 2008); even children as young as 10 will likewise avoid "seeing" race, even in contexts where race is relevant (Apfelbaum, Pauker, Ambady, Sommers, & Norton, 2008; for review, see Rattan & Ambady, 2013).

If majority group members are more prone to colorblindness, then it also makes sense that minority group members are more likely to believe in multiculturalism. This trend has been shown not only in the aforementioned studies based in the United States (Wolsko, Park, & Judd, 2006) but also in other countries with a substantive portion of immigrants (e.g., the Netherlands; Verkuyten & Thijs, 2002). As a result, some researchers have theorized that this may be due, at least in part, to the assumption that multiculturalism is primarily about ethnic minorities and that majority group members don't "count" in multiculturalism discussions (Plaut, Garnett, Buffardi, & Sanchez-Burks, 2011; for review, see Rattan & Ambady, 2013).

Practical Consequences of Multiculturalism versus Colorblindness

These aforementioned effects are not just "in people's heads." After all, prejudice and stereotyping are only two aspects of intergroup conflict; the third feature involves actions, or discrimination. Thus the next question is: How does ideology impact actual behavior?

In an interesting study, Deborah Son Holoien and Nicole Shelton (2012) looked to see how priming White participants with one ideology or the other shaped their subsequent interaction with ethnic minorities—in this case, Asians and Blacks. Similar to previous studies, the manipulation involved endorsing colorblindness or multiculturalism; afterward, independent judges rated how these (White) participants interacted with their partner (Holoien & Shelton, 2012). In addition, all participants also completed a Stroop task, which involved identifying the color of words that were written in a different hue and served as a reflection of cognitive performance (e.g., BLUE written in red font; Macleod, 1991; Stroop, 1935, as cited in Holoien & Shelton, 2012). They found that being primed with colorblindness led the ethnic minority partners of White participants to do worse on the Stroop task, while leading the White participants to show more prejudice during the interracial interaction (Holoien & Shelton, 2012). These findings suggested that colorblindness can also have practical consequences for both majority and minority group members in diverse contexts, leading majority group members to behave with more prejudice and minority group members to perform worse when subjected to such prejudice.

Moderators and Mediators: Explaining the Ideology-Prejudice Link

The fact that different studies have found different (and sometimes oppositional) findings on the relationship between colorblind and multicultural ideologies and prejudice suggests that, if anything, human beings are enormously complex in terms of how their beliefs shape their feelings about other groups (e.g., see Insight Box 10.1). Researchers have also taken note of the equivocal findings and have tried, in more recent years, to figure out what additional factors can change (i.e., moderate) or explain (i.e., mediate) the relationship between a person's ideology and prejudice level.

INSIGHT BOX 10.1

A Third Approach to Diversity?

Colorblindness and multiculturalism might be the two most often cited and studied approaches to diversity, but in recent years, a third possible approach has arisen—polyculturalism. Similar to multiculturalism, polyculturalism acknowledges the distinctions between groups; however, similar to colorblindness, it also emphasizes the shared commonalities between groups and the fact that different groups depend on, and influence, each other (Rosenthal & Levy, 2010). Citing historical work by Kelley (1999) and Prashad (2001), Rosenthal and Levy (2010) pointed out that polyculturalism is also different from conventional colorblindness in that it focuses on the historical and mutual influences that all cultures are subject to, and that no culture exists in a vacuum.

When Rosenthal and Levy (2010) went on to empirically test how polyculturalism related to other psychological processes, they found that it was related to a host of positive outcomes, including lower levels of social dominance orientation, greater endorsement with diversity, and increased interest in intergroup contact. This constellation of results was notable because multiculturalism and colorblindness did not yield the same consistently positive results—for example, although multiculturalism was linked to diversity appreciation, it was also linked to less intergroup contact, and although colorblindness was linked to less social dominance, this mainly emerged for majority group members (e.g., European Americans, and not other ethnic groups; Rosenthal & Levy, 2010). Polyculturalism's effects, however, held for all four ethnic groups that Rosenthal and Levy (2010) tested, including not only European Americans, but also Latino/a Americans, Black Americans, and Asian Americans. That said, polyculturalism and multiculturalism were also correlated with each other and relatively highly endorsed (in comparison to colorblindness), suggesting that these two different ideologies are not mutually exclusive (Rosenthal & Levy, 2010).

APPLYING WHAT WE KNOW: DIVERSITY AND PUBLIC POLICY

Countries vary widely in their approaches to diversity. On the one hand, some countries take a multiculturalism and integration approach. For example, in Canada, having immigrants maintain their origin cultures is widely accepted, and most Canadian immigrants endorse bicultural integration as their strategy of choice (Berry, 1984, as cited in Phinney, Horenczyk, Liebkind, & Vedder, 2001).

To this end, several factors have emerged. First, a person's own level of **ethnic identification** matters. As discussed in the previous chapter, ethnic identification refers to how strongly people feel like members of their own ethnic group and how important this membership is to their sense of self (Phinney & Rotheram, 1987). Some researchers have hypothesized that this sense of identification is crucial in determining how people react to their ideology and that for majority group members, multiculturalism can seem threatening to those who are strongly identified (Morrison, Plaut, & Ybarra, 2010). To test this idea, Morrison and her colleagues (2011) gave White participants either a manipulation that emphasized colorblindness or one that emphasized multiculturalism—the same one used previously by Wolsko et al. (2000); they also measured the extent to which the participants identified with being White American. Afterward, they gave them a **social dominance orientation** measure that assessed the extent to which these participants felt like some groups should naturally have more power than, and be superior to, other groups (Sidanius, Pratto, Stallworth, & Bertram, 1994). They found that highly identified White Americans responded to the multiculturalism condition by heightening their support for social dominance; subsequent follow-up studies showed that this translated to increased prejudice and less support for diversity-related organizations (Morrison et al, 2011). The researchers also found that if ethnic identification moderated the relationship between ideology and prejudice, then perceived threat mediated it; in other words, the reason highly identified White Americans reacted to multiculturalism so negatively was that they felt threatened (Morrison et al, 2011).

In contrast, other countries take a more assimilationist approach. The Netherlands, for example, had adopted an integrationist policy in the past—funding schools for immigrant children, providing state-sponsored language classes, and the like (Phinney et al., 2001). In more recent years, however, the Dutch have approved new integration laws that apply to both new and former immigrants; according to these new policies, all immigrants must pass a language and Dutch culture test before being allowed to stay permanently in the Netherlands ("Integration of newcomers," n.d.). Most controversially, the Dutch also passed a ban on wearing the burqa (photo 10.1), or Islamic veil, in certain public places, like schools, hospitals, and buses (Savela, 2014).

In the United States, both colorblind and multicultural practices exist. Studies on the efficacy of such programs have yielded a mixed bag of evidence. In a meta-analysis of the effects of multicultural education on outcomes, Stephan, Renfro, and Stephan (2004) did find that multiculturalism was linked to positive intergroup outcomes. However, these boons appeared largely to be the result of contact with outgroup members—essentially, supporting the contact hypothesis (Stephan et al., 2004). Consistent with this idea, Stephan et al. (2004) found that programs that emphasized experiential, hands-on techniques seemed to be more effective overall.

The Role of Intergroup Contact in Shaping Attitudes toward Diversity

Public policy is only one form of institutionalized attitudes toward diversity. In addition to public policy, individuals also respond to diversity on their own terms. The question, then, that researchers have been asking for decades is this: How do

PHOTO 10.1. In 2015, the Netherlands passed a controversial law regarding the burqa.

Source: iStock

interactions between members of different groups influence the way individuals within those groups feel about each other?

The Contact Hypothesis: Classic Studies

According to the classic **contact hypothesis** by Gordon Allport (1954), stereotypes exist because people do not have real interactions with members of other groups and, as a result, form (inaccurate) generalizations about them. Thus the idea is that contact would help people see other groups as actual individuals, thereby alleviating the prevalence of stereotypes. In other words, increasing interactions between groups should decrease stereotypes. That said, not all contact is created equal, and certain prerequisites are needed for contact to have its desired positive outcome—namely, the groups have to have comparable status and want the same things; they also have to cooperate and have institutional support from the larger society (Allport, 1954).

Since Allport's original theorization, numerous studies have been done to test the effect of contact on stereotypes and prejudice. When a meta-analysis was done across 515 studies on the contact hypothesis, the overall conclusion was that contact does moderately decrease prejudice overall (Pettigrew & Tropp, 2006). Interestingly, when the authors examined the role of specific contextual factors (e.g., having the same goals and status; being cooperative) that were supposed to increase the effectiveness of the contact hypothesis, they found no evidence that these contexts were necessary to reduce prejudice, and having them in place doesn't seem to increase the hypothesis's effects (Pettigrew & Tropp, 2006). When Pettigrew and Tropp (2006) compared studies where cooperation, comparable status, and the same goals were present versus absent, having those factors in place did not appear to make a significant difference (none of the studies lacked institutional support, which was a given across all studies on the contact hypothesis). Moreover, the effect of contact seemed to work equally well when the prejudice was against racial groups and nonracial groups (Pettigrew & Tropp, 2006).

Subsequent work has found that contact works to reduce prejudice through a three-pronged approach: (1) by helping individuals get to know the outgroup better, and such knowledge fights against existing stereotypes; (2) by alleviating anxiety about interacting with people from the outgroup, by seeing that such contact can be positive and productive, and (3) by helping individuals be able to see the world from the outgroup member's point of view (Pettigrew & Tropp, 2008). When Pettigrew and Tropp (2008) went back and did another meta-analysis on the contact hypothesis to test these ideas, they found strong support for all three mechanisms, especially the effects of anxiety reduction and empathic perspective-taking.

Contact Hypothesis: Newer Studies and Contradictory Evidence

Not all studies support the idea of the contact hypothesis, however. In fact, some studies actually show that contact between groups can backfire, and increase—not decrease—prejudice. Moreover, studying the contact hypothesis in controlled laboratory settings is really hard. Diversity, after all, is difficult to re-create in a lab space, and doing a realistic study that involves actual changes in real diversity—like making diversity hires or changing the demographic makeup of a neighborhood—is even harder. In recent years, Ryan Enos (2014), a government professor interested in public policy, decided to do a brilliant study: He hired Mexican nationals as confederates and asked them to ride the subway in the suburbs outside Boston (photo 10.2). Having Mexican families move into the predominantly white-collar, European American neighborhoods would have been difficult to pull off, but having Mexican individuals act as if they'd moved in—after all, they were riding the same commuter train to and from work every day—was much easier. Prior to the manipulation, he left political surveys at the train stations for people to complete; among the questions asked, he included ones about attitudes toward immigration; afterward, he asked the confederates—pairs of Mexican nationals living in the United States—to show up at the same time every day, dress in casual attire, and simply ride the train while conversing in their native language (Enos, 2014). They didn't have to interact with anyone; they simply rode the train with the regulars, and they did this for 10 days (Enos, 2014). Afterward, Enos's experimenters distributed another round of political surveys asking the same questions as before, and when they compared the two sets of responses, they found that contact with outgroup members—in this case, the Mexicans riding the train—produced more negative attitudes toward immigration (Enos, 2014). After the two weeks, people were less in favor of letting Mexican immigrants enter the United States and more favorable toward deportation (Enos, 2014).

Moreover, most of the classic studies on the contact hypothesis have been done on majority group members' attitudes toward minorities; very few studies have focused on how contact impacts minority group members' feelings toward majorities. To try to answer this question, a group of psychologists surveyed both majority and minority group members across three different European countries—Germany, Belgium, and England (Binder et al., 2009). As a result, they found a broad array of ethnic minorities: In Germany, they were primarily Turkish or others who had resettled; in Belgium, they were primarily Italians and Moroccans; in England, they were mostly Bangladeshi and African (Binder et al., 2009). Overall, they found support for the contact hypothesis among majority group members—having friends from minority groups reduced prejudice, and this was especially the case if majority group members thought that their ethnic friends were highly representative of their group (as opposed to anomalous; Binder et al., 2009). Interestingly, the researchers found no evidence for the contact hypothesis among minority group members, and having friends from the outgroup did little to change their attitudes toward the majority (Binder et al., 2009).

PHOTO 10.2. Enos's (2014) train study revealed the effect of contact with immigrants on immigration attitudes.

Source: iStock

The Jigsaw Classroom

A related approach to helping individuals cope well with diversity is the idea of the **jigsaw classroom**, which also relies on contact with other groups but does so in a highly structured setting (Aronson, Blaney, Stephin, Sikes, Snapp, 1978). As a paradigmatic example, the setup usually entails starting with a cohort of children from multiple ethnicities and both genders who are set out with a common learning goal (e.g., to learn about a specific topic). If this is a larger class, then dividing into multiple smaller groups may be helpful. Each group has an individual member who is in charge of learning about a particular topic and must ultimately master it and then teach it to the other members of the group; promoting a common goal (learning about a given topic) and mutual interdependence (each person needs to learn from the other members of their group in order to fully learn the material) sets the children up for responding positively to the diversity of their group members (Aronson et al., 1978). In addition to these features of interdependence and cooperation, most jigsaw classrooms also emphasize interactions between students rather than with teachers—after all, the point is that, rather than be dependent on an authority figure, each child is dependent on the other children in the room to learn—although supervision by a teacher is still needed (Aronson et al., 1978). Finally, similar to the premises under the contact hypothesis, it helps if the children have comparable status—that is, each topic or subtopic should be equally important (Aronson et al., 1978).

Similar setups have also been tested among adults and produced parallel positive outcomes. For example, studies on common ingroup identity have shown that it can be crucial in promoting cohesion. In a study by Gaertner, Mann, Murrell, and Dovidio (1989), participants met in trios, formed groups, and named their own group. Then they engaged in a cooperative activity—in this case, imagining that they were on a deserted location after a plane wreck in the middle of winter and deciding what would be the most important objects to take for survival (Gaertner et al., 1989). Afterward, two different groups had to join together and form a larger (six-person) group (Gaertner et al., 1989). In one condition, the original trios kept their names, but in another condition, the large group had to create a new identity and name; in still a third condition, the participants used names for themselves on an individual basis rather than as a group (Gaertner et al., 1989). At the end, researchers measured how biased the group members felt toward the other group (i.e., the one that they were not originally paired with); they found that when groups retained their original group names, they showed the most bias, but when they created a new group identity with a new name, they were the least biased (those who used individual names were in the middle; Gaertner et al., 1989).

Key Concepts

Colorblind ideology
Stereotype rebound effect
Melting pot vs. salad bowl vs. cultural mosaic
Ethnic identification

Social dominance orientation
Contact hypothesis
Jigsaw classroom

References

Apfelbaum, E. P., Pauker, K., Ambady, N., Sommers, S. R., & Norton, M. I. (2008). Learning (not) to talk about race: When older children underperform in social categorization. *Developmental Psychology, 44*, 1513–1518.

Apfelbaum, E. P., Sommers, S. R., & Norton, M. I. (2008). Seeing race and seeming racist? Evaluating strategic colorblindness in social interaction. *Journal of Personality and Social Psychology, 95*, 918–932.

Allport, G. W. (1954). *The nature of prejudice.* Oxford, U.K.: Addison-Wesley.

Aronson, E., Blaney, N., Stephin, C., Sikes, J., & Snapp, M. (1978). *The jigsaw classroom.* Beverly Hills, CA: Sage Publishing Company.

Associated Press (2016, July 4,). After 150 years, KKK sees opportunities in U.S. political trends. *Los Angeles Times.* Retrieved from http://www.latimes.com/nation/nationnow/la-na-ap-kkk-20160630-snap-story.html

Bachmann, A. S. (2006). Melting pot or tossed salad? Implications for designing effective multicultural workgroups. *Management International Review, 46*(6), 721–748.

Bennett, W. J. (1994). *The de-valuing of America: The fight for our culture and our children.* New York, NY: Simon and Schuster.

Binder, J., Zagefka, H., Brown, R., Funke, F., Kessler, T., Mummendey, A., . . . Leyens, J. P. (2009). Does contact reduce prejudice or does prejudice reduce contact? A longitudinal test of the contact hypothesis among majority and minority groups in three European countries. *Journal of Personality and Social Psychology, 96*(4), 843–856.

Brown, G. & Kidron, B. (1995). *To Wong Foo, thanks for everything Julie Newmar.* United States of America: Universal Studios.

Enos, R. (2014). Causal effect of intergroup contact on exclusionary attitudes. *Proceedings of the National Academy of Sciences, 111,* 3699–3704.

Gaertner, S. L., Mann, J., Murrell, A., & Dovidio, J. F. (1989). Reducing intergroup bias: The benefits of recategorization. *Journal of Personality and Social Psychology, 57*(2), 239–249.

Hirschman, C. (1983). America's melting pot reconsidered. *Annual review of sociology,* 397–423.

Holoien, D., & Shelton, N. (2012). You deplete me: The cognitive costs of colorblindness on ethnic minorities. *Journal of Experimental Social Psychology, 48,* 562–565.

Integration of newcomers. (n.d.) Government of the Netherlands. Retrieved from https://www.government.nl/topics/new-in-the-netherlands/integration-of-newcomers

Leyens, J. P. (2009). Does contact reduce prejudice or does prejudice reduce contact? A longitudinal test of the contact hypothesis among majority and minority groups in three European countries. *Journal of Personality and Social Psychology, 96*(4), 843–856.

MacLeod, C. M. (1991). Half a century of research on the Stroop effect: an integrative review. *Psychological Bulletin, 109*(2), 163.

Macrae, N., Bodenhausen, G., Milne, A., Jetten, J., (1994). Out of mind but back in sight: Stereotypes on the rebound. *Journal of Personality and Social Psychology, 67*(4), 808–817.

"Melting pot" America. (2006). BBC News. Retrieved from http://news.bbc.co.uk/2/hi/americas/4931534.stm

MLK's "content of character" quote inspires debate. (2013, January 20). CBS News. Retrieved from https://www.cbsnews.com/news/mlks-content-of-character-quote-inspires-debate/

Morrison, K., Plaut, V., & Ybarra, O. (2011). Predicting whether multiculturalism positively or negatively influences White Americans' intergroup attitudes: The role of ethnic identification. *Personality and Social Psychology Bulletin, 36*(12), 1648–1661.

Pettigrew, T. F., & Tropp, L. R. (2006). A meta-analytic test of intergroup contact theory. *Journal of Personality and Social Psychology, 90*(5), 751–783.

Pettigrew, T. F., & Tropp, L. R. (2008). How does intergroup contact reduce prejudice? Meta-analytic tests of three mediators. *European Journal of Social Psychology, 38*(6), 922–934.

Phinney, J. S., Horenczyk, G., Liebkind, K., & Vedder, P. (2001). Ethnic identity, immigration, and well-being: An interactional perspective. *Journal of Social Issues, 57*(3), 493–510.

Phinney, J. S., & Rotheram, M. (1987). *Children's ethnic socialization: Pluralism and development.* Newbury Park, CA: Sage Publications.

Plaut, V. C., Garnett, F. G., Buffardi, L. E., & Sanchez-Burks, J. (2011). "What about me?" Perceptions of exclusion and Whites' reactions to multiculturalism. *Journal of Personality and Social Psychology, 101*(2), 337–353.

Plaut, V. C., Thomas, K. M., & Goren, M. J. (2009). Is multiculturalism or color blindness better for minorities? *Psychological Science, 20,* 444–446.

Rattan, A., & Ambady, N. (2013). Diversity ideologies and intergroup relations: An examination of colorblindness and multiculturalism. *European Journal of Social Psychology, 43*(1), 12–21.

Rosenthal, L., & Levy, S. R. (2010). The colorblind, multicultural, and polycultural ideological approaches to improving intergroup attitudes and relations. *Social Issues and Policy Review, 4,* 215–246.

Rosenthal, L., & Levy, S. R. (2012). The relation between polyculturalism and intergroup attitudes among racially and ethnically diverse adults. *Cultural Diversity and Ethnic Minority Psychology, 18*(1), 1–16.

Ryan, C. S., Hunt, J. S., Weible, J. A., Peterson, C. R., & Casas, J. F. (2007). Multicultural and colorblind ideology, stereotypes, and ethnocentrism among Black and White Americans. *Group Processes & Intergroup Relations, 10*(4), 617–637.

Savela, T. (2014, May 22). Cabinet approves limited burqa ban. *The NL Times.* Retrieved November 4, 2016, from http://nltimes.nl/2015/05/22/cabinet-approves-limited-burqa-ban

Sidanius, J., Pratto, F., Stallworth, L., & Bertram, M. 1994. Social dominance orientation: A personality variable predicting social and political attitudes. *Journal of Personality and Social Psychology, 67*(4), 741–763.

Stephan, C. W., Renfro, L., & Stephan, W. G. (2004). The evaluation of multicultural education programs: Techniques and a meta-analysis. In W. G. Stephan & W. P. Vogt (Eds.), *Education programs for improving intergroup relations: Theory, research and practice,* (pp. 227–242). New York, NY: Teachers College Press.

Verkuyten, M. (2005). Ethnic group identification and group evaluation among minority and majority groups: Testing the multiculturalism hypothesis. *Journal of Personality and Social Psychology, 88,* 121–138.

Verkuyten, M., & Thijs, J. (2002). Multiculturalism among minority and majority adolescents in the Netherlands. *International Journal of Intercultural Relations, 26*(1), 91–108.

Wheeler, L., Reis, H. T., & Bond, M. H. (1989). Collectivism-individualism in everyday social life: The middle kingdom and the melting pot. *Journal of Personality and Social Psychology, 57*(1), 79–86.

Wolsko, C., Park, B., & Judd, C. M. (2006). Considering the tower of Babel: Correlates of assimilation and multiculturalism among ethnic minority and majority groups in the United States. *Social Justice Research, 19*(3), 277–306.

Wolsko, C., Park, B., Judd, C. M., & Wittenbrink, B. (2000). Framing interethnic ideology: Effects of multicultural and color-blind perspectives on judgments of groups and individuals. *Journal of Personality and Social Psychology, 78*(4), 635–654.

CHAPTER 11

Where Does Culture Come From?

As with most scientific inquiry in general and the study of cross-cultural differences in particular, discovering and documenting existing variation between groups is only the first step; the next, perhaps more compelling question grapples with how to explain these differences and the underlying mechanisms at hand. How can the existing cultural differences covered in the previous chapters be explained? This chapter covers the methodological challenges of identifying distal models (see below) that offer to explain the origins of cultural differences, and the existing paradigms used to study them, including priming of cultural conceptions and identifying key underlying cultural values or experiences theorized to account for cultural differences. This chapter will also discuss theoretical models of culture, including culture as a response to ecological conditions, a by-product of social learning, and an outcome of gene-environment interactions.

A Lesson from *Breaking Bad*

As of the writing of this book, AMC's original series, *Breaking Bad*, stands as the single, most highly rated show in the history of television in the United States (Li, 2013). When asked to sum up the monumental narrative of his award-winning series, the show's creator Vincent Gilligan simply said that it was the story of how "Mr. Chips became Scarface" (MacInnes, 2012). Now, you may or may not have seen firsthand what exactly he is referring to, but to bring everyone onto the same page, the premise of the *Breaking Bad* goes something like this: An overqualified high school chemistry teacher named Walter White finds out he has terminal lung cancer when his wife is unexpectedly pregnant with their second child, and they already have one teenage son who has cerebral palsy. Soon after his diagnosis, he runs into Jesse, a former student turned meth dealer. Walter offers to use his chemistry know-how to make their own brand of high-quality meth, as long as Jesse is willing to sell it. They go all in on this enterprise, and both terrific and tragic things ensue, including unplanned murders, run-ins with Mexican cartels, embroilments with the DEA (including Walt's brother-in-law, who just so happens to be a DEA agent), and the like. By the end, soft-spoken family man Walt has become powerful, brutal drug lord Heisenberg (his dealer name).

The question, then, as it relates to the topic of this chapter is simple: How did this metamorphosis occur? What explanations can the viewer arrive at to explain this radical change in TV's most-watched protagonist? Regardless of whether you've seen the show or not, you can likely come up with a myriad of explanations that range from immediate concerns a dying high school chemistry teacher with a wife and two kids might have (e.g., the mortgage) to long-term, overarching pressures (e.g., pride, success, achievement). The former we would call **proximal explanations**; the latter we call **distal explanations** (Scott-Phillips, Dickins, & West, 2011).

This distinction is important because the same is true with culture. If culture isn't magic (i.e., it doesn't just appear out of nowhere), then it must be able to be explained. If we want to explain culture, then we must consider both the immediate, short-term, proximal causes as well as the more long-term, distal ones.

A Brief History of Cultural Psychology

When two premier psychologists in the field—Steve Heine and Ara Norenzayan—set out to sum up the state of the discipline of cultural psychology back in 2006, they made this observation: The process of studying culture (much like the process of studying the content of any science) is twofold. The first step is invariably descriptive and involves pointing out important cultural differences in people's psychological tendencies (Heine & Norenzayan, 2006). The second step is much harder but also more interesting; it involves explaining everything you found in Step 1 (Heine & Norenzayan, 2006).

This two-step process described by Heine and Norenzayan (2006) largely reflects the actual field we're in. Since the rise of cultural psychology as a subset of mainstream psychology in the early 1990s, the focus for the first two decades has been primarily descriptive, outlining all the differences that have been found between cultural groups (although in this case, the overwhelming majority of such comparisons have largely been between European Americans and East Asians, as discussed in chapter 1; Heine & Norenzayan, 2006). After more than a quarter century, we now know that cultural variation exists when it comes to (1) basic cognitive processes like attention (e.g., Nisbett & Norenzayan, 2002); (2) social processes like our need for self-esteem (e.g., Cai, Brown, Deng & Oakes, 2007); (3) mental illnesses like social anxiety (Chang, 1997); (4) abstract, higher order cognitive processes like reasoning (e.g., Peng & Nisbett, 1999); (5) emotional processes like what affect valuation and empathy (e.g., Tsai, Knutson & Fung, 2006); (6) practical outcomes like how we act in close relationships (e.g., Rothbaum, Pott, Azuma, Miyake, & Weisz, 2000; for a review, see Heine & Norenzayan, 2006; for more recent reviews, see Kitayama & Cohen, 2010, and Taras, Kirkman, & Steel, 2010).

Nevertheless, descriptive psychology, or the psychology of documenting psychological phenomena—especially descriptives in the domain of culture—is not without its problems. Perhaps the single biggest issue is the one I've already mentioned—that after two decades, we know quite a bit about European Americans and

East Asians but not nearly as much about other populations (Heine & Norenzayan, 2006). A related issue is the one we share with the rest of psychology: that the overwhelming majority of psychology participants across the world are WEIRD (Western, Educated, Industrialized, Rich, and Democratic; Henrich, Heine & Norenzayan, 2010) and thus nonrepresentative. Although the Western critique is somewhat abated by cultural psychology's very nature, the other four features still apply to varying degrees. This is especially true considering that East Asian college students, like U.S. ones, also tend to be highly educated and middle class, often from well-developed, cosmopolitan areas (Heine & Norenzayan, 2006). This is especially problematic given that we already know that education/class are also forms of culture in and of themselves (see chapter 2).

Another issue with Step 1 that is especially relevant in cultural psychology is the tendency for Western (usually U.S.-based) psychologists to take something that has "worked" in this country and test to see if it replicates elsewhere (Heine & Norenzayan, 2006). In this sense, cultural psychology can be criticized as rather Eurocentric. This Eurocentric tendency is especially problematic in cases where psychological studies take on a prescriptive approach—that is, when researchers are not merely just describing the state of the world, but also suggesting—directly or not—that there is a way that the world should be and a way that it shouldn't.

One commonly cited example of the problem with **Eurocentricity** is in the case of attachment style. If you've taken a developmental psychology course (or even just an introductory one), you should be well aware of the Strange Situation (Ainsworth, Blehar, Waters, & Wall, 1987) and the division of babies into secure, insecure-avoidant and insecure-anxious attachment. While secure babies exhibit the normative behavior of showing some distress when the parent or caregiver leaves but is consolable and happy to see the parent return, insecure-avoidant babies react little, and insecure-anxious babies are upset throughout, even when the parent comes back (Ainsworth et al., 1978). In the United States, the idea that secure attachment is the ideal one is reflected in the actual population, and most American babies are indeed securely attached (van Ijzendoorn & Kroonenberg, 1988). However, meta-analyses of cultural studies have found cultural variation, and Western Europe versus Israel and Japan suggest a different pattern: While avoidant attachment was more common in Western Europe, ambivalence was more common in Israel and Japan, although across countries, secure attachment was the modal form of attachment style (van Ijzendoorn & Kroonenberg, 1988). Interestingly, longitudinal studies suggest that even in other cultures, avoidant attachment produces less than ideal relationships later in life (Grossman & Grossman, 1990).

Besides attachment, other commonly cited examples of Eurocentricity as a problem in psychology include domains like intelligence and morality. With intelligence, one possibility is that the tests developed in the United States and other Western countries may only reflect a very specific form of intelligence and one that may not necessarily apply or be valued in other cultural contexts (Sternberg & Grigorenko, 2004). With morality, the issue is similar: Some of the theories of moral development that Western psychologists developed—like the ones by Kohlberg (1971)—suggest that some forms of moral reasoning are superior to others. Namely, abstraction and individualistic reasoning are heralded by Kohlberg as higher moral strategy than following conventions or duties, but this again may be culturally bound. For example,

Miller and Luthar (1989) found that Indians are more likely to focus on interpersonal duties when making moral judgments, which, according to Kohlberg, might reflect more conventional moral reasoning rather than higher order, postconventional morality (see also Heine & Norenzayan, 2006, for discussion of this).

How, then, do we avoid at least some pitfalls of Step 1? As Heine and Norenzayan (2006) argued, more effort should be directed at raising up "grassroots" research in other cultures by members of those cultures; instead of always having American psychologists going abroad to study phenomena discovered in the United States, researchers in other countries could do the same.

If Step 1 is about description, then the next step is invariably about explanation; to this end, psychologists in more recent years have also tried to use differences in basic psychological processes (e.g., the way people see themselves, reason about the world, and value different things) to unpack more downstream or lower order cultural differences (Heine & Norenzayan, 2006). In this respect, three major types of explanations are possible: ones that rely on the physical environment (ecological), ones that rely on social transmission (epidemiological), and ones that involve gene-environment interactions (genetic) (for reviews, see Heine & Norenzayan, 2006; Gangestad, Haselton, & Buss, 2006; Nettle, 2009; and Schaller, 2006).

Culture as Ecology

Imagine that you're a caveman. First pretend you live in a world where your main food comes from big, speedy animals like, say, lions and leopards. Now, I hear leopards and lions are extremely hard to catch and very, very fast. So if you were a caveman in such a world, your success at acquiring dinner would be largely the luck of the draw (it is presumably very hard for you to catch lions and leopards with any kind of consistency); as such, if it weren't for your nice neighbors who were willing to share their food with you on days when you aren't able to catch a thing, or keep watch over you when you sleep so the lions and leopards don't come for you as their dinner, then you would surely die a slow, painful death.

Now pretend you're a caveman but you live in a different world where your food source primarily derives from small, furry animals—say, prairie dogs or squirrels. Presumably they are a little easier to catch than a lion is, and they're also less likely to eat you back. In this universe, you would not need your neighbor so desperately.

These are just illustrative examples, but the underlying idea has to do with **evoked culture**—the idea that different norms for how to act toward your neighbors arose under different environments, because different environments exerted different demands and pressures on people's survival (Tooby & Cosmides, 1992, as cited in Heine & Norenzayan, 2006). In the first world of lions and leopards, the need for sharing with and depending on your neighbors was strong; in the second world of dogs and squirrels, this was less the case. Over time, these environmental demands produced longstanding cultural values.

Other examples of culture as a response to the environment can be found in the growing number of studies on the relationship between disease and psychological processes. By comparing differences in the prevalence of different diseases and pathogens across the world, researchers have found that susceptibility to infection is related to a whole host of processes, including personality (e.g., openness and extraversion; Schaller & Murray, 2008), individualism-collectivism (Fincher, Thornhill, Murray, & Schaller, 2008), and mate preferences (Gangestad & Buss, 1993).

Culture as Social Epidemiology

If you've ever watched an episode of the *Real Housewives of* [insert city here] on Bravo (photos 11.1 and 11.2), you may have noticed a curious trend: The premise across each city-specific series is the same and the background is similar, but on

PHOTOS 11.1 AND 11.2. *Real Housewives of Atlanta* versus *Real Housewives of Beverly Hills*: A matter of transmitted culture?

Source: Photofest

each show the housewives have their own unique dynamics and norms. Despite being a mostly married with children, wealthy, beautiful, privileged, middle-aged bunch, those from New York don't look exactly like the ones from Orange County, and those from Orange County don't even look exactly like the ones from Beverly Hills, even though those latter two cities are just a stone's throw away from each other and share a similar ecology. Thus another explanation is likely social or **transmitted culture**: Rather than physical spaces exerting demands, other people are the source of the pressure. In other words, culture is socially transmitted from person to person, group to group (for review, see Heine & Norenzayan, 2006).

Psychologists are not the only ones who talk about cultural transmission either, nor is this a phenomenon that only applies to humans. As early as the 1970s, animal researchers noticed that different groups of the same species of bird would sing different songs based on when and where they lived (Jenkins, 1978). Birds who lived near each other would sing the same songs, and this was presumably because of transmission of songs between generations (Jenkins, 1978). Other researchers have applied the same idea of social learning to chimpanzees to explain why different groups of chimps also act differently—in their case, eat differently, "talk" differently, and use different objects as tools, also because at least part of what they learn is from each other (see Tomasello, 1990).

In more recent years, evolutionary psychologists have theorized that not all social learning is created equal. Instead, some kinds of socially learned information are more useful than others—you could learn to cook from your mother or you could learn from Martha Stewart, and the latter could arguably offer more useful information. People know this, and as a result, we are more likely to imitate some group members over others. Psychologists call it "prestige"; the average person calls it "popularity." Either way, the idea is the same: We learn information socially, and we are to pay special attention to social information from prestigious or popular members of our group because the information they can offer is presumably better (Henrich & Gil-White, 2001).

Culture as Gene-Environment Interactions

The third and final explanation for culture offered by Heine and Norenzayan (2006) is genes, but in their review, they largely cast doubt on the idea that any cultural differences we've observed in the last 20+ years could be attributed simply to genetic differences between groups. What is more likely is that culture and genes interact—a more nuanced argument that a growing number of psychologists are studying. Put simply, this is the notion that **gene-environment interactions** exist. Not all genes express themselves in the same way across different environments, and some environments are more conducive to some genetic variants than others (e.g., Kim et al., 2010). Below are several examples of culture and genes mutually influencing one another.

From a broad evolutionary perspective, culture and genes likely **co-evolved**: Different genes made different brains—some good at social learning in large groups, some less so—and the evolution of culture made it so that brains that were good at the former were naturally selected for (Chudek & Henrich, 2011). By selecting for brains that were essentially good at picking up culture, this, in turn, promoted further cultural transmission and development, because over time a growing number of members of the species had large, socially attuned brains that paid attention to information provided by other people; on a broad level, this kind of feedback loop is likely responsible for general features of the human psyche, like our penchant for cooperation and prosociality (for a review of these ideas, see Chudek & Henrich, 2011).

More specific instances of culture-gene interactions also exist. Take, for example, the oxytocin receptor gene. In a series of studies carried out in 2010 and 2011, Heejung Kim and her colleagues demonstrated that genetic polymorphism on this gene interacted with culture to predict people's behavior. First, some background: Oxytocin, generally speaking, is a hormone that has been associated with social bonding (Lieberwirth & Wang, 2014); thus, not surprisingly, different alleles of the oxytocin receptor gene have also been linked to how a person emotionally responds to other people (see Kim et al., 2010, 2011, for review of studies). Culture, likewise, also exerts many norms on people's behavior, including their social norms and sensitivities (see chapter 1). Kim et al. (2010, 2011) predicted that culture and genes would work together to influence how socially sensitive people actually were. In one set of studies, Kim et al. (2010) found that European Americans with the G alleles on their oxytocin receptor suppressed their feelings less and sought more social support, but Koreans with that same genotype suppressed their feelings more and were no different in their seeking of social support. This was presumably because in North American cultural contexts, being emotionally sensitive meant looking to others for support and not suppressing your emotions, but in Korean cultures, the emotionally appropriate response in social interactions was suppressing your emotions and not burdening others with your needs (Kim et al., 2010, 2011).

As another example, take the serotonin transporter gene, which has also been shown to interact with culture. Generally, serotonin is an important neurotransmitter involved in emotion, especially in relation to depression (Shopsin & Frank Feiner, 1984). When Joan Chiao and Katherine Blizinsky (2010) examined this gene in relation to context, they predicted that variations of the serotonin transporter gene likely co-evolved with basic cultural values like individualism versus collectivism. They based their argument on past work, citing studies showing that East Asians are more likely to have one type of serotonin transporter allele—the S allele—than Europeans (Gelernter, Kranzler, & Cubells, 1997), and that this S allele is associated with numerous types of negative emotional responding (e.g., Caspi et al., 2003); however, they also cite other studies suggest that depression and anxiety-related mental disorders are actually less common among Asians, not more so (Weissman et al., 1996; see Chiao & Blizinsky, 2010, for review of these studies). Thus, to solve this paradox, Chiao and Blizinsky (2010) argued that the rise of collectivistic values served to protect members of a genetically vulnerable group against depression and anxiety; consistent with this idea, they found that areas of the world with more S alleles were also more collectivistic and less likely to have high rates of depression or anxiety disorders.

Explaining Between-Culture Variation

We can apply the aforementioned principles in specific cases and use them to explain variation that happens both between cultures as well as within cultures. **Between-culture variation** refers to differences between different groups—different ethnicities, classes, regions, and so forth. To illustrate, consider taking a real or mental vacation to East Asia and contrast it with a similar type of vacation within the United States (to avoid the pricey airline tickets, you can simply do a Google image search for major cities in the United States versus those in Tokyo or other cities in Japan, and Korea). What do you notice?

East versus West: Explaining Differences in Thinking and Values

When Yuri Miyamoto, Richard Nisbett, and Takahiko Masuda (2006) did a study precisely on this premise, they took pictures of New York versus Tokyo, Ann Arbor versus Hikone (a medium-sized city in Japan), and Chelsea, Michigan, versus Torahime (a small city in Japan); they compared the view from schools, hotels, and post offices. Afterward, Miyamoto et al. (2006) presented these photos to Japanese and U.S. undergraduates and asked them to evaluate them on how complex they were. Japanese cities in general were rated as more complex than American ones (Miyamoto et al., 2006). Subsequent analysis using photo processing software revealed the same effect, with Japanese cities containing more objects than American ones (Miyamoto et al., 2006).

Miyamoto and her colleagues (2006) went on to use this evidence to explaining the longstanding observation that systematic differences in attention and thinking styles exist between the East and the West (see chapter 1). While people in the West tend to be focal, paying attention to the central objects in a scene or situation, those from East Asia tend to be highly contextual (Nisbett & Masuda, 2003). Thus the idea is that the physical world constrains and shapes the psychological one (photo 11.3) and living in a complex environment with many different objects makes for a contextual mind that is always paying attention to peripheral cues (Miyamoto et al., 2006).

Beyond looking at present-day differences between physical environments, researchers have also pointed to differences further back in history to explain East-West differences in thinking styles. In their seminal review of cultural differences in cognition, Richard Nisbett and his colleagues (2001) compared and contrasted the ancient Greeks versus the ancient Chinese: While the former excelled in fields like philosophy and physics—fields that tried to systematically describe and explain the world using stable, incontrovertible laws—the latter made advances in irrigation, porcelain, gunpowder, and pasta, more practical domains with aims of making social life possible. The Greeks relied on debate to know things, and through their debates arrived at the philosophical principles we continue to cite today; the Chinese avoided debates because doing so would disrupt harmonious social life (Nisbett, Peng, Choi, & Norenzayan, 2001).

Nisbett et al. (2001) went on to argue that these differences reflect divergences in the ways these ancient societies were set up: Ancient China was largely agrarian, and a society that evolved around farming was necessarily large, stable,

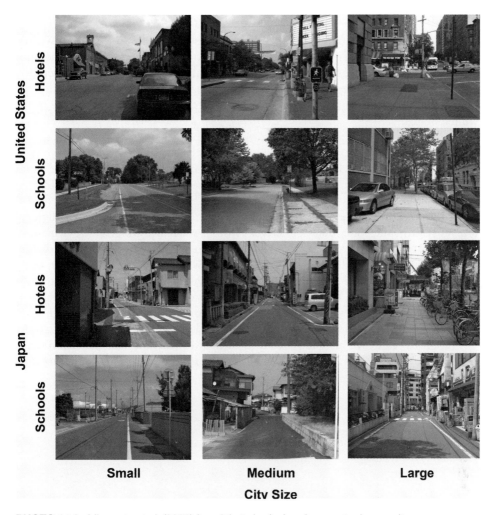

PHOTO 11.3. Miyamoto et al. (2006) found that physical environments shape culture.

and cooperative. Waiting for your crops demanded that you stay in the same location for extended periods of time, which allowed large societies to rise up (Nisbett et al., 2001). Ancient Greece, in contrast, was largely based on a fishing and herding economy (Nisbett et al., 2001). Since both fishing and herding are relatively solitary endeavors, Greeks were less tied to their neighbors and had more freedom and independence, and the fact that Greece functioned under largely self-ruling city-states (as opposed to China's system of emperors and bureaucrats) also gave Greeks more daily freedoms than the Chinese enjoyed (Nisbett et al., 2001). Nisbett et al. (2001) used these features to explain why the Chinese became so characteristically collectivist—after all, they depended on one another daily and lived under a strict hierarchy—while the Greeks became the starting point for Western individualism. They, in contrast, lived free from their neighbors (Nisbett et al., 2001).

Explaining Within-Culture Variation

Culture doesn't only differ between groups; it also varies within groups. **Within-culture variation** deals with the natural tendency for people who belong to the same "culture" to show deviations from one another. After all, not all group members act the same way, and within every group, systematic divergences exist. Below are two examples: the French (versus the rest of Europe) and class differences in the United States.

The Curious Case of the French Throughout this book, U.S. Americans have typically been referred to as European Americans, but not all of Europe looks the same, culturally and otherwise. To illustrate, take the case of France (photo 11.4). In their treatise on the American versus French self, Alain Ehrenberg and Louis Sass (2014) argue that the idea of the "self" is a highly American idea at the heart of (American) individualism, and one that is derived from Protestantism and the American Revolution. Ehrenberg and Sass (2014) go on to argue that American individualism and French individualism are not the same; while the former focuses on being an authentic person who is the same in private as in public and striving toward individual achievement, the latter is more connected to the rest of society and its authority figures. Thus, while Americans favor autonomy, the French are more skeptical of it because it might threaten "collective solidarity" (Ehrenberg & Sass, 2014).

Empirical evidence also supports this idea of distinctions between the French and the United States. When Oyserman, Coon, and Kemmelmeier (2002) compared

PHOTO 11.4. The case of the French as an example of within-culture variation

Source: iStock

the United States with other countries on individualism and collectivism, they found that the United States was somewhat more individualistic than France. When Marie-Anne Suizzo (2004) compared French and American mothers' attitudes toward parenting and their toddler children, they found that while French and American mothers both reported valuing self-reliance and autonomy, French mothers more than American ones also emphasized stimulation, or the idea of cognitive and social "awakening." French mothers were more likely to endorse less expressive and more suppressive responses in public—for example, telling their children not to cry publicly (Suizzo, 2004). This is consistent with other studies showing that relative to U.S Americans, the French are less likely to endorse expressing conflict (Ting-Toomey, 1991). Taken together, this suggests that not all European culture is identical, but nuanced variations exist between different types of Western cultural contexts.

Class Variation in the United States: Revisiting Soft versus Hard Individualism Recall that class remains a dividing force in American society (see chapter 2). When the anthropologist Adrie Kusserow (1999) looked at differences between working class families in the South Rockaway neighborhood of Queens and upper-middle class ones in Manhattan's Upper East Side's Carter Hill, she found systematic patterns relating to soft versus hard individualism. In South Rockaway, life was hard: Gangs, substance dependency, poverty, and single motherhood were normal facets of life (Kusserow, 1999). As a result, mothers had to teach their children to be strong in the face of hardship, and individualism arose out of necessity—to protect yourself from others, to refuse to succumb to outside pressures (Kusserow, 1999). This type of hard individualism emphasized self-reliance, and autonomy meant paying attention to one's own business and no one else's (Kusserow, 1999).

In contrast, Carter Hill was a world of luxury apartments and au pairs; families there typically consisted of two parents with college or advanced degrees and white-collar jobs (Kusserow, 1999). Consequently, parents taught their children a very different form of individualism, one that centered on their fulfilling their desires and expressing their true feelings (Kusserow, 1999). Individualism in this case was soft, a luxury that could be enjoyed, because it involved exploration, self-actualization, and feelings of confidence (Kusserow, 1999). In both cases, though, the underlying premise is the same: Within-culture differences emerged because not all people within a group have the same environments or experiences, and with divergent contexts come divergent values.

Class Variation in the United States, Continued: Explaining Class Effects via Money Recall also that not only does class produce distinct versions of American individualism but it is also responsible for different views toward greed and prosociality. Chapter 2 covered a number of different studies that demonstrated the negative effects of high social class on a host of social behaviors, including empathy and unethical behaviors: Relative to members of lower classes, people from upper classes (or who were simply made to feel like they were upper class) were often less empathic, less likely to stop for pedestrians, more likely to cheat and steal, and the like (e.g., Piff, Stancato, Cote, Mendoza-Denton, & Keltner, 2012). Why might that be? To be fair, there are many potential explanations, one of which may have to do with the psychological effects of having money. If one of the defining features of being upper class is having more resources, then this begs the question of what money does to the brain, and whether money's effects can be related to the effects of class.

A young teacher named Jesus, from Nazareth, once told a rapt audience that money (or at least the love of money) was the root of all evil; since then, others, like billionaire Warren Buffett, have begged to differ, declaring: "Rule Number One: Never lose money. Rule Number Two: Never forget Rule Number One" (Buffett & Clark, 2006). Psychologists have shown that in some ways, both men were right—money is associated with both positive and negative outcomes. On the positive side, it seems that money can substitute or compensate for other motivations—for example, it seems to contribute to a sense of meaning and can even help people feel less pain (Chang & Arkin, 2002; Zhou & Gao, 2008). On the negative side, money also appears to hurt people in social interactions. When Kathleen Vohs and her colleagues (2009) did a series of studies on the effects of reminding people about money versus not doing so, they found that the presence of even a subtle money reminder interfered with participants' sociality. In the experimental setup by Vohs, Mead, and Goode (2006), they simply had participants sit in front of a computer that either had a blank screen, a sea life underwater scene as a screensaver, or a pool of floating money as a screensaver. Afterward, Vohs et al. (2006) looked at how these individuals behaved in a variety of situations, including how far away they sat from a partner they had to talk to, and whether they chose to do a hard task (in this case, coming up with an ad) by themselves or with someone else. They found that being reminded of money made people more interpersonally distant—they preferred to work alone and be more distant from others (Vohs, Mead, & Goode, 2006). Taken together then, it may not be all that surprising that chronic access to money—a luxury enjoyed by the upper class—may make less-than-prosocial behaviors toward others more likely because these individuals are constantly finding themselves in situations where they feel distant from others. Over time, repeated experiences of being interpersonally distant may ultimately contribute to a culture where greed and lack of empathy are more normative.

Explaining Psychological Universals

Not only do differences demand explanation but similarities do as well. It is reasonable to ask ourselves, "Why are we different?" But it is just as reasonable to ask ourselves, "Why are we not more different?" Why are we, in some cases, very much the same? Addressing this question can take many forms, but for illustrative purposes, the last part of this chapter will go into two examples of psychological universals and the explanations that have been put forth for each one.

Explaining Universals in Incest Avoidance When Richard Shweder and his colleagues (1995) asked families from Orissa, India, and Hyde Park, Chicago, how to set up sleeping arrangements for a five-person family consisting of a mom, dad, two daughters (ages 3 and 14) and three sons (ages 8, 11, and 15), they found an incredible amount of cross-cultural consistency. Sometimes the family lived in a two-bedroom house and other times a three-bedroom one, but regardless, certain trends emerged: People everywhere seemed to base their choices on incest avoidance (Shweder, Jensen, & Goldstein, 1995). Within the same household, males and females were almost always separated (except for the mom and dad; Schweder et al., 1995). The fact that there is little cultural variation in this case strongly suggests a universal evolution of incest-avoidance (Shweder et al., 1995). Indeed, subsequent research has shown that people who lived together with members of the opposite sex during their childhood are even more opposed to incest than those who did not, presumably because living together is a good cue for family relatedness (Lieberman, Tooby, & Cosmides, 2003).

Explaining Universals in Mate Preference Avoiding sex with siblings is not the only thing that has universally evolved among people. Recall the host of universals in physical attractiveness covered in chapter 6. Presumably, the fact that men universally prefer healthy women who look like they have good genes is no accident, nor is the fact that women everywhere prefer men with those qualities as well, plus one more—resources. Ultimately, just about every specific feature of male and female physical attractiveness boils down to one of these signals: great DNA; a strong, disease-free body; and plenty of earthly belongings.

Consider the classic case of WHR, or waist-to-hip ratio. As discussed before, the ideal WHR the world over is 0.7, and this is because women with this magical ratio are more likely to be successful bearers of healthy children. They are more likely to get pregnant because they have more regular and frequent menstrual cycles (which translates into more opportunities for conception) (for review, see Singh, 1993), and they are also more likely to be able to raise the children that they have, because they also tend to be healthier in general; they are less likely to get a host of diseases, like kidney disease and some cancers (Chou et al., 2008; Huang et al., 1999). Moreover, they are more likely to have smart kids, as butt fat (but not abdominal fat) has been linked to fetal brain development (Lassek & Gaulin, 2008). Likewise, breast size offers a similar signal, and studies have shown that both WHR and breast size are good indicators of female hormones related to fertility—namely, progesterone and estrogen (Jasieńska, Ziomkiewicz, Ellison, Lipson, & Thune, 2004).

Women everywhere also seem to have universal preferences—namely, for older men; explanations for this desired age gap have largely centered on the idea that age is correlated with resources, and resources are important for survival (Kenrick & Keefe, 1992).

At this point, it's also important to acknowledge that even in the context of mating and attraction, nonreproductive sex is also a universal reality. Here it helps to return to the distinction between proximal and ultimate motives. When it comes to the explanations for universals in physical attractiveness, the reasons outlined here are almost exclusively **ultimate motives**—they are nature's intentions for our species, centering on reproduction and survival (Scott-Phillips et al., 2011). At the same time, **proximal motives** exist (Scott-Phillips et al., 2011), and people the world over engage in actions all the time for more immediate reasons—love, companionship, and/or a warm body at night.

The Bottom Line

The bottom line, once again, is this: Culture isn't magic; it doesn't appear out of the blue. It came from somewhere; it evolved over time. And that evolution made us smart, so now we can choose. The evolution of culture is a force, but it never tells us exactly where we go. Our brain makes the decision—and that's where you come in.

Key Concepts

Proximal vs. distal explanations
Eurocentricity
Evoked culture
Transmitted culture
Gene-environment interactions
Co-evolved (culture & genes)
Between- vs. within-culture variation
Ultimate vs. proximal motives

References

Ainsworth, M. D. S., Blehar, M. C., Waters, E., & Wall, S. (1978). *Patterns of attachment: A psychological study of the Strange Situation*. Hillsdale, NJ: Erlbaum.

Buffett, M., & Clark, D. (2006). *The Tao of Warren Buffett*. New York, NY: Scribner.

Cai, H., Brown, J. D., Deng, C., & Oakes, M. A. (2007). Self-esteem and culture: Differences in cognitive self-evaluations or affective self-regard? *Asian Journal of Social Psychology, 10*, 162–170.

Caspi A., Sugden, K. Moffitt, T. E., Taylor, A., Craig, I. W., Harrington, H., . . . Poulton, R. (2003). Influence of life stress on depression: Moderation by a polymorphism in the 5-HTT gene. *Science, 301*, 386–389.

Chang, L., & Arkin, R. M. (2002). Materialism as an attempt to cope with uncertainty. *Psychology & Marketing, 19*(5), 389–406.

Chang, S. C. (1997). Social anxiety (phobia) and East Asian culture. *Depression and Anxiety, 5*(3), 115–120.

Chiao, J. Y., & Blizinsky, K. D. (2010). Culture–gene coevolution of individualism–collectivism and the serotonin transporter gene. *Proceedings of the Royal Society of London B: Biological Sciences, 277*(1681), 529–537.

Chou, C. Y., Lin, C. H., Lin, C. C., Huang, C. C., Liu, C. S., & Lai, S. W. (2008). Association between waist-to-hip ratio and chronic kidney disease in the elderly. *Internal Medicine Journal, 38*(6a), 402–406.

Chudek, M., & Henrich, J. (2011). Culture–gene coevolution, norm-psychology and the emergence of human prosociality. *Trends in Cognitive Sciences, 15*(5), 218–226.

Ehrenberg, A., & Sass, L. (2014). Individualisms and their discontents: The American self versus the French institution. *Philosophy, Psychiatry, & Psychology, 21*(4), 311–323.

Fincher, C. L., Thornhill, R., Murray, D. R., & Schaller, M. (2008). Pathogen prevalence predicts human cross-cultural variability in individualism/collectivism. *Proceedings of the Royal Society of London B: Biological Sciences, 275*(1640), 1279–1285.

Gangestad, S. W., & Buss, D. M. (1993). Pathogen prevalence and human mate preferences. *Evolution and Human Behavior, 14*(2), 89–96.

Gangestad, S. W., Haselton, M. G., & Buss, D. M. (2006). Evolutionary foundations of cultural variation: Evoked culture and mate preferences. *Psychological Inquiry, 17*(2), 75–95.

Gelernter J., Kranzler H., Cubells, J. F. 1997 Serotonin transporter protein (SLC6A4) allele and haplotype frequencies and linkage disequilibria in African- and European-American and Japanese populations and in alcohol-dependent subjects. *Human Genetics, 101,* 243–246.

Heine, S. J., & Norenzayan, A. (2006). Toward a psychological science for a cultural species. *Perspectives on Psychological Science, 1*(3), 251–269.

Henrich, J., & Gil-White, F. J. (2001). The evolution of prestige: Freely conferred deference as a mechanism for enhancing the benefits of cultural transmission. *Evolution and Human Behavior, 22*(3), 165–196.

Henrich, J., Heine, S. J., & Norenzayan, A. (2010). The weirdest people in the world? *Behavioral and Brain Sciences, 33*(2-3), 61–83.

Huang, Z., Willett, W. C., Colditz, G. A., Hunter, D. J., Manson, J. E., Rosner, B., . . . Hankinson, S. E. (1999). Waist circumference, waist: Hip ratio, and risk of breast cancer in the Nurses' Health Study. *American Journal of Epidemiology, 150*(12), 1316–1324.

Jasieńska, G., Ziomkiewicz, A., Ellison, P. T., Lipson, S. F., & Thune, I. (2004). Large breasts and narrow waists indicate high reproductive potential in women. *Proceedings of the Royal Society B: Biological Sciences, 271*(1545), 1213–1217. Retrieved from http://doi.org/10.1098/rspb.2004.2712

Jenkins, P. F. (1978). Cultural transmission of song patterns and dialect development in a free-living bird population. *Animal Behaviour, 26,* 50–78.

Kendrick, K. M. (2004). The neurobiology of social bonds. *Journal of Neuroendocrinology, 16*(12), 1007–1008. doi:10.1111.1365-2826.2004.01262

Kenrick, D. T., & Keefe, R. C. (1992). Age preferences in mates reflect sex differences in human reproductive strategies. *Behavioral and Brain Sciences, 15*(01), 75–91.

Kim, H. S., Sherman, D. K., Mojaverian, T., Sasaki, J. Y., Park, J., Suh, E. M., & Taylor, S. E. (2011). Gene–culture interaction oxytocin receptor polymorphism (OXTR) and emotion regulation. *Social Psychological and Personality Science, 2*(6), 665–672.

Kim, H. S., Sherman, D. K., Sasaki, J. Y., Xu, J., Chu, T. Q., Ryu, C., . . . Taylor, S. E. (2010). Culture, distress and oxytocin receptor polymorphism (OXTR) interact to influence emotional support seeking. *Proceedings of the National Academy of Sciences, 107,* 15717–15721.

Kitayama, S., & Cohen, D. (Eds.). (2010). *Handbook of cultural psychology.* New York, NY: Guilford Press.

Kohlberg, L. (1971). Stages of moral development. Retrieved from http://info.psu.edu.sa/psu/maths/Stages%20of%20Moral%20Development%20According%20to%20Kohlberg.pdf

Kusserow, A. S. (1999). De-homogenizing American individualism: Socializing hard and soft individualism in Manhattan and Queens. *Ethos, 27*(2), 210–234.

Lassek, W., & Gaulin, S. (2008). Waist-hip ratio and cognitive ability: Is gluteofemoral fat a privileged store of neurodevelopmental resources? *Evolution and Human Behavior, 29*(1), 26–34. Retrieved from http://dx.doi.org/10.1016/j.evolhumbehav.2007.07.005

Lee, N. Y. L., and Johnson-Laird, P. N. (2006). Are there cross-cultural differences in reasoning? *Proceedings of the 28th Annual Meeting of the Cognitive Science Society,* 459–464.

Li, S. (2013, September 5). *Breaking Bad* named highest-rated TV series by "Guinness World Records." *Entertainment Weekly.* Retrieved from http://ew.com/article/2013/09/05/guinness-world-records-breaking-bad/

Lieberman, D., Tooby, J., & Cosmides, L. (2003). Does morality have a biological basis? An empirical test of the factors governing moral sentiments relating to incest. *Proceedings of the Royal Society of London B: Biological Sciences, 270*(1517), 819–826.

Lieberwirth, C., & Wang, Z. (2014). Social bonding: Regulation by neuropeptides. *Frontiers in Neuroscience, 8*(171). Retrieved from http://doi.org/10.3389/fnins.2014.00171

MacInnes, P. (2012). Breaking Bad creator Vince Gilligan: The man who turned Walter White from Mr. Chips into Scarface. *The Guardian.* Retrieved November 20, 2016, from https://www.theguardian.com/tv-and-radio/2012/may/19/vince-gilligan-breaking-bad

Miller, J. G., and Bersoff, D. M. (1995). Development in the context of everyday family relationships: Culture, interpersonal morality, and adaptation. In M. Killen & D. Hart (Eds.), *Morality in everyday life: Developmental perspectives* (pp. 259–282). New York, NY: Cambridge University Press.

Miller, J. G., & Luthar, S. (1989). Issues of interpersonal responsibility and accountability: A comparison of Indians' and Americans' moral judgments. *Social Cognition, 7*(3), 237–261.

Miyamoto, Y., Nisbett, R. E., & Masuda, T. (2006). Culture and the physical environment holistic versus analytic perceptual affordances. *Psychological Science, 17*(2), 113–119.

Nettle, D. (2009). Beyond nature versus culture: Cultural variation as an evolved characteristic. *Journal of the Royal Anthropological Institute, 15*(2), 223–240.

Nisbett, R. E., & Masuda, T. (2003). Culture and point of view. *Proceedings of the National Academy of Sciences, 100*(19), 11163–11170.

Nisbett, R. E., Peng, K., Choi, I., & Norenzayan, A. (2001). Culture and systems of thought: Holistic versus analytic cognition. *Psychological Review, 108*(2), 291–310.

Oyserman, D., Coon, H. M., & Kemmelmeier, M. (2002). Rethinking individualism and collectivism: Evaluation of theoretical assumptions and meta-analyses. *Psychological Bulletin, 128*(1), 3–72.

Peng, K., & Nisbett, R. E. (1999). Culture, dialectics, and reasoning about contradiction. *American Psychologist, 54*(9), 741–754.

Piff, P., Stancato, D., Cote, S., Mendoza-Denton, R., & Keltner, D. (2012). Higher social class predicts increased unethical behavior. *Proceedings of the National Academy of Sciences, 109*(11), 4086–4091. Retrieved from http://dx.doi.org/10.1073/pnas.1118373109

Rothbaum, F., Pott, M., Azuma, H., Miyake, K., & Weisz, J. (2000). The development of close relationships in Japan and the United States: Paths of symbiotic harmony and generative tension. *Child Development, 71*(5), 1121–1142.

Schaller, M. (2006). Parasites, behavioral defenses, and the social psychological mechanisms through which cultures are evoked. *Psychological Inquiry, 17*(2), 96–137.

Schaller, M., & Murray, D. R. (2008). Pathogens, personality, and culture: disease prevalence predicts worldwide variability in sociosexuality, extraversion, and openness to experience. *Journal of Personality and Social Psychology, 95*(1), 212–221.

Scott-Phillips, T., Dickins, T., & West, S. (2011). Evolutionary theory and the ultimate-proximate distinction in the human behavioral sciences. *Perspectives on Psychological Science, 6*(1), 38–47. Retrieved from http://dx.doi.org/10.1177/1745691610393528

Shopsin, B., & Frank Feiner, N. (1984). Serotonin and depression. In J. Mendlewicz, B. Shopsin, & H. M. van Praag (Eds.), *Serotonin in affective disorders* (pp. 1–11). Basel, Switzerland: Karger.

Shweder, R. A., Jensen, L. A. & Goldstein, W. M. (1995). Who sleeps by whom revisited: A method for extracting the moral goods implicit in practice. *New Directions for Child and Adolescent Development, 67*, 21–39. doi:10.1002/cd.23219956705

Singh, D. (1993). Adaptive significance of female physical attractiveness: Role of waist-to-hip ratio. *Journal of Personality and Social Psychology, 65*(2), 293.

Sternberg, R. J., & Grigorenko, E. L. (2004). Intelligence and culture: How culture shapes what intelligence means, and the implications for a science of well-being. *Philosophical Transactions of the Royal Society B: Biological Sciences, 359*(1449), 1427–1434. Retrieved from http://doi.org/10.1098/rstb.2004.1514

Suizzo, M. A. (2004). French and American mothers' childrearing beliefs: Stimulating, responding, and long-term goals. *Journal of Cross-Cultural Psychology, 35*(5), 606–626.

Taras, V., Kirkman, B. L., & Steel, P. (2010). Examining the impact of Culture's consequences: A three-decade, multilevel, meta-analytic review of Hofstede's cultural value dimensions. *Journal of Applied Psychology, 95*(3), 405–439.

Ting-Toomey, S. (1991). Intimacy expressions in three cultures: France, Japan, and the United States. *International Journal of Intercultural Relations, 15*(1), 29–46.

Tomasello, M. (1990). Cultural transmission in the tool use and communicatory signaling of chimpanzees? In S. Parker & K. Gibson (Eds.), *Language and intelligence in monkeys and apes: Comparative developmental perspectives* (pp. 274–311). Cambridge, U.K.: Cambridge University Press.

Tsai, J. L., Knutson, B., & Fung, H. H. (2006). Cultural variation in affect valuation. *Journal of Personality and Social Psychology, 90*(2), 288–307.

Van Ijzendoorn, M., & Kroonenberg, P. (1988). Cross-Cultural patterns of attachment: A meta-analysis of the Strange Situation. *Child Development, 59*(1), 147–156. Retrieved from http://dx.doi.org/10.2307/1130396

Vohs, K. D., Mead, N. L., & Goode, M. R. (2006). The psychological consequences of money. *Science, 314*(5802), 1154–1156.

Weissman, M. M., Bland, R. C., Canino, G. J, Faravelli, C., Greenwald, S., Hwu. H.G., . . . Yeh, E. K. (1996) Cross-national epidemiology of major depression and bipolar disorder. *Journal of the American Medical Association, 276*, 293–299.

Zhou, X., & Gao, D. G. (2008). Social support and money as pain management mechanisms. *Psychological Inquiry, 19*(3-4), 127-144.

CHAPTER 12

Culture and the Brain
Frontiers in Cultural Neuroscience

The brain was an inscrutable black box for centuries, but neuroscience is the next great frontier; its technology offers new ways of understanding the brain, and culture is no exception to this developing trend. This chapter will cover the newest studies on how culture shapes the biology of the brain, and how the brain can, in turn, shape culture. It will discuss both the theories derived from anthropology, cultural psychology, neuroscience, and neurogenetics that can inform how we understand the relationship between culture and the brain, as well as the methodological issues (e.g., defining culture, designing appropriate experimental tasks for the scanner, comparing neuroimaging data from different populations) involved in cultural neuroscience.

A Brief History of Neuroscience

Four thousand years before Christ, the ancient Sumerians discovered the psychedelic, mind-altering effects of poppies (Brownstein, 1993). In the year 177 CE, the famous Greek philosopher-turned-doctor named Galen gave the world's first neuroscientific lecture, aptly titled, "On the Brain" (Millon, 2004). Neurons were discovered in the 1800s, soon after scientists realized that cells were the building blocks of life (Shepherd, 1991), but it wasn't until the early 1990s that scientists developed a machine that used giant magnets to show what the brain looked like when it was thinking (see Smith, 2012, for a brief review of this history of brain imaging). This technique, known as **functional magnetic resonance imaging**, or **fMRI**, uses the oxygenation of blood to track brain activity—after all, blood contains oxygen, and the brain—like every other organ in the body—requires blood, so if you simply followed where the blood went you could get an insight into what the massive piece of meat previously referred to as the "black box" was thinking.

Since then, fMRI techniques have largely transformed our understanding of humankind's arguably most important device. Over a thousand studies later, we now know just how localized the brain is, and where; we've also gained some insight into how our brain is organized. For example, the discovery of mirror neurons told us that our sociality is inbuilt in our very minds because they respond in the same way regardless of whether someone else is doing something or whether we are doing it ourselves (Acharya & Shukla, 2012). And neuroimaging studies of ostracism found that physical pain and emotional pain very much feel (and look) the same, at least in our minds (Eisenberger, Lieberman, & Williams, 2003). The fact that scientists now use neuroimaging methods to study longstanding social processes is nothing new. As humans, both social and biological forces drive our behavior, and the distinction between them is often more imaginary than real. Even apart from brain studies, a host of other subfields have also attested to the fact that social interactions can drastically shape numerous biological processes, including cardiovascular reactivity, immune responses and the progression of disease, and genes (see previous chapter; see also Cacioppo, Berntson, Sheridan, & McClintock, 2000, for review).

The rise of the field of **social neuroscience**—or using fMRI techniques to study social questions typically reserved for social psychologists—looks a bit like the rise of cultural psychology. Prior to the 1990s it was a nonexistent field, and in a relatively brief period of time, the number of studies on the topic has exploded. Over the past two decades, social neuroscience has been used to elucidate the processes and brain structures that underlie empathy (Decety & Ickes, 2011), education (Immordino-Yang & Damasio, 2007), risk taking (Steinberg, 2008), and development (Baron-Cohen, Lombardo, & Tager-Flusberg, 2013), just to name a few. Yet the kinds of problems that plague social neuroscience are also similar to the ones that applied to mainstream psychology before cultural psychology came along: The overwhelming majority of studies using neuroscientific methods come from universities and institutions in the Western hemisphere with very little representation from the rest of the world (Chiao, 2009). Still, the small but growing subfield of social-cultural neuroscience exists, and the rest of the chapter will cover some of the highlights in this new domain.

Your Brain, on Culture: Universals across Ethnic Contexts

As with the rest of the human psyche, there are both commonalities and differences when it comes to the brain across cultural contexts. It's a given that all humans share the same basic brain structures and features—we are all born with the same lobes and executive functions, the same myelin sheaths and neurotransmitters, receptors, and neurons. On a deeper level, there are additional commonalities in terms of how our brains respond to the social world.

Responses to Ingroup versus Outgroup Faces

Take, for example, the seminal work done by Joan Chiao and her colleagues (2008) when they scanned the brains of Japanese and European Americans while showing them photographs of different faces. Half the faces Chiao et al. (2008) used were of an ingroup member—that is, a fellow Japanese if the participant was Japanese; a fellow European American if the participant was European American. Also, Chiao et al. (2008) varied the faces in terms of their emotional expressions: Some were happy while others were angry and still others were fearful or neutral. Their primary research question was this: Do all brains respond in the same way to emotional faces, whether those faces belong to an ingroup or outgroup member? (Chiao et al., 2008).

They found that across cultures, everyone tended to exhibit stronger brain responses in the amygdala to ingroup members showing fear; no differences between ingroups and outgroups emerged on any other emotion or in the neutral condition (Chiao et al., 2008). The argument was that fearful ingroup members are especially telling; if a member of your group is afraid, chances are there is danger nearby and that danger likely applies to you (Chiao et al., 2008). Thus it appears that universally, people's brains are finely tuned to pay special attention to threatening emotions from familiar people in their own groups (photo 12.1) because of the meaning that this kind of information carries (Chiao et al., 2008).

PHOTO 12.1. How you respond neurologically to an emotional face may depend on whether it belongs to an ingroup or outgroup member.

Source: iStock

Other studies, however, have shown different pattern of findings. Hart et al. (2000) found increased activity in the amygdala to outgroup faces relative to ingroup ones among Black and White participants—specifically, the amygdala habituated to ingroup faces over time but sustained response to outgroup faces, resulting in an overall stronger reaction to outgroups toward the end. Other research, in contrast, has found increased brain activity in response to ingroup faces compared to outgroup ones. When van Bavel, Packer, and Cunningham (2011) manipulated faces to be either associated with an ingroup or an outgroup, they found increased brain activity when responding to unfamiliar ingroup faces than outgroup ones—not just in the amygdala but in a host of other areas as well (e.g., the fusiform gyri, orbitofrontal cortex, dorsal striatum). In a follow-up study, they also found increased activity in a specific area of the brain geared toward processing face information (the fusiform face area; van Bavel, Packer, & Cunningham, 2011). Consistent with this ingroup advantage or preference idea, other studies have found that both European Americans and Japanese showed greater activity in the areas of the brain that engage in mind reading (in this case, posterior superior temporal sulci) when the target is an ingroup face than when it is an outgroup one (Adams et al., 2010).

Your Brain, on Culture: Cultural Differences by Ethnicity

Self-Construals

Some of the basic distinctions between Eastern and Western selves discussed previously (chapter 1) have been further supported by fMRI studies. Take the case of the Western individualistic, independent self and the Eastern collectivistic, interdependent self. Markus and Kitayama (1991) originally outlined this crucial distinction, and subsequent studies have shown that bicultural individuals can frame-switch between the two selves when primed with one culture or another: Put them in a Western mindset, and they act more like individualists; put them in an Eastern mindset, and they act more like collectivists (Hong, Morris, Chiu, & Benet-Martínez, 2000). Then, in 2010, a group of researchers from the City University of Hong Kong and Peking University decided to see if these distinctions were also reflected on the neural level (Ng, Han, Mao & Lai, 2010). So Ng et al. essentially replicated Hong et al.'s frame-switching study in the scanner: They exposed (bicultural) Hong Kong Chinese to images taken from either the East or the West (think Bruce Lee versus James Bond; Ng et al., 2010). Afterward, they asked them to decide whether a list of adjectives described themselves or their loved one (in this case, their mother; Ng et al., 2010). They found that the Eastern prime led to brain activity patterns that looked the same whether the participant was thinking about himself or his mother, but the Western prime led to a pattern that looked different, particularly in the ventral medial prefrontal cortex, or VMPFC (Ng et al., 2010). Specifically, the Western prime led to increased VMPFC activity when thinking about the self (Ng et al., 2010). A related study showed that while the VMPFC is the primary place the self is represented in European American brains, the MPFC is where the self—and close others—is represented in Chinese brains (Zhu, Zhang, Fan, & Han, 2007).

Related to independent versus interdependent selves is the finding that Western selves tend to value dominance whereas Eastern ones tend to place more value on submission (e.g., Triandis & Gelfand, 1998; see Freeman, Rule, Adams, & Ambady, 2009 for review). When Freeman et al. (2009) examined how East Asian and European American brains responded to pictures of people demonstrating dominant versus submissive body language, they found that in both cases, the reward center of the brain—the mesolimbic area—was more active when viewing culturally normative behaviors. So European Americans showed more mesolimbic activity when seeing people display dominant stances, whereas Japanese showed more activity when seeing submissive ones (Freeman et al., 2009). This suggests that everyone responds to socially prescribed behaviors, but the content of what is rewarded differs as a function of cultural norms.

Language and Reading

Cultures differ in many ways, and one of the most obvious is in matters of language. Thus it may not be surprising that different languages produce divergent patterns of brain activation. In a pair of neuroimaging studies done by Siok, Perfetti, Jin, and Tan (2004), the researchers found that Chinese dyslexics exhibit a distinct neural response to (Chinese) words. Siok et al. (2004) argued that given that Chinese characters are fundamentally different from the English alphabet—the former is based on pictures and is logographic, and the latter is based on sounds and is phonemic—language processing recruits different areas of the brain in the two cultural contexts. When reading Chinese, the left middle frontal gyrus is more active because this area is responsible for translating graphic stimuli to meaning systems, whereas in English, the left temporoparietal region is more active, because this area is responsible for translating phonemes (Siok et al., 2004). Thus dyslexia among Chinese-speakers is marked by a disruption of the former, but dyslexia among English-speakers is marked by a disruption of the latter (Siok et al., 2004). This suggests that in matters of a disorder like dyslexia, culture may play a critical role in determining the implicated brain areas.

The Same, but Different (Again)

By now, you should be well aware of the reality that people are infinitely more complex that we imagine, and in matters of culture this is no exception. If the story of culture is that we are both the same and different, then this has also been shown to be reflected in our brains. To illustrate, consider the studies.

Theory of Mind

How does culture impact the way we understand others? Although numerous behavioral and self-reported studies have documented distinctions as a function of our different cultural selves, few had looked to see whether this is reflected on the neural level until Kobayashi, Glover, and Temple's 2006 study of European Americans and Japanese Americans who were asked to engage in **Theory of Mind** (ToM) while inside the scanner. Recall that ToM refers to the fundamental human ability to know the minds of others and realize that not all minds think alike (e.g., Frith & Frith, 2005). In their study, Kobayashi et al. (2006) had participants scanned while being presented with a series of **false-belief tasks**—vignettes that involved characters whose minds thought differently about the same thing; European Americans read these in English, while bilingual Japanese Americans read them in English or Japanese. Results showed that both universals and culture-specifics emerged. In terms of universals, several brain areas proved to be active for both groups when engaging in ToM: the medial prefrontal cortex (mPFC), the right anterior cingulate cortex (ACC), and the right medial frontal gyrus (MFG)/dorsolateral prefrontal cortex (DLPFC; Kobayashi et al., 2006). In terms of culture-specifics, a number of differences emerged between the two groups in terms of a variety of other brain areas—for example, European Americans had more activity in the right insula and right mPFC, whereas the Japanese American group had more activity in the interior frontal gyrus (Kobayashi et al., 2006). Although it remains unclear whether these distinctions were driven more by language (e.g., the fact that the Japanese Americans were bilingual whereas the European Americans were monolingual) or other features of culture (e.g., self-construal), it nevertheless suggests that on a neural level—just like on a behavioral one—members of different groups are both alike and different.

The Aging Brain

In a separate line of research, fMRI studies show that aging appears to have similar effects on the brain cross-culturally. In a series of studies, Goh et al. (2007) examined the brain activity of young and old East Asians and European Americans when viewing different scenes that varied either in terms of the central, focal object or in terms of the background (e.g., a lion in a desert or an ostrich in a desert). Across both cultural groups, elderly participants showed less activity in memory and visual, object-processing centers of the brain—namely, the hippocampus and the occipital area (Goh et al., 2007). Given that age has long been associated with cognitive deficit in just about every domain (with the exception of vocabulary; Novak, 2012), this finding is not surprising. Nevertheless, this research was helpful in confirming the expected universality of the aging brain. At the same time, however, this study also found a cultural difference: Elderly East Asians showed less activity when processing central objects compared to elderly European Americans (although no cultural difference in object processing occurred among young participants; Goh et al., 2007). This finding was consistent with the longstanding idea that East Asians are more background-focused, whereas European Americans are more object-focused; however, the fact that this difference only emerged among the elderly suggests that some cultural distinctions may take a lifetime of experience to emerge (Goh et al., 2007).

Additional Forms of Culture, Revisited

Given the relative newness of the field of cultural neuroscience, just about every "cultural" study involving fMRI techniques has relied exclusively on the traditional form of culture as ethnicity, and on the most popular ethnic comparison—East Asians versus European Americans. Still, there are a handful of studies that have used neuroimaging to study the effects of other forms of group membership.

Religion as Culture

Like ethnicity, religion also changes the brain. In a study comparing Catholics with atheists and agnostics, Wiech et al. (2008) found that Catholics responded to pain differently when provided with a religious image, and this was reflected on both a neural as well as a behavioral level. Neurally, the ventrolateral PFC was at play—an area involved in pain inhibition, and behaviorally, Catholics reported that seeing a religious image helped them cope with the pain better.

Other research provides further evidence of the neurological power of religion. A group of participants were given the classic Stroop task (i.e., color words presented in colored font that either matched or mismatched the word it spelled) while an **EEG** cap recorded their neuron firing activity (Inzlicht, McGregor, Hirch, & Nash, 2009). Those who professed greater belief in God responded with less brain activity after a mistake was made (Inzlict et al., 2009). In particular, Inzlicht et al. (2009) looked at a specific kind of **event-related potential**, or a group of neurons firing at the same time: the error-related negativity, or ERN. The ERN reflects what it sounds like—a strong neural response after a mistake—in an area of the brain that is involved in anxious responses and self-control, the anterior cingulate cortex, or ACC (Inzlict et al., 2009). Taken together, these findings suggest that religion's buffering effects against anxiety can be seen on the neural level (Inzlicht et al., 2009).

Class as Culture

In addition to ethnicity and religion, class apparently also shapes the brain. Recall the findings discussed in chapter 2 about how lower socioeconomic status is linked to increased prosociality and empathy. Recent neuroimaging studies confirmed this difference: Across two studies that looked at perceived (subjective) social status in college and actual SES (i.e., household income and parental education), researchers found that lower class was associated with increased brain activity in areas involved in **mentalization**—that is, representation of other people's thoughts and experience, primarily in parts of the prefrontal cortex and posterior cingulate cortex. In addition, brains of lower class individuals also showed stronger emotional reactions (e.g., in the amygdala) in response to angry faces (Muscatell et al., 2012). This latter finding of increased responding to threatening faces among low SES individuals has also been shown in other studies with different samples. Interestingly, in a similar study by Gianaros et al. (2008), they found that college students' perceptions of their parents' social status predicted their own amygdala response to angry faces; interestingly, the participants' own SES—in this case, their income or employment status—did not make a difference.

If lower SES produces brains that are more adept at knowing and responding to the minds of others, it also comes with liabilities. In a separate line of work, developmental psychologists have found that low SES was associated with smaller brain volume in two particular areas—the amygdala and the hippocampus—among children and teens (Noble, Houston, Kan, & Sowell, 2012). In this study, the participants' parental educational achievement (i.e., number of years of schooling) predicted the size of the amygdala (the emotional center of the brain): Less educated parents had children with larger amygdalas, potentially because lower SES is linked to greater stress, and chronic exposure to stress can lead to a more developed emotion center of the brain (Noble et al., 2012). In addition, the ratio of the participants' family income divided by the national poverty cutoff predicted the size of the hippocampus, the part that plays a key role in memory; kids from poorer families had smaller memory centers, potentially also because of stress (Noble et al., 2012).

Gender as Culture

Perhaps the most studied form of "culture" in the context of neuroimaging research has been gender, and a number of fMRI studies have now lent support to the idea that males and females may engage in distinct brain areas when responding to the same task. To illustrate, when given a virtual maze to navigate, men responded with activity in the hippocampus, but women responded with activity in the PFC and parietal lobe, a finding that is consistent with the longstanding and reliable gender difference in spatial orientation (Gron, Wunderlich, Spitzer, Tomczak, & Riepe, 2000). Stress also seems to elicit different patterns of brain activity in men and women. When asked to do a series of math problems in the scanner (as a stressor), women engaged their limbic system more whereas men engaged their PFC more (Wang et al., 2007), suggesting that the two groups may rely on different strategies—for example, emotional versus cognitive responses—when dealing with difficult situations.

Studies on gender and emotional responses show both similarities and differences in neural response patterns. When Lee et al. (2002) showed men and women pictures of happy, sad, and neutral faces in the scanner, they found similar activation of brain regions in response to the happy faces (e.g., in the frontal and parietal lobes), with slight variation in other areas (e.g., the occipital and temporal lobes); in response to the sad faces, however, gender differences were more pronounced, with men showing frontal lobe activity but women showing a lack thereof. In a related study on how men and women responded to a series of emotional and empathic tasks—including recognizing emotion in faces, viewing emotional social scenes, and reading about emotional situations—researchers once again found both similarities and differences (Derntl et al., 2010). Namely, Derntl et al. (2010) found that although men and women recognized emotions in faces equally well, they showed different activation patterns, suggesting that their brains relied on distinct processes to arrive at the answers. In terms of the empathic tasks, both groups responded with activation in the amygdala, but overall, women appeared to have a stronger neural response (Derntl et al., 2010). This suggests once more that men and women may rely on different strategies when responding to the same task.

Key Concepts

functional magnetic resonance imaging (fMRI)
Social neuroscience
Theory of Mind
False-belief task
EEG
Event-related potential
Mentalization

References

Acharya, S., & Shukla, S. (2012). Mirror neurons: Enigma of the metaphysical modular brain. *Journal of Natural Science, Biology and Medicine, 3*(2), 118–124.

Adams Jr., R. B., Rule, N. O., Franklin Jr., R. G., Wang, E., Stevenson, M. T., Yoshikawa, S. . . . Ambady, N. (2010). Cross-cultural reading the mind in the eyes: An fMRI investigation. *Journal of Cognitive Neuroscience, 22*(1), 97–108.

Baron-Cohen, S., Lombardo, M., & Tager-Flusberg, H. (Eds.). (2013). *Understanding other minds: Perspectives from developmental social neuroscience* (3rd ed.). Oxford, U.K.: Oxford University Press.

Brownstein, M. J. (1993). A brief history of opiates, opioid peptides, and opioid receptors. *Proceedings of the National Academy of Sciences, 90(12), 5391–5393.*

Cacioppo, J. T., Berntson, G. G., Sheridan, J. F., & McClintock, M. K. (2000). Multilevel integrative analyses of human behavior: Social neuroscience and the complementing nature of social and biological approaches. *Psychological Bulletin, 126*(6), 829–843.

Chiao, J. Y. (2009). Cultural neuroscience: A once and future discipline. *Progress in Brain Research, 178,* 287–304.

Chiao, J. Y., Iidaka, T., Gordon, H. L., Nogawa, J., Bar, M., Aminoff, E., . . . Ambady, N. (2008). Cultural specificity in amygdala response to fear faces. *Journal of Cognitive Neuroscience, 20*(12), 2167–2174.

Decety, J., & Ickes, W. (2011). *The social neuroscience of empathy.* Cambridge, MA: MIT Press.

Derntl, B., Finkelmeyer, A., Eickhoff, S., Kellermann, T., Falkenberg, D. I., Schneider, F., & Habel, U. (2010). Multidimensional assessment of empathic abilities: Neural correlates and gender differences. *Psychoneuroendocrinology, 35*(1), 67–82. doi:10.1016/ j.psyneuen.2009.10.006

Eisenberger, N. I., Lieberman, M. D., & Williams, K. D. (2003). Does rejection hurt? An fMRI study of social exclusion. *Science, 302*(5643), 290–292.

Freeman, J. B., Rule, N. O., Adams Jr., R. B., & Ambady, N. (2009). Culture shapes a mesolimbic response to signals of dominance and subordination that associates with behavior. *Neuroimage, 47*(1), 353–359. doi:10.1016/j.neuroimage.2009.04.038

Frith, C., & Frith, U. (2005). Theory of mind. *Current Biology, 15*(17), R644–R645. doi:10.1016/j.cub.2005.08.041

Gianaros, P. J., Horenstein, J. A., Hariri, A. R., Sheu, L. K., Manuck, S. B., Matthews, K. A., & Cohen, S. (2008). Potential neural embedding of parental social standing. *Social Cognitive & Affective Neuroscience, 3*(2), 91–96. doi:10.1093/scan/nsn003

Goh, J. O., Chee, M. W., Tan, J. C., Venkatraman, V., Hebrank, A., Leshikar, E. D., . . . Park, D. C. (2007). Age and culture modulate object processing and object—scene binding in the ventral visual area. *Cognitive, Affective, & Behavioral Neuroscience, 7*(1), 44–52.

Grön, G., Wunderlich, A. P., Spitzer, M., Tomczak, R., & Riepe, M. W. (2000). Brain activation during human navigation: Gender-different neural networks as substrate of performance. *Nature Neuroscience, 3*(4), 404–408.

Hart, A. J., Whalen, P. J., Shin, L. M., McInerney, S. C., Fischer, H., & Rauch, S. L. (2000). Differential response in the human amygdala to racial outgroup vs ingroup face stimuli. *Neuroreport, 11*(11), 2351–2354.

Hong, Y. Y., Morris, M. W., Chiu, C. Y., & Benet-Martinez, V. (2000). Multicultural minds: A dynamic constructivist approach to culture and cognition. *American Psychologist, 55*(7), 709–720.

Immordino-Yang, M. H., & Damasio, A. (2007). We feel, therefore we learn: The relevance of affective and social neuroscience to education. *Mind, Brain, and Education, 1*(1), 3–10.

Inzlicht, M., McGregor, I., Hirsh, J. B., & Nash, K. (2009). Neural markers of religious conviction. *Psychological Science, 20*(3), 385–392.

Kobayashi, C., Glover, G. H., & Temple, E. (2006). Cultural and linguistic influence on neural bases of "Theory of Mind": An fMRI study with Japanese bilinguals. *Brain and Language, 98*(2), 210–220. doi:10.1016/j.bandl.2006.04.013

Lee, T. M., Liu, H. L., Hoosain, R., Liao, W. T., Wu, C. T., Yuen, K. S., . . . Gao, J. H. (2002). Gender differences in neural correlates of recognition of happy and sad faces in humans assessed by functional magnetic resonance imaging. *Neuroscience Letters, 333*(1), 13–16. doi:10.1016/S0304-3940(02)00965-5

Markus, H. R., & Kitayama, S. (1991). Culture and the self: Implications for cognition, emotion, and motivation. *Psychological Review, 98*(2), 224–253.

Millon, T. (2004). *Masters of the mind: Exploring the story of mental illness from ancient times to the new millennium.* Hoboken, NJ: John Wiley & Sons.

Muscatell, K. A., Morelli, S. A., Falk, E. B., Way, B. M., Pfeifer, J. H., Galinsky, A. D., . . . Eisenberger, N. I. (2012). Social status modulates neural activity in the mentalizing network. *NeuroImage, 60*(3), 1771–1777. doi:10.1016/j.neuroimage.2012.01.080

Ng, S. H., Han, S., Mao, L., & Lai, J. C. (2010). Dynamic bicultural brains: fMRI study of their flexible neural representation of self and significant others in response to culture primes. *Asian Journal of Social Psychology, 13*(2), 83–91. doi:10.1111/j.1467-839X.2010.01303.x

Noble, K. G., Houston, S. M., Kan, E., & Sowell, E. R. (2012). Neural correlates of socioeconomic status in the developing human brain. *Developmental Science, 15*(4), 516–527.

Novak, M. (2012). *Issues in aging.* Boston, MA: Pearson.

Shepherd, M. G. (1991). *Foundations of the neuron doctrine.* New York, NY: Oxford University Press.

Siok, W. T., Perfetti, C. A., Jin, Z., & Tan, L. H. (2004). Biological abnormality of impaired reading is constrained by culture. *Nature, 431*(7004), 71–76.

Smith, K. (2012). Brain imaging: fMRI 2.0. *Nature, 485*(7392), 24–26. doi:10.1038/484024a

Steinberg, L. (2008). A social neuroscience perspective on adolescent risk-taking. *Developmental Review, 28*(1), 78–106. doi:10.1016/j.dr.2007.08.002

Triandis, H. C., & Gelfand, M. J. (1998). Converging measurement of horizontal and vertical individualism and collectivism. *Journal of Personality and Social Psychology, 74*(1), 118–128.

Van Bavel, J. J., Packer, D. J., & Cunningham, W. A. (2008). The neural substrates of in-group bias a functional magnetic resonance imaging investigation. *Psychological Science, 19*(11), 1131–1139.

Van Bavel, J. J., Packer, D. J., & Cunningham, W. A. (2011). Modulation of the fusiform face area following minimal exposure to motivationally relevant faces: Evidence of in-group enhancement (not out-group disregard). *Journal of Cognitive Neuroscience, 23*(11), 3343–3354.

Wang, J., Korczykowski, M., Rao, H., Fan, Y., Pluta, J., Gur, R. C., . . . Detre, J. A. (2007). Gender difference in neural response to psychological stress. *Social Cognitive and Affective Neuroscience, 2*(3), 227–239. doi:10.1093/scan/nsm018

Wiech, K., Farias, M., Kahane, G., Shackel, N., Tiede, W., & Tracey, I. (2008). An fMRI study measuring analgesia enhanced by religion as a belief system. *Pain, 139*(2), 467–476. doi:10.1016/j.pain.2008.07.030

Zhu, Y., Zhang, L., Fan, J., & Han, S. (2007). Neural basis of cultural influence on self-representation. *Neuroimage, 34*(3), 1310–1316. doi:10.1016/j.neuroimage.2006.08.047

CHAPTER 13

Predicting the Future
Tracking Cultural Change

Perhaps the single most defining and challenging thing about culture is that it changes as people change; it remains a forever moving target. This chapter will cover various forms of cultural change, including change as a function of modernization, globalization, travel, contact with members of different cultural groups, and historical shifts or events. It will end with a series of future, unanswered questions about culture in the future (i.e., knowing what we do not know).

Mechanisms for Cultural Change

What drives cultural change? A number of researchers have suggested that cultural change demands certain prerequisites in place. On the most basic level, if culture itself is the result of learned and socially transmitted responses to particular environments, then culture can change any time environment changes or social learning occurs. In this respect, cultural change can happen easily and often, and anthropologists like Boyd and Richerson (1996) have noted that many animal species, including baboons and birds, have shown evidence of this kind of social learning in practices like song singing and tool use (Lefebvre & Palameta, 1998; and Wrangham et al., 1994, as cited in Boyd & Richerson, 1996). However, Boyd and Richerson (1996) go on to argue that this type of cultural change common in animals is not the same as the type of mass-scale cultural change we see in humans. Human cultural change is "cumulative," meaning that it builds on itself over generations and results in far more complex changes than what typically happens in the animal kingdom (Boyd & Richerson, 1996). Further, they argue that **cumulative cultural change** is the result of human's propensity for **observational learning** (Boyd & Richerson, 1996; see also Henrich & McElreath, 2003).

Other researchers have gone on to elaborate on this idea and propose that one particular mechanism for cultural evolution is through the use of **inadvertent social information**, or **ISI**—that is, information people provide unintentionally, often simply by letting other people watch what they are doing (Danchin, Giraldeau,

Valone, & Wagner, 2004). Danchin et al. (2004) contend that much of this ISI occurs in public contexts and, as a result, becomes a vehicle for cultural transmission. That is, members of a species do things in public and other members see what they are doing; depending on the outcomes, those watching may adopt what they see and, over time, this can take on the form of widespread cultural change (Danchin et al., 2004). Interestingly Danchin et al. (2004) make their argument for cultural evolution in animal contexts, offering an important counterpoint to other researchers' contention that systematic cultural changes primarily happen in humans.

Cultural Changes within the United States

If culture is by definition dynamic and a natural extension of the people that create it, then it naturally follows that as people change, so must the culture around them. The idea of cultural change, then, is often—but not necessarily—slow and painful; in recent years, we've seen extraordinary shifts in widely shared social attitudes in a relatively brief period of time, without requiring large-scale societal warfare. Often, these changes involve moving away from more traditional values and toward more modern ones, but this is not always the case (Inglehart & Baker, 2000). The rest of the chapter will outline some of the systematic efforts to study cultural change and what they have revealed, both within the United States and globally.

Mating Patterns

One of the better studied cultural trends is in mating preferences. Back in 2001, Buss, Shackelford, Kirkpatrick, and Larsen did a large-scale study of people's desires for their ideal mates. They compared self-reported mate values of men and women between 1939 and 1996 across different regions in the United States, including in the South, Midwest, West, and New England (Buss et al., 2001). They found evidence for stability and variation across regions, gender, and time (Buss et al., 2001). Regionally, participants from the South appeared to value religion and religious values (e.g., chastity) more than those from the other regions, and this difference remained over time (Buss et al., 2001). Still, there were also similarities across regions, and people everywhere in this country appeared to place comparable levels of emphasis on the importance of having a physically attractive mate, although this was stronger among men than women (Buss et al., 2001).

More generally across the United States, strong evidence for changes over time also emerged in the Buss et al. (2001) study. For both genders across time, people found love and attraction to the other person to increase in importance, along with other desirable features like intelligence, social skills, and the ever-important physical attractiveness (Buss et al., 2001). If the desire for smart, outgoing, beautiful mates increased, then other values conversely decreased—features like neatness and sexual purity became less important over time (Buss et al., 2001). Buss and his colleagues (2001) also found that other mate values, though, did not change much. Over the 20th century, people continued to care about mates they could rely on and who had good personalities, and people also continued to not care about whether their mates belonged to the same political party as they did (Buss et al., 2001). At the same time, many of the evolutionarily important, gender-specific values discussed in previous chapters (e.g., see chapter 4) remained: As always, men cared about health and beauty more, whereas women cared more about drive and a stable financial future (Buss et al., 2001).

Psychological Correlates of Aging

What is your stereotype of the elderly? On the one hand, there is the negative stereotype that older people are less competent and more unhappy (e.g., impaired; curmudgeonly; see Cuddy & Fiske, 2002). This notion might be based on a grain of reality—namely, the one that says that aging does come with bodily and cognitive declines in terms of body fat, muscle tone, hair loss, bone density, and various cognitive abilities (Saxon, Elten, & Perkins, 2014). On the other hand, the psychological research on aging also suggested a far rosier picture: Older people also tend to be happier (Mroczek & Kolarz, 1998). Thus, for a while, the longstanding assumption was that aging came with both cognitive declines and emotional benefits—you may be slower, but you will be happier, presumably because life's troubles are long behind you.

This silver lining in aging, however, might be changing. A recent study that compared happiness levels by age group from the U.S. General Social Survey found that over the past four decades—1972–2014—the correlation between age and happiness has gone down each year (Twenge, Sherman, & Lyubomirsky, 2016). Interestingly, the authors also found that declines in happiness are happening primarily in older adults but not in younger ones; among 18–29-year-olds, happiness levels have, if anything, increased in recent years, but among those above 30, happiness has been decreasing in recent years (Twenge et al., 2016).

Twenge et al. (2016) go on to argue that this cultural shift may be explained by the **revolution of rising expectations** and **income inequality**. Citing other research showing that people's expectations for their jobs and relationships may not align with reality (e.g., Twenge & Kasser, 2013), Twenge et al. (2016) suggest that this gap between expectations and actual attainment may be especially problematic and salient for older, but not younger, individuals. This is related to the other cited factor of income inequality, given that older adults who are out of school and working are more likely to suffer from economic declines related to the recent recession (Twenge et al., 2016).

Cultural Changes Outside the United States

Despite the relative newness of the field of researchers who study cultural change, a limited number of studies have also emerged on cultural contexts outside the United States, and the shifts in values that have occurred in other countries over time.

Mating Preferences in Asia

As with the aforementioned Buss et al. (2001) study on changes in mating preferences among Americans, both stability and variation have also been documented in who people want to spend their lives with, in other countries. One such case is India, which presents itself as a particularly interesting cultural context in which to examine mating and change because it has a long history of arranged marriage and is a culture in which marriage and weddings are treated very seriously (Heitzman

& Wordern, 1995, and Banerjee, Duflo, Ghatak, & Lafortune, 2009, both as cited in Kamble, Shackelford, Pham, & Buss, 2014). When Kamble et al. (2014) looked at Indians' preferences for a mate, they compared two groups—one sampled in 1984 and another in 2009. In both cases, participants answered a series of questions about their ideal marriage partner similar to the ones used previously by David Buss, completing both rankings of mate qualities and a separate set of ratings for each individual characteristic in terms of its importance (Kamble et al., 2014).

Similar to the American data, the Indians also showed both stability and change in their preferences over the quarter-century time gap (photo 13.1) between the first sample and the second one (Kamble et al., 2014). Kamble et al. (2014) also found that some mate preferences grew in importance over time—for example, both Indian men and women increasingly valued mates who were artistic, creative, domestically skilled in cooking and housekeeping, ambitious, and industrious. At the same time, other preferences like physical attractiveness diminished in value for both genders, and still others remained relatively stable—for example, gender differences in the emphases on financial resources and its correlates (e.g., education, intellect) persisted, with women valuing these more than men (Kamble et al., 2014). Finally, some qualities remained important for everyone across time, like mutual attraction, a good personality (namely, kindness and understanding), and good health (Kamble et al. 2014). The fact that some mate preferences like love and attraction seem immune to the effects of time and cultural practices (like arranged marriage) is especially noteworthy.

Similar patterns of cultural consistency and change also emerged in a different Asian culture: China. When Chang, Wang, Shackelford, and Buss (2011) asked two

PHOTO 13.1. Kamble et al. (2014) showed that mate preferences among Indians have both changed and remained stable over time.

Source: iStock

cohorts of Chinese participants spaced a quarter century apart about their mate preferences, they found that gender differences between men and women remained stable. As always, men preferred youth and beauty while women preferred resources (Chang et al., 2011). Cultural differences also emerged; in general, people gave less value to chastity (here defined as virginal status) and more value to final prospects (Chang et al., 2011).

Global Trends in Cultural Change

The aforementioned studies of cultural stability and change beg an important question: Is there a universal direction that all cultures appear to be headed toward? Are there trends in cultural change that are happening everywhere? The jury may still be deliberating, but so far there is some preliminary evidence to suggest that there may be a few potential "universal" change trends.

Happiness Levels

One of them is changes in overall levels of happiness, or at least the valuation of happiness. Relying on data from the World Values Survey, a more recent analysis of data from 1981 to 2007 found that at least in the 45 countries for which data are consistently available, happiness is on the rise (WVS, 2016). The researchers behind the WVS suggest that part of this trend can be explained by the growing economies and social and political freedoms that have also been on the upswing over the past three decades; however, outliers still exist, and happiness levels in certain countries have also gone down during that time frame (WVS, 2016).

Economic Development

How do modernization and economic development change culture? When Ronald Inglehart and Wayne Baker (2000) set out to answer this question at the dawn of the new millennium, they compared two possibilities. They argued that on the one hand, in line with theorists like Karl Marx, economic change should herald massive cultural changes (e.g., see Marx's *Das Capital* or *Communist Manifesto*)— in other words, changes in economy are what promotes the stuff of cultural revolution (Inglehart & Baker, 2000). On the other hand, consistent with the ideas of philosophers like Max Weber, culture should remain relatively stable (Weber, 1904, as cited in Inglehart & Baker, 2000), independent of what is happening economically in a society. To assess whether economic development in modern times and cultural change go hand in hand, Inglehart and Baker (2000) turned to the WVS, one of the most large-scale and comprehensive international survey studies done to date. They accessed data collected over nearly two decades, from 1981 to 1998, from six continents and 65 countries; of particular interest was how these nations differed in their values over time, and to this end Inglehart and Baker (2000) focused on two particular dimensions of interest. They called one the secular-traditional dimension, and the other the survival-self-expression dimension (Inglehart & Baker, 2000). In terms of the former, Inglehart and Baker (2000) defined traditional values as embodying religion, respect for authority, and nationalism (with secularism being the opposite); in terms of the latter, they defined survival values as emphasizing physical resources and de-emphasizing psychological well-being (with self-expression values being the opposite). Inglehart and Baker (2000) found strong support for the first idea—that economic patterns and cultural change appear to go together. People from wealthier nations hold different values than those from poorer ones, and the latter tend to focus more on tradition and survival, whereas the former focus on rationality and self-expression (Inglehart & Baker, 2000).

These authors also found a strong effect of time on cultural values. Of the 65 original nations Inglehart and Baker (2000) examined, 38 of them had data over time (i.e., from 1981 to 1998); and when they compared within-country shifts in value over those 17 years, they found that many of these places moved toward increases in self-expression and secularization (e.g., Germany, Sweden, Belgium, Switzerland, Australia, Mexico, Japan). Interestingly, a small number of countries also went in the opposite direction (Inglehart & Baker, 2000). For example, Russia and Belarus moved toward survival and tradition; still others only moved along one dimension or the other (e.g., Hungary became more secular but not any more expressive, whereas India became more expressive but not more secular), and at least one country—Nigeria— did not appear to change their values by much (Inglehart & Baker, 2000).

Time, however, was not the only powerful force that Inglehart and Baker (2000) found. They also came across strong evidence that culture—particularly religious culture—exerted strong effects over people's values even when economic conditions are taken into account (Inglehart & Baker, 2000). In other words, although economic development did change values, it did not produce identical value systems across all countries; instead, economic development produced different patterns of cultural change in each country that seemed to differ as a function of that country's religious traditions; whether a country was historically Christian or Muslim or Confucian made a substantive difference (Inglehart & Baker, 2000).

Urbanization and Individualism

Related to the idea that cultures become more secular and expressive over time is the broader notion of individualism. After all, if you recall from chapter 1, expressing the self is one of the core tenets of being an individual (Markus & Kitayama, 1991). Similar to the above work by Inglehart and Baker (2000), other researchers have also found mass-level cultural changes, but on a broader time scale. For example, work by Greenfield (2013) found that striking cultural shifts have occurred in the last two centuries across two Western nations—the United States and Great Britain—most likely due to broad societal changes from rural to urban environments. Citing the theory that cultural values are responses to different ecologies, Greenfield (2013) argues that as societies become more wealthy and technologically advanced, people are less grounded in collectivistic, communal concerns like duty, obligation to others, religious devotion, and obedience to authority, while also becoming more oriented toward individualistic priorities like personal wealth and choice.

To demonstrate this change, Greenfield (2013) used Google Ngram to track the content of English-language books from 1800 to 2000 published both in the United States and the U.K.—resulting in a corpus of more than a million books in the case of the former and about a third of that number in the case of the latter. In the American context, Greenfield compared the frequency of words like "obliged" versus "choose," "give" versus "get," and "act" versus "feel"; in the British context, she did the same with similar words, including "choose," "decision," "acquisition," and "emotion" versus "benevolence" and "deed." She also looked at additional concepts like "individual," "self," "unique," and "child" versus "obedience," "authority," "belong," and "pray" across both cultural contexts (Greenfield, 2013). Moreover, Greenfield (2013) also looked at the percentage of the population living in rural versus urban areas based on Census Bureau and World Bank data; in both the United States and the U.K. a growing proportion of people lived in cities over time. Consistent with predictions, individualistic words that focused on choice, feelings, acquiring things, and being unique increased over time (just as urbanization increased), whereas collectivistic words that focused on obligations, giving, actions, obedience, and authority decreased over time (just as rural dwellings decreased); this pattern was the same across both cultures studied (Greenfield, 2013; see figure 13.1).

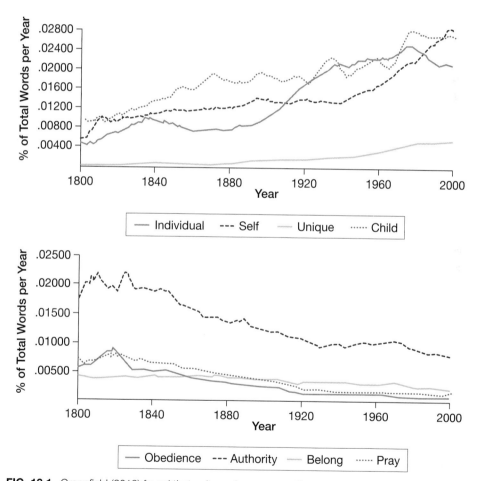

FIG. 13.1. Greenfield (2013) found that culture changes over time.

Source: Based on Greenfield, P. M. (2013). The changing psychology of culture from 1800 through 2000. *Psychological Science, 24*(9), 1722–1731.

Similar effects emerged in other contexts. When Zeng and Greenfield (2015) did a similar study in China also using Google Ngram, they found that words reflecting individualistic ideals and values increased over four decades—from 1970 to 2008. Along similar lines, words reflecting collectivism also decreased during the same time frame (Zeng & Greenfield, 2015). Thus it appears that the trend toward increasing individualism may be occurring on a broad scale across multiple cultural contexts.

Globalization and Identity Changes

Beyond becoming more secular and urban over time, the world is also ever increasingly global. Modernization, economic development, and technological growth have now made it easier than ever to be connected—either literally or virtually--to other cultural contexts. How does this feature of modern society—globalization—affect our psyches?

To answer this question, Jeffrey Jensen Arnett (2002) tracked some of the changes that have affected young people around the world over the past several decades. Between 1980 and 2000, educational attainment for both males and females consistently went up in every country Arnett (2002) examined, including not just those in the United States and Europe (Germany, Italy, Poland) but also Latin America (Argentina, Mexico), Africa (Nigeria), the Middle East (Egypt, Turkey), and Asia (China, India); between 1970 and 1995, access to the media via TV and phones increased exponentially in every region of the world, sometimes by incredible magnitudes. Arnett also cites additional evidence that traditionally collectivistic cultures might be changing their cultural practices: Sexual liberation is on the rise while household size is on the decline in many parts of Africa; emigration out of the country and delays in starting a family are becoming more popular throughout Asia (Naito & Gielen, 2002, and Santa Maria, 2002, as cited in Arnett, 2002).

Arnett (2002) goes on to argue that these changes in globalization have produced at least two major psychological changes: (1) the increased prevalence of biculturalism and (2) identity confusion. In terms of biculturalism, Arnett (2002) specifically argues that young people will likely have both what he calls a **global identity**—a general awareness of what it means to be part of a connected and diverse world—and a separate **local identity**—which is a direct product of the specific regional cultural traditions that they grew up with. He also notes that in addition to local and global identities, there may also be an increasing number of cases involving a **hybrid identity**, which is what happens when a person combines both the local and global features of their identity into one, thereby creating a new identity (see also Hermans & Kempen, 1998, as cited in Arnett, 2002). Alternatively, another possibility is that the onslaught of different cultural exposures makes people less—not more—connected to a particular cultural identity, resulting in **identity confusion** (Arnett, 2002). Arnett relates this idea to a number of similar and related processes; recall, for example, the issue of marginalization, which happens when people neither feel like they belong to their host culture nor their origin culture (see chapter 9). Similarly, **cultural distance** happens when a person's cultural values and his or her own beliefs don't align, and **culture shedding** involves discarding certain parts of one's culture (Berry, 1997, as cited in Arnett, 2002). Finally, another alternative to is opt for a **self-selected culture**—one that does not go along with the existing global culture but represents a unique manifestation of a particular configuration of other cultural values, often centered around a religion (as in the case of religious fundamentalists) or something totally secular (as in the case of other subcultures, like that of heavy metal; Arnett, 2002).

Conclusion

I have a five-year-old whom I play Good News, Bad News with. I always say, "So you want the Good News or Bad News?" He's an optimist, and he always asks for the GN. But I'm a psychologist, so I know better and I tell him that GN and BN are two sides of the same coin: They're the same thing. So here's your GN/BN: The future is uncertain, because we are in an era of unprecedented cultural change.

Consider how long it took for women to get the right to vote. The women's suffrage movement started in 1848, the year of the first women's rights convention in Seneca Falls, New York. It took 70 years—until 1919—to finally get the 19th Amendment passed, which gave women the right to vote. Meanwhile, there was the fight for Black Americans to get the same rights as White Americans. If you start this battle at the Civil War, this itself took more than four years and included at least 237 named battles fought. But any historian will tell you that the end of the war did not mark the end of the battle, and the African American civil rights movement took at least another 14 years, from 1954 to 1968. Some say the fight is not yet over. If you consider the LGBTQ movement, the first state to legalize gay marriage was Massachusetts in 2003, and it took 12 years for the Supreme Court to finally come on board. So if you're an optimist, then the good news might be this: Cultural change appears to happening faster now than ever before. But here's the great news: You get to choose the direction of change that comes next. Because you are your culture, you get to choose.

Key Concepts

Cumulative cultural change
Observational learning
Inadvertent social information (ISI)
Revolution of rising expectations
Income inequality
Global, local, and hybrid identity
Identity confusion
Cultural distance and shedding
Self-selected culture

References

Arnett, J. J. (2002). The psychology of globalization. *American Psychologist*, *57*(10), 774–783.

Berry, J. W. (1997). Immigration, acculturation, and adaptation. *Applied Psychology*, *46*(1), 5–34.

Boyd, R., & Richerson, P. J. (1996, January). Why culture is common, but cultural evolution is rare. *Proceedings of the British Academy*, *88*, 77–94.

Buss, D. M., Shackelford, T. K., Kirkpatrick, L. A., & Larsen, R. (2001). A half century of mate preferences: The cultural evolution of values. *Journal of Marriage & Family, 63,* 491–503.

Chang, L., Wang, Y., Shackelford, T. K., & Buss, D. M. (2011). Chinese mate preferences: Cultural evolution and continuity across a quarter of a century. *Personality and Individual Differences, 50*(5), 678–683.

Cuddy, A. J., & Fiske, S. T. (2002). Doddering but dear: Process, content, and function in stereotyping of older persons. In T. D. Nelson (Ed.), *Ageism: Stereotyping and prejudice against older persons* (pp. 3–26). Cambridge, MA: The MIT Press.

Danchin, É., Giraldeau, L. A., Valone, T. J., & Wagner, R. H. (2004). Public information: From nosy neighbors to cultural evolution. *Science, 305*(5683), 487–491.

Greenfield, P. M. (2013). The changing psychology of culture from 1800 through 2000. *Psychological Science, 24*(9), 1722–1731.

Henrich, J., & McElreath, R. (2003). The evolution of cultural evolution. *Evolutionary Anthropology: Issues, News, and Reviews, 12*(3), 123–135.

Hermans, H. J., & Kempen, H. J. (1998). Moving cultures: The perilous problems of cultural dichotomies in a globalizing society. *American Psychologist, 53*(10), 1111–1120.

Inglehart, R., & Baker, W. E. (2000). Modernization, cultural change, and the persistence of traditional values. *American Sociological Review,* 19–51.

Kamble, S., Shackelford, T. K., Pham, M., & Buss, D. M. (2014). Indian mate preferences: Continuity, sex differences, and cultural change across a quarter of a century. *Personality and Individual Differences, 70,* 150–155.

Lefebvre, L., & Palameta, B. (1988). Mechanisms, ecology and population diffusion of socially-learned, food-finding behavior in feral pigeons. In T. Zentall & B. G. Galef, Jr. (Eds.), *Social learning, psychological and biological perspectives* (pp. 141–165). Hillsdale, NJ: Erlbaum.

Markus, H. R., & Kitayama, S. (1991). Culture and the self: Implications for cognition, emotion, and motivation. *Psychological Review, 98*(2), 224–253.

Mroczek, D. K., & Kolarz, C. M. (1998). The effect of age on positive and negative affect: A developmental perspective on happiness. *Journal of Personality and Social Psychology, 75*(5), 1333–1349.

Naito, T., & Gielen, U. P. (2002). The changing Japanese family: A psychological portrait. In J. L. Roopnarine & U. P. Gielen (Eds.), *Families in global perspective* (pp. 63–84). Boston, MA: Allyn & Bacon.

Santa Maria, M. (2002). Youth in Southeast Asia. In B. B. Brown & R. W. Larson (Eds.), *The world's youth: Adolescence in eight regions of the globe* (pp. 171–206). Cambridge, U.K.: Cambridge University Press.

Saxon, S. V., Etten, M. J., & Perkins, E. A. (2014). *Physical change and aging: A guide for the helping professions.* New York, NY: Springer.

Twenge, J. M., & Kasser, T. (2013). Generational changes in materialism and work centrality, 1976–2007: Associations with temporal changes in societal insecurity and materialistic role modeling. *Personality and Social Psychology Bulletin, 39*(7), 883–897.

Twenge, J. M., Sherman, R. A., & Lyubomirsky, S. (2016). More happiness for young people and less for mature adults: Time period differences in subjective well-being in the United States, 1972–2014. *Social Psychological and Personality Science, 7*(2), 131–141. Retrieved from https://doi.org/10.1177/1948550615602933

World Values Survey (2016). Retrieved August 4, 2016, fromhttp://www.worldvaluessurvey.org/WVSContents.jsp?CMSID=Findings

Wrangham, R. W., McGrew, W. C., DeWall, F. B. M., & Heltne, P. G. (1994). *Chimpanzee cultures.* Cambridge, MA: Harvard University Press.

Zeng, R., & Greenfield, P. M. (2015). Cultural evolution over the last 40 years in China: Using the Google Ngram Viewer to study implications of social and political change for cultural values. *International Journal of Psychology, 50*(1), 47–55.

EPILOGUE

Where does this tour of culture leave us? This last chapter brings it all together, delineating that though there may not be one singular "human nature," there are, in fact, many human natures. Our job as decent, curious people is to simply figure out what those natures are and what to do with ourselves now that we know. Here we deal with the difficult question and critique of how the study of culture diverges from the study of stereotypes, and what the science of culture has to say about how we understand others and ourselves.

Culture Is Not Destiny

Recall this common critique of cultural psychology: "All we did all semester was learn about stereotypes" (this was an actual comment I received in a teaching evaluation the very first semester I ever taught Cultural Psychology, and it forever changed the way I teach). I started this book by telling you that the study of culture is not simply the study of a long and illustrious history of stereotypes, because culture, unlike stereotypes, is prone to change and can be self-selected. In case you were still not fully convinced, here is some cold, hard evidence that your culture is not your destiny.

Situations Trump Culture

On the one hand, culture is all around us; it's ubiquitous and far-reaching, like water is to fish. On the other hand, culture is a terribly fragile construct and one that can easily be overridden by other forces. Studies show that even small cues from the environment can overturn dominant cultural tendencies. Take, for example, one of the biggest and most well-established cultural differences to date—the tendency for European Americans to have high self-esteem and to self-enhance, versus the tendency for East Asians to have low(er) self-esteem and to self-criticize (e.g., Heine & Hamamura, 2007; see chapter 1 if you've forgotten). But consider what happens when European Americans are placed in Japanese contexts and Japanese are placed in European American contexts: voilà! Both groups are likely to change. Japanese who have traveled abroad are more self-enhancing than Japanese who have never left their island, and second generation Japanese have more self-esteem than first generation Japanese (see Heine & Lehman, 2004; Hetts, Sakuma, & Pelham, 1999). What's more, you don't even have to travel or immigrate to see these effects: When Kitayama, Markus, Matsumoto, and Norasakkunkit (1997) simply asked Japanese in Kyoto and European Americans in Eugene (Oregon) to *imagine* themselves put in daily situations created by other Japanese or European Americans, they found that being exposed to a situation created by an European American led to self-enhancement and being exposed to a situation created by a Japanese person led to self-critique. Other studies have shown that priming European Americans with affiliation cues can exert similar effects and make them more interdependent (Oyserman & Lee, 2008; Oyserman, Sorensen, Reber, & Chen, 2009). This is not to say that travel is overrated but, rather, that slight situational cues—no matter where you are—can powerfully change the cultural behaviors you exhibit.

Studies on frame-switching further confirm this idea. Take bicultural individuals and expose them to icons reflecting one of their cultures; doing so will likely lead them to behave in ways consistent with the culture you primed (Hong et al., 2000). Researchers have demonstrated this effect with Hong Kong Chinese by exposing them to either the American flag and the White House, on the one hand, or a Chinese dragon and a pagoda, on the other; afterward, testing their cognitive styles revealed that the White House made participants engage in more dispositional attributions (blame the person) whereas the pagoda made them engage in more situational attributions (blame the context; Hong et al., 2000; Wong & Hong, 2005). The same effect has been shown with Mexican bilingual participants, with language as the prime; speaking in English made them more self-enhancing (they rated themselves as more agreeable) but speaking in Spanish made them more modest (they rated themselves as less agreeable but nevertheless acted with more simpatía; Ramirez-Esparza et al., 2008).

A Lesson from Baboons

Back in the early 2000s, the auto insurance company Geico came out with a series of widely popular and effective commercials with the tag line, "So easy a caveman can do it." The message was simple—switching car insurance was the most straightforward of tasks and so effortless that our less sophisticated ancestors could've done it. This brings us to a broader idea that we can likewise apply to culture: If species less developed and intelligent than the latest model of homo sapiens can figure out something, then whatever it is, it shouldn't be that hard for humans to do as well.

This widely accepted idea, although commonsensical and intuitive, appears harder when actually applied to real situations. Take, for example, the ancient quandary: How do you establish world peace? I ask this to my multicultural class students each semester, and each semester I get the same bewildered looks in return. Some of the more optimistic students will offer up abstract but slippery ideas having to do with love conquering all or blanket tolerance for everyone; the more pessimistic ones, in turn, will just shake their heads.

PHOTO 14.1. What can we learn from baboons?

Source: iStock

But consider this: Baboons (photo E.1) are commonly known as one of the most brutal and violent of primate species. There is widespread abduction, abuse, and rape (Pines & Swedell, 2011; for review, see Alvarez & Bachman, 2013) among them. As such, for the longest time, violence was assumed to be an integral part of "baboon nature," one that evolution and millions of years of socialization bred into them.

Then along came Robert Sapolsky and Lisa Share, who started observing a troop of savanna baboons from Kenya in the late 1970s; they reported in the 1980s that a group of the most aggressive male members of the troop went to a nearby tourist lodge in search of food (see Sapolsky & Share, 2004). Given that the edible goods that humans left behind were widely coveted by other baboon troops, Sapolsky and Share (2004) found that only the strongest and most aggressive males could successfully attempt the dumpster-dive. On one such ill-fated trip, the males came across leftover meat contaminated with bovine tuberculosis; all the baboons who ate it died (Sapolsky & Share, 2004). This essentially took out half the adult males in the entire troop but didn't do so randomly; only the most aggressive males perished, because it was only by their violence and strength that they got access to the infected meat in the first place (Sapolsky & Share, 2004). This left behind a troop populated with only females and less aggressive males, and what happened next changed how we understood baboon nature forever.

When Sapolsky and Share (2004) compared their observations of this troop of baboons from the 1990s with their earlier observations from the late 1970s/early 1980s, they noticed striking differences in how the animals acted. The more recent troop (post-tuberculosis) was less likely to aggress against females, more likely to groom one another, and less likely to attack low-ranking males; moreover, the low-ranking males—which typically show elevated levels of stress hormones because of their lack of status and, as a result, suffer from a host of illnesses like hypertension and ulcers—were also healthier and less stressed (Sapolsky & Share, 2004). There also didn't seem to be "side effects" from this lack of violence and domination in the new troop—pregnancy and birth rates were as high as ever (Sapolsky & Share, 2004).

Sapolsky and Share (2004) go on to argue that the enduring effects of this new peaceful culture among this particular baboon troop appears to be the result of social transmission (remember culture as epidemiology?). When new teenage baboon males join the troop, the females treat them with the same warmth and kindness they treat the other members; over time, this appears to be effective in perpetuating the new affiliative culture (Sapolsky & Share, 2004).

What does this mean for human beings? If culture isn't destiny, then this means that we have a hand in the construction of our own futures; we get to pick. After millions of years, humans may have become used to the idea that our own natures are irrevocably prone to perpetual conflict and recurrent warfare—to intolerant backlashes even as we seem to progress toward tolerance. Perhaps it is easy to become too used to our own ideas of human nature and too resigned to hope for enduring change. But if baboons can do it, then this should give us hope and insight into the mechanisms that may allow for similar revolutions in our own cultures.

References

Alvarez, A., & Bachman, R. (2013). *Violence: The enduring problem*. Los Angeles, CA: Sage Publications.

Heine, S. J., & Hamamura, T. (2007). In search of East Asian self-enhancement. *Personality and Social Psychology Review*, 11(1), 4–27.

Heine, S. J., & Lehman, D. R. (2004). Move the body, change the self: Acculturative effects on the self-concept. *Psychological Foundations of Culture*, 8, 305–331.

Hetts, J. J., Sakuma, M., & Pelham, B. W. (1999). Two roads to positive regard: Implicit and explicit self-evaluation and culture. *Journal of Experimental Social Psychology*, 35(6), 512–559.

Hong, Y. Y., Morris, M. W., Chiu, C. Y., & Benet-Martinez, V. (2000). Multicultural minds: A dynamic constructivist approach to culture and cognition. *American Psychologist*, 55(7), 709–720.

Kitayama, S., Markus, H. R., Matsumoto, H., & Norasakkunkit, V. (1997). Individual and collective processes in the construction of the self: Self-enhancement in the United States and self-criticism in Japan. *Journal of Personality and Social Psychology*, 72(6), 1245–1267.

Oyserman, D., & Lee, S. W. (2008). Does culture influence what and how we think? Effects of priming individualism and collectivism. *Psychological Bulletin*, 134(2), 311–342.

Oyserman, D., Sorensen, N., Reber, R., & Chen, S. X. (2009). Connecting and separating mind-sets: Culture as situated cognition. *Journal of Personality and Social Psychology*, 97(2), 217–235.

Pines, M., & Swedell, L. (2011). Not without a fair fight: Failed abductions of females in wild hamadryas baboons. *Primates*, 52(3), 249–252.

Ramírez-Esparza, N., Gosling, S. D., & Pennebaker, J. W. (2008). Paradox lost: Unraveling the puzzle of Simpatía. *Journal of Cross-Cultural Psychology*, 39(6), 703–715.

Sapolsky, R. M., & Share, L. J. (2004). A pacific culture among wild baboons: Its emergence and transmission. *PLoS Biology*, 2(4), e106.

Wong, R. Y. M., & Hong, Y. Y. (2005). Dynamic influences of culture on cooperation in the prisoner's dilemma. *Psychological Science*, 16(6), 429–434.

Index

acculturation, 28, 199–200
Ache, 129
achievement, 31, 58, 63, 107, 165, 203–4
acting White effect, 203
affect. *See* emotion
affect valuation theory, 9–10
African Americans, 18–24, 164–65, 167–73, 179–81, 185–86, 199–200, 214–16
age, 202
aging, 248, 255
agency detection, 83–85
aggression, 95–96, 122, 143
Allport, G., 218
American Indians, 28–32
amok, 17, 142
amygdala. *See* neuroimaging
analytic thinking. *See* cognition, cognitive styles
anxiety. *See* mental health
Arnett, J., 260
Aronson, J., 108–9, 165–66, 221–22
Asians, 4–17, 166, 171–73, 181, 186, 199–200, 215–16, 227, 232, 244–48, 256–57, 260, 263–64
assimilation, 200, 213, 217
ataque de nervious, 28
attachment style, 227
attention, 14, 78, 104 226, 232
attitudes: explicit versus implicit, 22, 168; Implicit Association Test (IAT), 27, 35, 164–65, 169, 171, 174, 182
attraction. *See* mating
awe. *See* emotion, emotional experience

baboons, 265–66
Baker, W., 257
Barrett, J. 76
Beach, S., 139
Bennett, W., 37, 212
Berscheid, E., 189–90
bilateral symmetry. *See* physical attractiveness
Biernat, M., 183–84
Bin Laden, Osama, 161–62
Blizinksky, K., 231
body mass index. *See* physical attractiveness

Breaking Bad, 225–26
Brown v. Board of Education, 179
burqa, 217
Buss, D., 131, 140, 145–46, 150–51, 254–56

Canada, 216
categorization. *See* stereotype
Chiao, J., 231, 244
Christianity, 69, 71, 78, 81
choking, 172–73
Clark, K., 179–80
Clark, M., 179–80
class, 49–63; classism, 61; differences by class, 50–58, 61–62, 235, 249; environmental threats, 130; objective social class, 50; subjective social class, 50
Cohen, D., 121–23
Cohen, G., 167
collective action, 204
collective self-esteem, 21, 35
collective threat, 167
collectivism. *See* individualism-collectivism
Connolly, W., 37
contact hypothesis, 218–219
contextualism. *See* cognition, cognitive styles
cognition: attribution, 14, 124, 201, 264; categorization, 14, 36, 161, 163–64, 197; cognitive styles, 13, 15–16, 21, 26, 30, 56–57, 185, 226, 232, 248, 264; cognitive development, 31, 96; complexity, 57
cognitive dissonance, 124
colorblindness, 34, 212–17
comorbidity, 106
control: compensatory control, 85; personal/self-control, 56–57, 62, 78, 81
Correll, J., 169–70
cortisol, 122
cultural change, 253–60
culture of honor. *See* Southern culture

Darwin, C., 148
Davis, K., 180
depression. *See* mental health
deterministic fallacy, 59

dialecticism. *See* cognition, cognitive styles
discrimination, 22–23, 27, 163–64, 171, 173, 198–99, 201–4, 206, 215
dhat, 17, 142
Diallo, A., 169
diathesis-stress, 19, 127
disidentification. *See* identity
distal versus proximal explanations, 226
diversity, 35–36, 62, 143–44, 163, 202, 211–13, 216–17, 219, 221
Dolezal, R., 205
Dong, Mao Zhe, 161
dyslexia, 247

East Asians. *see* Asians
ecology. *See* evoked culture
economic development, 257
egalitarianism, 36, 53, 130
Elliot, J., 71
emotion: contagion, 55; distress, 17, 19, 23–24, 27–28, 31, 102, 105, 128; emotional experience, 10, 30, 55, 75, 102, 226, 249; expression/suppression, 10–12, 20, 25, 245; gender differences, 101–3; ideal versus actual, 25; physiological reactions to emotion, 103; recognition, 12–13, 19, 30, 250; regulation, 25–26, 76, 102–3, 106
empathic accuracy, 13, 56, 103, 226
Enos, R., 219–20
epidemiology. *See* transmitted culture
ethnicity, 1, 197, 215, 248–49; ethnic identification, 198–99, 217
eurocentricity, 227
evoked culture, 131, 228–29
evolutionary psychology, 128–31

fairy tales, 4
falling-out, 23
family: compadrazgo, 24; fictive kin, 24; la familia, 24
femininity. *See* gender
fertility, 149–50, 237
Fitzgerald, F., 53
fMRI. *See* neuroimaging
frame-switching, 201, 246, 264
fraternity members. *See* Greek system
fundamental attribution error, 14, 124

Garcia, J., 167
gender: differences, 96–97, 100–10,
    144, 157, 182, 186–87, 201, 250;
    femininity/masculinity as cultural
    dimensions, 18; identity, 99;
    inequality, 107–10; intensification
    hypothesis, 106; socialization, 95;
    versus sex, 97
genes, 58, 97, 106, 136, 142–43, 154
    230–31, 237
ghost sickness, 32
Gladwell, M., 169
globalization, 260
Google Ngram, 258, 260
gratitude. *See* emotion, emotional
    experience
Gray, J., 97–98
Green, M., 183–84
Greek system, 183
gun rights and laws, xii, 119, 121

happiness, 96, 255, 257
Harrell, A., 147
Heine, S., 8, 138, 226–28
health outcomes, 198, 202
helping. *See* pro sociality
hex, 23
Hitler, A., 162
holistic thinking. *See* cognition,
    cognitive styles
Hofstede, G., xiv, 18
Hokkaido, 124–25
hope. *See* emotion, emotional
    experience

IAT. *See* attitudes
identity, 31, 195; bicultural
    identity, 199–202, 260; ethnic
    identification, 217; global versus
    local versus hybrid identity,
    260; identity confusion, 260;
    identity threat, 203–4; White
    identity, 33–37
illusory correlation, 164
implicit cognition. *See* attitudes
immigration: 28, 199–203, 220;
    immigrant paradox, 200; types
    (voluntary immigrant, refugees,
    asylum seekers, sojourners), 201
inadvertent social information, 253–54
incest avoidance, 236–37
independent self. *See* self,
    self-construal
individualism-collectivism, 18–19,
    130, 181, 185, 229, 231, 233, 246,
    258–60; French versus American
    individualism, 234–35; soft versus
    hard individualism, 51, 53, 235
inequality, 57–59, 62, 255
Inglehart, R., 257

ingroup, 21–22, 35, 130, 221, 244–46;
    ingroup derogation, 181–85
interdependent self. *See* self,
    self-construal
intergroup conflict, 162–74
internalization. *See* identity
Islam, 78, 217
ISIS, 70

Japan, northern frontier, 124
Jedi-ism, 70
jigsaw classroom, 221–22
Johns, M., 173–74
Judaism, 81

Khan, G., 161
Kim, H., 5, 231
King, R., 169
Kitayama, S., 8
koro, 17
Ku Klux Klan, 211

Latino/a Americans, 19, 24–28,
    171, 174, 181, 199–200, 202–3,
    214, 216
language, 13, 17, 20, 25, 28, 154–55,
    202, 217, 219, 247
Lehman, S., 8
Louima, A., 169

mal puesto, 28
Markus, H., 5, 8, 51
Martens, A., 173
mascots, 29
Masuda, T., 232
The Matrix, 188–89
mating: preferences, 130–31, 229,
    237, 254, 256; racial bias, 171–72;
    universals in, 140, 143–51
media, 6, 29, 97, 169, 182, 192, 260
meditation, 78
melting pot. *See* multiculturalism
mental health: culture-specific
    disorders, 17, 23, 28, 32, 142;
    diagnoses, 23, 28, 32, 62;
    disparities versus gender, 103–4;
    disparities by race, 16, 23, 27–
    28, 32, 61–62, 231; disparities
    between urban/rural dwellers,127;
    outcomes, 32–33, 61–62, 78, 198
mentalizing. *See* Theory of Mind
mere exposure effect, 135,
    138–39, 145
microaggressions, 167–68, 171
minimal group paradigm, 198
Miyamoto, Y., 232
money, 236
moral typecasting, 84

morality, 80, 152–153; Moral
    Foundations Theory, 155; Social
    Intuitionist Model, 154
Moreland, R., 139
multiculturalism, 211–13

Napoleon, 161
nationality, 197
naturalistic fallacy, 59
neuroimaging, 77–78, 103, 171; EEG,
    239; fMRI, 243–244; mirror
    neurons, 244; neural responses to
    ingroups/outgroups, 244–245
Netherlands, 217
Nisbett, R., 14–16, 122–23, 232–233
Norenzayan, A., 76, 80, 138, 142,
    226–28, 230
numeracy, 138

Obama, President Barack,
    36–37, 195–96
Odde Ori, 23
OKCupid, 172
Olsteen, J., 69
Olympics, 6
oxytocin, 231

pain, 20, 56, 84, 143, 236, 244, 249
parenting, 51, 105, 235; authoritarian,
    2; authoritative, 2; permissive, 3
parental investment model, 144
passing, 206
pathogens, 130–31, 140, 148
personality, 52, 229–30, 256; Big Five,
    24, 156. *See also* mental health
phobia. *See* mental health
physical attractiveness, 131, 140,
    147–48, 189–92; bilateral
    symmetry, 148–50; Body Mass
    Index, 149–51; Waist-to-Hip
    Ratio, 148–50, 237
Piff, P., 59
Pitt, B., 69
police: officers, 170–71;
    shootings, 169–70
polyculturalism, 216
power distance, 18
prejudice, 82, 163–65, 167, 174, 215–16,
    218–19; envious prejudice, 173
Pride & Prejudice, 139–40
public policy, 216–17, 219
Prisoner's Dilemma, xiii–xiv, 82
Protestant Work Ethic, 74
pro sociality, 77, 79–80, 82, 126, 231,
    235–36, 249

race, 1, 168, 170, 172–74, 180–81, 185–87, 195–97, 205–6, 212–15; racial identity, 1, 196, 205–6; racism, 35–37, 61, 161, 168, 181, 211; transracialism, 206; versus ethnicity versus nationality, 197
religion, 69–86, 102, 146, 156–57, 249, 257–58, 261; Big Four religious dimensions, 156; religiosity, 156–57; religious universals, 156–57
reference group effects, xvi
refugees. *See* immigration
response bias, xvi; moderacy bias, xvi; extremity bias, xvi; acquiescence bias, xvi
revolution of rising expectations, 255
root-work, 23
Routledge, Veronica, xi
Rudder, C. *See* OKCupid
rumination, 102, 105–6

Sanberg, S., 182
Sapolsky, R., 265–66
saving face, 12
schadenfreude, xv
Schmader, T., 173–74
secularization myth, 73
segregation, 179–80
self, 4; self-construal, 5–8, 11–12, 18–19, 24, 29, 34, 50–52, 246–48; self-esteem, 8–9, 21–22, 29–30, 32, 61, 167, 174, 185, 199, 204, 226, 259, 263–64; self-stereotyping, 183–84
self-fulfilling prophecy, 189–92
serotonin, 231
sexual identity, 99

Share, L., 265–66
Shweder, R., 236–37
simpatia, 24–25
Snyder, M., 189–90
social dominance orientation, 216–17
social facilitation, 138
Social Identity Theory, 198–99
social loafing, 138
social support, 79, 86, 102, 204, 231
somatic, 13, 20; somatization, 17, 23, 28
spirituality, 74–75
sorority members. *See* Greek system
Southern culture, 117–23; culture of honor, 119, 121; history, 121; homicides, 119–21
Steele, C., 165, 186–87
stereotype: and categorization, 163, 197; versus culture, 136, 263; endorsement, 181, 214, 218–19; lift (positive stereotypes), 109, 166, 172–73, 199; versus prejudice/ discrimination, 163–64; rebound effect, 212; shifting standards model, 173, 199; threat, 108–9, 165, 167, 173–74, 186–88, 199, 203–4
stigma, 17, 21–22; stigma consciousness, 174
Strange Situation. *See* attachment style
stress, 27, 61, 97, 105–6, 122, 127–28, 249–50, 265–66
substance abuse, 28, 61, 104–6
susto, 28
Swami, V., 151–52
Syria, 162
system justification, 184–85, 192

Taijian kyuofusho, 17
Tanke, E., 189–90
Terror Management Theory, xiii, 83
testosterone, 97, 99, 122, 143
Theory of Mind, 77, 247–49
Tiger Mom, 2
time orientation, 18
Tovee, M., 151–52
Tsai, J., 9–10
translations, xv
transgender. *See* gender identity
transmitted culture, 229–30, 266
transracial. *See* race

uncertainty avoidance, 18
universals, 135–57, 236–37; Four Fs (fighting, fleeing, flirting, feeding), 142–52; levels of universality, 138–42
urban: versus rural distinction, 126–28; urbanization, 258–59

Vaillant, G., 126
validity, xv, 202
van Doren, M., 8, 136
Vescio, T., 183–84
Vohs, K., 236
voluntary settlement hypothesis, 124
voodoo, 23

Wald, R., 117–18
WEIRD, 137
well-being, 11, 22, 27, 31–32, 55, 61, 76, 78, 109, 198–200, 258
White identity. *See* identity
within-culture variation/within-group heterogeneity, 129, 136, 234–35
World Values Survey, 257–58